GERMAN CONQUISTADORS IN VENEZUELA

GERMAN CONQUISTADORS IN VENEZUELA

The Welsers' Colony, Racialized Capitalism, and Cultural Memory

GIOVANNA MONTENEGRO

University of Notre Dame Press
Notre Dame, Indiana

Published in the United States of America

Paperback edition published in 2025

Library of Congress Control Number: 2022946247

ISBN: 978-0-268-20321-4 (Hardback)
ISBN: 978-0-268-20322-1 (Paperback)
ISBN: 978-0-268-20323-8 (WebPDF)
ISBN: 978-0-268-20320-7 (Epub)

This book has received the Weiss-Brown Publication Subvention Award from the Newberry Library. The award supports the publication of outstanding works of scholarship that cover European civilization before 1700 in the areas of music, theater, French or Italian literature, or cultural studies. It is made to commemorate the career of Howard Mayer Brown.

The author gratefully acknowledges the financial assistance provided for this publication through the generosity of donors to the Harpur College Advocacy Council Faculty Development Endowment—an endowed fund that invests deeply in the research, creative activities, and professional development of Harpur College of Arts and Sciences faculty at Binghamton University.

GPSR Compliance Inquiries:
Lightning Source France,
1 Av. Johannes Gutenberg,
78310 Maurepas, France
compliance@lightningsource.fr
Phone: +33 1 30 49 23 42

Para mi madre, Neida Montenegro Juarez

CONTENTS

LIST OF FIGURES AND TABLES

FIGURES

TABLES

ACKNOWLEDGMENTS

This book would not have been possible without the tremendous support I have received from many individuals and institutions throughout the years.

Fellowships from the Newberry Library, the Herzog August Bibliothek, the Huntington Library, the Omohundro Institute, the Fulbright program, and the American Association of University Women have allowed me to complete research on this work. Likewise, at Binghamton University, internal support from the Institute for the Advanced Study of the Humanities, the Harpur College Dean's Office, the Presidential Diversity Fellowship, and the SUNY Dr. Nuala McGann Drescher Program gave me time off from teaching for writing. I am deeply grateful to all.

I thank Eli Bortz, editor-in-chief at the University of Notre Dame Press, for believing in this project and for his editorial support throughout the revision process. I am deeply grateful to Karen Stolley for her extensive comments and suggestions on two rounds of this manuscript. I also thank the anonymous reviewers for their thoughtful feedback and suggestions.

Elisabeth Krimmer (University of California, Davis) and Ivonne Del Valle (University of California, Berkeley) were wonderful graduate school advisers who guided me at the inception of this project and provided insight, comments, and support throughout the years. I thank them for believing in the promise of the work and what I as a young scholar had to say to the fields of Latin American Colonial Studies and Early Modern German Studies. At the University of California, Davis, I wish to also thank Gail Finney for her support and for inspiring me to be a comparatist working in German Studies. Andres Resendez, Katie Harris, Leo Bernucci, Chuck Walker, Zoila Mendoza, Seth Schein, Brenda Schildgen, Juliana Schiesari, and Ari Friedlander provided mentorship and training. I also thank the Davis Humanities Institute for mentorship, the Mellon Early Modern Fellowship at UC Davis for writing and research support, and the Tinker Fellowship from the Hemispheric Institute of the Americas at UC Davis for travel research funds.

At San Francisco State University, Dane Johnson encouraged me when I was a young master's degree student and read my work with care. All of his thoughtful marginalia made a difference. Volker Langbehn, encouraged my journey through German Studies, beginning with German 101. Both advisers encouraged me to look at connections between German and Latin American literatures. I am also grateful to the California State University Sally Casanova Pre-Doctoral program and the many research and networking opportunities it offered.

For the feedback and conversations that I have had over the years at conferences and workshops and over coffee, drinks, and dancing, I thank Alison Bigelow, Daniella Bleichmar, Thomas Bremer, Kathleen Brosnan, Caroline Egan, Christophe Giudicelli, Mark Häberlein, Hermann Hiery, Martha Howard, Dyani Johns Taff, Françoise Knopper, Frédérique Langue, Vicente Lecuna, Pete Mancall, Yolanda Martínez San-Miguel, Kelly McDonough, Kitty Millet, Ana More, Jennifer Nelson, Daniel Nemser, Ana Peluffo, Sonia Rose, Jennifer Saracino, Kathryn Sederberg, Tomás Straka, Mariana Cecilia Vazquez-Pérez, Toni Veneri, Alina Dana Weber, Adriana Méndez-Rodenas, *gracias por mapear conmigo*, thank you for your feedback, support, mentorship, and laughter. To Nicole Legnani, a big thanks for guiding me through the publication process. I also thank the National Center for Faculty Development and Diversity for mentorship through their Faculty Success Program. A big thanks to Badia Ahad for editing the book proposal and Kate Epstein for manuscript editing.

I am particularly indebted to the librarians and staff members at the many libraries and archives I consulted in my research, including the Biblioteca Nacional de Venezuela; the Archivo General de la Nacion (Venezuela); the library of the Universidad Central de Venezuela; the Biblioteca de la Casa de Estudio de la Historia de Venezuela Lorenzo A. Mendoza Quintero in Caracas; and the library, maps department, and newspaper archive of the Academia Nacional de Historia (Venezuela). I also thank the Special Collections at the National Autonomous University of Mexico; the library of the Museum of Anthropology in Mexico City; the Real Biblioteca del Monasterio de San Lorenzo de el Escorial; the Bibliothèque Nationale de France; the library at the University of Toulouse-Mirail; the library of the University of Salamanca; the special collections at the Würtembergische

Staatsbibliothek, the Staatsbibliothek in Berlin; the Iberoamerican Institute library in Berlin; the library of the Free University, Berlin; the City Archives of Ulm and the City Archives of Augsburg; in Seville, the Archivo General de las Indias and the Residencia de Investigadores as well as the Biblioteca Americanista de Sevilla; the libraries at UC Davis and UC Berkeley; the German Historical Institute Library in Washington, DC; and the Special Collections and Cartography sections of the Library of Congress. In Wolfenbüttel, Germany, at the Herzog August Bibliothek, I thank Gerlinde Strauss for hosting a lively community of scholars and Volker Bauer for answering my questions on genealogical trees.

In Chicago, at the Newberry Library, I thank Jim Akerman, Susan Schmidt, and Lia Markey for pointing me to amazing maps and early modern German books.

At the Freie Universität, I thank the Peter Szondi Institute for Comparative Literature, which hosted me during my Fulbright grant as a doctoral student, and the members of the Mittelalter-Renaissance-Frühe Neuzeit Forum, who graciously allowed me to join their seminars (and their trip to the Dürer exhibit). Also, to Oliver Lubrich, my thanks for affiliation letters, which allowed me to travel to Germany on many occasions.

I would like to acknowledge that Binghamton University is located on the unceded homelands of the Onondaga and Oneida Nations of the Haudenosaunee (Iroquois) Confederacy.

To my colleagues at Binghamton University (BU) in the comparative literature department. Special thanks to Luiza Moreira, my Chair, for her continued support. Jeroen Gerrits, for all of the conversations, collaborations, and Baltimore shuttle rides, Brett Levinson, Neil-Christian Pages, Tarek Shamma, and Zoja Pavloskis-Petit. Kathleen Stanley for her administrative support throughout the years. Though you are longer with us, thank you Gisela Brinker-Gabler and María Lugones. María, *extraño tu sonrisa*. A special thanks to my colleagues in Romance Languages, Dana Stewart, Ana Ros, Sandra Casanova-Vizcaíno, Bryan Kirchen, Robyn Cope, Jeanette Patterson, and Brendan Hennessey. To the BU Latin American and Caribbean Area Studies (LACAS) community, including Nancy Appelbaum, Gladys Jiménez-Muñoz, Carmen Ferradas, Josh Price, Gabriela Veronelli, Brad Skopyk and many others, my thanks for being an intellectual and fun *familia*. AT BU's Center for Medieval and Renaissance Studies, CEMERS, a special thanks to Olivia Holmes, Marilynn Desmond, Sean Dunwoody,

Rosmarie Morewedge, Bridget Whearty, Tina Chronopoulos, and John Kuhn. I thank my colleagues Sydney Dement and John Cheng for the initial publishing conversations. I also thank the many colleagues who participated in the NEH grant writing groups over the years, sponsored by IASH.

To Nancy Um, my thanks for mentorship and for encouraging me to work more with digital methods. To Amy Gay, thanks for all of the work you do encouraging more work on DH.

To Birgit Rasmussen and Barrett Brenton, thank you for giving more space for Indigenous studies at Binghamton.

Tim Schmidt, graduate student, assisted with editing and obtaining reproduction rights. A big thanks to my undergraduate research assistants, Yuri Lee and Terry Han. To graduate and undergraduate students whom I have had the pleasure of teaching, I thank you for your comments and insights. A big thanks to Ali Almajnooni, Ali Alshhre, Mushtaq Bilal, Badreddine Ben Othman, Chia-Hsu Chang, Xiomara Damour, Giovanni Dettori, Isabel Dietrich, Daimys García, Alison Jones, Kazuki Ochiai, Alan Palacios, John Santare, Harper Sherwood-Reid, Adama Sakho, Daniela Valle, Diana Ventura, Daiki Yoshioka.

To my writing group—Sonja Kim, Kate Martineau, Yi Wang— thanks for including me in an amazing supportive community of women scholars. Also the National Center for Faculty Development and Diversity for their mentorship.

To the Binghamton *comadres* María Chavez, Aja Martínez, and Odilka Santiago, thank you for your friendship and support. Roberta Strippoli, Lubna Omar, and Joe Citriniti, thank you for making Binghamton fun. To my California-in-NY crew, Marguerite Wilson, David Renfrew, and Hayley Mann, thanks for bringing sunshine to the long winters.

I also thank my dear Catherine (Cassie) Hopkins; my dear friends Michelle Karell and Ruta Katinas; my amazing Davis crew, Jessica (Sissi) Chin Foo and Pauline Maillard; my San Francisco ladies, Sara Berman (Pyorre), Elizabeth Everhart, Andrea Mikonowicz, Abigail Harwood, Clara Brandt, and Heather White; and my Berlin crew, Margaux Meunier, Maryna Shuklina, Alexander Zverev, Cristina Sitja-Rubio, and Vladimir Bourdine.

In Possagno (TV), Italy, the Zattas, especially Lorena and Ivano. To my dad, Tony Tovena, for teaching me that languages are fun.

To my mother, Neida Montenegro, who made this journey happen and who encouraged me to follow my dreams. My brother Gianpier, and the many, *tías, tíos*, and *primx* of the Montenegro family. To my grandparents Hugo and Rosa (*q.e.p.d*). My fur baby, Lavender, has made the tedious editing process that much more bearable.

A few chapters have appeared previously as articles, though they have since been expanded and revised: A version of chapter 6 appeared as "'The Welser Phantom': Apparitions of the Welser Venezuela Colony in Nineteenth and Twentieth-Century German Cultural Memory," *Transit: A Journal of Travel, Migration, and Multiculturalism in the German-speaking World* 11, no. 2 (2018): 21–53, http://transit.berkeley.edu/2018/montenegro/. It was published in Spanish as "'El fantasma de los Welser': Apariciones de la colonial Welser de Venezuela en la memoria cultural alemana de los siglos XIX y XX," in *Trópico Absoluto*, October 10, 2020, http://tropicoabsoluto .com/2020/10/10/el-fantasma-de-los-welser-apariciones-de-la-colonia-welser -de-venezuela-en-la-memoria-cultural-alemana-de-los-siglos-xix-y-xx/.

A version of chapter 5 appeared as "La representación de los Welser en la historiografía colonial venezolana," *Boletín de la Academia Nacional de la Historia* 102, no. 408 (2019): 190–220, www.anhvenezuela.org.ve/bo -letinesanh/.

A version of chapter 3 appeared as "Conquistadors and Indians 'Fail' at Gift Exchange: An Analysis of Nikolaus Federmann's *Indianische Historia* (Haguenau, 1557)," *MLN* 132 (2017): 272–90.

Introduction

This book investigates one of the strangest episodes in the conquest and colonization of the Americas, the governance of the province of Venezuela by German bankers in the sixteenth century. It also recovers the production of this episode's cultural memory on the German and Venezuelan sides in subsequent centuries. The 1528 contract between the Habsburg emperor Charles V (he was also King Charles I of Spain) and agents of the Welser Company from Augsburg stipulated that the Germans would provide their assistance to "pacify the land and to place it in our service in a manner that we can profit from it" (fig. I.1). The Welsers had high hopes for expanding their business beyond banking to colonization and the slave trade in the Spanish Indies, but the colony failed. In 1556 Spain was officially governing the territory again; the 1528 contract had been dissolved. I argue that in the sixteenth century amid a nascent European-centered globality that saw the demand for world commodities by an increasing number of European consumers, German, Genoese, and Flemish merchant capitalists provided needed capital to European monarchs such as Charles to embark on the colonization of the New World. In the case of the Welser Company, the German bankers would lend money to Charles and soon after receive certain privileges that gave them carte blanche for many commercial ventures, including the production and trade of commodities such as sugar in Madeira, La Palma (Canary Islands), and Hispaniola; the exportation of illicit New World drugs such as balsam; the trafficking of humans in the Atlantic slave trade; and the conquest of Indigenous peoples in the province of Venezuela.

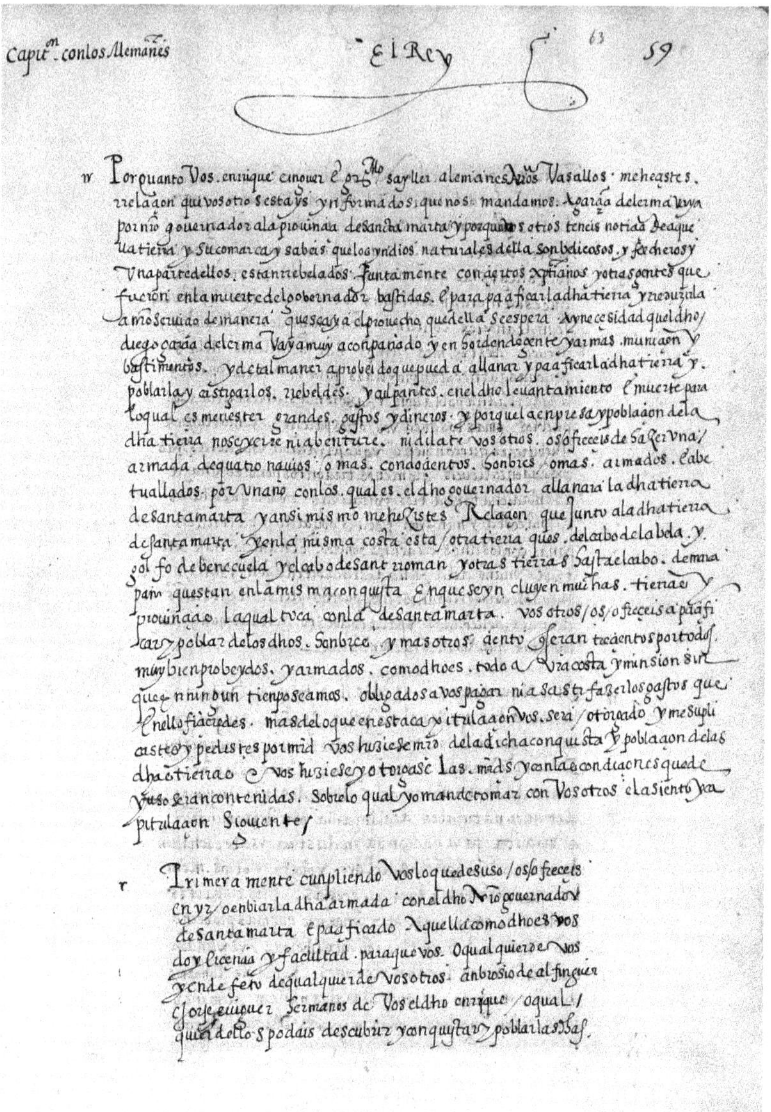

Capitn. con los Alemanes El Rey 63 59

Porquanto vos enrrique einguer e geronimo sayller alemanes nuestros vasallos me heçistes
relaçion que vosotros estays ynformados que nos mandamos a garçia de lerma yr
por nuestro governador a la provinçia de santa marta y porque vosotros teneis notiçia de aquella
tierra y su comarca y sabeis que los yndios naturales della son belicosos y ferozes y
una parte dellos estan rrebelados juntamente con algunos xpianos y otras gentes que
fueron en la muerte del governador bastidas e para paçificar la dha tierra y reduzirla
a nuestro serviçio de manera que sea ya el provecho que della se espera ay neçesidad que el dho
diego garçia de lerma vaya muy acompañado y en orden de gente y armas muniçion y
bastimentos y de tal manera aprobeido que pueda allanar y paçificar la dha tierra y
poblarla y castigar los rrebeldes y culpantes en el dho levantamiento e muerte para
lo qual es menester grandes gastos y dineros y porque la enpresa y poblaçion de la
dha tierra no se yerre ni aventure ni dilate vosotros os ofreceis de hazer una
armada de quatro navios o mas con doçientos honbres o mas armados e abe
tuallados por un año con los quales el dho governador allanara la dha tierra
de santa marta y ansi mismo me hezistes relaçion que junto a la dha tierra
de santa marta y en la misma costa esta otra tierra que es del cabo de la bela y
golfo de beneçuela y el cabo de sant roman y otras tierras hasta el cabo de mara
pan que estan en la misma conquista en que se yncluyen muchas tierras y
provinçias la qual toca con la de santa marta vos otros os ofreceis a paçifi
car y poblar de los dhos honbres y mas otros dentro que seran treçientos por todos
muy bien probeydos y armados como dhos es todo a vuestra costa y minsion sin
que ni ningun tienpo seamos obligados a vos pagar ni a satisfazer los gastos que
en ello fiçieredes mas de lo que en esta capitulaçion vos sera otorgado y me supli
castes y pedistes por merçed vos hiziese merçed de la dicha conquista y poblaçion de las
dhas tierras e vos hiziese y otorgase las merçedes y con las condiçiones que de
yuso seran contenidas sobre lo qual yo mande tomar con vosotros el asiento y ca
pitulaçion siguiente/

Primeramente cunpliendo vos lo que de suso / os ofreceis
en yr o enbiar la dha armada con el dho nuestro governador
de santa marta e paçificado aquella como dho es vos
doy liçençia y facultad para que vos o qualquier de vos
y en defeto de qualquier de vosotros anbrosio de alfinguer
e jorje einguer hermanos de vos el dho enrrique o qual /
quier dellos podais descubrir y conquistar y poblar las dhas

FIGURE I.1. Contract between the Welser agents Enrique Ehinger and Hieronymus Sailer and Emperor Charles V for the governance of the province of Venezuela. "Capitulación con Enrique Einguer y Jerónimo Sayller," 27 March 1528 (Madrid). Archivo General de las Indias (AGI), Seville, Spain, INDIFERENTE_0415,L.1,F.63R-66R. (Pictured, 66R, first page). Used with permission.

The Welsers and Charles V engaged in racialized capitalism that tried to satisfy the growing European demand for commodities such as sugar and gold, which depended on the labor of Indigenous and African slaves. As the Chicana geographer Laura Pulido (2017, 4) writes, the racist capitalist "ideology that constructed indigenous peoples as less than fully human was entirely necessary for the colonial project." And wanting to be part of the nascent globality, the Welsers traded in both slaves and agricultural commodities. German merchant capitalists helped finance the conquest of the Americas and procured the licenses to export African slave labor into the newly conquered islands of the Antilles as well as Central America and northern South America, which at the time was called, broadly, Tierra Firme (fig. I.2). This book presents a micro history of what occurred between 1528 and 1556 during the Welser governance in Venezuela, which began soon after the Welsers received one of the first Spanish-sponsored permissions to trade in African slaves. German merchant capitalists dominated the financial market in southern German free imperial cities (subject only to the Holy Roman Emperor), especially Augsburg; bankers of the Habsburgs, the Welsers wanted to also engage in the trade of New World commodities and the privilege of New World conquest. The Welsers were active in Spain, the Atlantic islands of Madeira and La Palma (Canary Islands), and Hispaniola and Venezuela. The company's endeavors in Madeira and La Palma would influence the Welsers' colonial actions on Hispaniola and Venezuela. They used the labor of enslaved Africans in the extraction and production of sugar, which would result in the environmental degradation of the region.

The example of the donations to Charles's campaign to become Holy Roman Emperor by the Fuggers, Augsburg's rival mercantile banking family dynasty, and the Welsers shows that big donors received what seemed at first lucrative lending and business opportunities with the crown, yet often those deals turned sour when the crown defaulted on its loans. Welser agents were part of an economic network that was centered in Seville and received contracts from the crown for colonial endeavors in exchange for credit. However, Charles's bankers and financing activities in sixteenth-century Europe created anxieties surrounding not only the influx of New World gold but also the ethics of high exchange rates and high-interest lending, especially the charge of usury against the Catholic Habsburgs. As the historian of trade and capitalism Rowena Olegario (2016, 229) reminds us, while the concepts of lending and borrowing are relatively easy to grasp, there are many types

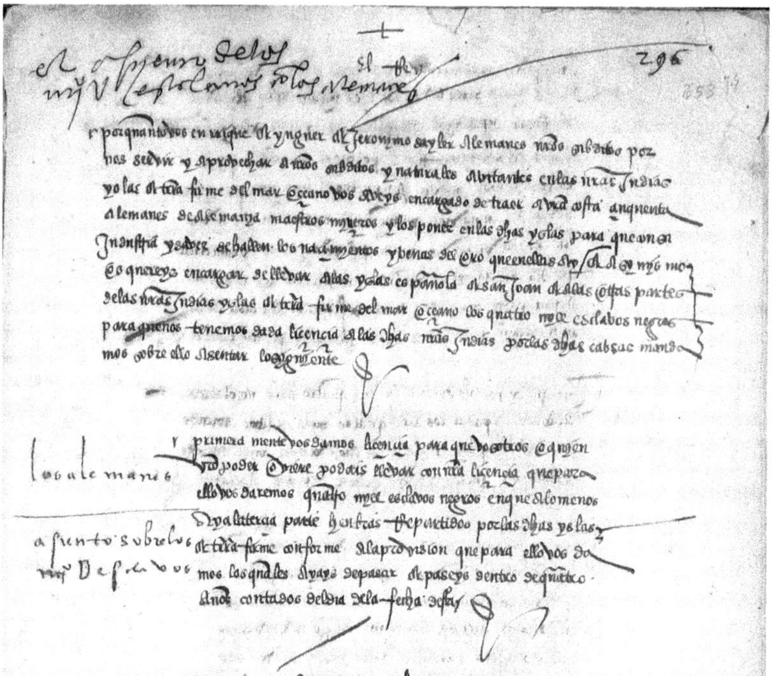

FIGURE I.2. License to export 4,000 African slaves given to the Welsers. "Asiento con Enrique Ehinger y Jerónimo Sayler," 12 February 1528 (Burgos). AGI, INDIFER-ENTE, 421,L.12.F.296R-297R. Used with permission.

of credit and a single definition is elusive. The *Oxford English Dictionary* gives one definition of *credit* as "trust or confidence in a customer's ability and intention to pay at some future time, shown by allowing money or goods to be taken or services to be used without immediate payment."[1] Olegario's (2016, 229) definition of public credit as "a government's ability to borrow on the strength of its credibility and reputation" works best for my purposes. The Holy Roman Emperor had the credibility and power to borrow from the Augsburg bankers, but he often defaulted on his loans throughout the time the Welsers colonized Venezuela.

Cartographers in Seville and farther afield in Venice traced the Welsers' credit flow to the Spanish crown in their maps of the province of Venezuela, showing an early modern globality in which the exchange of cartographic and financial information was as common a practice as the exchange of currency and goods—despite the attempt by various European monarchs to keep their geographic information secret. The appeal of maps during the early modern period reflected an interest in space and goods that in the Middle Ages had been expressed in written form as itineraries, sailing directions, and written chorographies. According to Karl Offen and Jordana Dym's introduction to *Mapping Latin America* (2011, 6), a map can be defined as a "graphic representation of space (real or imagined, terrestrial or otherwise) that organizes, presents, and communicates spatial information visually. Maps are simultaneously material and social, real and physical products that reflect cultural concerns, values, and communication arts and technologies of the society that produced them." In the Renaissance the image was related to a profound fascination with both the written word and the object. As the geographer David Woodward (2007a, 19) has written, cartographic visual culture coexisted with the text; both served imperial purposes through the colonial and religious expansion of Europe. In the case of Charles V's Spain and its imperial imaginations of Asia filtered through the Americas, Ricardo Padrón, in *The Indies of the Setting Sun* (2020), reminds us that Spanish official maps visualized a tangible transatlantic and transpacific spatial experience that in turn nourished a unique imperial geopolitical imaginary (18).

Mapmakers first show Venezuela as "Castilla del Oro," a sort of El Dorado full of natural resources to exploit, but later they created powerful narratives about the Welser Company's possession of Venezuela and the subsequent Welser family's nostalgia for it in their maps. These early examples of cultural memory show how entrenched genealogy, and family blood, would become with colonial soil in a cartographic project. In the German realms, the colony would become part of the Welser's nostalgic family history through what I term the relationship between Welser blood and colonial soil. Augsburg and the German lands went through much discord and war, including Reformation conflicts that later turned into the deadly Thirty Years' War (1618–48), and the colony was remembered mainly by the Welser family. In the nineteenth century, as the German Empire (1871–1918) unified a disjointed country under two confessions, the Germans sought to become an imperial power along with the British and the French, who had established colonial empires, to rapidly colonize "the blank spaces" of Africa and the Pacific Ocean on European-produced maps. German colonialists recalled the Welser period with particular flourish at this time. Through the creation of maps and genealogical materials, the Welsers archived nostalgic possession of the Venezuela colony where Welser blood had been shed.

Although people on both sides of the Atlantic have remembered this colonial history in literature, maps, and cultural monuments and rituals, the Iberian story has dominated most of colonial Latin American literature and history. From the infamous conquistadors Hernán Cortés to Francisco Pizarro, the story of the conquest of the Americas has been that of Hispanic domination, Indigenous resistance and submission, and the importation and exportation of African slaves who survived the Middle Passage. The German Welsers' short-lived governance became the subject of legend in Spanish historiographical sources, especially in light of the Reformation. This project also uncovers the Spaniards' deep distrust of German governance, fearing the Welsers were followers of Martin Luther's new faith. Although Juan de Castellanos's epic poem *Elegías de Varones Ilustres de Indias* (written in 1578–1601) celebrates the German conquerors and depicts them as heroes, one of the most widely translated works critical of the Spanish conquest, Friar Bartolomé de Las Casas's 1552 *Brevísima relación de la destrucción de las Indias* (A Short Account of the Destruction of the Indies), had portrayed most of the German governors as barbaric tyrants, using a famous pun, "animal/aleman" (animal/German).

Venezuela was regarded by Spain as one of its unimportant colonies for two hundred years after the Welser governance ended; many Spaniards blamed the Welsers for their tendency to conquer rather than colonize.

Venezuelans themselves would forever remember this episode as a blemish on its "Spanish" history. Later, in independent Venezuela, historians and fiction writers tried to continue to "translate" it for Venezuelans not familiar with this non-Hispanic conquest.

The short-lived colony continued to have an impact on cultural memory in the twentieth century. While in their historiography Venezuelans expressed gratitude for being colonized by the Spanish instead of the barbarous Germans, in Germany during Nationalist Socialism some of the German governors the Welsers installed became Aryan heroes in parades celebrating Germany's past. The Welser episode has important implications for the ways Germans rethink their colonial history today. Germany looked back on the Welser episode with nostalgia as it reimagined itself as a colonial power from the imperial era through the Nazi period. More recently, university students and activists in Germany have started to think about the decolonization of their monuments and streets. Much like the ongoing debate in the United States surrounding Confederate monuments, Germans are asking how to remember difficult chapters in their colonial history.

German, Spanish, and Venezuelan writers and historians have published scholarly and popular works dealing with this episode. While some scholars treat the study of the Welsers' participation in Eurocapitalism (Armani 1985) and examine the ties between cosmography and trade (Johnson 2008), many studies take a historical approach and examine the economic history of the Welsers (Haebler 1903; Friede 1961; Simmer 2000; Häberlein and Burkhardt 2002).[2] Only a few have addressed the cultural implications of the episode (Denzer 2002; Schmölz-Häberlein 2002; Zantop 1997). Moreover, little attention has been given to the early modern visual culture that reproduced images of New World peoples in the Germanophone realms; Stephanie Leitch's *Mapping Ethnography in Early Modern Germany* (2010) remains an exception. In addition, Carina L. Johnson's *Cultural Hierarchy in Sixteenth-Century Europe* (2011b) examines how Mexican and Ottoman peoples and cultural goods circulated through the Habsburg realms during the sixteenth century. The only monographs on the Welser Venezuela colony are Juan Friede's *Los Welser en la conquista de Venezuela* (1961) and Götz Simmer's published dissertation, *Gold und Sklaven* (2000). Friede's work was innovative for its time and corrected much of the misinformation that existed in Spanish sources; Simmer's is more complete, taking into account the Welsers' strategy of "mobility" and emphasis on expeditions. Neither book has been translated into English.

Largely missing are studies of the importance of genealogy and territorial possessions for the Welsers, which I consider through the connection of lineage and land, or blood and soil. This book addresses this gap for English-language readers, as the subject is key to understanding the history of "foreign" conquest in "Spanish" America and its reception on both sides of the Atlantic. The book also seeks to contribute to the growing literature on postcolonial reckonings with Germany's colonial past.

THE CONQUEST AND DEFINITION OF VENEZUELA

This is not an ethnohistorical work, but the materials I examine reveal information about the territory that Arawak and Carib groups, including the Caquetíos, Guaycaries, and Xaguas, among others, called home and their strategies of resistance. In 1498 Christopher Columbus sailed near the Orinoco Delta around the Gulf of Paría off the northeastern coast of South America. Franciscan friars from Spain established a colony in Cumaná in eastern Venezuela in 1515 that would later become part of the province of New Andalucía. In 1517 the island of Cubagua would become the site of the city of New Cádiz. The particularly brutal exploitation of native divers for pearls would destroy the environment and decimate the native populations of Cubagua by 1537, when a hurricane and an earthquake drove out the last settlers.[3]

The Spanish explorer Alonso de Ojeda made two voyages to the northern coast of South America, in 1499 and 1502. Around the peninsula of Paraguaná, he entered a gulf he called Venezuela, or Little Venice, because the native populations built their houses on stilts over the water. This expedition allowed Ojeda to enter Lake Maracaibo and land at Cabo de la Vela. Soon after, Diego Caballero contracted an *asiento* (short-term contract) and a capitulación to explore the peninsula of Paraguaná all the way to the Cabo de la Vela in the Guajira peninsula, and Martín Fernández de Enciso received a capitulación to conquer and settle the region of Cabo de la Vela. Neither of those capitulations was actually carried out.

An order of Emperor Charles V established the province of Venezuela in 1527. Juan Martínez de Ampíes (d. 1533), an officer in the Spanish army, founded the colony of Santa Ana de Coro there and became its first governor. The Welser governors would take over in 1528. Other provinces Spain

established in the area were Margarita (1525), Trinidad (1532), Nueva Andalucía and Guayana (1568), and Maracaibo (1676). Administered first by the
Royal Audiencia of Santo Domingo, much of Venezuela would later become
subject to the viceroyalty of New Granada and then finally to the captaincy
general of Venezuela. The captaincy was an administrative district of colonial Spain created in 1777 to provide autonomy to the provinces of Venezuela, and its creation was part of the Bourbon reforms that made the
province of Maracaibo subject to the province of Caracas, where the Real
Compañía Guipozcoana held economic monopolies from 1728 to 1785. On
5 July 1811, seven of the ten provinces of the captaincy declared their independence from Spain. A series of failed republics followed, until Simón Bolívar led a campaign to liberate New Granada from Spain in 1819–20, which
led to Venezuela's independence as part of Gran Colombia.

The latter part of this book is about the cultural memory of this Welser
period of governance in a wide array of media. In cartography we see the
tension between German nostalgia for the "lost" Venezuela colony and the
Spanish amnesia that enacts a total memory loss surrounding this "strange"
episode of Spain's colonial history. To tell that story, we must consider how
that amnesia was already represented in sixteenth- and seventeenth-century
maps. These manuscript maps scribbled in ink reveal a story of how Spanish
conquistadors and explorers saw Venezuela's topography and the peoples
who occupied it. While they depict the colonies that the Germans governed
(Coro) or founded (Maracaibo), many of the maps cannot fully represent
the political realities or histories of the region.

The *Mapa de Venezuela, parte costera* (fig. I.3), a hand-drawn manuscript map held at the Archivo General de las Indias (AGI; General Archive
of the Indies) in Seville, is dated to sometime after 1552 (likely after 1555),
soon after the Welsers stopped governing the province, and does not show
the Welsers' presence. The Pueblo de Coro appears as a Spanish colony, with
its "Iglesia" (church) and port. A road, or "camino a laguna," runs from Coro
to the Pueblo de Maracaybo, which the Welser governor Ambrosius Alfinger
founded in 1529. Maracaibo is depicted by four houses on the western bank
of the "laguna de mar," or lake, and Indigenous settlements are marked by
the famous huts built over the water on stilts (the *palafitos* that Ojeda
thought resembled Venetian homes on the canals). While "Sierras," or
mountains, dominate the area east of Maracaibo, other settlements such as
Tocuio (Tocuyo, founded in 1545), which would be the site of the execution

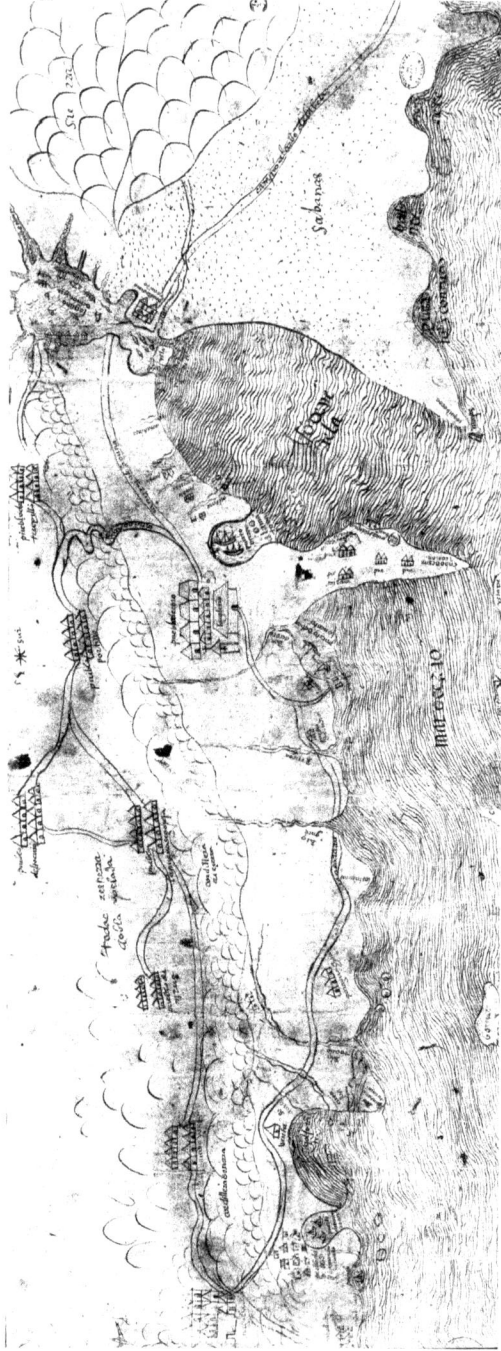

FIGURE I.3. *Mapa de Venezuela, parte costera* (after 1552). AGI, MP-VENEZUELA, 3 (ca. 1548) (Figure MP-Venezuela 3). Used with permission.

FIGURE I.4. Emmanuel Stenglin, *Venezuela Provincia in America Occidentali Quam olim Dni. Velseri Patricij Augustani possidebant, a Carolo V. Imperatore ipsis Consignata Venezuela.* [Nürnberg]: Wolfgang Mauritius Endter, 1682. Included in *Genealogical Table of the Family von Welser* (1666) with engravings by Georg G. Strauch and Emanuel Stenglin. Library of Congress (LOC), Special Collections, CS629.W4. Used with permission.

of the Welser governor Philipp von Hutten and son of the head of the Welser Company, Bartholomäus Welser VI, also appear on the map.

It is telling that this Spanish manuscript map does not mention the Welser governance. Only a German-made map from the seventeenth century commemorates the Welsers' governance of the province in nostalgic terms. The map, which I discuss in detail in chapter 4, was made by an Augsburg-based printer, Emmanuel Stenglin (fig. I.4). In order to appreciate the powerful pull of that nostalgia, I investigate the most powerful patrician families in the financial capital of Europe in the sixteenth century, Augsburg.

THE WELSER FAMILY HISTORY

The relationship between capitalism and clan-based social systems in the southern German lands, which the Welsers exemplified, informs how I consider the practice of Augsburg's business kinship, enacted through elite families' intermarriage, that helped develop mercantile culture and global trade networks. I argue that patrician families' interest in documenting their genealogy drove the Welsers to commemorate their family line through their blood that was shed in the Venezuelan territory.

The Welsers had been a prominent patrician family in the city of Augsburg since the late Middle Ages. A Bartholomäus Welser (d. 1346) appears in the city books in 1311. In the fifteenth century the Welsers had business posts and branches throughout Europe, including Antwerp, Genoa, Zaragoza, Valencia, Seville, and Lisbon, as well as Cologne, Rome, Leipzig, and Vienna. They were active in mining and the trade of silk textiles, spices, leather, and precious metals (Simmer 2000, 30). The Welsers' merchant strategy involved the establishment, with the Vöhlin family, of the eponymous Welser-Vöhlin Company in 1496, which operated first in Memmingen and then in Augsburg. The Welsers and Vöhlins formed what the German sociologist Hermann Mitgau (1968) called a "closed marriage circle," a typical strategy of the patriciate (*Herren*) in imperial German cities to keep strict hold of their genealogical present and future until the Industrial Revolution.[4] The early Augsburg Welser-Vöhlin society dealt in commerce, banking, textiles, and the spice trade in Lisbon (Cramer-Fortig, Fleischmann, and Herde 2006, 82–83). As they became involved in the pepper trade, one of the firm's employees, Balthasar Sprenger, traveled with the Portuguese fleet to India and published a richly illustrated travel narrative of his experiences. Soon after, the Welsers opened a branch on the island of Madeira that would be devoted to the sugar trade, as well as a branch on the island of Hispaniola in Santo Domingo. After the 1520s they wanted to expand to Tierra Firme (northern South America), which was rumored to be awash in gold. Because of their extensive lending relationship with Emperor Charles V, they held certain privileges within Spanish territory. For example, in July 1525, Jacob Cronberger and Lazarus Nürnberger, representatives for the Welsers and other German businesses, were the first German agents to receive permission from the emperor to conduct business in the Indies (Wüst 2011, 57). Consequently, the Welsers expanded their business first throughout Spain, then in the lucrative overseas market in Santo Domingo, to which they also imported goods from Europe, until finally they became governors of the Venezuelan province in Tierra Firme.

While Anton I Welser (1451–1518) headed the company in Augsburg, after a family dispute in 1517, Jakob Welser I (1468–1541) and his sons formed Jakob Welser & Söhne in Nuremberg, which focused on mining. Despite the conflict between members of the Nuremberg and Augsburg Welser families, they would remain closely linked in their trade of metals, textiles, spices, and extension of credit. Jakob's sons would found the Nuremberg Welser line, named Welser von Neunhof und zu Beerbach. Anton's sons, Bartholomäus V (1484–1561) and Anton II (1486–1556), would be left with the Augsburg company (figs. I.5, I.6). Both men's portraits reveal their status and power. Christoph Amberger, who painted Augsburg's powerful patricians, painted Anton. Amberger's portrait shows Anton in rings and a golden chain, along with coins at his hands that depict his wealth and merchant trade. However, Bartholomäus V would be head of the Augsburg branch and would be responsible for the Welsers' "golden age" in the sixteenth century.

FIGURE I.5. Portrait of Bartholomäus Welser V, head of the Welser Company in Venezuela. Oil painting on canvas by anonymous artist. Courtesy of the Freiherrlich von Welsersche Familienstiftung. Signatur A 38. Photograph by Helmut Meyer zur Capellen.

FIGURE I.6. Christoph Amberger, *Portrait of Anton Welser d.J. (the Younger)*, brother of Bartholomäus, 1527. Oil painting on canvas. Courtesy of the Freiherrlich von Welsersche Familienstiftung. Signatur A37. Photograph by Helmut Meyer zur Capellen.

Sometime during this golden age, the Welsers began showing a certificate of nobility signed by Emperor Charles V stating that they were from noble stock, though later it was determined to most likely have been fake (Bock 2008, 97), reflecting a preoccupation with the family's history that is evident in its many genealogical histories, tables, and trees. One seventeenth-century Welser family tree, which I discuss in detail in chapter 4, a copper engraving made by Georg Strauch, served as a template, with various copies to which the family could add names of later offspring and, in one version, even the aforementioned Stenglin map of Venezuela (fig. I.7). The betrothal of Bartholomäus Welser V's niece, Philippine von Welser (1527–80), and Ferdinand II, archduke of Austria (1529–95), the second eldest son of Maximilian and nephew of Emperor Charles V, prompted the emperor to validate the family's noble status, although the dynastic House of Habsburg excluded Philippine's descendants from hereditary rights (Auer 1998, 39–40).

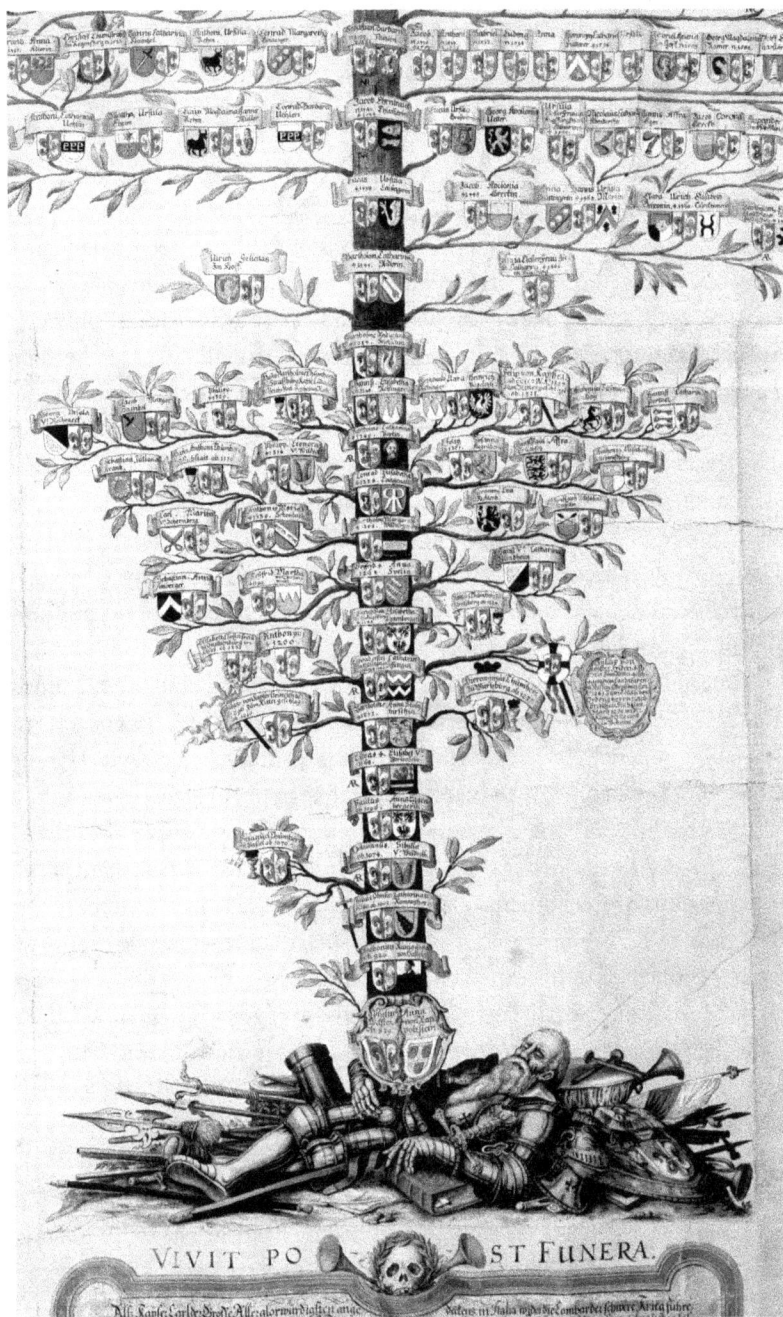

FIGURE I.7. Georg Strauch, Detail from *Genealogical Table of the Family von Welser* 1666, with engravings by Georg G. Strauch and the map of Venezuela by Emanuel Stenglin with the title, *Venezuela, provincia in America occidentali. Quam olim Dni Velseri patricii Augustani prossidebant, a Carolo v. imperatore ipsis consigna-ta.* 96 x 266 cm, 12 leaves hand-colored and mounted on canvas. Courtesy of the Library of Congress, Special Collections, CS629.W4

THE RISE OF AUGSBURG AND THE ONE PERCENT

According to Wolfram Baer (1978, 15), no other German city changed so much in its economic character as Augsburg in the late fifteenth and early sixteenth centuries. Commerce and mining were the dual engines of change. Located at the confluence of the Wertach and Lech Rivers, the city provided navigable transport routes as well as alpine passes that allowed it to become a main access point to Italy, with Venice the main destination. Its role in the mining industry in the fifteenth century allowed Augsburg to compete with the Genoese bankers in high-finance lending. Nonetheless, the city played a secondary role to Nuremberg in cosmopolitanism, famous for being the home of the artist Albrecht Dürer and the humanist Hartmann Schedel. The humanist circle that Schedel led published the *Nuremberg Chronicle*, which would remain influential for Augsburg bankers eager to do business globally before and after Columbus sailed to the Americas.

Augsburg had been a bishop's seat and was under ecclesiastic rule until it gained the status of free imperial city in the Middle Ages. In contrast to other free imperial cities, though, the bishop controlled the right to mint money until the emperor implemented a change on May 27, 1521. While not part of the royal nobility, Augsburg's oligarchy was composed of patricians who had ruled the city since Emperor Friedrich Barbarossa granted the city the status of free imperial city. For example, Augsburg's *Stadtrecht*, the civic code of 1276, stated that members of patrician stock would comprise the city council. As Kathy Stuart (1999, 33) documents in her study of early modern Augsburg, patricians like the Welsers aggressively guarded their status against encroachment by the more recently rich. Throughout the fourteenth century, there were conflicts between the increasingly wealthy guilds (the most powerful of which were those of merchants, weavers, and goldsmiths) and the old patrician guard, including the Augsburg guild revolt of 1368, as well as conflicts in Speyer, Mainz, Worms, and Ulm. In 1383 the city's leading patrician circle became impenetrable; only in the 1500s did this elite group open to nonelites who had prospered financially. The outcome of the Augsburg guild revolt of 1368 was that guilds co-governed with patricians, but the latter were still overrepresented in the ranks of city power (Blendinger 1984, 151).[5] Between 1368 and 1548 Augsburg's guilds sent twelve representatives to the Great Council and thirty-four guild masters, including weavers, bakers, and butchers, to the Small Council (Jecmen and Spira 2012, 28; Stuart 1999, 35). Yet even within these classes the economic elites were more engaged in the business of trading their wares than their production. As Stuart (1999, 35) explains, "The guilds were at once political corporations and economic associations that regulated the production and distribution of a commodity." To show how stratified Augsburg society was, Katarina Sieh-Burens (1986, 20) provides statistics for the "Wirtschafts-metropole" (economic metropolis), as Augsburg was called at the end of the fifteenth century. For example, Franz Bäsinger, *Münzmeister* and father-in-law of Jakob Fugger, a Welser competitor, contracted with Duke Sigismund of Tirol for a loan of 35,000 florins in exchange for the exploitation of silver mines. This would be typical of the mixing of credit and mining that characterized such contracts by the Fuggers and Welsers (Kießling 1984a, 177).

Augsburg overtook Nuremberg as one of the most important financial centers in Europe, becoming a hub in the first decades of the sixteenth century known for international trade, banking, and mining. It also became the site of monopolies and cartels in the second half of the sixteenth century (Sieh-Burens 1986, 20).

Augsburg's prominence in the late fifteenth century reflected other factors. The first is that the Habsburgs financed many offensives against the Ottoman Turks and relied on Augsburg's willing financial support. The second is that since 1456 trade increased between Augsburg's patrician and guild members with the Habsburg emperor (Frederick III) and the pope. The contract between the Fuggers and Habsburg duke Sigismund from Tirol in 1456 was an example of such trade. Habsburg archduke Maximilian came through Augsburg to receive money as well as a patrician escort for his wedding journey to Burgundy (Schnith 1984, 163). Thereafter he preferred to purchase armor produced in Augsburg (Jecmen and Spira 2012, 30). Soon after, the Fuggers provided Emperor Frederick III and his entourage with cloth and silk fabric when they passed through the city.

In the Holy Roman Empire's social circles, the elite patricians of "golden Augsburg" stood close to the Habsburg dynasty and aspired to the nobility, complicating Augsburg's status as a "free" imperial city that remained subject to the emperor. Emperor Maximilian elevated Jakob Fugger and his nephews to the title "imperial Barons" of Kirchberg in 1511 and then "Counts" in 1514, which in 1526 was confirmed as a hereditary title (Häberlein 2012, 202). As previously mentioned, the Welsers also certified their nobility through their close relations to Emperor Charles V, even though Philippine von Welser's 1557 secret morganatic marriage to Ferdinand II, archduke of Austria, would become the stuff of romantic fairy tales in the eighteenth and nineteenth centuries. Yet the tangible difficulties symbolized by the inter-marriage of members of the patrician and royal social classes (punishable by law) only showed how the Habsburg royals of the highest imperial rank viewed the patrician and guild member class in terms of a hierarchy they were eager to uphold. The patricians of Augsburg were the city's elite, but they were not royalty with whom to seal strategic alliances.

CITY AND LINEAGE

In exploring Augsburg's elite classes, I delve into the leading patriciate, of which the Welsers were members. After the guild constitution of 1368, the patriciate developed into its own closed class, and only male members could inherit patrician status. Moreover, in comparison to cities like Nuremberg, Augsburg had no territorial possessions surrounding it (Baron 1937, 628). By the 1530s, only seven of the original elite groups remained: the Welsers, Rehlingers, Herwarts, Langenmantels (two lines), Ilsungs, Hofmairs, and Ravensburgers. The Welser, Rehlinger, and Herwart clans still played an important economic role in the city, but after 1538 members of the mer-chant class could ascend into the patrician class. Augsburg's complex social and political rules demanded wealth in material and social forms;[6] after all, Augsburg was a free imperial city led by a powerful minority who saw them-selves as equal to the highest nobles.

There was also another social circle: the *Mehrer*. This term is difficult to translate, but it roughly means "friends" of the patricians. Through marriage with a patrician's daughter or another Mehrer's daughter, a male member of the merchant class could also reach the status of Mehrer but never the patri-ciate (Reinhard and Häberlein 1996, xv). It was in this circle that the Fuggers first began to participate in the active political and social life of Augsburg in the Lords' Drinking Room Society (*Herrentrinkstubengesellschaft*), also known as the Lords' Room (*Herrenstube*), an elite club that admitted mem-bers of the patriciate and their in-laws and was created to avoid social min-gling with undesirable citizens from the lower strata of Augsburg society. According to Ann Tlusty (2001, 28), by the sixteenth century the Lord's Room had become "the social center of Augsburg's privileged society"; there, new city council members were sworn in, visiting dignitaries honored, politics debated, and patricians' entertained.

Most of the Mehrer members between 1548 and 1618 were employees of merchants' firms. The biggest group of elites came from the merchant class, with the *Kaufleutezunft*, or Merchants Guild, comprising a large part of Augsburg's well-to-do citizens in 1538, but patrician and Mehrer circles remained tight. A list of the members of the *Kaufleutestube*, or Merchant's Ale House, from 1541 shows it could only be accessed through hereditary right or marriage. The prosographic work of Häberlein and Reinhard on Augsburg's elite in the sixteenth century, which identifies the financial links between 1,545 powerful Augsburg citizens, reflects the role of connection and birth in the dealings that made Augsburg a financial capital of early modern Europe.[7]

THE FUGGERS OF AUGSBURG

No book on sixteenth-century Augsburg and the Welsers can fail to mention their competitors, the nouveau riche Fuggers. The Fuggers represented one of the most typical cases of social climbing in the early modern period (Stuart 1999, 36). Originally from the weaving class, one of their family members, "Jakob the Rich" (1459–1525), became one of the richest men that had ever lived. Katarina Sieh-Burens (1986, 90) describes the Welsers and the Fuggers as examples of two very different models of Augsburg patrician families, the first from the older patrician stock and the latter the product of social ascendancy due to massive wealth. Both families were intent on documenting their social status and honorable genealogy; the Fuggers remained loyal to the emperor and produced beautifully illustrated genealogical books, while the Welsers commemorated their older family line and the blood they shed in Venezuela in a genealogical tree.

The Fuggers' wealth led Emperor Charles V to declare them his official lenders, which afforded them the special privileges of association with him. Ramón Carande Thobar's three-volume *Carlos V y sus banqueros* (1965) reveals just how important their capital and loans were to the Habsburg monarch (see ch. 1). Perhaps it was their new entry into Augsburg's patrician class and their position as social climbers that led them to fervently oppose the Reformation and remain Catholic even as the Holy Roman Emperor, leader of free cities and rulers, would prepare the "Augsburg Confession," an affirmation of Lutheran faith produced for the Imperial Diet in 1530. In general, the Fuggers remained loyal to the emperor and his Catholic faith, and they proposed a series of measures that would disband the Reformation-oriented guilds and instead reward them as elite members of the patriciate who could now lead the city's affairs.

The Fuggers were among other companies competing with the Welser-Vöhlin Company around 1500. However, while the Fuggers mostly traded mining products (Tyrolian and Slovakian silver and copper), the Welsers relied more on the trade of spices, textiles, and dyes. The different business interests meant that there was less rivalry between the two family firms, except in their dealings with the Roman curia and their interests in overseas expansions. When Vasco da Gama's expedition to India secured the ocean route between Europe and India, Augsburg's merchants paid attention. The Augsburg city secretary, Dr. Conrad Peutinger, gathered news reports about India and translated them with his brother-in-law Christoph Welser (Häberlein 2012, 51). The Portuguese crown at this time allowed foreign merchant participation through investment in the outfitting of the expeditions, and the inclusion of German merchants with mining connections was further welcome as the Indian market desired copper and silver. The Welser-Vöhlin Company was the first to establish an outpost in Lisbon in 1502, which its agent, Lucas Rem, would direct. In 1504, an agreement was signed allowing southern German merchants, including the Fuggers and the Welsers, as well as Genoese merchants, to participate in outfitting the fleet of Francisco de Almeida, which would travel from Lisbon to India the following year. While the Welsers contributed most of the money, the Fuggers contributed a small sum. However, soon after the Portuguese declared a crown monopoly in 1506 it became more difficult for German merchants to pursue commercial activities there (Häberlein 2012, 52). Instead, they would look toward Spain. In 1519 the Fuggers, like the Welsers, financed the election of Charles I of Spain to Charles V, Holy Roman Emperor, and became his trusted lenders. The Fuggers would lead in the amount of funds owed by the crown (19.54 percent), with the Welsers second at 15.01 percent (Tracy 2002, 101). In return, they too received the lease of land owned by the *maeztrasgos* (chivalric orders), but they had to wait for the influx of New World gold and silver as payment for their loans from the crown (see ch. 1). Like the Welsers, the Fuggers secured a contract with the Spanish Council of the Indies in 1530 to conquer and settle an area of South America. Their colonization contract extended from the Straits of Magellan to Chincha in Peru (all of present-day

Chile and part of southern Peru), but for unknown reasons (perhaps they got wind of the Welsers' difficulties in Venezuela), the Fuggers did not undertake the project.

THE RISE OF INEQUALITY IN AUGSBURG AND DECLINE OF PATRICIAN MEMBERSHIP

While Augsburg became an important financial and artistic center in the sixteenth century, the ruling classes initially had looked to Nuremberg's humanistic circle for inspiration. Augsburg was an important city for the empire, with many Imperial Diets (governing bodies) meeting there. In the Diet of 1518 Martin Luther came to answer questions on the Ninety-Five Theses posed by a papal delegate, Cardinal Cajetan (Jecmen and Spira 2012, 34). In the Diet of 25 June 1530 the emperor received Philipp Melanchthon's Augsburg Confession, the twenty-eight articles that constitute the basic confession of Lutheran churches, which remains one of the most influential documents of Protestant theology. Augsburg would remain most famous for the Peace of Augsburg, which took place at the Diet of 1555 and which brought Emperor Charles V together with the princes who made up the Schmalkadic League, which ruled that the prince of each territory could determine the preference for either Lutheranism or Catholicism.

Augsburg would enter a period of stagnation in the 1530s that greatly affected its citizens. At the beginning of the sixteenth century Augsburg had around 30,000 inhabitants and about 5,000 taxpayers. Ten years later, the population grew to around 50,000 inhabitants, with 10,000 taxpayers. All in all, around 1500 the polarization of Augsburg's population into rich and poor could no longer be ignored by its citizens (Kießling 1984b, 246); in terms of social stratification, Augsburg's underclass (made up of weavers, servants, day laborers) grew by 10 percent in a fifty-year period (1490s–1550s). As Augsburg's artisans and patricians became wealthier, the underclass of weavers and day laborers, who had once enjoyed relative stability, became poorer, increasingly living hand to mouth.

Some elite guild members married members of the patrician class and participated in patrician activities. This new reality united old patricians such as Simund Grossembrot and Jörg Herwart with the guildsmen Ulrich Fugger and Franz Baumgartner in the copper business and, later, in trade with the East and West Indies (Kießling 1984b, 244). The transformation of the *Herrentrinkstube*, or Gentlemen's Drinking Hall, into the *Mehrer der Gesellschaft* in 1568 and the attending opening up of membership to individuals from the elite guilds who had capital reflected the decline of the patrician class (Jahn 1984, 191). The older order of patrician families of which the Welsers were part had decreased from fifty families to seven, prompting the opening of the patrician class to the ruling merchant families in 1538. It was at this time that the Fuggers became a patrician family.

Augsburg's decline may have contributed to the Welser Company's downfall; even as it veered toward bankruptcy and after it attempted to record the family's honorable lineage and turned to nostalgic commemorative projects that marked their imperially sanctioned colonization of Venezuela. Scholars such as Sieh-Burens (1986) and Stuart (1999) have shown that religion and honor played a primary role in maintaining the stratification of Augsburg society in the early modern period. Even as the city became a commercial center in the sixteenth century, the patricians represented an elite group that valued "honor" to such an extent that it excluded those who could be labeled "dishonorable" either because of their work (e.g., skinners, executioners, and grave diggers) or by association with a member from one of these outcast classes. Dishonor and honor were inherited through generations, which made genealogy vital for keeping the family reputation intact for members of patrician and merchant circles. Large quantities of genealogical materials related to the Augsburg patrician and merchant families that emphasize their ascendancy and aristocratic caste still exist. Elites such as the Fuggers and Welsers kept this genealogical history in books such as *Geheim Ehrenbücher, Geschlechterbücher, Stammesbeschreibungen,* and *Cronica.* I argue that this genealogical information remains crucial to understanding the many narratives of the Welser's Venezuela colony that are being told even today. While the Welsers' project of colonization in Venezuela began in 1528 and officially extended until 1556, their decline in the colony had already begun in the 1530s. The Welser Company would go bankrupt in 1614.

METHODOLOGY AND CHAPTER OVERVIEW

My approach as a comparatist and a scholar of the literature and history of colonial Latin America and the early modern Germanophone realm is interdisciplinary. I rely on travel narratives, translations, judicial records, and letters from archives including the Archivo General de las Indias, as well as maps, prints, and photographs based on research conducted on both sides of the Atlantic in Spanish, German, French, Italian, and other languages. This approach sheds light on the Welser episode in ways that analyze the various genres that contribute to the production of a cultural memory about the colony.

However, I am also aware of the many limitations and silences of this book. Achille Mbembe (2002, 19) reminds us that not all documents are destined for archives and that archives mainly keep documents related to the work of the state. Ann Stoler (2002, 90) has criticized the way that archives are mined for ethnographic content related to colonial histories, rarely examining the archives' "peculiar form or context." Daniel Nemser (2015, 131) has powerfully demonstrated that the AGI was founded to defend Spanish colonialism and to become *the* holder of the discourse on Indigenous peoples of the Americas. Made with materials from the colonies, the AGI building literally embodies resource extraction and exploitation, and its administrators practiced marginalization and dispossession of eleven families that called the building home. If, as Nemser (2015, 137) writes, "the documents held at the AGI are the residue of a long history of dispossession, the grimy, partial and always fragmented build-up left behind by countless acts of violence, coercion and exploitation that accompanied Spanish colonial rule," what are we to make of that violent corpus? What are we to make of the corpus of documents in the Venezuelan National Archive and libraries that celebrate the positivist "mestizo" nation and whitewash Indigenous and Afro-Venezuelan stories? To answer these questions, I incorporate the work of anthropologists and ethnohistorians who have tried to re-create the lives of the peoples who were exterminated in genocidal campaigns of conquest and whose stories survive despite enslavement.

This book has seven chapters in which I strive to situate the Welser colony in its historical and social background, its visual and literary representations, and its cultural memory. The book has three parts that are loosely organized by background, chronology, and place. The first part of this book addresses the economic and social history of the Welsers amid a racialized merchant capitalism (chs. 1 and 2). According to Pulido (2017, 3), "A focus on racial capitalism requires greater attention to essential processes that shaped the modern world, such as colonization, primitive accumulation, slavery, and imperialism." I examine the lending relationship between the banking family and Emperor Charles V to contextualize the Welsers' racialized capitalism in Venezuela within the larger scope of their mercantile activities in Iberia and the Atlantic islands of Madeira and La Palma. The European taste for sugar and other commodities opened up a market in which the Welsers wanted to take part and which depended on the Indigenous peoples and the African slave trade. The Welsers' colonization of Venezuela occurred while there was growing unease concerning the destabilizing effects of an inrush of American gold and silver into European financial markets and increasingly high loan interest rates and fees for currency exchange.

Part II of this book deals with narrative and cartographic representations of the Welsers in Venezuela during the sixteenth through eighteenth centuries (chs. 3, 4, 5). Nikolaus Federmann's narrative of conquest, the *Indianische Historia* (1557), reveals much about colonial violence in the province of Venezuela and the way in which gifts and translated words are tools of empire but also how they are used by native subjects to resist conquest (ch. 3). Translation in colonial Spanish America revolved around using it as a tool of conquest for the Spanish crown; translation of religious texts from Spanish to Indigenous languages assisted the crown in the conversion and assimilation of Indigenous peoples to Catholicism. Federmann also "translated" his report for German readers. And while chapter 4 focuses on narratives, chapter 5 looks at the way imperial cartography, like translation, served to promote the Welsers' conquest and colonization of Venezuela. Through the genealogical memorabilia of the Welser family as well as empire-sponsored cartographic projects, I show how the Welsers became invested in showing the relationship between their family's blood and the colonial Venezuelan soil. Colonial Spanish historiographers from the sixteenth to eighteenth century also "translated" the Welser episode for a Spanish readership. Authors such as Bartolomé de Las Casas (1555), fray Pedro Aguado (the 1570s), and José de Oviedo y Baños (between 1705 and 1723) described the Welser governance as so foreign that its agents were called "animals" (ch. 5).

Part III (chs. 6 and 7) takes up the question of remembrance and the performance of this Welser history through cultural memory in the present in Germany and Latin America. As the German scholar of English literature and cultural memory Aleida Assmann (2016, 14) defines it, cultural memory is often made up of media, events, and materials that create memory across generations within a culture. In independent Venezuela historians and fiction writers have tried to continue to "translate" this episode for Venezuelans not familiar with this non-Hispanic conquest. From romantic drama, including Adolfo Briceño Picón's *Ambrosio de Alfinger* (ca. 1887), to the postmodern José Ignacio Cabrujas's *El camino del Rey* (1967) to historical novels such as Francisco J. Herrera Luque's *La luna de Fausto* (1983) and William Ospina's *Ursúa* (2005), the Welsers sometimes appear as the antiheroes of the Hispanic conquest of the region, but they are also used to highlight the idiocy of conquest and the corrupt state of affairs in Venezuela and in Colombia. In Germany in the nineteenth century, colonial newspapers indicated imperial Germany's desire to colonize parts of Africa and the Pacific and so too sometimes recalled the Welser episode with nostalgia. Later, the Welsers became immortalized as Aryan heroes: the 1938 Day of German Art parade (which Hitler attended) featured a Welser float as an example of German entrepreneurship and imperialism.

The conclusion and the postscript demonstrate the relevance of the Welser colony and its cultural memory to projects in the twenty-first century concerning venture capitalism, colonialism, cultural memory, and the restitution of artifacts taken during the colonial era, inviting additional debate over the legacy of capitalism and colonialism throughout the world today.

PART I

The Welsers
A History of Their Racialized
Merchant Capitalism

CHAPTER 1

Colonization, Commerce, Commodities, and Imperial Credit

> Try what my credite can in Venice doe.
> —William Shakespeare, *Merchant of Venice*

The conquest of Venezuela depended on currency exchange and the extension of credit. Charles depended on the Welsers and other bankers to exchange and move currency in Europe and the Indies to finance that conquest. There were many currencies and measuring systems in sixteenth-century Europe, and these currencies fluctuated. Sven Schmidt (2015), in *Das Gewerbebuch der Augsburger Christoph-Welser-Gesellschaft (1554–1560)*, looks at the account books of the Welsers and Fuggers and finds differences in each company's exchange rate for Spanish currency. But from 1545 to 1560 there was relative stability, with a general devaluation of Spanish currency of about 15 percent. This all pertains to the theory of price revolution and the idea that increased mining output from Europe, combined with the influx of gold and silver from the New World, caused inflation and devaluation. Table 1.1 lists exchange rates for the currencies mentioned in this chapter.

Before the Welsers of Augsburg were granted the rights to conquer and govern the province of Venezuela by King Charles I of Spain (1500–1558),

Table 1.1. Exchange rates in Europe in the 1500s

1 Rheinisch florin	60 kreuzer
100 Venetian ducats	140 Rheinish florins
100 scudi (Italian crowns)	150 Rheinish florins
100 Portuguese ducats (cruzados)	167 Rheinish florins
100 Spanish/Hungarian ducats	167 Rheinish florins
100 Flemish pounds	420 Rheinisch florins
100 Flemish pounds	600 Carolus florins
Spanish currency (from Castilla)	
1 ducat	375 maravedís
1 peso de buen oro / de mina	450 maravedís
1 real	34 maravedís
1 peso de ocho / castellano	272 maravedís
1 peso ensayado	450 maravedís or 1.65 pesos de ocho

later Holy Roman Emperor Charles V of the House of Habsburg, they sought ventures in Portugal's and Spain's colonies in the Atlantic world. As I show in this chapter with the diary of the Welser agent Lukas Rem, the Welsers' merchant activities in the sugar islands of Madeira and La Palma would be an experiment in early merchant capitalism that relied on a racialized workforce for the production of sugar, which is the crop they tried to produce and export with little to some success in the increasingly environmentally degraded islands of Madeira, La Palma, and Hispaniola. These experiences would later influence the Welsers' attitude toward the exploitation of natural and labor resources in their conquest and governance of the province of Venezuela. Moreover, the Welsers' lending practices to Charles, including loans for his campaign to secure the title Holy Roman Emperor, show the ways in which private capital from Augsburg and other parts of the empire would shape and influence policy during Charles's reign in Europe and the New World territories. Amid anxieties surrounding the influx of New World gold into Spanish and European markets, multiple exchange rates, and predatory lending interest rates, the Welsers exemplified an early modern merchant capitalist mentality that sought economic advancement through participation in new global racialized and exploitative ventures meant to increase the company's and Spain's capital. Printed treatises that addressed the ethics of banking and usury appeared in Spain between 1540 and 1570. Even Charles's daughter, Princess Joanna of Austria (1535–73), was alarmed about the excessive interest rates demanded by the bankers. In the end the crown's dependence on foreign capital extended to the permissions or privileges granted to individuals for certain business ventures on Hispaniola and Tierra Firme, and the Welsers would be granted the capitulación to govern the province of Venezuela. Perceptions of foreignness would continue to have an impact on the German Welsers, who were viewed as an alien force in Spanish colonization efforts in the Americas—especially as the Protestant Reformation raged in the Habsburg realms.

LUCAS REM IN THE SUGAR ISLANDS OF MADEIRA AND LA PALMA: PRACTICING FOR THE AMERICAS

Lucas Rem (1481–1541), a member of a patrician Augsburg family, worked for the Welser-Vöhlin Company from 1499 to 1517 and was an exemplary factor (company manager who connected buyers and sellers as well as creditors and debtors). He documented his commercial activities and business travel on behalf of the company in a diary, which serves as a source of information on the Welsers' affairs in Lisbon, Portugal, where he was the factor from 1503 to 1508, as well as the Canary Islands and Madeira. Rem's diary, I argue, demonstrates that the Welsers' investments in the sugar business in the Atlantic islands of Madeira and La Palma are examples of merchant capitalism that relied on racialized labor.

The diary also details the young merchant's training in Venice, where he apprenticed with Guido D'Angelo and Ulrich Ehinger, and his hopes and frustrations throughout his career with the company in Portugal, Spain, France, and Flanders, in cities such as Lisbon, Lyon, Zaragoza, and Antwerp, as well as the Atlantic islands. He represented the Welser Company at the Lyon merchants' fair and traveled through France and Spain trading in spices and Moroccan saffron on the company's behalf.

In France and Flanders, Rem toured Moulin, Tours, Blois, and Bruges, recording that he had a "wonderful trip in good company [that was] useful to collect debts for the Welsers" (Rem 1861, 6).[1] He went on to Geneva, Freiburg, and Bern to collect payments owed from his managers (7).[2] These were payments owed on goods delivered by the Welsers. When he returned to Augsburg in 1501 he recorded, "I had so much to do in so many places, that in 24 days I did not stay home [in Augsburg]" (7).[3] In August 1501 he returned to Lyon and became extremely ill with pestilential fever (7). Yet he writes that he continued to work tirelessly on behalf of the Welsers. On 7 October 1502, he recorded, "Even sick I rode [to "Alvages," i.e., Albi in Occitania in France] and made useful business with Moroccan Saffron" (7).[4] Later, after traveling through the Pyrenees and Spain, he conducted business with the Spanish king, Phillip I. He made it to Valencia in January 1503, writing that he had "a good deal of money to receive and exchange" (8).[5] He arrived on 8 May 1503 in Lisbon, the hub for expedition and merchant voyages to western Africa and the East Indies. He was again "sick with fever" and had to rely on "a foreigner" for "help and advice," "as I knew no one there" (8).[6] It appears the advice was useful as on 1 August he signed a contract on behalf of the Welsers with the king of Portugal, Emmanuel I (Manuel I), to stock three ships for India (8).[7] Of the plague ravaging the Iberian Peninsula in 1503, he wrote, "God help us! The pest is again at home, and many merchants are dying."[8] Perhaps because he had been ill, the entries between 1503 and 1508 contain fewer details than other parts of the diary.[9] But he wrote that in Portugal he sold copper, quicksilver, cinnabar, and lead. He also began to make preparations for business in the Atlantic, namely, the islands of Madeira, Cabo Verde, and the Azores, as well as the northern African Barbary coast.[10]

His physical discomfort and homesickness must have been so dire that when Rem returned to Augsburg in January 1508 he begged his employers "not [to] send me to Portugal anymore" (10).[11] The Welsers, likely recognizing the difficulty of reestablishing the connection with King Emmanuel, were unsympathetic, and after traveling south to Venice and Rome and then on to Avignon and Lyon, Rem received a message from his employers that he should "travel by sea or land to Lisbon, Madeira, [and] La Palma for the benefit of the company" (12).[12]

Gifted in accounting and administration, Rem was employed to open outposts for the Welser Company that would deal in sugar in Madeira and the Canary Islands, which Portugal and Spain, respectively, had conquered in the 1500s. From Lisbon, Rem sailed on to Funchal, the capital of Madeira, on 8 September 1506, a voyage that took five days. He met with Leo Ravensburger and Hans Schmid there,[13] but the factory and books were in disarray, and Rem installed Jacob Holzbock as the administrator.[14]

Madeira was the first place where the sugar industry developed in the Atlantic, and it would become an important site for the model of colonization that the Welsers would follow on Hispaniola, especially in regard to sugar production. Sugar planting and trade of the commodity was already in place in the Funchal market in the late fifteenth century, with "foreigners" (in this case, individuals who were not Portuguese) from Flanders and Genoa doing the planting and trading of the crop there. According to Alberto Vieira (2004, 75), just as in the Canary Islands and later in Venezuela, foreigners were allowed to plant and trade sugar in Madeira, although periods of xenophobic bans interrupted such activities during times of economic depression within the Portuguese realms.

As sugar became a desired commodity on the European market, the crop's production and refining methods were rapidly industrialized; it demanded intensive capital and reliable labor power and resulted in degradation of the land. The highest yields in Madeira's sugar production occurred in 1506; however, the industry's decline and the environmental degradation of the island would follow especially between 1516 and 1537. According to Shawn William Miller (2007, 79), Madeira, named for its "single, all-encompassing forest," "excellent soils," and "abundant fresh water," was turned into a barren island where an early seventeenth-century observer "could not find a single tree on the colony's entire 740 square kilometers." Soil erosion, insects that decimated the crops, and a labor shortage led more Madeirans to abandon sugar for grape planting destined for wine production (Vieira 2004, 61). At the same time, Madeirans sought other sugar-growing opportunities in the Canary Islands that were suited for such planting, Tenerife, Gran Canaria, and La Palma.[15]

Merchant traders such as the Welsers and the Claaes followed a similar pattern of participation in the sugar trade that would begin in Madeira and then move to the Canary Islands and finally to the Caribbean and Atlantic markets on Hispaniola and in Brazil. Agents such as Lucas Rem (for the Welsers) and Erasmo Esquet (for the Claaes) lived in Lisbon and had local agents in Funchal, who were usually chosen first from within the merchant family itself, then from compatriots who had their residences in Funchal, and finally from among the Portuguese (Vieira 2004, 77). During the beginning of Madeira's sugar decline of 1508–9, from 17 to 21 September 1509, Lucas Rem sailed from Madeira to La Palma with Hans Egelhoff, Jacob Holzbock, and Bartholme Kelli (or Keller). Madeirans had begun to promote the sugar industry on the Canary Islands, having brought over the first plantings. For example, in 1507 in Tenerife 34,545 *arrobas* of sugar had been produced,[16] and in La Palma, 2,727 arrobas; the sugar trade was alive and well in La Palma when the Welsers decided to invest directly in the ownership of a sugar mill and plantation. Thus the Welsers completed the move from Madeira to the Canary Islands when their representative, Egelhoff, bought the Tazacorte plantation in La Palma on behalf of the Welser Company through Italian intermediaries, Bono Bronzoni and Juan Augusto.[17] Rem would leave Egelhoff as representative of the Welser Company there.

The Tazacorte plantation's history was intertwined with the Spanish conquest of the island. The first Spaniard to take ownership of Tazacorte after the Spanish colonization of La Palma was Juan Fernández de Lugo, nephew of the conquistador don Alonso Fernández de Lugo, the "Adelantado de las Islas Canarias," who conquered La Palma and Tenerife. In the *repartimiento*, or distribution of conquered lands administered by Spanish authorities, Tazacorte figures in 1502 as "land, natural pool and waters, and 5 plots of land" (Viña Brito 2004, 548).[18] This follows a popular model on the Canary Islands that granted Spanish conquerors and important creditors desirable land with access to fresh water that would be used for water-intensive sugar planting and production. The native islanders were excluded from owning such desirable properties. Levin Bonoga, a "mercader flamenco" (Flemish merchant) who had a close relationship with Férnandez de Lugo, was renting the land from De Lugo when Tazacorte was sold first to Jácome Dinarte. Then Tazacorte was sold to Egelhoff, the Welser agent.

Rem's diary entry reveals his scorn for the plantation: "Tassacorte" was nothing but a "damned land,"[19] and by his account he was eager to leave as fast as possible (Rem 1861, 13). Rem supervised construction projects on the plantation by day and worked on the accounts by night. His diary acknowledges that he should have stayed longer to put the plantation in working order but that his priority was to return to Spain before winter weather at sea blocked his return to the Iberian Peninsula.[20] Rem eventually returned to Lisbon and had an audience with King Emmanuel to seek better global business prospects. The Welsers entrusted Rem to handle the affairs between the king and the Welser Company concerning the trade in India, as well as large shipments of sugar from the Azores and Madeira.[21]

Rem's less than lukewarm affection for Tazacorte may have persuaded the Welsers to sell the property four years later; the Welsers had bought

Tazacorte for 1,700 ducats in 1509, yet it was not until 1513 that Empress Isabella issued a royal decree confirming the transfer of ownership (Viña Brito 2004, 551). That same year Jacob Groenenberg from Cologne (also known as Groenenborch before he changed his name to the Hispanicized Monteverde) bought the sugar plantation for 8,000 gold florins (Viña Brito 2004, 545).[22] Groenenberg also purchased the industrial machinery to process the sugarcane, livestock, a blacksmith and coppersmith shop, and the enslaved Africans attached to the plantation, which the sale records as "all of the blacks of either sex" (Viña Brito 2004, 555).[23]

Enslaved people were used in sugar production in both Madeira and the Canary Islands, and the Welsers followed this pattern in Tazacorte, though a mixed labor force of enslaved and freedmen would have worked in the sugar mills of Madeira. Alberto Vieira (2004, 69) warns that it is important to view the islanders' use of slave labor according to landholding structures on Madeira and various sugar islands of the Canary archipelago as it differed in the Portuguese and Spanish contexts. Madeirans were active participants in the Atlantic slave trade because of the need to import labor, as the island was not populated when the Portuguese encountered it in 1419. The island's location close to West Africa provided easy access to the slave market during periods of high demand for sugar. In periods of decline, the number of manumissions rose (Vieira 2004, 69). The situation on the Canary Islands was different from Madeira in that there was a conquered population, the Indigenous Guanches in Tenerife, who served as the first slaves. But the islands' proximity to West Africa made it possible for Berber and Sub-Saharan African peoples to be enslaved and imported there. In fact, the highest concentration of enslaved people in the archipelago was ultimately on La Palma. The Welsers' experience on Madeira and the Canary Islands may have been the reason that the Spanish crown gave the Welser Company one of the first contracts to export enslaved Africans to Venezuela. The Welsers proved to have a clear interest in participating in the lucrative slave trade.

Rem's diary reveals this mélange of merchant capitalism, processing of raw goods, and environmental resource transformation and degradation, as well as the use of racialized slave labor that would mark the Welsers' expertise as merchants involved in Atlantic trade and colonization. Despite the Welsers' unproductive experience on the Canary Islands and Madeira, they would continue to follow mercantile opportunities on Hispaniola in the

Caribbean where sugar planting had also begun in earnest. The Welsers would have many factors handling their affairs in Hispaniola's Santo Domingo as Rem had done in Madeira's Funchal, before they turned to colonizing Venezuela.

THE WELSERS IN SANTO DOMINGO

Christopher Columbus had brought the first sugarcane to Hispaniola from La Gomera in the Canary Islands in 1493 as an experiment to determine what crops would do well in the West Indies. While the first attempts to grow sugarcane started in earnest in 1503 in the area of the plain of Vega Real, problems with transportation and a need for technologically sound sugar mills would halt those efforts. However, the importation of expensive machinery and "sugar masters and mill technicians" from the Canaries and the mainland in 1515 enabled the first sugar mill to begin to operate in earnest (Ratekin 1954, 6). To keep the mill working after the decimation of the native Arawaks, planters began to use enslaved Africans to work in a sugar economy that would quickly multiply to include many sugarcane plantations, known as *ingenios* to colonial administrators. Emperor Charles V would grant permission to Hispaniola's royal judge, Rodrigo de Figueroa, who in 1519 had taken over as governor from the Hieronymite commission led by Luis de Figueroa and Alonso de Santo Domingo, to grant loans of 6,000 gold pesos to anyone who wanted to build a mill. In the 1530s there were about thirty-four mills, which operated until the collapse of the industry in the 1570s (Ratekin 1954, 11).

Sugarcane cultivation and processing resulted in environmental degradation of the sugar islands in both the Atlantic and the Caribbean. While the first plantings took from twelve to eighteen months to achieve maturity, subsequent crops still took around twelve months. According to John F. Richards (2003, 328), "To maximize their investment in the crushing mills, animals, and slaves, the early Hispaniolan planters learned to stagger plantings of individual fields so that the crop would not ripen all at once." The monocrop landscape resulted in soil erosion and habitat fragmentation. Sugar processing, which requires large quantities of timber, was an industrial operation that depended on the investor's capital, human labor power, and plenty of water to boil the sugar (Richards 2003, 413). As a result, deforestation and pollution from water runoff was rampant. Moreover, the enslaved

Black African population grew as the industry required immense human resources. Ultimately, the Welsers' buying and selling of the Tazacorte plantation in La Palma within a span of three years and their involvement with the slave trade and the sugar industry in Santo Domingo point to their interest in reaping quick returns from their investments.

On Hispaniola, the Welsers hoped to finally succeed in reaping the benefits from sugar processing that had failed at Tazacorte, but first they relied on the business from their imports to the island. The types of products that the Welsers imported to Hispaniola were similar to those of Spanish and Italian agents: wine, flour, olive oil, ham, soap, and textiles. They exported sugar and tropical medicinal drugs (Simmer 2000, 36). However, the sugar business would become increasingly important for the Welsers after Sebastian Rentz purchased one-half of the Santa Barbara sugar mill (Simmer 2000, 36).[24]

The Welsers' experiences in the sugar islands and later in Venezuela would be emblematic of the capitalocene, which, as Jason Moore (2016a) defines the term, signifies "capitalism as a way of organizing nature—as a multispecies, situated, capitalist world-ecology" (6). What Moore dubs "cheap nature," cheap labor and energy, allowed for the the Welsers' and Spain's accumulation of global capital in Madeira, the Canary Islands, Hispaniola, and Venezuela.[25] Tazacorte in La Palma and Santa Barbara in Hispaniola reflect the Welsers' desire to profit from colonial production and trade and to diversify their investments. Credit histories, the contract for conquest and governance, and the mixed Spanish-German administrative system may have caused the Welsers to adopt a strategy of maximizing short-term profits. Yet in Venezuela their preferred "search and destroy" methodology and their engagement with the slave trade would win over agricultural production and processing of raw goods. They had received permission from Charles V to import four thousand African slaves to the Indies before he gave them the capitulación for governance in Venezuela, suggesting the emperor wanted the Welsers to focus on the slave trade rather than the sugar trade; that is, he wanted them to supply the labor rather than manage the plantations.[26] Their engagement in the slave trade in the Canary Islands prepared the Welsers to take advantage of the labor of human chattel in the shortest amount of time and to the greatest extent (Marx 1976, 377). Globality here was intertwined with exploitative practices and the circulation of credit. In what follows, I analyze the Welsers' and Charles's entangled webs of credit that depended on exploitation and appropriation of the New World's resources.

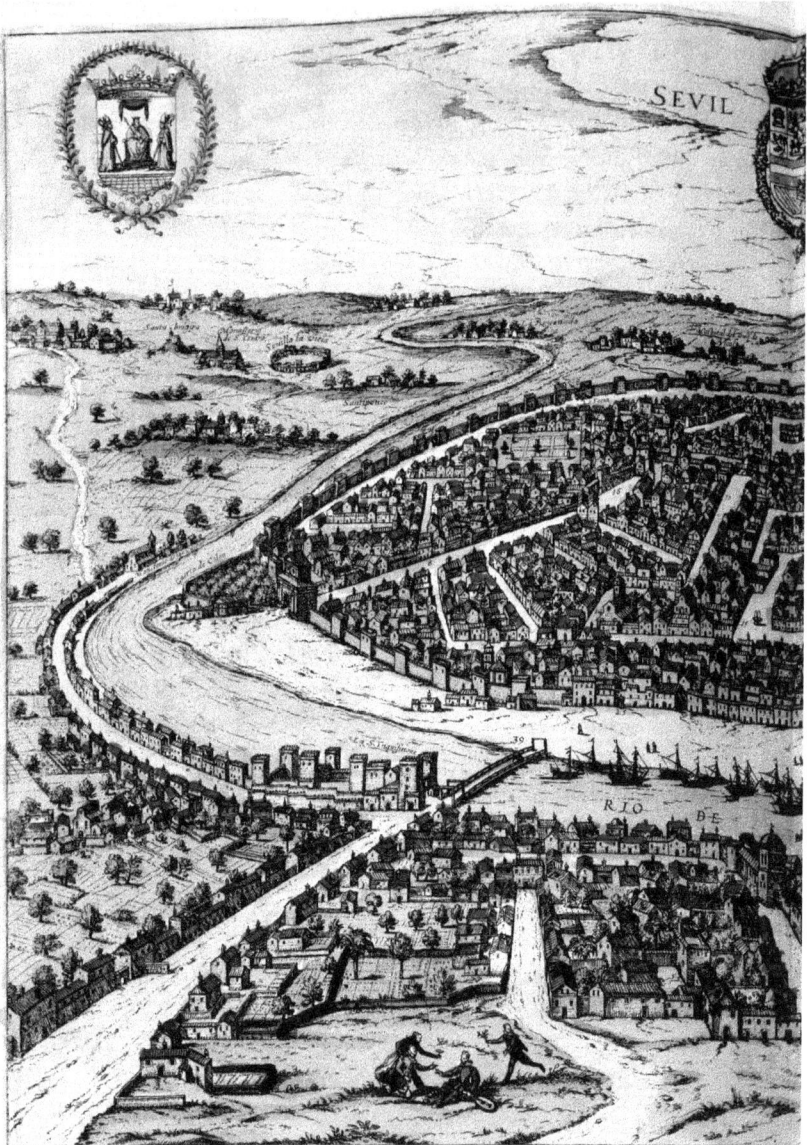

SEVIL

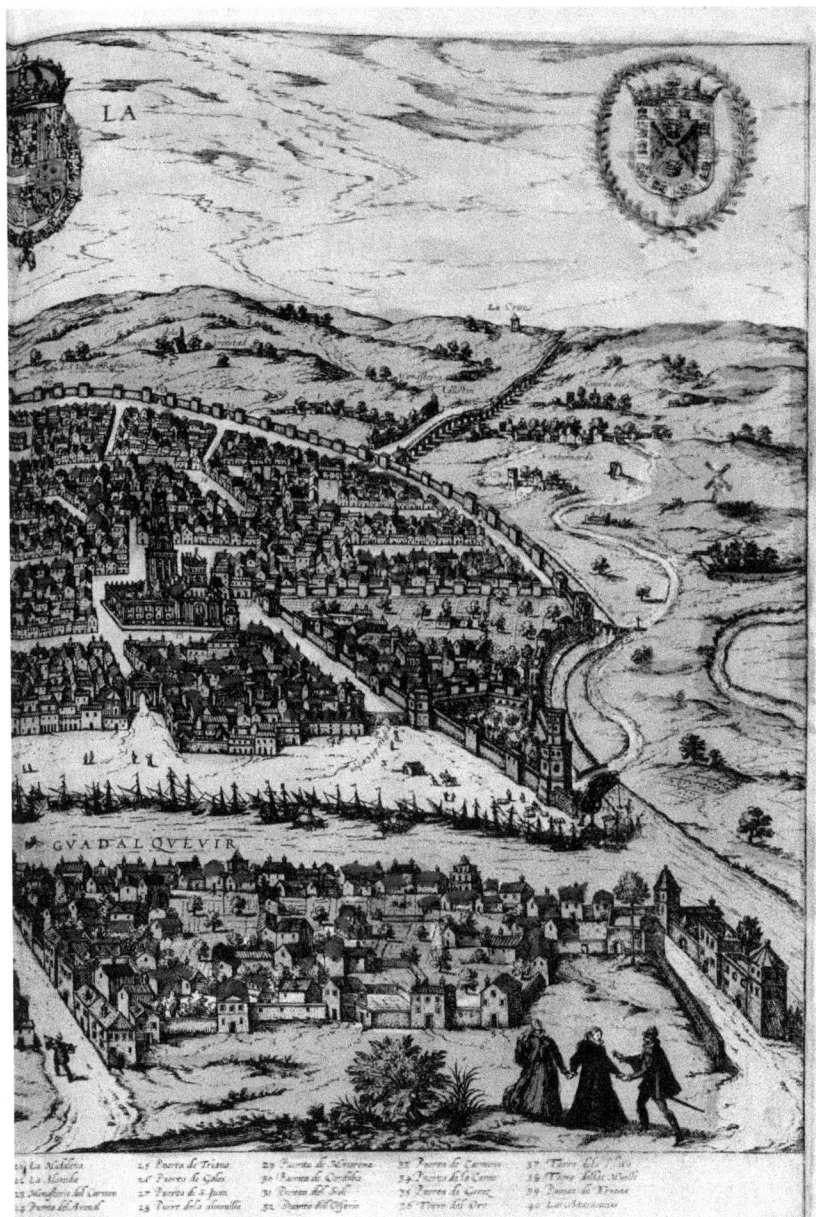

FIGURE 1.1. "Sevilla," 1617. In Georg Braun and Franz Hogenberg et al., *Civitates Orbis Terrarvm*. [Coloniae Agrippinae: apud Petrum à Brachel, sumptibus auctorum, 1572–1618, 6 vols.] Book 4: *Urbium praecipuarum totius mundi, liber quartus*). Map. Retrieved from Library of Congress, www.loc.gov/item/2008627031/.

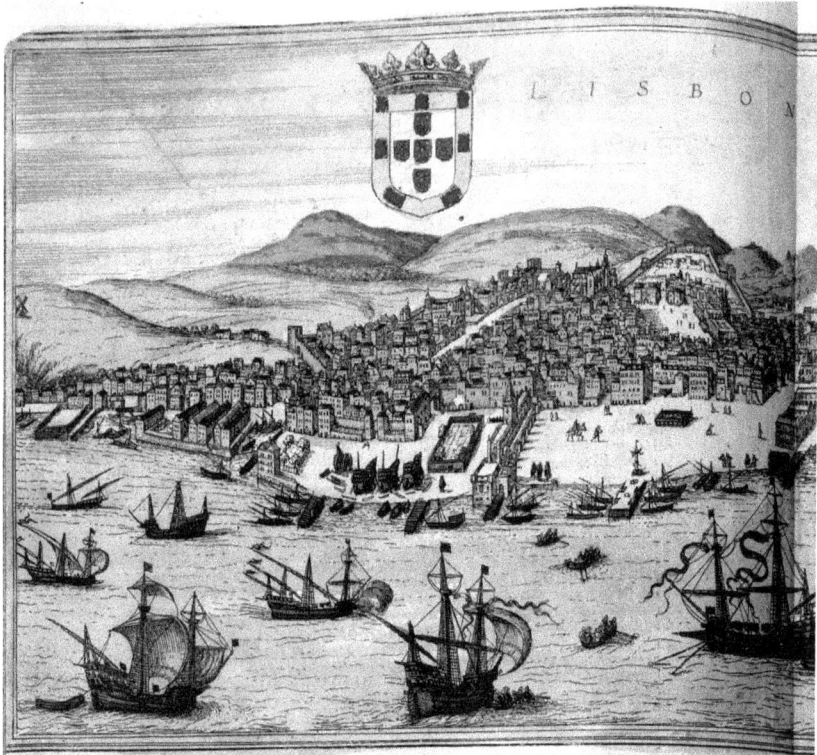

LISBON

CASCALE Lisbonæ opp.

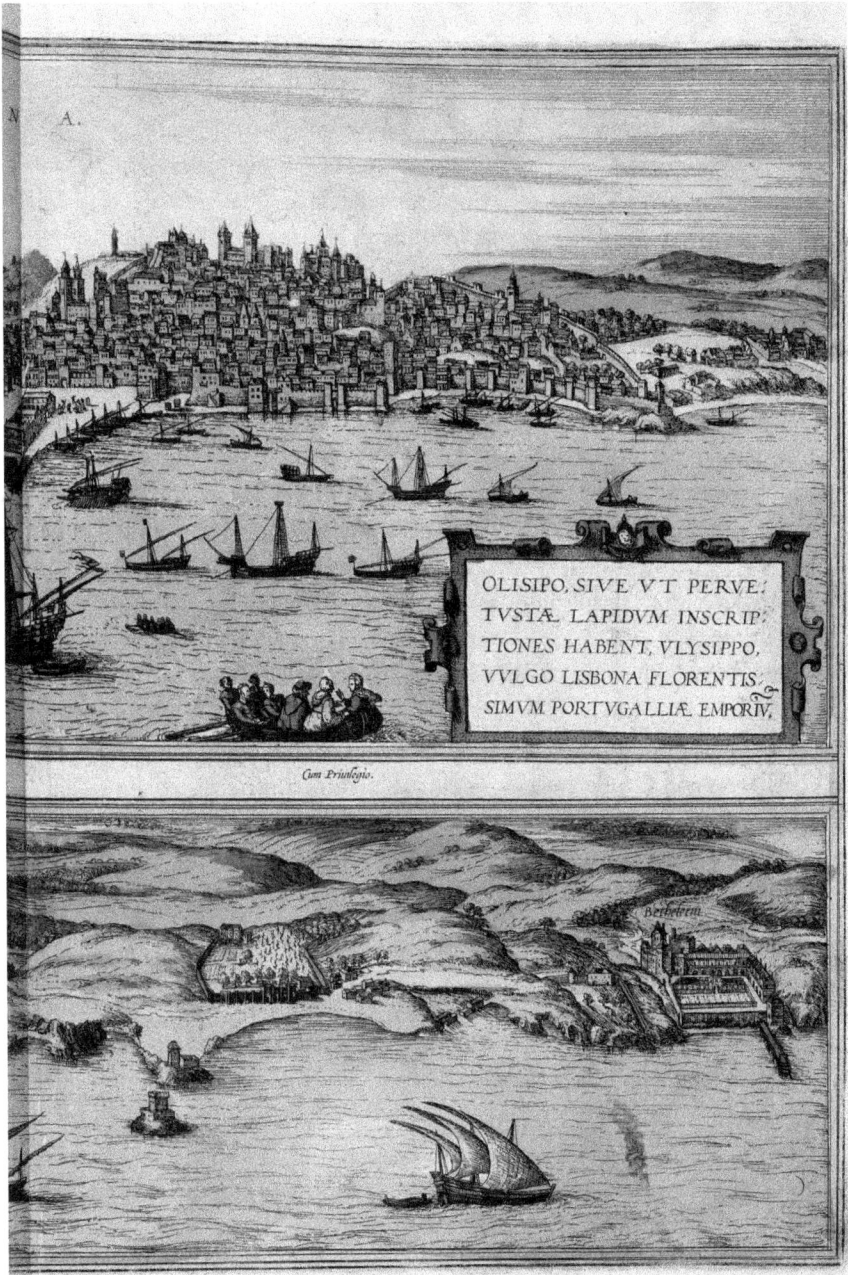

OLISIPO, SIVE VT PERVE-
TVSTÆ LAPIDVM INSCRIP-
TIONES HABENT, VLYSIPPO,
VVLGO LISBONA FLORENTIS-
SIMVM PORTVGALLIÆ EMPORIV,

FIGURE 1.2. "Lisbona." In Georg Braun, Franz Hogenberg et al., *Civitates Orbis Terrarvm*. [Coloniae Agrippinae: apud Petrum à Brachel, sumptibus auctorum, 1572–1618, 6 vols.] Book 1, *Civitates orbis terrarum, liber primus* (59 plates, colophon dated 1612). Map. Retrieved from Library of Congress, www.loc.gov/item/2008627031/.

THE WELSERS AND CHARLES V: A PROBLEMATIC LENDING RELATIONSHIP

During the sixteenth century, the amount of credit southern German bankers extended to Spain determined the relationship between Spain and the free cities of the Holy Roman Empire, including Augsburg and Nuremberg, which were under the Habsburgs' control. King Charles I of Spain depended on loans from patrician and merchant families in Augsburg and Nuremberg to fulfill his imperial ambitions. His election as Charles V, Holy Roman Emperor (1519), further solidified the financial links between southern Germany, Spain, Italy, Portugal, and Flanders.[27] The complex relationship between the cash-starved emperor and the Fuggers and Welsers drew the bankers and the emperor into an endless circle of credit extensions and delayed repayments. For the Welsers, it would secure entry into the Indies.

While the Fuggers were Charles's major backers, the Welsers were the second largest contributors, supplying 143,383 florins, or almost 17 percent of the total funding, to his electoral campaign, which gave them considerable leverage. Nine years later, in 1528, the emperor granted the Welsers exclusive rights to the exploration and colonization of the Venezuelan province on Tierra Firme. Charles found himself relying on the Augsburg Welsers and Fuggers and the Genoese Grimaldi for credit, ultimately deepening Spain's debt. As James D. Tracy writes in *Emperor Charles V, Impresario of War*, Charles's fundraising activities continued throughout his rule, and Augsburg and Nuremberg would provide the bulk of his credit largely to pay for his intra-European conflicts and wars (2002, 98). Mining in the Austrian mountains had long allowed Augsburg's merchant and banking families to loan money to Habsburg rulers. As major creditors, the Welsers were able to win many contracts from the emperor to conquer the new continent. A struggle between the Welsers and the Spanish crown on all matters related to governance in the province of Venezuela reflects both parties' anxieties about maximizing their profits.

To colonial historians, the Welser Venezuela period would be emblematic of administrative chaos, as well as the enslavement of Indigenous peoples. Debates in Spain concerning the enslavement of Amerindians, Indigenous resistance to the Spanish, and the crown's interference in the Welsers' administration created a chaotic situation in the colony of Coro in

Venezuela. In addition, the Welsers actively participated in the coastal In-digenous slave trade as well as the African slave trade.[28] Whereas the crown, conscious of protectors like the Dominican friar Bartolomé de Las Casas who defended the rights of Indians, began to respond to claims of unjust conquest in the Indies, the Welsers took their capitulación to heart. If they were going to pacify the Indians in order to extract profit from the land on behalf of the Spanish crown, they would seek to exploit the Indigenous slave trade to the fullest extent.

The Welsers' experience with intra-European and overseas trade, espe-cially the Portuguese spice trade, made them reliable and trusted contractors and creditors. In Europe, Charles could depend on his Habsburg, Burgun-dian, and Genoese connections for the mobilization of money across the empire at a time when political strife had limited his access to Lyon, Flor-ence, and Venice, which had been banking centers in Europe since the Middle Ages. To the north, Antwerp flourished as a banking and trade city in the sixteenth century, and the emperor would increasingly rely on his Flemish connections. Hence private capital from the empire would shape and influence policy during Charles's reign. The emperor was the first ruler who took advantage of the bourgeoning financial markets and exchange houses in Europe; while he effectively used this funding for his wars, he also drew criticism for his reliance on foreign capital. Scholars even in the twen-tieth century, who viewed Charles as the most foreign of Spanish kings, cri-tiqued him for his pan-European attitude and lack of Castilian manners.[29] The loans gave the firms power to influence Spanish policy. As Tracy (2002, 308) notes, Charles had little choice, as the firms in Augsburg and Genoa such as the Grimaldi "were . . . the only ones with wide networks of reliable agents [who could] ensure the remittance of money for the emperor's pay masters more or less on schedule." The need to exchange money across cur-rencies and to mobilize it across territories led Charles to establish a special relationship with the Welser and Fugger families as well as the Grimaldi in Genoa. At the same time, the banking families were pressured to grant the emperor "imperial" lines of credit with not much guarantee of return.

As I wrote in the introduction, lenders' extension of credit depended on the credibility of the debtor. However, Charles as Spanish monarch and Holy Roman Emperor often defaulted on his loans. In 1776 Adam Smith noted in the *Wealth of Nations* that war requires borrowing (2003, 1158), and of course credit was important to Charles to fund his wars (despite the general apprehension about usury). Smith discussed the advantages of lending money to government: "The merchant or monied man makes money by lending money to government, and instead of diminishing, increases his trading capital" (1158). The Welsers and Fuggers did reap special privileges as a result of granting loans to the emperor, but as time went on and the crown continued to delay loan payments to its creditors, the privilege of being Charles's bankers must have often felt like a curse.

Christine Johnson (2008) and Elvira Vilches (2010) also have written about the importance of credit for the emperor and the Welsers. Johnson aptly titles a chapter on Bartholomäus Welser's difficult relationship with the emperor in her *German Discovery of the World*, "The Sorrows of Young Welser." According to Johnson (2008, 179), merchant houses such as the Fuggers' and Welsers' were often forced to loan the emperor money, and they were certain to never see it again. The emperor could repay the loan whenever he wanted, lower the interest rates, and substitute the terms of repayment. Credit in the end was subject to political and social hierarchies, though creditors such as Jakob Fugger also exerted influence over the court and the emperor's policies.[30]

The Fuggers at the beginning of the 1520s held court with the emperor and were involved in a number of Spanish ventures. For example, they were to collect revenue from the Spanish crown directly as payment of their loans, including those from the religious military orders, which were known as maestrazgos. Jakob Fugger "kindly reminded" Charles who had put money toward his elections when it appeared that they were not going to be able to lease out their revenue from the maestrazgos (Häberlein 2012, 65). Jakob Fugger also invested 10,000 ducats in García de Loaysa's expedition to the Moluccas soon after the circumnavigation of the globe was achieved by Fernando Magellan's fleet (1519–22). However, the seven ships that sailed from La Coruña in July 1525 never returned (Häberlein 2012, 66).

Charles also ruled in favor of German merchants when they were accused of violating anti-monopoly laws. The Imperial Diet of Nuremberg (1522–23) tried to investigate and attack merchants' monopoly on the spice trade because of the sudden wealth they enjoyed and the increasing costs of the spices (Tracy 2002, 174). The imperial estates debated on limiting the capital stock of companies to 50,000 florins and limiting all outside capital investment, which would have severely limited companies such as that of the Fuggers and Welsers. But humanists came to the rescue of the banker-merchants and effectively argued against trade regulations. Conrad Peutinger (1465–1547), for example, argued that the European spice trade was so complicated that no corporation could manipulate the process, and in any case, spices were luxury goods. In the end, the imperial estates decided to not put a ceiling on the capital stock of merchant companies but passed a 4 percent import duty (Häberlein 2012, 66). Soon after, in 1523, the imperial prosecutors filed suit against the Fuggers, Welsers, Höchstetters, and other Augsburg firms for violating the laws against monopolies. After sending a delegation on behalf of the Augsburg merchants, Charles ruled in favor of the merchant companies in an edict in 1525 stating that the companies' mining activities were providing employment and sustenance to thousands of people within the empire (Häberlein 2012, 67).

In 1524, with the celebration of the Courts of Madrid, a period of financial renewal had begun that saw an attempt at reducing the debt, especially the money loaned to Charles by his foreign creditors, as well as guaranteeing the availability of liquid assets that could finance the endeavors of the monarchy (Carretero Zamora 2000, 168). A letter from Empress Isabella, also queen of Portugal, who often acted as regent of Spain during her husband Charles's many absences, discusses this repayment plan. On 1 June 1530 she wrote to Bishop Zamora, treasurer Gutiérrez, and Fernando de Guevara (a member of the Treasury Council) that the monarchy was thinking about diverting funds received through provincial tributes from Granada, collected before the Reconquista, to pay the Fuggers and the Welsers for the credit they extended to Charles, including the loan of 1.5 million ducats conceded on 18 February 1530 (Carande 1967, 2:362).[31] Hence the crown attempted to honor the terms of their creditors' loans.

Borrowing in general happened through perpetual bonds and lifetime annuities known as *juros* and *asientos*, short-term loans issued against the general credit of the king (Drelichman and Voth 2011, 1208). Spain also employed an austerity plan that would reduce the number of juros through their eventual amortization;[32] however, political problems in the empire, including tensions in central Europe and pressure from Turks and Berbers in the Mediterranean, halted those plans. The situation was particularly difficult in 1535 when the courts met in Madrid. Charles was looking for ways to pay off the accumulated debt and not worry about raising any more funds. Subsequently, the crown authorized the *secuestro* (ransom) *de Indias* in 1536 and 1537, giving the crown the right to take the gold and silver that arrived from the Americas (Carretero Zamora 2000, 171). Bartholomäus Welser was one of the unlucky "obligated lenders" (*obligado prestamista*) whose New World profits were held by Charles (Carretero Zamora 1995, 199).

FOREIGN CREDITORS AND CHARLES V: BETWEEN USURY AND CONVENIENCE

From the time of the conquest in 1492, the sovereigns of Castile had the right to grant permits for the exploration and conquest of the Americas, which led to the crown's concession of land to private individuals or companies. If the individual could not finance his conquest, he had the option of finding credit on his own or of coming together with other, more powerful investors who would then come before the crown to ensure financial responsibility for the conquest. If the investor was not the actual conquistador, or *empresario*, he usually would remain in Seville, though sometimes he would send a companion with the conquistador to guard his interests.

Charles also used "private enterprise" and encouraged high-risk venture capitalists' conquest contracts in the New World. According to Alberto Armani (1985, 19), Charles's concept of imperial sovereignty led him to favor a pan-European, thus foreign, outlook rather than a Spanish nationalist policy. In fact, the individual member territories had to pay for the empire's constant wars. Charles's decision to open the American market to non-Castilians in 1525 likely stemmed from his desire to fund his expensive European political endeavors, including the quest to become emperor and his many wars.[33] Ramón Carande, author of the detailed three-volume financial history of Charles V and his reign, *Carlos V y sus banqueros* (1943), during archival research assembled a series of five hundred asientos that detailed the loans Charles V received from foreign creditors from which Carande constructed detailed charts (tables 1.2–1.4). He identifies four periods in Charles's financial relationship with his bankers. The data show patterns regarding the Welsers' and Fuggers' loans to the emperor that detail how they were his preferred creditors—especially at the beginning of his reign. This period was of course the one in which the Welsers received the capitulación to govern Venezuela as well as the license to trade four thousand enslaved Africans in the Indies. The first period, the "Formative Years," encompasses

Table 1.2. Number of contracts (asientos) from each year, with the amount of the loan and its interest rate (first period).

Number in the Series	Year				Germans			Spaniards			Italians		
		Quantities Borrowed (Ducats)	Fees (%)	Owed or Paid Amount	Quantities Borrowed (Ducats)	Fees (%)	Owed or Paid Amount	Quantities Borrowed (Ducats)	Fees (%)	Owed or Paid Amount	Quantities Borrowed (Ducats)	Fees (%)	Owed or Paid Amount
1	1520	4,454	4.85	4,670				3,454	3.12	3,562	1,000	10.80	1,108
2–6	1521	55,834	16.87	65,255							55,834	16.87	65,255
7–12	1522	156,502	7.78	168,678	103,656	11.22	115,292	46,846	—	46,846	6,000	9	6,540
13–32	1523	348,103	11.01	386,446	99,335	14.90	114,140	23,925	3.32	24,721	224,843	10.11	247,585
33–35	1524	60,858	15.05	70,023	35,333	9.21	37,689				25,525	26.67	32,334
36–38	1525	172,415	22.98	212,048				72,415	35.39	98,048	100,000	14	114,000
39–46	1526	358,224	15.91	415,229	68,424	26.04	86,246	165,000	12.53	185,682	124,800	14.82	143,301
47–56	1527	472,917	9.97	520,084	265,000	9.75	290,850				207,917	10.25	229,234
57–68	1528	599,668	11.96	671,427	260,000	10.56	287,469	152,334	9.93	167,470	187,334	15.56	216,488
69–80	1529	794,567	18.89	944,659	145,600	16.41	169,500	72,800	16.44	84,770	567,167	19.82	690,389
81–85	1530	830,467	14.62	951,898	660,000	15.74	763,900	65,000	7.50	69,875	105,467	12	118,123
86–91	1531	904,406	37.24	1,241,239	686,550	44.86	994,583	47,856	14	54,556	170,000	13	192,100
92–98	1532	620,638	675.15	675,715	270,637	11.55	301,915	160,000	—	160,000	190,001	1.52	213,800
Total Amount		5,379,053		6,327,371	2,594,531		3,161,584	809,630		895,530	1,974,888		2,270,257

Table 1.3. Total amounts for each period and interest rates calculated by percentage of amounts borrowed versus those paid; separated by contributions and renumerations for each group of bankers.

	Germans			Spaniards			Italians			Flemings		
	Quantities Borrowed (Ducats)	Fees (%)	Owed or Paid Amount	Quantities Borrowed (Ducats)	Fees (%)	Owed or Paid Amount	Quantities Borrowed (Ducats)	Fees (%)	Owed or Paid Amount	Quantities Borrowed (Ducats)	Fees (%)	Owed or Paid Amount
First Period	5,379,053	17.63	6,327,371	809,630	10.61	895,530	1,974,888	23.22	2,757,137			
Second Period	5,437,669	21.27	6,594,365	616,239	13.61	700,128	2,237,440	22.72	2,688,637	30,500	3.11	31,450
Third Period	8,397,616	27.86	10,737,843	2,249,618	13.58	2,555,248	2,490,971	37.07	3,414,482	773,998	14.40	885,491
Fourth Period	9,653,869	48.81	14,351,591	857,042	9.70	940,229	4,901,214	67.40	8,204,911	1,570,156	26.19	1,981,453
Total Amount	28,858,207	28.89	38,011,170	4,532,529	11.87	5,091,135	11,604,513	42.58	16,546,787	2,374,654	14,56	2,898,394

Table 1.4. Participation of each group of bankers and the totals within each specified period (relative value).

	Germans		Spaniards		Italians		Flemings	
(Proporciones)	Quantities Borrowed (Ducats)	Owed or Paid Amount	Quantities Borrowed (Ducats)	Owed or Paid Amount	Quantities Borrowed (Ducats)	Owed or Paid Amount	Quantities Borrowed (Ducats)	Owed or Paid Amount
First Period	48.23	49.97	15.05	14.15	36.72	35.88		
Second Period	46.95	47.09	11.33	10.62	41.14	41.81	0.56	0.48
Third Period	34.33	36.15	26.79	23.80	29.66	31.80	9.22	8.25
Cuarto Tramo	24.01	22.47	8.89	6.55	50.82	57.17	16.28	13.81

Note: Tables 1.2–1.4 have been translated and adapted from Ramón Carande Thobar, *Carlos V y sus banqueros* (1965).

the time between Charles's imperial election and coronation, 1520 to 1532. Lutheranism rose in this period, and there were various conflicts in Italy, including with the papacy. Suliman's Ottoman forces arrived in Vienna, and Jakob Fugger pressured Charles to repay his loans.

Over the second period, "The Crucial Years," from 1533 to 1542, the debt increases as Charles continues to borrow money. This is the period when Spain saw large shipments of New World gold. Spain expected it to create immediate wealth, but in fact it destabilized the economy, leading to an economic crisis. In *New World Gold*, Vilches writes that the influx of American gold destabilized Spanish ideas and representations of value (2010, 24). Moreover, an explosion of economic writing responded to the financial crisis of the era. Spaniards realized that Spain was an indebted nation and saw that gold, either as money or as bullion, did not function as a stable, reliable value (Vilches 2010, 1). Vilches examined the anxiety that Spaniards experienced on the arrival of the New World gold: at times they thought the Spanish economy depended exclusively on gold rather than credit (16). The German free imperial cities were in a similar situation, as there was a high demand for precious metals, which meant that the Fuggers' and Welsers' silver and trade market flourished while the effects of the bullion of gold and silver from the New World destabilized financial markets at home. Charles V also thought that the influx of precious metals would solve all of his financial problems (29); as we see in the example of the Welsers, Spain's colonial expansion depended on credit, and the crown and the merchant class were indebted to one another (30). The influx of gold and silver from the Indies could not free the emperor from dependence on credit. The "Crucial Years" were also characterized by Charles using the crown's "royal fifth" percentage from bullion coming from the New World and a secuestro de Indias of 800,000 ducats (Carande 1943, 18). He had invented the secuestro, or ransom, of rare metals coming from the Indies in 1534 as a means of repaying his creditors that effectively penalized Seville's merchants by seizing gold that was supposed to be theirs.

During the "Years of Uncertainty," 1541 to 1551, Charles continued to pay down his debt from the bullion that came from the Americas, including silver from Potosí. "Licencias de saca" issued by the emperor were permissions to be paid in gold or silver, used to pay outstanding debts (Carande 1943, 19). Asientos decreased, but a civil war erupted in Peru that blocked the treasury. During this time, in 183 asientos Charles borrowed almost one million ducats per year (a total of 8,397,616 ducats). More Spanish bankers loaned the emperor money than in previous years, which meant that at least the crown saved on the exchange fees.[34]

The "Afflictive Years," 1551 to 1556, represented crisis and rising interest, deficit, and privatization (Carande 1943, 20). Charles borrowed 9,643,869 ducats, but the interest rate increased to 33.42 percent. The creditors would be reduced to a select few, and they would put in place new conditions that would allow them to collect their old debts. As Charles prepared to abdicate the throne to his son Philipp II, the only financial success appeared to be the incorporation of the income gained by the maestrazgos into the royal coffers.

Tables 1.2, 1.3, and 1.4 show that the Fuggers and the Welsers were active lenders to the emperor from the 1520s to the 1550s. But the Genoese surpassed them in the fourth period, and the Flemings, who were not present during the first period, became active lenders. The data show that while the German bankers eagerly loaned funds to Charles soon after his 1519 election as Holy Roman Emperor, in the last period the Genoese took over as Charles's bankers when the Welsers' governance of the Venezuela colony reverted to Spain. The first period, from 1520 to 1532 has the Germans lending 2,594,535 ducats, as compared to 1,974,888 ducats for the Italians and 809,630 for the Spanish. The Flemings did not extend any loans during this period. The second period, from 1533 to 1542, has the Germans lending 2,553,490 ducats, compared to 2,237,440 for the Italians and 616,239 for the Spanish. The Flemings enter the picture with their first loan to the emperor, 30,500 ducats, in 1541. The third period, 1543–51, has the Germans lending 2,883,029 ducats, compared to 2,490,971 for the Italians, 2,249,618 for the Spanish, and 773,998 for the Flemings. The last period, 1552–56, has the Germans in second place, lending much less than the Italian Genoese bankers, with 2,315,457 ducats to the Italians' 4,901,214 ducats; in four years the Genoese loaned the emperor twice as much as they had in the preceding eight years. The Flemings also increased their loans, to 1,570,156, while the Spanish decreased to 857,042, less than half of what they had loaned in 1543–51.

Over the period 1520 to 1556, the Genoese bankers lent 11,604,513 ducats, while the Germans loaned 10,346,511 ducats. However, interest as well as banking and exchange fees differed significantly. German, Spanish, and Fleming bankers charged 12 percent; the Italians charged 14 percent. Due to banking and exchange fees, the German bankers thus would recover

13.4 million for the 10.3 million ducats they paid out, while the Genoese recovered 16.6 million on 11.6 million ducats. Thus the Germans increased their funds by 29 percent, while the Genoese increased theirs by 43 percent.

The Spanish crown was aware of the high lending fees; royals, humanists, theologians, and popular writers all had something to say about merchants and usury. For example, Charles V's daughter, Joanna of Austria, princess regent, sent instructions in 1554 in a letter to the accountant Antonio de Eguino so that he could petition the emperor on her behalf:

> On the topic of the excessive interest rate that the bankers charge, the exchange rates from Italy are 26% (first rate) and then on top of this there is an additional fee of exchanging ducats per escudos, that's another 7%, in the difference of currency, and then there is an additional 10%, so that in the end the money ends up costing 43% more, and then if there is a delay in payment there is an additional 14% and because the contracts are to be paid in three, four, or five years, that means that those 339,00 escudos taken by the ambassador in Genova, becomes 898,000 more or less, and because of this excess and disorder, there is so much loss that there are no royal coffers that can take this loss. (Quoted in Carande 1967, 3:22)[35]

Perhaps Charles would have benefited from taking his daughter as a financial adviser. Princess Joanna's calculations of the loan prices the Genoese exacted were part of the ongoing debates on usury in Spanish culture after the 1540s.

According to Domènec Melé's "Early Business Ethics in Spain," the period was marked by "monarchs [who] granted privileges and monopolies to private parties, as well as to national and foreign bankers, as compensation for funds donated to defray royal expenses" (1999, 176). During this time, Spain, affected by a population decline due to the plague and emigration, as well as migration to the cities, suffered a price revolution that was worsened by the influx of New World gold (176). Moreover, "the expansion of business and the growing expenses of the states always in financial difficulties," "work done by craftsmen and farmers on credit advanced by merchants," and "the diffusion of home-based production systems" resulted in "spectacular development in credit operations" (176). Yet the social anxieties surrounding the granting of credit and the charge of usury led many to seek the advice of theologians and priests.

Three different treatises on "exchange and usury" published in Medina del Campo, Valladolid, and Toledo between 1541 and 1547, all of which had several printings, discussed these calculations. These were Cristóbal de Villalón's *Provechoso tratado de cambios* (Treatise on Exchanges) (Valladolid, 1541, 1542, 1546); Luis Sarabia de la Calle's *La instrucción de mercaderes* (The Instruction of Merchants) (Medina del Campo, 1544, 1547); and Luis de Alcalá's *Tratado de los préstamos* (Treatise on Loans) (Toledo, 1543, 1546). Written in the vernacular Castilian, these treatises were the first in Spain that addressed the ethics of banking and usury. The high inflation of the 1540s generated interest in the topic and further publications, although priests rather than merchants were the primary audience. These texts included Juan de Medina's *De Poenitentia, restitutione et contractibus* (On Penance, Restitution, and Contracts) (Alcalá, 1545) and Domingo de Soto's treatise *De Iustitia et Iure* (On Justice and Law) (Salamanca, 1553), as well as the economic analyses of exchange rates and tables offered in Martín de Azpilcueta's *Comentario resolutorio de cambios* (Resolutory Comment on Exchange) (Salamanca, 1557). The latter three treatises were meant to be guides for priests who were unsure how to deal with financial matters in merchants' fairs and markets (Reeder and Perdices de Blas 2003, 353).

Azpilcueta's *Comentario* is an account of practices concerning the exchange of money across currencies and the extension of credit internationally as seen from sixteenth-century Spain. It attempted to be a moral guide and explained the credit and money exchange customs of each country (France, Italy, Spain, Flanders) while citing canonical law (Azpilcueta uses about a thousand references). The *Comentario* explained that currency exchange made it possible for moneychangers to commit "usuria e injusticia" by charging too much (Azpilcueta 1965, 85). Azpilcueta condemned the common practice among moneychangers of emitting a *cédula*, or contract of payment, for Rome, Lisbon, Lyon, Flanders, or Venice, stating that a quantity of money should be paid in a certain time or at a specific fair (*feria*) with full knowledge that the payment would not be made but that they would collect fees on the transaction (42).

Azpilcueta drew on Scholastic traditions to support the profession of the moneychanger through a Christian perspective. He wrote that while Aristotle frowned on the business of money exchange, St. Thomas described the "art of exchange [*mercadear*] [as] lawful as long as the goal[s] are moderate profits, enough to sustain oneself and one's household." Azpilcueta also recognized that the profession of currency exchange "brings some profits to the republic," categorizing it as a legitimate national practice and denying the notion "that profiting from the exchange of money is illicit."[36]

While it is unclear whether merchants themselves actually read treatises like Azpilcueta's,[37] Sarabia de la Calle wrote in his treatise on usury that he did not want to discuss the practice of exchange that merchants employed because it might give people who would become lenders ideas about the market (Reeder 2003, 354). Tomás de Mercado's *Suma de tratos y contratos* (Compilations of Deals and Contracts) (Seville, 1571) glosses over what constituted usury on the grounds that merchants were too busy thinking about their profits to think about ethics. After all, exchange rates were so complicated that even Domingo de Soto recognized that merchants changed exchange and credit practices often to make it hard for the layperson to understand them (Reeder 2003, 354). Most of the contemporary writers on the subject of ethics in banking blamed the economic decline in Spain on merchants' greed. As Reeder (2003, 355) notes, most of the writers were apparently ignorant of the fact that the influx of gold and silver from the Americas may have also caused the rise in exchange rates.

The circulation of money—including loans and currency exchange—would prove crucial to the conquest of Venezuela. Charles depended on his German and Genoese bankers to move currency around Europe, and he needed them in the Indies to finance conquest and colonization projects. However, Azpilcueta suggested that the influx of New World gold and silver had affected the value of money and contributed to the high cost of living in Spain. This quantity theory of money implies that changes in the quantity of money tends to lead to inflation. As Azpilcueta writes:

> While like in lands where there is a scarcity of (circulating) money, all of the other sellable goods, as well as men's labor, are given for less money than where there is an abundance of money; like what is seen in France where there is less money than in Spain, goods such as bread, wine, cloth, labor costs a lot less money. And, even in Spain, during the time when there was less money, sellable goods and labor were to be had at a lesser expense, than *after when the Indies were discovered Spain was covered in gold and silver.* The cause of which *is that money is worth more where it is scarce than where it is abundant.* And when some say that the scarcity of money reduces the price of goods, this originates from the fact that its quick rise in value makes it appear much lower [*subida haze parecer lo al mas baxo*], as when a short man near a tall man appears shorter than when near one equal to his size. (My emphasis.)[38]

The abundance of money affected all of Europe in what became known as the price revolution. While the influx of New World gold and silver permeated the Spanish market, other Europeans saw price increases as a result of the decrease in all economic transactions between Spain and the rest of Europe.[39] The venture capitalists of the early modern period funded projects aimed to maximize profits, like the joint-stock companies of England and Holland, the Dutch West India Company and the East India Company, even as they recognized the high risk of shipwrecks, piracy, and armed conflict.

"FOREIGNERS" IN THE SPANISH INDIES

Despite early efforts to exclude them, which stemmed from xenophobia, discrimination against religious beliefs, and a desire to protect state secrets, foreign merchants eventually secured their place in the Spanish Indies. The Catholic kings had drafted laws in 1505 preventing anyone not from Castilla or León from going to the Indies unless they were married and had lived in Seville, Cádiz, or Jerez for at least fifteen years. *Conversos*, Jews who had converted to Christianity before the 1492 deadline, could not go as either passenger or sailor. In 1511 the right to travel was extended to the Aragonese, but Genoese individuals who attempted to undertake the venture of conquest were often returned to Spain. Rafael Cataño, a Genoese from the Cattaneo family, obtained permission to go to Hispaniola to settle financial accounts but was ordered to return as soon as he finished his business with Christopher Columbus. There may have been other exceptions. One of the Genoese bankers from the Grimaldi family, Bernardo Grimaldo, managed to stay in Hispaniola. Ferdinand the Catholic (Ferdinand II of Aragon) had begun to conduct business with the Grimaldi Genoese bankers, and Charles would also continue to do so (Carande 1967, 1:456).

Charles, despite having been labeled the most foreign of Spanish monarchs, permitted foreign participation in the Spanish colonies intermittently, reversing the ban and then renewing it twice. He allowed a number of foreign parties and individuals, mostly Genoese, Aragonese, and Germans (German-speaking individuals from the Habsburg realms), into the New World. However, he always permitted these parties to engage in commerce even if there was a ban at the time.[40] The Spanish crown barely saved itself from financial catastrophe by employing foreigners with financial links to Castile for purposes of conquest at various times during Charles's rule.

While he could not demand national allegiance, Charles and the Spanish crown could still profit from foreign-financed ventures by demanding the royal fifth.[41] In the case of the Welsers in Venezuela, the Kingdom of Castile retained political and judicial authority over the territories and certain economic gains, including taxes, tributes, and subsoil mineral resources. The Germans would govern the region, though their governor had to have a Castilian lieutenant.

Carande hypothesizes that Charles enacted a policy of allowing the Fleming and German merchants to enter the Spanish Indies because of their reputation for competence and their superior financial infrastructure. However, he writes that the Welsers proved a significant disappointment in Venezuela.

The Welsers' wretched performance in Venezuela would prove that he [Charles] overestimated their talents. On the other hand, the same foreign merchants, who conducted business in the Indies, despite many announcements to the contrary, would quickly realize that they could reap the benefits of the Indies without actually being there.[42]

It is possible that the Welsers' lack of autonomy and Spain's constant monitoring contributed to that failure. The lack of autonomy certainly led to the confrontations between the Welser governors and the Spanish administrators that made up the *cabildo* (council) of the city of Coro. Because of this strife, Bishop Rodrigo de Bastidas came from Santo Domingo (the Spanish crown's judicial center in the Indies remained there in the Audiencia Real) to Coro to see if the rumors about and denunciations of the Welsers were true (Farías 1997, 299). Later, and perhaps because of the Welsers' example, many foreign merchants realized that amid fears of foreign encroachment they would do better to conduct the business of colonization from outside the Indies.

But the figures show that the crown earned money in the province and that the Welsers, though they considered their profits low relative to their investments, smelted gold and sold slaves for a profit. Between 1529 and 1532 the Welsers brought thirteen ships to Venezuela; seven came directly from Spain, the rest from Santo Domingo.[43] These ships brought 40,000 pesos worth of goods, and the taxes on these goods earned the Spanish crown 2,947 pesos, the first earnings received from this young governance (Farías 1997, 299). The smelting of gold, which Farías calls the primary objective of the Welsers and every other Spanish governor, brought in some of the highest earnings in the province in the colonial period. In the first year of their arrival the Welsers gathered 1,116 pesos; in the second year, almost 10,000; and in 1533, the all-time high of 39,225. In the period between 1529 and 1538 the smelting of gold brought 89,080 in fine gold pesos (Farías 1997, 299–300). The Welsers also enslaved about 1,005 Amerindians valued at 7,500 pesos, which Farías considers an extremely low price, as the Welsers probably made a profit at least three times that. Most of these native Indians were sold in the slave market in Santo Domingo (Farías 1997, 300). Also between 1529 and 1538, the Welsers brought in goods totaling 77,285 pesos on which they paid an *almojarifazgo*, or customs tax, to the crown of about 5,046 pesos, despite their protests that their original contract did not include these payments. These goods were sold in Coro, where the colonists complained about the Welser monopoly on trade and the exorbitant prices charged. Ultimately, the Welsers profited from the land through the slave trade and the smelting of gold, although they complained that there was not enough mineral wealth to be found.

As I have made clear here, the Welsers' exchange of currency throughout Europe and extension of credit to Charles were both part of their merchant capitalist endeavors. Lukas Rem's account of his work as factor for the Welsers in Madeira and La Palma showed the company's first forays into the commodity trading of sugar, which depended on an increasingly racialized and colonized labor force. Yet Spanish society was often anxious about this new era of high finance and divided over the ethical implications of lending money and usury to the point that a whole new literature on the ethics of finance appeared. As we shall see in chapter 5, these Spanish anxieties about usury would later be compounded by antiforeign sentiment and accusations of heresy against the Welsers. The next chapter continues this microhistory by examining the networks of privilege that allowed the Welsers to thrive in the business of conquest. The Welsers expanded their mercantile activities and engaged in the Indigenous and African slave trade once they received the capitulación to govern the province of Venezuela.

CHAPTER 2

The Welsers in Venezuela

Early Modern Slavery

¿para qué habia de ser como los cristianos, que eran malos?
—Cacique Hatuey, quoted in Bartolomé
de Las Casas, *Historia de las Indias*

La plata y el oro de América penetraron como un ácido corrosivo, al
decir de Engels, por todos los poros de la sociedad feudal moribunda en
Europa, y al servicio del naciente mercantilismo capitalista los empre-
sarios mineros convirtieron a los indígenas y a los esclavos negros en un
numerosísimo "proletariado externo" de la economía europea.
—Eduardo Galeano, *Las venas abiertas*
de América Latina

The Welsers' governance of Venezuela was a merchant capitalist endeavor
that, as I argued in the previous chapter, depended on the extension of credit
and was profit oriented. The Welsers' long-distance trade, which required a
large investment of capital in the hope of receiving large profits, defined
their merchant capitalism. Part of the secret formula of merchant capitalism

was to secure monopolies, exclude competitors, and control markets (Fulcher 2004, 4). In thinking about merchant capitalism, I find the German historian Jürgen Kocka's definition useful.

> These early merchants' intense relationship to the market and their strong profit orientation, the relative independence enjoyed by commercial actions and institutions, the significance of investment and accumulation that used credit and were profit oriented, the formation of enterprise (at least in Europe), and finally the dynamic way that capitalist developments radiated beyond long-distance trade (at least in Europe), even into the rudiments of production—all this compels categorizing these phenomena as capitalist. (2016, 52)

The Welsers operated an enterprise that was part of a nascent racialized capitalism. They secured the monopoly on the trade of enslaved Africans, they attempted to exclude competitors such as the Genoese merchants who traded slaves and balsam from operating in Santo Domingo, and they controlled markets for their imports into the Indies, including foodstuffs. The Welsers successfully protested against protections proposed by the Spanish crown for Indigenous peoples living in the province whom they enslaved and sold within the Caribbean. The Venezuela capitulación allowed the Welsers' unprecedented access to extractive enterprises meant to exploit the province's natural resources by accumulating gold and sapping balsam trees.

In this chapter I show how the crown's capitulación with the Welsers for the conquest and colonization of Venezuela sparked their exploitation of Indigenous slaves. Moreover, the capitulación granting them a monopoly on the importation of African slaves into the Spanish Indies drove the Welsers' racialized merchant capitalism. First, I analyze the language of the capitulación and the terms of the Welsers' Venezuela governance. I then turn to the Spanish crown's 1503 "Cannibal Law," which basically encouraged the enslavement of Indigenous peoples, who would labor in mining operations in the province and plantations on Hispaniola and other islands. Accusations of cannibalism contributed to the racialization first of the anthropophagous Caribs, who of course were labeled guilty of resisting conquest and juxtaposed to the benevolent Taíno, but later this othering was extended to most Indigenous peoples in the circum-Caribbean as well as Brazil. Moreover, the Welser's license to monopolize the import of enslaved Africans into the

Spanish Indies completed their colonial business as essentially a capitalist enterprise that commodified racialized bodies (both African and Indigenous). I conclude by describing who was in charge in the colonial town of Coro.

The Venezuela capitulación[1] signed by representatives of the Welsers and the Spanish crown in Madrid on 27 March 1528 was a response to a *relación,* or report, of problems relating to conquest efforts in the neighboring province of Santa Marta due to "bellicose Indians armed with arrows."[2] The Welsers were required to provide their services to "pacify that land and to place it in our service in a manner that we can profit from it."[3] The royal contract was actually addressed to Enrique Inger (Heinrich Ehinger, 1484–1537), one of the most powerful German merchants in Spain, and Gerónimo Sayler (Hieronymus Sailer; 1495–1559), who would go on to gain entry into Augsburg's closed patrician circle through his marriage to Felicitas Welser (1513–69), Bartholomäus Welser V's daughter (figs. 2.1, 2.2). Entry into this patrician circle (discussed in the introduction), along with access to the Welser Company itself, was clearly beneficial for both Sailer and the Welsers. It remains unclear whether the contract was made to Ehinger and Sailer individually or, as is most likely, as representatives of the Welsers. In any case, the contract to pacify Venezuela was officially transferred by Charles V to Bartholomäus Welser and Anton Welser on 17 February 1531.

Seville's networks of privileges granted to private entities demonstrate how enterprise was responsible for the investment of large amounts of capital required for risky colonial ventures in the hope of the private accumulation of wealth (of which the crown would receive a cut). Mercantile network mapping created by the economic historian Montserrat Cachero Vinuesa is helpful for understanding what she has labeled "the economy of privilege" in early modern Spain (fig. 2.3). Her project analyzes "the political, legal, and economic institution of privilege by examining the prerogatives granted by the Spanish Crown for the colonization of the New World. . . . The Crown used privileges as an incentive to attract private resources for undertaking these tasks, since it did not have the means to do so independently."[4] Cachero used data from more than five hundred privileges or entitlements granted to about 250 individuals from 1492 to 1556, the year in which Charles V abdicated. She then coded the data and represented the nodes as agents, and each node was sized according to how many privileges were granted to them. Specifically, the biggest nodes are the ones that are

FIGURE 2.1. Christoph Amberger, *Portrait of a Patrician* (Hieronymus Sailer). Painting, 1537, ResMüG0005. (The painting was previously at Residenz München, Grüne Galerie.) L 255. © Bayerische Schlösserverwaltung Sibylle Forster

between the king and queen. Cachero states that these nodes/agents are symbolic of "High betweenness centrality," which is "associated with being in the position to observe or control the flow of information and goods." This was the case for Ehinger and Sailer, who were able to negotiate privileges even when the king was absent at court. Ehinger and Sailer received twenty-

FIGURE 2.2. Christoph Amberger, *Portrait of a Patrician* (Felicitas Welser). Painting, 1537, ResMüG0006. (The painting was previously at Residenz München, Grüne Galerie.) Munich, Schloss Nymphenburg, Hauptverwaltung. © Bayerische Schlösserverwaltung Sibylle Forster

four privileges from Charles V and three from Isabella of Portugal. Bartholomäus Welser received eight privileges from Charles V and three from Isabella. Through Ehinger and Sailer, the Welsers' enterprise remained firmly entrenched in an increasingly global world that began producing soft commodities such as sugar in the Atlantic islands and the New World.

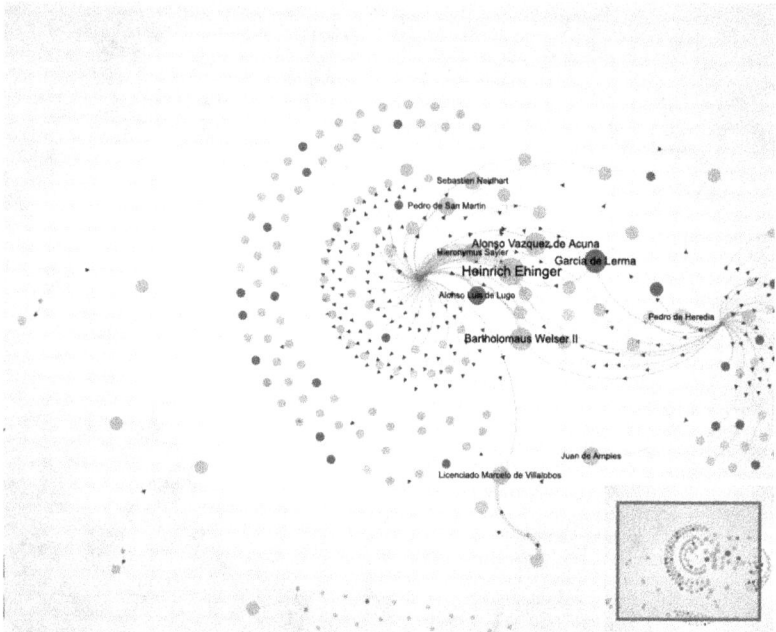

FIGURE 2.3. Montserrat Cachero Vinuesa's visualization of the "Economy of Privilege" (2016) shows Heinrich Ehinger and Bartholomäus Welser as primary figures to whom Royal Decrees were granted—even when Charles was absent. https://histecon. fas.harvard.edu/visualizing/privileges/. Screen shot used with permission.

THE LANGUAGE OF THE CAPITULACIÓN

The language of the capitulación shows that Venezuela remained a risky venture for the Welsers despite their hope of high profits. The 1528 contract states at the beginning that Ehinger and Sailer were "offer[ing] [them]selves to pacify and settle the land."[5] Charles writes that he gave them this opportunity because they had "begged and asked [him] for the mercy of conquest"[6] so that the Germans could "discover, conquer, and settle" the land between the governorship of Santa Marta and Cabo de la Vela (northwestern Venezuela; no southern limit was specified).[7] They were to found two or more towns, and each man was to take three hundred men and build three forts. The recruits had to be allowed to enter the Indies—the ban on foreigners was in place at the time even if the Germans were an implicit exception—and they were to found settlements within the first two years of their arrival. In addition to six hundred colonists, they were to bring fifty master German miners who would extract gold, silver, and other metals from the land. The capitulación further states that the Indigenous peoples who continued to rebel even after they had been warned and read the *requerimiento* could be taken as slaves.

The requerimiento was a written text that was read to Amerindians before conquest; it demanded the acknowledgment of the Spanish monarch as their king and of the supremacy of the Catholic faith. The only options were submission or warfare.[8] However, the capitulación does include a provision regarding the good treatment of natives that the king had signed in Granada on 17 November 1526; this was the "General Provision of Statutes on Observations Needed on the Population and Discovery."[9] The capitulación noted that it had been drafted during the conquest "because of the mistreatment of Indians."[10] Above all, the stipulation that the Welsers read the requerimiento was a reminder that they had to act according to Spanish administrative custom. They had to consider the Indigenous peoples' spiritual salvation through their conversion to the Catholic faith, and they had to set an example through their governance so that the Indians would have a "desire to be [Spain's] vassals, subjects, and naturals."[11] The Indians were to be entrusted to a cleric's charge (*encomendados*) for instruction in the Catholic faith so that they might give up their "special vice of consuming human flesh."[12] Of course, the German settlers could act in self-defense and wage war on those who refused to obey.

The Welsers could introduce horses to the colony, and they would be excluded from paying a tax on salt or customs (almojarifazgo). The capitulación bumped the royal fifth to a royal tenth on mining and extraction of precious metals for four years, after which the percentage paid in taxes would increase until they were paying the full royal fifth beginning in the tenth year. The crown often made concessions like these that benefited the Welsers. In a cedulario from 12 December 1528, Charles decreed that the Welsers had the right to stock ships that brought "sugar, cañafístola [golden shower, *Cassia fistula*], palo santo [holy stick, *Bursera graveolens*], leathers and anything that was not gold nor silver nor pearls nor any other metal or precious stones" directly to Flanders or any other port they desired, bypassing the customary stop in Seville (Otte 1984, 316–17). While unlike other asientos the Welsers received the right to bypass mandatory port of entry rules as well as major breaks in expected contributions to the crown, they paid a price in their lack of autonomy in the colony.

INDIGENOUS SLAVERY UNDER
WELSER GOVERNANCE

The link between capitalism and colonialism has long been discussed. Marx and Engel saw capitalism's origins in Europe, as opposed to other world regions, as related to climate. In 1989 the geographer Jim Blaut (1989, 266) argued that capitalism was developed in Europe and not elsewhere because even though before the sixteenth century Europe had no advantage over Africa or Asia in the development of feudalism toward capitalism, Europe's close proximity to America, as well as the conquest of Indigenous peoples, "provided European protocapitalists (merchants, artisans, acquisitive landlords, freehold peasants, and others) with massive capital accumulation which they used to dissolve feudal relations" in Europe. The Egyptian world-systems analyst Samir Amin (1990, 70) agreed with Blaut that "the proto-capitalist evolution of mercantile Europe was inseparable from the conquest of the Americas." The geographer Eric Sheppard summed up Blaut's link between capitalism and colonialism as ultimately one tied to the use of slave labor.

> Europe's rise to dominance as the heart of nineteenth century industrial capitalism, he [Blaut] maintains, is a result of geographical chance: access to the rich resources of the New World, as a source of gold and silver and other resources delivered cheaply on the back of slaves, as a place to experiment with labor relations in plantations that became the basis of the factory system, and as a sink for surplus European populations, gave Europeans a leg up over other sites of incipient capitalism. (2005, 965)

The "Cannibal Law" passed in Spain in 1503 distinguished good Indians from bad ones depending on whether or not they practiced cannibalism, although colonizers would label any Indigenous people who resisted as cannibals to legitimate their subjugation as slaves. This law is an example of how race came into play in the colonial merchant capitalist system. Colonial administrators were invested in a racialization of Indigenous, and later Black, bodies who could be used as cheap labor. Moreover, their land could be confiscated.[13] Bodies could be labeled dangerous, animalistic, and part of a nature, including land, that needed to be managed in an appropriate manner. Europeans procured "excess resources from the environment to export for an external market and the creation of a commodity" (Hayes and Timms 2012, 12–13). According to John Richards (2003), the allocations of land to Spanish settlers under the encomienda system in Hispaniola meant they obtained land and property rights over Taíno chieftains and their people located within or adjacent to the grants. The Taínos were to serve the settlers by mining, planting their family plots known as *conucos*, or by employment in their personal service (Richards 2003, 321). Of course, the Taínos on Hispaniola became nearly extinct as they succumbed to smallpox and forced labor. In 1508, there were about sixty thousand Taínos left on Hispaniola (321). Slave raids had continued in the Antilles to replenish the ever-dwindling number of Taínos who worked the gold mines of Hispaniola. Royal permits issued for slave raids in the lesser Antilles of Curaçao, Aruba, and Trinidad and Tobago began enslaving supposedly cannibal Caribs (325). The coast of Venezuela, especially the eastern coast close to the areas of pearl exploitation in Cubagua, became known as the site of natural resource and labor exploitation. Although the crown did not directly authorize the trade of Indigenous peoples from this area, the direct exploitation of pearl fisheries gave rise to the Indigenous slave trade (Jimenez 1986, 122).

Nevertheless, in the 1530s the enslavement of unruly natives became a controversial subject, even if they were "proven" cannibals. In fact, the shift to categorizing Indigenous peoples who resisted conquest from "cannibal" to "rebellious" would become an important bureaucratic legal tool for the Welsers as the crown redrafted protocols concerning Indigenous slavery in Venezuela. Charles and his wife, Queen Isabella of Portugal (referred to here as empress), debated with Spaniards whether those natives who resisted Spanish rule could be taken prisoner. For example, on 25 January 1531 the empress, from afar, handled the affair of a *cacique* (Indigenous leader) who had been taken with two hundred of his people to the island of Cubagua by Spanish slave traders. She demanded that the Cubagua governors punish those who initiated the enslavement of peaceful Indians and the lynching of one Indian (Otte 1982, 31).[14] While her cedulario to those responsible referenced justice, she also referenced practical concerns: "Many times [Cubaguan slave traders] go over to incite the coast and those Indians that are peaceful and in our service turn to war. They are then enslaved, killed and much trouble is caused in the disservice of God, us, and the destruction of the land. . . . From here on no person will go to incite the Indians and not make problems in [the coast of the province of Venezuela]." However, on the same day the empress also wrote a cedulario addressed to the governor that specifies that the royal fifth of the slaves' value captured in the *entradas* (expeditions) should be paid to the crown: "As such, I order you to pay to our officials, without any excuse, the 'fifth' of the slaves [value] that until now have belonged to us and been taken" (Otte 1982, 38).[15] Whatever qualms Empress Isabella may have had about the enslavement of nonrebellious Indians, the monarchs expected to profit from their sale. Hence while she was presenting herself as a monarch who was concerned about the Indians and could appease their defenders such as Friar Antonio de Montesinos in Hispaniola, she sought a hard-line rule against the traffickers and demanded money from the illegal trade. This polemical period between the decree of the Laws of Burgos (1512) and the New Laws (1542), which saw the powerful petitions from Friar Bartolomé de Las Casas to the crown, was characterized by official inconsistencies regarding the treatment of the crown's Indigenous subjects.

In 1530 the Indigenous slave trade in the Indies should have experienced a respite. The Cedulario Real (Royal Decree) of 2 August 1530 remains one of the most controversial in reference to the province of Venezuela. Written by Empress Isabella while Charles was absent from Spain for a few years, it condemns the native slave trade and the depopulation of the Venezuelan province. It treats the question of Spaniards' enslavement of Indians and supports the policy of the Catholic Kings, who "with good reason" thought to enslave those Indians who refused to follow the Catholic faith. It notes that the conquistadors' greed and disservice to God had led them to take Indians prisoner regardless of their refusal to convert to Christianity, leading to chaos in human trafficking. The empress's cedulario concludes:[16]

> However, considering the great and intolerable damages that have been made in the disservice of God, our Lord, that continue every day due to the chaotic greed of the conquistadors and others who have procured to make war and capture the said Indians unjustly and immoderately, they have enslaved, bought and had many of the said Indians [as prisoners] who really are not. (Otte 1982, 92–93)[17]

The regents were aware of the conquistadors' slave raids on the coast and their enslavement of Indigenous people, including those who were considered peaceful, such as the coastal Caquetíos. At this point, the Indigenous slave trade had proliferated and Spanish slave raiders wiped out the population on the coasts of northern South America; the Welser governors continued this practice. In fact, there were two different ways in which native slave labor was used. Indians were enslaved and sold within and outside the province; others were enslaved for the purposes of interior conquest (Simmer 2000, 173). It was common practice for the Welser governors and the soldiers who went with them on their unsuccessful entradas into the interior to enslave the Indigenous guides on their return so that they could sell them in Coro and turn a profit.[18]

Among the more horrific practices was Alfinger's method of chaining Indigenous slaves on these expeditions. The slaves were chained together by their necks, and if a slave in the chain became sick or exhausted, his head was cut off so that the chains would not have to be opened. Federmann continued this practice in the entrada depicted in his narrative of conquest, the *Indianische Historia* (1557). A witness who testified in the *juicios de residencia* stated that he was responsible for cutting off the heads of those enslaved people who were exhausted so that they did not hold back the line (Simmer 2000, 175). Las Casas and other *crónica* (chronicle) authors wrote about this as well and considered it emblematic of the Germans' treatment of the natives.

Naturally, the Welsers complained about the empress's 2 August 1530 cedulario, stating that it would be impossible to govern the land and make a profit without the ability to enslave Indigenous peoples and trade them. The Welser agents complained that the empress's cedulario violated the terms of the capitulación that allowed the Welsers to take rebellious slaves. This suggests why they were eager to label natives "rebellious." Moreover, the Welsers often argued that the situation on Tierra Firme was different, that the natives were rebels and cannibals. According to Otte, Charles's policy had been to tolerate the practice of enslavement until Empress Isabella, pressured by the debates for and against just conquest by Las Casas and others, issued the polemical cedulario on 2 August 1530 (1982, xxxiii). The empress, in response to her critics, dictated yet another cedulario that exacerbated the situation of the enslavement of Indians on Tierra Firme. On 10 May 1531 she made clear that the previous cedulario should not apply to the province of Venezuela until the issue could be clarified. This cedulario maintained that they could legally enslave Indians but could not trade them out of the province (Jimenez 1986, 221).

After a hiatus, eventually policy was drafted that further complicated the situation of the Indigenous slave trade on the Venezuelan coast. It involved the reimplementation of the requerimiento to invent rebellious Indians for the purposes of Welser conquest. Charles returned to Spain in 1533, and when he met with his council in Toledo in 1534, they pressed him on the subject. The resolution they reached was a ridiculous and theatrical attempt to justify war against rebel Indians that applied only to the province of Venezuela: conquistadors had to follow a specific protocol in which a bishop and another priest agreed that the Indians were truly rebels and the conquest truly just (Otte 1982, 129–32). Interpreters would read the requerimiento when they first encountered the natives; if the natives then refused to submit to the Spanish, the conquistadors could make war on them and enslave the survivors (Otte 1982, 133).

Charles eventually reinstituted the intra-Venezuelan slave trade, but he prohibited the exportation of slaves to other markets; however, in doing so, he essentially gave his official blessing to what was already a large and flourishing Indigenous slave trade in Venezuela (Otte 1982, 67). Charles in effect maintained the existing intraprovincial indigenous slave trade that flourished in the Spanish Indies by relying on Indigenous slaves acquired in Venezuela; they just had to undergo the theatrics of the requerimiento test.

The problem of native slavery was debated in Castile, and many laws were drafted for and against it. Both the Indigenous and the African slave trade were linked to the Welser governance in the province of Venezuela. There is a record of the enslavement and sale of 150 Indians whom the Welsers captured in Venezuela and then sold in Santo Domingo in 1530, before the special trade rules were drafted. This is the beginning of a slave trade that hardly ever paid the royal fifth to the crown because the Welsers were flouting the crown's requirement of oversight by a *veedor* and a priest, as well as documentation by a notary (Simmer 2000, 177).

THE WELSERS AND THE EARLY AFRICAN SLAVE TRADE

The triumph of early modern capitalism, according to Kocka, was due to a "massive *increase in free labor*" (2016, 66; original emphasis). While slave labor started with Indigenous slaves mining for gold (Hispaniola) and silver

(Potosí), the demand for agricultural commodities finished the cycle (Kocka 2016, 66). The Welsers' traffic of slaves was not limited to the Indians; they were also given one of the first contracts for the Spanish transatlantic slave trade. Perhaps 11 to 12 million Africans were exported to the Americas beginning in 1450 and continuing for four centuries to satisfy European demand for agricultural commodities that included sugar, tobacco, cotton, ginger, coffee, indigo, arrowroot, nutmeg, and lime (Beinart and Hughes 2007, 22–23).

On 18 August 1518 a license was given to import four thousand enslaved Africans to Baron de Montenay, Lorenzo Gramenot, which he eventually transferred to Genoese merchants. Ten years later, the Welsers were the recipients of the monopoly over the African slave trade, which would allow them to import four thousand enslaved African to the Indies. This asiento was granted to "Enriqque Eynguer and Jerónimo Sayler" and was signed by the king in Burgos on 12 February 1528, more than a month *before* the capitulación for the governance of Venezuela was also granted to the Germans. After the Genoese and Portuguese, the Welsers were among the first slave traders to negotiate between Spain, Africa, and the Americas. This contract gave the Welsers the right to bring slaves "from this Kingdom or the Kingdom of Portugal or any part of the territories and islands of the Great King of Portugal." It stipulated that of the four thousand enslaved Africans, a third must be women and that they should be sold for the price of 55 ducats each. The crown expected to collect 20,000 ducats on the sale of the slaves (5,000 ducats each year of the four years of the contract) (Otte 1984, 242).

On this latter point, the cedulario of 23 September 1529 addressed to "Enrrique Eynger" and "Gerónimo Sayler" references the asiento that allows for each enslaved African to be sold at 55 ducats.[19] In another cedulario written on 23 September 1529, the empress states that the "neighbors of Española" (*vezinos de la isla Española*) should ignore the quality of the enslaved people. She admonished

> that some people and residents of the island and other parts have wanted to choose, and so they want to take them [the slaves] this and no other way, and if this happened [the buyers' right to choose] they [the traders] would incur *irreparable losses* and they would not be able to comply with what they were assigned nor would they be able to take

the chosen slaves. . . . The people who will buy them should take them [regardless of their condition], as not all of them could be alike, at the price of 55 ducats each, because [traders] take a loss from those [slaves] who die at sea and at shore before they are sold, or how my mercy would have it." (Otte 1984, 324–25; my emphasis)[20]

This cedulario has the empress advocating on the slave traders' behalf so that they could receive the correct price for the sale of the human chattel that survived the Middle Passage and recoup losses on the many enslaved people who died at sea. The enslaved Africans are nothing more than merchandise, labeled equal in price, though not equal in labor "value." For the crown, the priority was ensuring that the price of the remaining enslaved Africans was not negotiable—perhaps given the pressure from the slave traders. The empress assured the traders that on docking at each island port, they could take any slave to work in the mines or do other work who had not been sold within fifteen days. She acknowledged that "if a lot of time was spent keeping them to be sold [keeping them alive and in captivity] it would cost more than their worth." She gave them carte blanche to take any slave not sold "to other islands and lands that you want and sell them at the price that you can, and do with them what you want and what you see for good" (Otte 1984, 325).[21] Thus profit was the only real concern; there were no effective limitations on the geography of the intra-Caribbean slave trade, including Tierra Firme.

However, officials in Santo Domingo complained about the quality of the slaves brought over by the Germans. A letter, which I have not been able to locate at the AGI or other archives in Spain, written to the king on 19 July 1530 by the *oidores* of Santo Domingo, Gaspar de Espinoza, Alonso Zuazo, and Antonio Serrano, complained that these enslaved people were "malísimos" (very bad) and that despite the need of their labor no one bought them (*nadie los compraba*) (cited in Cortés López 2004, 41–42).

The Germans welcomed the exclusive agreement for trade in Venezuela; after all they were the only party technically allowed to import enslaved Africans into the Indies for a period of four years (though the Genoese-Sevillian traders were the first to import enslaved Africans for Spain in 1518). However, another cedulario reveals that the slave market was saturated and that the crown was struggling to collect its portion: "Many traders and other persons have imported many slaves, without permission or desire from our part and against the *asiento*, and because of this they cannot sell the slaves that they brought" (Otte 1984, 331).[22] The slave trade was still productive for the Welsers though, because in addition to the four thousand enslaved Africans they were allowed to sell in the Indies, the crown extended the right to import eight hundred additional enslaved Africans to work just in the province of Venezuela. Moreover, on 21 June 1533 Charles wrote a cedulario that permitted those additional enslaved people to be sold elsewhere in the Spanish Indies.[23] Specifically, they should be sold in this allotment: 300 in Hispaniola, 300 in Cuba, and 200 in Tierra Firme.[24] Given the lawlessness that occurred, it was unlikely this directive was followed.[25]

In summary, the crown's decrees on the province of Venezuela show the desire for increasing profits at the same time that the crown is nervous about the Indigenous slave trade. The cedulario that grants power to Bartholomäus Welser VI, Enrique Eynguer (Heinrich Ehinger), and Jéronimo (Hieronymus) Sailer specifies that the crown will read an account about this *governación* and that the emperor's secretary must "state in it what you think that would benefit our service and increase our income and the good of our subjects in those parts [proveays en ello lo que os paresçiese que conviene a nuestro serviçio e acrescentamyento de nuestras rentas e al bien de nuestros súbdictos e de aquellas partes]" (Otte 1982, 47).

Competition for profits between the Welsers and the crown led to conflicts. It motivated the German bankers to make money as fast as possible because of the precarious nature of their government contract. For the Spanish crown, political and economic realities made bullion from the Indies a needed revenue source with which Charles could fund his European wars. Charles and the Welsers were involved in an increasingly futile pattern of forced borrowing that resembled extortion, while the Welsers desperately tried to recoup their funds through the conquest of Venezuela. The lives lost on both sides, many enslaved people and a few masters, remain embedded in the soil along with their histories.

Finally, the Welser colonization of Venezuela encouraged Spanish xenophobia about foreigners' encroachment on the Indies. The contested narrative of violent German conquest that would be revived even in the nineteenth century was fueled by sixteenth-century Castilian debates over proper treatment of the Amerindians and particularly by German, English, and Dutch translations of Las Casas's defense of the Indians (though infamously not of Africans). The 1550 Valladolid debate organized by Charles to determine whether Indigenous peoples were capable of self-governance was fought between Ginés de Sepúlveda, who proposed that Indians were natural slaves, and Las Casas, who argued that they were free men.

German translations of Las Casas's works appeared in the aftermath of the debate. The publisher, translator, and city of publication of the first German edition of Las Casas's *Brevísima relación* in 1597 are unknown; a Latin version appeared in Frankfurt in 1598 (De Bry).[26] The second German edition was published in 1599 by an unknown translator of Flemish origin who took an anti-Spanish stance during the Flemish-Spanish war. While Las Casas characterizes the Welsers as cruel, the real barbarians are still the Spaniards in the original text. Hence the work contributes to promoting the Spanish Black Legend, furthered by the inclusion of Theodor de Bry's famous seventeen engravings that accompany other versions of this text.[27] The text promoted the Black Legend about specific "Spanish" mistreatment of the natives that had been promoted in England and Flanders as well.[28]

Though Las Casas actively engaged with the ideas of "just" enslavement and conquest, in the first German translation (1597) the translator changes Las Casas's original Spanish text,[29] especially the sections that compare the German Welser governors to tyrannical conquerors. The translation and the printed marginalia show the pro-German, anti-Spanish editorial perspective, with the Spaniards the perpetrators of all the violence. Examples of added printed editorial marginalia, absent from the original Spanish text, show the editorial choices that make the Spanish, rather than the German Welsers, responsible for the violence inflicted on Venezuela's Indigenous peoples: "Venezuela zu Grund verwüstet und erösiget; *Spanier* fangen den Oberherrn in Venesuela / und bringen die Indianer immerlich umb" (Las Casas 1597, 76; Venezuela deserted and depopulated to the ground; the Spanish imprison the cacique in Venezuela and kill the Indians deplorably).[30] Due to the Reformation and the Lutheran princes' defeat by Charles in the Schmalkadic War, anti-imperial feelings caused anti-Spanish sentiment in the German lands. German humanists were also preoccupied with Catholic and Lutheran theology, as well as the corruption of the empire and the Catholic Church during the Reformation; however, they did not thoroughly debate the treatment of the Indigenous in the New World as they would do in the Netherlands, where Catholic and Spanish rule over the Indigenous were read as emblematic of the Netherlands' semicolonial relationship to Spain as it sought to obtain their independence from Habsburg Spain.[31]

Certainly, the Welser governors were subject to the laws of Castile, and Federmann's later response to accusations that he mistreated the Indigenous peoples suggest that he was aware that their mistreatment was illegal unless they were deemed cannibals and rebels. However, Federmann, like many others, often used the term "cannibal" to refer to groups of Amerindians he wanted to enslave. Clearly, the Welser agents knew there was money to be made in enslaving Indians. Federmann often enslaved whole "nations" of peoples in service of his project of finding gold and access to the Pacific, royal decrees against enslaving those who were not rebellious be damned.

THE WELSER GOVERNORS AND THE SPANISH ADMINISTRATION

Exercising a racialized capitalism in Venezuela meant that the Welser governors used Indigenous porters to carry equipment on inland expeditions, plundered many Indigenous settlements, and, in addition to selling enslaved Africans, engaged in the capture, enslavement, and sale of Indigenous peoples. Before analyzing in the next chapter Federmann's account detailing these activities, I find it necessary to give a short account of who was in charge during the tumultuous period of the Welser governance of Venezuela. Often because the Welser governors were on expeditions, lieutenant governors and others took charge. Yet the Welser governors never truly had full autonomy in Venezuela; the Spanish crown insisted on sending their own officials to administer the crown's funds and over time Spaniards' xenophobia toward the Germans only grew.

When the Welsers attempted to assert themselves by forcing out the Spanish governor Juan Martínez de Ampiés (1527–29), an ensuing conflict between the Spanish and the Welsers further curtailed the Welsers' autonomy. The Welsers' contract stipulated they were under the judicial domain of the courts at the Audiencia Real in Santo Domingo and the administrative local Spanish council, or cabildo, in Coro. In addition to the the mayor (*alcalde*), Bartolomé Zarco, and the notary public (*escribano público*), Alonso de la Llana, the all-Spanish council was made up of three administrators of the Royal Treasury (Hacienda), including the accountant (*contador*), Antonio de Naveros; the treasurer (*tesorero*) Alonso Vázquez de Acuña; and the manager (*factor*), Pedro de San Martín. When the conflict between the cabildo and the Welser governors escalated in 1533 to a full rebellion, the bishop from Santo Domingo, Rodrigo de Bástidas (1497–1570), came to Venezuela in 1534 in his capacity as governor and judge of a commission on a fact-finding mission concerning the chaotic governance and the abuse of Indigenous Caquetío allies (Farías 1997, 300).

During the Welser period, 1528–57, the overview of who was in charge reads as a confusing history of constant changes in governor and lieutenant governor appointments of Spaniards and Germans— all men intent on finding financial gain to justify the difficult crossing of the Atlantic Ocean and daily life in a new colonial village. Ambrosius Alfinger was the first governor the Welsers sent; for the Welsers this was a logical choice as Alfinger had experience working as a manager for the Welser Company in Santo Domingo. Driven by the prospect of finding gold, he left his governorship in the colony of Coro in August 1529 to embark on more exciting inland expeditions around Lake Maracaibo with 180 men, leaving Luis Sarmiento as his deputy. In the meantime, Nikolaus Federmann arrived in Coro in 1530 with 123 Spaniards, 24 German miners, and 10 horses on a Welser ship. The Welsers, believing Alfinger dead, sent Hans Seissenhofer (Juan Alemán) as acting governor; he arrived with 300 men on 18 April 1530 and made Federmann his deputy. On 3 May 1530 Alfinger returned sick with only 110 men after spending nine months in the area of Lake Maracaibo. He brought with him 9,586 pesos of gold and resumed the governorship. Still ill, Alfinger left Coro to rest in Santo Domingo, leaving Federmann as his deputy. A month later, on 12 September 1530, Federmann took a treasure-finding expedition with 16 Spanish horsemen, 98 Spanish soldiers, and 100 Caquetío porters into Venezuela's interior, leaving the colony in the hands of Bartolomé de Santillana. On 27 January 1531 Alfinger returned to Coro from Santo Domingo and reassumed his post as governor. In March 1531, Federmann's troops returned from the interior. Alfinger exiled Federmann for a period of four years as punishment for leaving his post.

Alfinger went on a second interior expedition in 1531, reappointing Bartolomé de Santillana (Sailer) as his deputy. The expedition that set out to explore and penetrate the area west of Coro (around Lake Maracaibo and the Guajira peninsula) to the border of the nearby Spanish colony of Santa Marta was marked by brutality against Indigenous nations, a lost golden treasure, and the miraculous survival of a few soldiers. Around 27 May 1533 a member of the Chimila or Chitarero nation struck Alfinger with a poisoned arrow near Chitacomar (the present-day municipality of Chinácota), and he died four days later.

Due to diverging agendas for the administration of the colony and the best way to extract profit from it, the cabildo overthrew and imprisoned the German Santillana (Sailer) after Alfinger's death in 1533 and named Francisco Gallegos and Pedro San Martín as interim leaders until 1534. What the Venezuelan historian Demetrio Ramos called "la Revolución de Coro" temporarily ended German rule in the colony and had profound implications for the freedoms given to municipal authorities.

In part, Spaniards were motivated by their own search for racialized capitalism as the Spaniards wanted access to encomiendas. Spanish officials of Coro, Luis González de Leiva and Alonso de La Llana, representatives of the citizens of Coro, left for Spain to petition Charles to be given Indians in encomiendas and repartimientos, as the German governor had not done so; they also asked the crown not to be sent foreign administrators. Their objections, presumably, in addition to the xenophobia and struggles for power, arose from a desire for access to Indigenous labor and tribute through an encomienda. According to James Lockhart, the original *encomendero* (holder of a tribute grant) primarily received draft seasonal labor, though later tribute to the Spanish was often added. As encomenderos became established, they "became the center of almost all kinds of business except import-export; they and their employees were the core of the local Spanish market" (Lockhart 2003). However, in the second half of the sixteenth century Indigenous draft labor was distributed among Spaniards through the repartimiento. Spaniards in Venezuela, eager to replicate the wealth that these grants had given their compatriots in Peru and Mexico, sought this privilege in Venezuela.

At that time the Audiencia Real of Santo Domingo sent Bishop Bastidas as interim governor to assess the situation. Bastidas was struck ill, and he left Alonso Vázquez de Acuña in charge as lieutenant governor and returned to Santo Domingo, taking Gallegos and Sarmiento as prisoners with him. Soon after, the new German governor appointed by the Welsers, Georg Hohermuth von Speyer (ca. 1500–1540), known as Jorge Spira, arrived in Coro on 6 February 1535 with 700 men and took over the governorship. He went to Santo Domingo to obtain goods for yet another inland expedition, which he undertook with Philipp von Hutten. This expedition, begun in 1535, would go through the Venezuelan plains until it reached the Apure

River, which it would not be able to cross. After experiencing hunger, sickness, and the death of 300 of their companions, only 100 soldiers (80 foot soldiers and 20 on horseback) would return three years later, in 1538. Hohermuth's party would return with only 1,594 pesos of fine gold. Hohermuth found Antonio Navarro, the *juez de residencia* who had been appointed by the Audiencia of Santo Domingo, governing in Coro. He reassumed the governorship with permission from the Spanish crown and remained in charge until his death in 1540; at the time he was preparing another entrada. In the meantime, Federmann, back in Venezuela, had left Coro in 1537 on another expedition that reached the high plateau of Bogotá in 1539. However, he found the Spanish conquistadors Gonzalo Jiménez de Quesada and Sebastián de Belalcázar there. In 1540 Federmann left for Europe with all three men to claim their conquest of the territory, but neither he nor any other agent of the Welsers was ever able to claim the Kingdom of Nueva Granada.

The entradas reflect the Welsers' repeated attempts to expand the reach of their racialized capitalism. The Welsers used Indigenous slaves on most of the entradas as guides and porters, but we know they also brought enslaved Africans on their entradas inland in Venezuela. In Coro, after Hohermuth's death, Bishop Rodrigo de Bastidas, named interim governor again by the Audiencia of Santo Domingo, designated Philipp von Hutten (1505–ca. 1546) general captain of a new expedition. Barthomomäus Welser VI (1512–ca. 1546), the son of the merchant leader, would accompany Hutten on the expedition, with only one hundred Spaniards and a number of Indigenous porters. Neither man returned; they were murdered at the behest of Juan Carvajal, a Spaniard who had certified documents from the Audiencia Real in Santo Domingo to take over the territory after Hutten had been absent from Coro for a number of years. During Hutten's absence, Enrique Remboldt had been named by the Welsers as governor to substitute for Bastidas. However, Remboldt died in 1544, and the Coro magistrates Bernardino Manso and Juan de Bonilla replaced him. The Audiencia Real in Santo Domingo then appointed Juan de Frías, who because of other business on Margarita, left his own deputy in place in Coro, the infamous Juan de Carvajal. Carvajal had taken those families that were left in Coro to found the city of El Tocuyo in a fertile valley suitable for farming. Naturally, on Hutten's return, the Germans and Carvajal's men disputed Carvajal's legitimacy, which resulted in Carvajal ordering two enslaved African men to behead both Germans. Many accounts document the barbarity of Carvajal's crime (including mention of the dull blades used for the execution). Some call Juan Carvajal a traitor, others a savior who rescued Venezuela from German rule. The crown was firmly with the former; after news had reached the Audiencia Real in Santo Domingo, a brief trial ensued in El Tocuyo. The judge, Pérez de Tolosa, condemned Carvajal as a traitor, and he was executed in 1546.

The gruesome beheadings of Bartholomäus Welser VI and Philipp von Hutten are examples of the violent struggle for power that was common in the conquest of the Americas and the crown's increasingly futile attempt to control and govern each individual territory and its subjects from the metropole through the Audiencia Real in Santo Domingo. Prince Philipp II, who was handling royal affairs at the time, was truly outraged at the murder of the Welser governor and Bartholomäus Welser VI. On 20 September 1548, he recognized that Hutten "had discovered with great work on his part and at the Welsers' cost" that Carvajal had earlier wanted to gain the riches that belonged to Hutten and the Welsers.[32] The situation in Coro had been no different from the more infamous civil strifes such as that of the Pizarros in Peru. The 1533 Spanish Coro rebellion against the Welsers was an early mark of the strife between the German governors and the Spanish administrators due to their diverging approaches to seeking wealth: while the Welsers plundered gold on their violent inland expeditions and engaged in Indigenous slavery, the Spaniards wanted access to the profitable encomiendas and repartimientos.[33]

The deaths of Philipp von Hutten and Bartholomäus Welser VI effectively ended the Welsers' governance of the province of Venezuela, although they did not stop demanding governorship of the territory in the Spanish courts until 1557. Part I of this book focused on the economic and sociological background of the Welsers. In the next part I turn to narrative and cartographic representations of the Welsers in Venezuela during the sixteenth through eighteenth centuries.

PART II

Narrative and Cartographic
Representations of the Welsers in Venezuela,
Sixteenth to Eighteenth Century

CHAPTER 3

Nikolaus Federmann's *Indianische Historia*

*Gifts and Translation as Strategies of the
Welser Conquest of Venezuela*

Those who exchange presents with one another
Remain friends the longest
If things turn out successfully.
                    —Marcel Mauss, *The Gift*

Conquistadors from Christopher Columbus to Nikolaus Federmann employed gifts, friendship, and translation as strategies of conquest. Like Columbus's letters and diaries, Federmann's *Indianische Historia* reveals significant information about gifting as a strategy of war, not just peace. The narrative, written in German by Federmann (he also knew Spanish), reveals how translation and interpretation were used as a strategy of war and resistance in a region populated by Indigenous peoples of the Arawak, Carib, and Chibcha linguistic families.

In his diary, Columbus describes the gift exchange between his party and the first Indians he encountered, on October 13, 1492, on Guanahaní island (in the Bahamas). Columbus wrote, "They give everything they have for whatever we give them, even pieces of broken bowls and glass cups they will barter for" (1990, 33; "Mas todo lo que tiene[n] lo dan por qualquiera cosa que les den, de fasta los pedaços de las escudillas y de las taças de vidro rotas rescatavan" [32]).[1] He describes the natives' eagerness to barter "balls of cotton thread and parrots and spears" (31; "ovillos de algodón filado y papagayos y azagayas" [30]), stating that "they gave anything in exchange for whatever was given to them" (33; "y todo davan por qualquiera cosa que se lo diese" [32]). The original diary was lost in the sixteenth century, but excerpts from a biography by Hernando Colón, Columbus's son, and an abstract copied and translated by Las Casas have been circulating as Columbus's diary. The text went on to gain canonical status in the nineteenth century and was eventually published in translation as the *Journal of the First Voyage of America*. Many subsequent New World conquest narratives repeated the motif of the valuable gift traded for one worth little. Most scholars today argue that these exchanges, which typically followed first contact, favored the European invaders. For example, Vilches (2004) examines Columbus's representation of bartering in the Indies and finds that he used exchange to gain slaves for the Spanish royals. When Columbus took some of them to the Old World by force, they were brought as "profane tokens of holy grace and wealth" (2004, 202). On 14 October Columbus kidnapped a group of seven Taíno Indians to serve as translators to facilitate exchange and exploitation. Translation was an instrument of conquest and empire, though it could also be one of resistance.

Federmann also engaged in forced exchange with the nations he wished to conquer. He was a German who came to the province of Venezuela in 1529 as an agent of the Welser Company. His adventurous travel narrative, *Indianische Historia* (Indian History), remains one of the few contemporaneous accounts of the sixteenth-century German conquest and colonization of the province. A conquest narrative written as a defense for Federmann's actions and for would-be conquerors at home in Europe was published by Sigmund Bund in Haguenau in 1557 with the subtitle, *Ein schöne kurtzweilige Historia Nikolaus Federmanns des Jüngern von Ulm erster raise so er von Hispania un[d] Andolosia ausz in Indias des Occeanischen Mörs gethan hat und was ihm allda begegnet bis auff sein widerkunfft inn Hispaniam auffs kurtzest beschriben, gantz lustig zu lesen* (A Nice, Amusing Account from Nikolaus Federmann Junior from Ulm's First Voyage from Spain and Andalusia to the

Indies of the Ocean Sea, which Describes Briefly All That He Has Done and Encountered until His Return to Spain, Very Amusing to Read).

Federmann used violence and demanded obedience through gift exchange throughout Tierra Firme. His descriptions of his encounters with Indigenous nations and his frustrated gift exchanges with them reveal the failure of reciprocity and mutual exchange between the conquistador's men and the Amerindian nations they encountered. Federmann's linguistic manipulations and thwarted attempts at diplomacy through gift-giving constitute astute psychological maneuvers important to understanding the Welser conquest and colonization of Venezuela. Federmann's *Indianische Historia* relates in narrative form the violent encounters between the German-Spanish troops and the Indigenous populations of Venezuela that the cedularios detail in legal form.

Translation is fundamental to Federmann's "Indian" experience as he travels through northern South America. The text's focus on the Indigenous populations that Federmann encountered in Tierra Firme, which scholarship has ignored in favor of better-known Indigenous civilizations such as the Aztecs and the Incas, holds much ethnohistorical value. Indeed, translation forms the backbone of the text's depiction of German-Spanish violence against Indigenous agents. Federmann enslaves interpreters who translated from various Indigenous languages into Spanish and requires a Spanish notary to interpret the various experiences in an official format recognizable and suitable for the Spanish administrative system that was so intent on record keeping. Federmann's *Indianische Historia*, much like other colonial travel narratives, recounts how colonizers used language for the purpose of violent conquest. The Indigenous subjects, whom Federmann deprives of liberty, interpret and produce messages and codes. Words of war in Spanish, German, and various Indigenous languages are mixed and matched in a never-ending chain of coercion. No one is allowed to remain silent. Interpreters must produce the required information about topography, the location of gold and gems, and friendly and unfriendly Indigenous populations, as well as the availability of food for the German-Spanish crew.

Scholars such as Patricia Palmer and Vicente Rafael have argued that translation is an essential practice of empire. For example, in her analysis of English-Irish translation Palmer (2015, 358) writes, "Colonial translation didn't just operate under the sign of violence; it was an essential accessory to violence. Translation was central to both intelligence gathering and to cultivating the 'art of war.'" And in his analysis of the Spanish Empire's use of translation into vernacular languages for evangelization and Spaniards' hesitation surrounding the mistranslation of sacred terms, Rafael (2015, 88) argues, "Translation, as the process and product of exploiting the native languages for foreign ends, intensified the risk of native languages subverting those ends." Recently, however, scholars such as Anna Brickhouse (2015) and Allison Bigelow (2019) have sought to recover Indigenous agency from "motivated mistranslations." For example, Brickhouse has sought to dispel the myth that while translation went hand in hand with conquest and imperialism, Indigenous "lenguas," or interpreters, had no diplomatic agency. In fact, she discusses a series of "motivated mistranslations" dispatched by a collective of Indigenous interpreters to control their own or their peoples' destinies (Brickhouse 2015, 21). Bigelow takes up Brickhouse's concept of mistranslations to discuss how Indigenous mining technology was mistranslated first via a hybrid language, Quechuañol (Quechua + Spanish), and then in various European treatises. Mistranslation is a way to recover Indigenous technical literacies as well as to read how colonial ideologies of race and color stemmed from those mistranslations of vocabulary on the purity of metals (Bigelow 2019, 242). Federmann's narrative relies on interpretation and translation for conquest in the Canary Islands and in the province of Venezuela. However, we read about Indigenous interpreters' strategies of linguistic resistance and Federmann's own frustration at being led astray. In this chapter, after offering a summary about Federmann as the most polemical Welser governor in Venezuela, I examine his *Indianische Historia*. My analysis of Federmann's text sheds light on untimely gifts or gifts gone wrong as well as mistranslations in the initial conquest encounter between the Welser governors and Indigenous peoples such as the Guaiqueries (Arawak), Quiriquires (Carib), Caquetíos (Arawak), Achaguas (Xaguas-Ajagua-Arawak), Jirajara (Jirajara Ayaman, possibly Arawak), Cuibas (Arawak), and Cyparicotes (Chipas, possibly Carib) in the province of Venezuela. I conclude with an account of the work's publishing history in order to argue that "Indian" stories remained popular in the Habsburg realms. They were marketed strategically and with adequate dedications and patronage claims, thereby reinforcing the Christian mission of conquest at a time when the Lutheran Reformation divided the Germanophone world and censored voices in print.

NIKOLAUS FEDERMANN, THE MOST PROBLEMATIC
WELSER GOVERNOR

Little information remains about Federmann, but we know he easily navigated both Spanish and German mercantile and bureaucratic milieus. He was twenty-four when the Welsers appointed him to assist in conquering and sacking the Venezuelan province. He came from the free imperial city of Ulm, which joined the Schmalkaldic League in 1536 and thereby committed to a Lutheran statement of faith. In 1551 the city favored Lutheranism, and Federmann's anti-authoritarianism was posthumously tied to his birthplace.[2] As Juan Friede (1961) writes, Ulm had a tremendous impact on the formation of the character of Ambrosius Ehinger, who was Federmann's compatriot. Friede describes the Ulm conquistadors as "conscious of their personal worth, arrogant and independent because they lived in an environment where the traditional power of the nobility did not play an epoch-making role." He gives Federmann as an example because he "nobly" rebelled against the Welsers, "the patricians of Augsburg" (Friede 1961, 76).[3] According to Friede, Federmann's Protestantism allowed him to protest against his employers. Indeed, Federmann was represented as a rebel commandant well into the twentieth century. The *Historical Dictionary of Venezuela* has an entry on Federmann that describes him as "ambitious and eager to earn his reputation," stating that he therefore left his post as acting governor in Alfinger's absence, against the latter's orders, in 1530. It describes him again "disobeying the orders of his superior" and later "disputing who had the right to the conquest of" Bogotá (Rudolph and Rudolph 1996, 280–81). The portrait of contention and audacity most likely used Spanish sources. Federmann was taken prisoner in Flanders in 1540 on the basis of the Welsers' accusations. He was released and went to Madrid in February 1541, and he died in Valladolid on 22 February 1542 before the court could render a final ruling on the complaints of the Welsers and the emperor against him.

In 1529, when he stepped onto Venezuelan soil, Federmann brought 150 men with him, including the first German miners. All of the early chroniclers describe Federmann as an experienced soldier and captain, although there is no indication in the archives that he was either; he was merely a Welser Company agent. Just after Federmann's arrival in Coro, yet another Welser agent, Hans [Juan] Seissenhoffer, came with the first group of German and Spanish women, and despite Federmann's young age, he appointed Federmann deputy governor. After Governor Alfinger returned to Coro and before he left to recover from malaria in Santo Domingo, he made Federmann interim governor and general captain and mayor (*alcalde mayor*). At the time the colony of Coro would have benefited from stable governance, as power had changed hands between the Spanish and Welser representatives a number of times, and not in the friendliest manner (Alfinger had forced out the first Spanish governor, Juan de Ampiés). In fact, Federmann stated that Seissenhofer came to return the colony to German hands as a Spanish lieutenant had governed Coro while Alfinger embarked on an eight-month expedition and was believed to have perished in the jungle. Already in this period, the Welser agents responded quickly to interceding rule, for the acting governor was the Spanish lieutenant Luis Sarmiento, "welcher ein Hispanier was, und mehr auff sein dann auff deren nutz ersehen solte" (who was a Spaniard, and who looked more to his own interests than those of the Welsers) (Federmann 1557, 15). However, rather than establish confidence in German governance in Coro, Federmann undertook a long expedition, for which he would be punished as Alfinger had not granted him permission to do so. As a result, Federmann was exiled from the province for four years and sent home, though he eventually received the governance of Venezuela, however briefly, and would return to embark on yet another entrada.[4]

Federmann wrote his *Indianische Historia* based on his experiences conquering the interior of Venezuela in his first expedition of 1531.[5] He may have written it between 1531 and 1535 when he was exiled in Augsburg. The trials and tribulations in this narrative are designed to clear his name. The main source document for the *Indianische Historia* was a report that Federmann's Spanish notary had compiled during their expedition into Venezuela's interior that has never been found. The notary's report was intended for the king and was a normal administrative undertaking. Federmann translated the report and embellished it in Spanish; later he made the report more appropriate for a German audience. It was published posthumously in 1557. Federmann's access to both Spanish and German allowed him to be a cultural commentator on the conquest of the Americas. The portrait that emerges from Federmann's self-fashioning in the *Indianische Historia* is that of an astute and ruthless conqueror and manipulator.

The General Archive of the Indies has a transcription of testimony presented in court that also gives a portrait of Federmann—as he would like to be seen; it is clearly meant to be exculpatory. Addressing the Audiencia General in Santo Domingo in 1535, Federmann fashions himself as a benevolent leader, prey to harmful defamation, and called on various witnesses who had lived with him in Coro to testify to his positive qualities.[6] It is titled "Proof of the merits and services that Nicolaus Federmann performed in the conquest and pacification of the Province of Venezuela."[7] Federmann states that his purpose is to rectify his tarnished reputation because "Your Majesty was given an adverse account of my behavior,"[8] opining that Charles would benefit from having a truthful account of Federmann's service (1557, 2). He clearly chose his character witnesses well: Federmann's handpicked witnesses confirmed his absolute benevolence, popularity, and charity. According to their testimony, Federmann was an exemplary leader who cared for his soldiers and who dutifully fulfilled the task of pacifier and governor set out in the capitulación. For example, Francisco de Bastidas testified:

> He had served diligently and faithfully in a way that would convene the service of his Majesty and in regards to the well-being of the land and of the pacification and settling of it and to the good treatment of the natives . . . and that all agreed that when Federmann went on an entrada with certain Spaniards some of the particular things that were said about him upon his return, were that if there was a sick man among them and Federmann had something good (to eat) he would leave the sick man to eat it and if [the sick man] could not walk [Federmann] would give him a horse that he could ride so as to not leave him behind. (18–19)[9]

In this testimony, Bastidas presents Federmann as a faithful vassal who fulfilled his duty to pacify and settle the land and who treated the Indians and the soldiers well during the arduous expeditions into the interior. In the testimony, Bastidas allows that most Spaniards looked upon Federmann, and previously Ambrosius Alfinger, negatively. Federmann knew exactly what charges his enemies made against him and which ones would violate the contract between the crown and the Welsers. Hence, he used the Spanish legal system to profess his innocence before being charged guilty in the juicio de residencia. The portrait of Federmann that emerges in this process differs from the one Federmann presented in his narrative. In his recollection of his journey to Venezuela and his conquest expeditions, he fashioned himself as a caring helper and nurse rather than the ruthless conqueror he is in his narrative.

Indianische Historia.

In schöne kurtz-
weilige Historia Niclaus Federmanns des Jüngern von
Vlm erster raise so er von Hispania vñ
Andolosia auß in Indias des Occeanischen Mörs gethan hat / vnd
was ihm allda ist begegnet biß auff sein
widerkunfft inn Hispaniam / auffs
kurtzest beschriben / gantz
lustig zü lesen.

M D LVII·

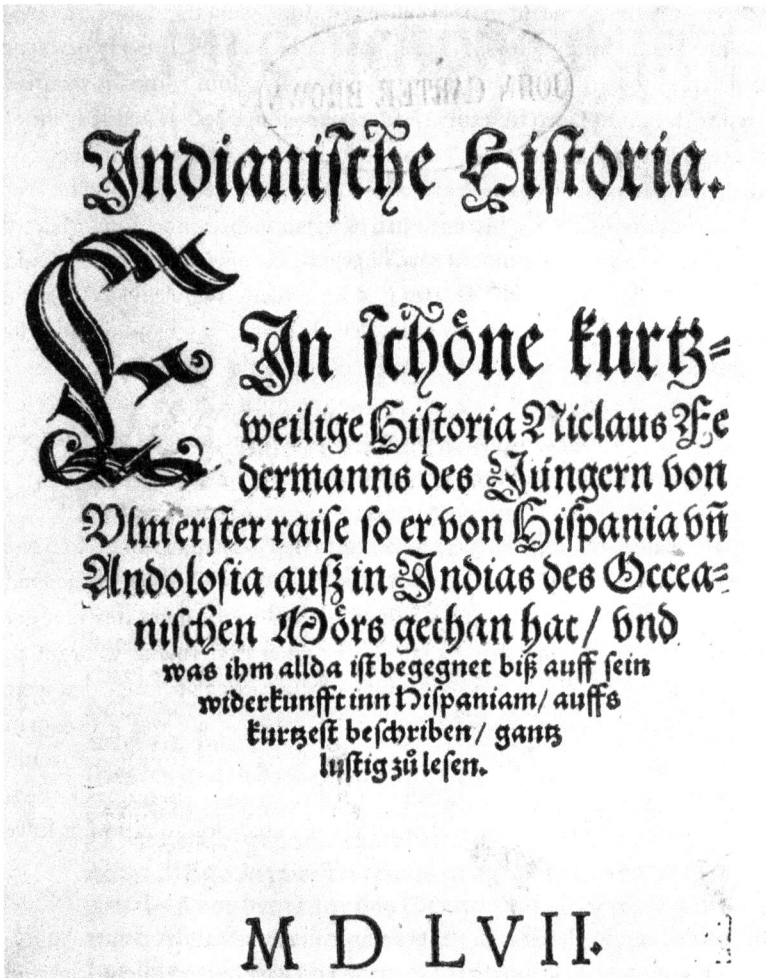

FIGURE 3.1. Title page of Federmann's *Indianische Historia*. It was published in quarto format (the pagination here uses this page as the first). Courtesy of John Carter Brown Library at Brown University. Internet Archive. Creative Commons License.

THE CANARIES AND THE MORISCOS: PURLOINED LETTERS, WORDPLAY, AND NARRATION

Navigators and explorers on their way to the Spanish Indies typically stopped in the Canary Islands. It was there that Federmann first encountered non-Christians. After facing many storms and traveling 300 miles over twenty-one days on a trip that normally took ten at most, Federmann anchored his boat at an unusual port on Lanzarote island and searched for badly needed fresh water. There he encountered Moroccan Berbers. As he wrote:

> es war aber, alls es unser unglück also erfordert und Gott gestattet, zu der zeit grosse dürre in diser Insel, hette lang nit geregnet, hetten die Arabier, so auß Barbaria, welche 17 meyl gegen der Insel über gelegen, und an ainem ort diser Insel, ihr wohnung zuhaben, und ihr viech, gaiß und kamelthier, aldar zu graßen und waiden, wurde vergonnet, von dannen sie in Barbaria ihre Contract und geschäfft oder handthierung mit dem viech und genieß derselben, als milch und keß, haben und treiben, darumb sie dem hauptmann der Insel, ihnen solches zu gestatten, ihren tribut geben, gesagts ihr viech an diesem Port Rabicon, da wir angefahren dem Wasser zü lieb, dessen sie an Otyen, da sie ihre gewohnliche wässerung haben gebrecht hintriben und uns erfahen, vermainend, wir weren franzoßen. (Federmann 1557, 5)

> In this time, however, we were unfortunate, and because God allowed it, there was a great drought on the Island and it had not rained for a long while. The Arabs from Barbary, that's located 17 miles from this island, had settled there and they let their cows, goats, and camels graze. In Barbary the Arabs trade milk and animal products, such as milk and cheese; because of this they pay a tribute to the governor of the island so that they can let their animals graze in this port of Rabicon, since the water was scarce in Otyen where they normally let their animals drink, they came when we arrived and caught us, thinking we were Frenchmen.

At the time, the Canaries were already under Spanish rule and Spain was at war with the French. The Berbers, whom Federmann calls "Arabier oder Moriscos" (Arabs or Moriscos) (6), taking Federmann's men for French enemies, hurled stones at them, injuring Federmann and killing three of his men (7). This incident was typical in the Atlantic in-betweens. As I wrote in chapter 1, for Europeans, the Canaries existed as a site for experimental conquest and colonization.

Federmann's description of this encounter suggests the language and wordplay that is prominent throughout his narrative. The phrase "Arabier oder Moriscos" exemplifies a style of translation that Federmann uses throughout the text to identify terms in both German and Spanish.[10] While the aim is to clarify to his reader what the terms actually mean, it also allows Federmann to dutifully re-create a Spanish context, or rather situate German history within a Habsburg Spanish setting. Moreover, as the text was created with the help of a Spanish notary for the Habsburg monarch, the translation retains terms that would be understood in an administrative Castilian and colonial context. In this case, however, "Morisco" has a specific Muslim Castilian significance that underlines the Iberian nature of Federmann's references. His enemies are infidels, though "Moriscos" conveys that they are Moors who converted to Christianity in sixteenth-century peninsular Spain.[11] It is not clear here if Federmann made a lexical mistake, but even if he did, it invokes the otherness and trickiness of the Moriscos: "es seer ein ring volck, schnels lauffs von und zum mann wie ein hirsch springt" (they are a fast people, they run fast from man to man, like a jumping deer) (6). Here and elsewhere, Federmann compares the islands' inhabitants to animals.

The Berbers are more aggressive than the docile natives Federmann would encounter in Santo Domingo. Yet this attack on Federmann, his crew, and the Berber traders sets up a linguistic motif that reappears throughout Federmann's *Indianische Historia*. Tellingly, Federmann's captivity at the beginning of the narrative inverts what will occur later in the Indies. In the Canaries, the stone-throwing, quick Moriscos almost beat Federmann and his men. Their willingness to negotiate for ransom conforms to the piracy tactics the Berbers used along the Mediterranean coast.

Federmann's savvy strategies and the power of written language save him and his crew. This marks the first instance of the suppleness with which he uses language. Later in his life, Federmann would use testimony and the written word to legitimate his power and to portray himself to both of his employers, the Welsers and the Holy Roman Emperor, as a good leader, despite rumors from the Spanish administration that he was a Lutheran. Federmann uses translation to gain power, whether it is political power with the Habsburg authorities and the Welser agents at home or power in a local context to gain an advantage over the subjects he exploits. While the Berbers kidnap Federmann in the hope of obtaining ransom, Federmann uses language to secure his crew's safety through his missives. He also shows his power as a captain and a leader to the governor, who eventually rescues him and his loyal crew members. Finally, Federmann demonstrates his linguistic mastery to his readers. In this instance, the kidnapped Federmann communicates with his estranged crew in coded written missives.

> die Arabier, deren gefangener wir waren, allein Rescat, oder Schatzung und losung, unserer Personen von uns verhuften und darumb uns enthielten, ließ ich mich gegen ihnen mercken, wollte mich mit dem hauptmann des schiffs (welches ich selbs sein ihnen verlaugnet) bereden. (7)
> ———
> The Arabs who had imprisoned us hoped to get a ransom, or a treasure, so I let myself be noticed by them, and that is why I proposed to speak to the Captain of the ship (I didn't tell them it was actually me).

The aside to the reader, the inside knowledge that Federmann himself is the "captain" of the ship to whom he writes, is an effective strategy. The "Arabs," as he refers to them, do not let him approach the ship to *speak* to the captain but they do allow him to *write* a letter addressed to him. The letter allows Federmann to give his crew instructions so that they can deliver himself and his men from captivity: "ich sollte deßhalb ahns schiff schreiben, und mein mainung dem hauptmann anzeigen, so wollten sie denen im schiff zeichen geben lassen, das sie an land schickten, die brieff zuholen, doch mit dem geding, dass ich müsste geloben, nit anzüzeigen wa wir gefangen lägen" (I should write to the ship and give the Captain my opinion, so they wanted to give a sign to those on the ship that they should come on land to retrieve the letter with the condition that I would not let them know where we were imprisoned) (7). Through the power of the word in the letter, Federmann unites with his men against his enemies. The sender, Federmann, and the addressee, the captain, are one and the same. Federmann's writing act allows him to regain control over his crew: the letter metaphorically reunites the head (or the captain) with the body (the crew).

Moreover, Federmann proves to be a master of interpretation and translation. The kidnappers stipulate that Federmann cannot reveal the whereabouts of their hiding place and that, after the ship receives a hand signal, only two men may retrieve the letter destined for the fictitious captain. The crew proves to be astute: they send as representatives of the ship men able to interpret the words of the captors for Federmann: "und als auff mein schreiben, auß dem schiffe kamen zwen mann, ein balbirer uns züverbinden, der ander ein Kriech, welcher die Arabische sprach kundte, darmit wir doch, den Arabiern unwisend, was sie unserhalb mit einander redten, in irer sprach auch kuntschafft hetten" (in response to my words two men disembarked from the ship: A barber who bandaged us and a Greek who could speak Arabic, [came] so that we could know what the Arabs said about us amongst each other unbeknownst to them) (7–8). While we do not know if Feder- mann specifically asked that these two sailors come to negotiate his release, the crew, at least, give him the tools to play a game of interpretation to gather secrets unbeknownst to the captors. Federmann recognizes that lan- guage and interpretation can be used as weapons. He later applies this lesson in his first Venezuelan inland expedition when he encounters native subjects with whom he cannot communicate. The role of the barber will prove to be important. "Ein balbirer" is a Spaniard in disguise and, as a member of Federmann's crew, loyally bound to "uns" (the agents of the Welser Com- pany). We do not know whether the kidnappers recognized the role that this character played in sabotaging their plan to collect ransom, but Federmann certainly recognized the advantage of having individuals in his service who share linguistic and cultural identities with his enemies and therefore can spy on them. Moreover, Federmann knew that such linguistic and cultural iden- tities could be acquired and disguised. The Greek, another imitator and speaker of Arabic, conveys the captors' plans to Federmann. Language re- leases Federmann from his chains. He will later use it to bind natives to reveal the location of secret treasures. In the province of Venezuela, language literally enslaves natives to Federmann.

THE CONSEQUENCES OF BAD GIFTS

The *Indianische Historia* details events from 1529 to 1533, covering Fed- ermann's journey to the recently settled Spanish colony of Coro in the province of Venezuela. A year after arriving in Coro, Federmann began his entrada, searching for El Dorado and the Pacific within present-day north- western Venezuela. He traveled through the nations of the Xideharas (Jira- jaras), Ayamanes, Cayones (Gayones), Xaguas (Achaguas), and Cyparicotes (Cipamotes), as well as the Caquetíos, who were allied with the Spanish and therefore friendly and off-limits to enslavement. It also took him through the nations of the rebellious Cuybas, who fought with poisoned arrows, and the Guaycaries, who resisted Federmann's conquest. He was aware that by order of Empress Isabella he was only to make war with "rebellious" Indians; however, he does not heed that stipulation. Federmann's narrative also recounts his return to Coro and his journey to Spain, then ends with his coming home to Augsburg. Federmann describes giving gifts during the expedition, but he also expects to receive gifts of value from his Indigenous hosts.

Theories on the gift have abounded since anthropologists and philosophers such as Claude Lévi-Strauss and Jacques Derrida (*Given Time: Counterfeit Money*, 1992; and *The Gift of Death*, 1995) rediscovered Marcel Mauss's *Essai sur le don* (*The Gift*, 1950). More recent studies have focused on European gift-giving in literature and culture in early modern England (Ben-Amos 2008; Klekar 2009) and France (Zemon Davis 2000). Valentin Groebner, in his *Liquid Assets, Dangerous Gifts* (2002), has focused on municipal gifts presented by the city of Basel in the fifteenth and sixteenth centuries. Groebner (2002, 10) sees the use of Mauss's gift concept as a utopian model that does not apply to the commodity- and purchase-oriented European reality. Almudena Pérez de Tudela and Annemarie Jordan Gschwend (2007, 420) have traced how the Habsburg court both in Iberia and in Austria demanded exotic animals in its desire to collect New World treasures. The Habsburgs' gift-giving practices helped unite people with objects in an intimate matter and also served as diplomatic tools across courts (Pérez de Tudela and Jordan Gschwend 2003, 29). Carina Johnson (2011a, 84) has also investigated how the Habsburgs, specifically, Emperor Maximilian, depicted his treasury in the monumental print projects, the Triumphal Arch and the Triumphal Procession. Johnson also describes how New World gold, including Inca treasure, was smelted rather than kept in its original form in order to pay for Emperor Charles V's wars against the Ottoman sultan Suleiman (97). The work of these scholars situate Federmann's motives: conquistadors sought gold bullion to accumulate but also gifts and exotica with which to impress their political leaders at home.

Federmann often emphasizes the importance of the ritual of giving and receiving gifts. These rituals conform to Mauss's assertion in *Essai sur le don* that no gift is really free: the giver always obliges the giftee to regift in due time. In *The Gift* Mauss quotes a few stanzas from the Havanal (from the Scandinavian *Edda*) to describe the role of gift exchange in interpersonal relationships.[12]

Those who exchange presents with one another
Remain friends the *longest*
If things turn out successfully.
(Mauss 1990, 1; my emphasis)

The poem implies that equal gift exchanges nurture friendship. The length of friendship, the poem suggests, hinges on the "successful" gift exchange. Mauss addresses the economy of the gift exchange and its attending socio-logical practices in his anthropological research on the North American Haida and Tlingit peoples. Federmann's text is one of the few existing sources from the region that documents Indigenous allegiances and wars with neighboring groups as well as Spanish conquerors, but I am not sug-gesting that Federmann's work constitutes anthropological research in the mode of Mauss's.[13] The gift exchange is a strategy that Federmann places in his narrative to eradicate any suspicion that he is a soft-handed hero. Given the political implications for the Welser agents, of whom the Spanish colo-nists were already distrustful, Federmann wanted to fashion himself as a conqueror on equal footing with the Spanish.

Mauss describes the potlatch system of exchange among Native Ameri-cans of the Northwest as a system of "total services" present also in the *kula* system of gift-giving in Melanesian society: "Presents are exchanged for any and every reason, for every 'service,' and everything is given back later, or even at once, and is immediately given out again" (Mauss 1990, 42).

Mauss describes the gift economy in his analysis of Polynesian society, showing that clans and parties exchange gifts to guarantee peaceful social relations between two Polynesian societies, writing that groups "have no option but to ask for hospitality, to receive presents, to enter into trading, to contract alliances, through wives or blood kinship" (13). He notes that the obligation to give is equally important. In this context, then, "to refuse to give, to fail to invite, just as to refuse to accept, is tantamount to declaring war" (13).

A similar dynamic existed between Indigenous groups in Venezuela. Federmann exploited Indigenous gift-giving practices, both to find allies and to seek hospitality (Arellano 1987, 415). He engaged in gift exchange to enforce a temporal contract with the recipient, that is, a contract that needed to be paid back after a certain amount of time. Federmann used the giving and receiving ritual to exploit Amerindians through unequal exchanges. Some of his trades obtained food for himself and his conquistadors or information about the topography of land he sought to travel in, but a larger number involved taking gold, gems, and pearls in exchange for glass beads. Federmann took advantage of the rules of gift-giving that existed among Indigenous groups; he relied on linguistic manipulations to subjugate Amerindians and to extract slave labor as well as treasure.[14]

Federmann always expected to receive more than he gave. For example, a typical trade occurs when Federmann meets the Ayamane nation. He states, "gabe inen auch erliche Schanckunge / von eisen hacken und glässere Paternoster, so bei uns (wie bewüßt) klaines werdts sein / aber bei ihnen / alls ain frembd ding/groß geacht ist" (I gave them true gifts from metal hooks and glass beads, which with us (as is known) are of little value, but to them, as a strange thing [gift], is highly valued) (Federmann 1557, 24–25). In the same town, Federmann's party takes "Mahis, Juca, Batata, Ayama" (corn, yucca, potatoes, and squash) (26). He claimed they "ainen überflufs funden" (found an abundant source) and helped themselves. They do not have to resort to violence because of their hosts' willingness to give. As the ethnohistorian of Venezuela Morella Jimenez (1986, 64) argues, the Indigenous peoples in this area were accustomed to extensive trade and exchange so it was hardly a surprise when conquistadors offered them gifts, which they would immediately exchange with those in their possessions. However, the intent from both parties was not the same.

Federmann complains when he does not acquire valuable gifts. For example, he walks through Ayamane land and finds nothing worth taking.

Uns ward under diser nation wenig Present oder schanckung von goldt, dann sie dessen kainen reichthumb oder ja vast wenig haben, dann sie sich nur der schwartzen glitzender körner, angefasset, wie die Pater noster, zu ihrer zier gebrauchen, auch gebrauchen sy sich etlicher Mariscos oder mörmuscheln, so sie von andern Nationen erkauffen, welchs ihnen als die dem mör ferr, seltzam seind, dann sie von dem mör nichts wissen, auch dahin nicht kömmen. Ist ein volck das mit dem umb sitzenden Nationen, ihren nachparn feinde seind, auch nicht ferr raißen, und sich aine Nation der andern termines und herrschung nicht gebrauchen. (Federmann 1557, 40)

———

From this nation we received few presents or gifts of gold, because these people have almost no riches, because they do have as adornments bright black beads, like the Paternoster (beads), and mussels that they buy from other peoples and that appear strange to them as they are far away from the sea. They do not know anything about the sea and do not travel there. They are a people that are encircled by enemy nations and one nation does not travel far and does not cross over the dominion of another nation.[15]

This passage is typical in that Federmann describes how he calculates the value of every nation he encounters, and the Ayamanes hold little of worth. However, he would make them useful by having them intercede with a less friendly nation, the Cayones. The Ayamane interpreters fear the Cayones, yet Federmann seeks to convince them that he has only friendship for both groups.

> Denn es vo mir allein darumb angesehen was, darmit sie unserer gerechten fraindtschafft, destweniger zweifletten, und auch erkennten, das wir umb ihres hail willen alda weren, dann sonst hette wir wolleiden mögen das je einer des andern feind gewesen weren, dann destweniger hetten wir uns irer versamlung die uns hette mögen schaden, besorgen dürffen. (38)

> ———

> What was more important was that they not doubt our just/fair friendship and that they knew that we were here to save them. Or else, it would have been the same to us if they were enemies, then we would not have feared their conspiracies against us so much.

Federmann decides he has a right to the possessions of the nations he meets, and in keeping with Mauss's description, he interprets the absence of gifts as an invitation to war. Accordingly, he takes up arms when the Guaycaries deny him gifts. Thus he practices "just war": according to Spanish custom and as a German conqueror working for both the Welsers and the Spanish crown, he could take the natives as semislaves or encomendados. As part of the encomienda system, the Spanish (or in this case, the Germans working for the Spanish crown) were entrusted to teach the natives Catholic doctrine, and they were also responsible for giving them food, shelter, and clothes. In exchange for this protection *indios encomendados* had to work and pay tribute to their encomenderos. According to Juan Friede (1960, 84), "el código del derecho del conquistador" (the conquistador's code of rights) legitimately demanded gifts and labor from the conquered, which included transport of their goods and interpretation of their language.

Derrida writes in *Given Time* (1992) of Mauss's concept of the gift that time or temporality was the gift's *essence*.[16] Time, that is, a specific restitution in due time, sets the fundamental rhythms and rules of the gift economy. Reception and restitution regulate what Derrida calls "the madness of the gift": "Here is, it seems, the most interesting idea, the great guiding thread of [Mauss's] *The Gift*: For those who participate in the experience of gift and countergift, the requirement of restitution 'at term,' at the delayed 'due date,' the requirement of the circulatory differance *is inscribed in the thing itself* that is given or exchanged" (1992, 40; original emphasis). As Derrida suggests, Mauss's descriptions show that the gift *demands time*: the gift has to be restituted during a specific amount of time, not too hastily but not too late either. Federmann often "buys" time with gifts to stave off an attack on his conquistadors. The temporal aspect of the gift remains integral to the conquistador and the nations with whom he negotiates. The time inscribed within the gift allows both parties to meet under the pretense of friendship, form alliances, and buy time before one party decides to wage war on the other. When he encounters the Xidehara nation, Federmann refers to a gift paid back in time. He describes the meeting thus: "Diser Nacion, gleich-wohl mehr auß forcht, dann auß geneigtem willen, woll empfangen, und was sie mir von Proviant auch ein thail golds gegeben, haben thon müssen" (This nation received us well more out of fear than out of their inclination, and they had to give us provisions and a portion of their gold) (Federmann 1557, 18). Here, it is the Xideharas who buy time from Federmann through gift giving. He declares war against them later, but they use the time to prepare for battle; as such, the purchase of time prevents immediate violence if not subjugation.

Time used as collateral fails Federmann in the gift exchange with the Cayone Nation. He believes he exchanges his friendship for gold and food: "un[d] vermeint, das wir die Present oder schänckung, in pfandt der freund-schafft gegeben weren, un[d] uns wurde von ihnen wie vo andern Pueblos oder flecken, glauben gehalten, hette sich der Cacique oder herr, mit all sei-nem volck, weib und kind, bei nacht haimlich absentiert oder weg gethon" (and we thought that the gifts were a pledge to assure friendship, and that we would be obliged to them as in other Pueblos, but the Cacique left clan-destinely during the night with all the people, women and children) (40).

"Pfandt" here refers to a pledge, assurance, or collateral that binds the Cayones to Federmann and vice versa; he thought he made a gift contract, which he feels Cayones break when they leave. Thus the Cayones bought time to leave with their gifts. While Federmann took their gifts as an investment or deposit, they turn out to be a delaying tactic by the givers.

Federmann raids the village where the Cayones hide, killing many and taking forty-three prisoners, including the cacique. He emphasizes broken trust in describing his treatment of the leader: "Den ließ ich in ein kettin schmiden zu andern, die ich in eisen füret, als der wider sein zusage, glauben gebrochen hette" (I had him welded by a chain to others that I led bound in irons so as to reiterate that he had broken our trust) (42). Federmann believed he and the Cayone cacique had enacted a pact of alliance. If the contractual obligations of giving one's word result in the cacique's imprisonment when he takes his word back, then the cacique's speech act, that of *giving* his word at the same time as his presents, needs to be reconsidered in light of Federmann's expectations that to "give one's word" implied a legal contract between two parties.[17]

The speech act of giving one's word (of making a promise), demonstrates the original gift-as-word that allowed Federmann to believe he was entering into a mutual contract with the cacique. In essence, the cacique takes back his word, thus taking back his gift of the Cayones' alliance with Federmann. He does so because he expects Federmann will treat the Cayones violently. Moreover, I invoke the German meaning of the word *Gift*, which is "poison" in English translation; Federmann counters the cacique's act of disobedience with his own gift of poisonous violence. As Federmann continues his expedition of conquest through Venezuela, he sends Indigenous prisoners ahead with gifts to meet other nations. Naturally, these chained messengers tell the Indigenous recipients that Federmann will probably enslave them, but the ongoing abandonment of Indigenous villages that follows repeatedly surprises Federmann and his hopes for unequal exchange.

It is useful to turn to Brickhouse's reading of mistranslation in Columbus's diary. As the seven Taíno interpreters give Columbus "an overwhelming stream of information that proves singularly unhelpful, even to the extent of obstructing the voyage's further progress" (Brickhouse 2015, 27), the Indigenous interpreters reveal Federmann's tactics and obstruct Federmann's slave raids. However, the Caquetíos, traditional allies of the Spanish who first conquered the coast, do not flee and give gifts willingly. The historical alliances between the Caquetíos and their leader, the cacique Manaure, and the Spanish founder of Coro, Juan Martínez de Ampiés, explain this. This relationship had resulted in mixed Spanish-Caquetío towns (Lovera Reyes 2011). Federmann describes the first encounter with the Caquetíos thus:

> Inn allem bewisen sie uns gutte freundschafft, unnd haben uns in disem Pueblos oder flecken diser provintz Variquecimeto, schankunge geben, aber ongenöttigter und willkuriger verehrung, ob drei tausent Pesos golds, welches bein 5000 gulden Rheinisch thut, dann es ain reich, unnd an vilem golde ain tractieret oder gewerbig volck ist, von denen mans auch refratiert und erkaufft. (Federmann 1557, 52)

> They manifest good friendship, and they gave us presents in this Pueblo or village of this province of Variquicimeto [present-day Barquicimeto], they gave us 3,000 pesos in gold or 5,000 Rhein gulden, but out of unforced and voluntary adoration. They are a rich people who work with gold so that they can trade and sell it.

The Caquetíos shower Federmann in gold and willingly trade their riches for Federmann's metal trinkets: "Und so man ihnen gegenschankungen von eisen, als hacken, oder äxten, messer, und dergleichen, das dann ihnen vast nott ist, vil goldt und grosser reichtumb zu bekommen were" (So we gave them gifts of iron such as hooks, axes, knives and the sort, that they have a need for, for which one can get a lot of gold and riches from them) (53).

Federmann sees the Caquetío as a trustworthy, easily exploitable nation.[18] Their home in a fertile valley offers many riches. Federmann writes that the Caquetíos "sovil Present und schankungen *auß guttem willen gaben*" (gave us so many presents out of *their own goodwill*) and that they do so "*nicht* wie inn andern flecken und vorfürgeraisten nationen, *aus forcht*" (*not out of fear* as in other Pueblos and previous nations we visited) (53; my emphases). He attributes this warm welcome to their faith and trust and puts them above other peoples he meets because of this lack of hostility and plentitude of valuable gifts. There is an apparent absence of coercion. Federmann acknowledges that the Caquetíos need European tools, but we have the sense that he as narrator is in league with his sixteenth-century German reader. Even though Federmann (finally) acknowledges the reciprocal expectation through his *gegenschankungen* (reciprocal gifts) to the Caquetíos, both parties know who received the gifts of greater value. Of course, Federmann's "good" treatment of the Caquetíos may have to do with the Caquetíos' relationship with the Spaniards (Arellano 1987, 407). Nonetheless, Federmann is again exposed as a trader/traitor/narrator who gives reciprocal gifts, or *gegenschankungen*, of European metalware for 3,000 pesos' worth of gold. Federmann as conquistador and narrator needs the ritual of gift exchange, but he knows it is all a hoax.

CONDITIONS OF FRIENDSHIP

Throughout his expedition of conquest, Federmann recounts his obsession with the diversity of language. For example, in the passage below Federmann expresses his frustration at the failure of translation and the disintegration of language as he attempts to speak through multiple interpreters.

> Biß züerraichung der Caquetios, wir einander zuverstehen, uns haben müssen behelffen, dann ich allein der ersten sprach, alls der Caquetios zwen Christen und vertrawte Tolmetschen die dieselbig sprach fast wol kundten, bei mir hette, und hernach bei den Xiderharas durch zwen, bei den Ayamones durch drei, bei den Cayones durch vier, und bei den Xaguas dürch fünff personen reden müsste. Derhabeln ist nicht züzweifflen, bis einer den andern verstanden, und also biß in die fünffte zungen sagt, wie ihm von mir ist befolhen, das ye einer etwas darzü setz oder darvon nimpt, also das unther zehen wörter so ime beuolhen, kaum eines meines gefallens, unserer notturft gemeß geredt wurde, welches ich nicht für ain klainen oder wenigen gebrach, und der uns offt an erfarung, viler heimlicheit des lands darumb wir dann maist außgeraißt, verhindert spüret. (35)

> ―――――

> I had spoken to the Caquetíos through two Christian interpreters that I trusted, and who mastered that language, but then I needed to speak through two interpreters with the Xideharas and, three with the Ayamanes, four with the Cayones and finally through five interpreters with the Xaguas. There is no doubt that after my statements had made their way to the fifth person, each person had changed or added something,

in a way that out of ten of my words only one was correct, which was not a small problem, since it prevented us from obtaining correct information about the land that we were traveling through.

Federmann's observations on what is essentially a game of "telephone" highlights the limits of intercultural understanding. This chain of miscommunication emphasizes the unreliability of human recollection and the subjective experience of understanding. On the other hand, it is perhaps in this moment where Federmann loses his power: his native interpreters translate each other's speech, losing Federmann's message. Like Columbus's captive translators who use translation "to engage in acts of political diplomacy" (Brickhouse 2015, 18), Federmann's multiple indigenous translators explicitly fail his translation request and produce "motivated mistranslations" (to use Brickhouse's term) as a form of resistance to Federmann's conquest.

The premise of friendship remains at the heart of Federmann's tactic of conquest. I have already described what happened to the cacique who broke his word: he was publicly shamed and enslaved. Federmann employs a similar logic when the Ayamanes do not come on "friendly" terms when he summons them but attack him instead. He sends three "Indios" to tell them that

> warumb wir darkomen weren, ihne(n) ahnzeigen solten, auch darneben berichten, so sy zu mir khämen, und sich wie freünd guttwilig ergeben, wölle ich ihn das vergangen schon verziegen haben, und für freünde ahnnemen, auch ihr freündt sein, unnd sie von ihren feinden helffen schutzen unnd erretten. (28)

> they should show them why we came [to show them friendship] and tell them that if they come to me as friends I would receive them as friends as I would forget the past, and I would be their friend and help protect them against their enemies.

Federmann uses the same tactics that he employed against the Berbers: a messenger or interpreter delivers the good and the bad news. Naturally, the good news is an offer of friendship on condition that they do as Federmann says. Federmann states what would happen if they refuse to accept.

Wa aber das nicht und sy sich meiner angebotner freündschafft widern
thette(n), wölle ich ihnen nachstellen, auch sie, ihre landt und veld-
gebew, verhergen un verprennen, auch sie und ihre weib und kinder
fahen, jha für Eschlavos und verkauffte leüt haben und vergeben, und
in allem wie ain rechter abgesagter feindt gegen ihnen leben un(d) mich
erzaigen. (28–29)

If they did not come and if they refused my offered friendship, then I
would destroy and burn their land and their fields and I would capture
them, their wives, and children, and sell them as slaves, and I would
show myself to be a true enemy.

In effect, he declares war on them. By using a Hispanicized term (*Eschlavos*)
for "slaves," Federmann shows himself to be in league with the traders of
Venezuela's Indigenous peoples. When Federmann meets the Guaycaries
they refuse to enter into an agreement with him; the ensuing battle leaves
five hundred natives dead. Federmann's men find the Guaycarie cacique
who broke faith with him and take him back to Coro as a slave. Just as with
the Cayone cacique, Federmann humiliates the oath breaker.

Also fingen sie den Cacique oder Herren und drei und zweintzig per-
sonnen manne un[d] weiber, der meist principalen oder fürnempsten,
den ließ ich zur straff, dieweil er mir dreimal den glauben gebrochen,
in ein ketten schmiden, und hab also ihn und auch die andern so mit
ihme gefangen, biß gen Coro gefürt, und die weiber den Christen zu
dienen anßgetailt. (94)

And so they took prisoner the cacique and twenty-three men and
women, most of them important people, then I punished him and put
him in chains because he had broken his word three times, and I took
him and the others captured with him to Coro and divided the women
among the Christians so they may serve them.

Federmann takes his captives to Coro and, likely, sells them into the Indigenous slave trade. He mentions women were to serve his men personally as
slaves. In this, as in all other instances, Federmann gives so that he may
receive. If he does not receive, Federmann interprets the refusal as an invitation for the use of force.

Federmann's gifts extend to women. The cacique of the Ayamane nation gives him a bride: "Verehreten mir auch ettliche Presentes oder shanckungen von goldt, prasentiert und schankt auch der Cacique oder Herr, mir ein zwergin bei vier spannen lang, fast schöner und gutter proportz oder gestallt, die er sagt sein Weib sein" (They gave me also presents or gifts of gold. The cacique also gave me or presented me with a female dwarf, four spans long, well-built or proportioned, that he said was his wife) (37). (Federmann characterizes the nation as "klain volck, und zwergen" [23], small people and dwarves.) Federmann forces the woman to accompany him on his subsequent travels and eventually leaves her in Coro before returning to Europe "darumb das sie und alle ander Indios, auß ihrem vaterland, und sonderlich in kalten landen, nit lang leben" (because she, like the other Indios, would not live long outside of their homeland, especially in cold lands) (37). His rationalization of the value of the gift frames the bride as a necessary companion for his *Indianische Historia* but as one who would be worthless in Europe. He also complies with the geographic theories that posit that marvels and monsters, such as this "dwarf-bride," should be left in the tropics. It seems likely that she was either sold into the rampant Indian slave trade on the Venezuelan coast or stayed in Coro and became the slave of another conquistador.

This is certainly not the only evidence of Federmann kidnapping Indian women. In the juicios de residencia against the Welsers, a witness, Bernardino Manso, gives the following testimony incriminating Federmann.[19]

Fuele preguntado que si vió el dicho Federman tomase algunas indias de principales por se hermosas para llevar y consigo y echarse con ellas dijo que vió que tomó una hija de uno de los principales de Cayarna que el dicho tiene la cual lleva ya consigo y que es público y notorio que se echa con ella y asímismo oyó decir que procuró e hizo buscar ciertas indias en Paraguaná pero que la intención para qué no la sabe. (Morón 1977, 174–75)

He was asked if he had seen Federmann take some Indian women from the principals because they were beautiful and to lay with them and he did see him take the daughter of one of the principals of Cayarna and Federmann has her with him and this is public knowledge that he lays with her and he also heard that he made his men search for certain

Indian women in Paraguaná but with what intention he [the witness] did not know.

According to Jimenez (1986), the crown tried to control the activities of the Germans when it first commissioned Hernán Martínez de La Marcha to conduct a juicio de residencia against Federmann and Pedro Limpias in 1537. However, Dr. Antonio Navarro was named *juez de residencia* in 1537. Jimenez analyzed the regular correspondence between Bishop Rodrigo de Bastidas, who tried to regulate his Venezuelan diocese from his home in Santo Domingo, and the crown. The correspondence shows Bastidas's increasing worry about the depopulation of Venezuela given Federmann's and Limpias's treatment of the Indigenous populations. Navarro took *la residencia* of every major official involved in the Venezuela governance from 1529 to 1538, including the deceased governor, Ambrosius Alfinger, who was accused of grave offenses against the Indigenous peoples on his expeditions. For example, in the town of Tamara he corraled two hundred Pacabuyes and refused to give them food or water until family members brought him gold (Morón 1977, 232). There was a charge of torture of a cacique from the town of Yjara who had been imprisoned for six months because he had nothing left to trade (232). In addition, there was a charge of taking Indians in chains and cutting off the heads of the sick and tired so as to not detain the expeditions (232). The "surprising" final sentence, despite the serious charges, was that the Welsers pay the royal fifth of the 222 Indian slaves who were taken from friendly nations.

Navarro began his juicio de residencia against Federmann on actions conducted in the expedition to Maracaibo between 1529 and 1530, detailed in the *Indianische Historia*, and the expedition to Cabo de la Vela as Spira's (Georg Hohermuth von Speyer's) lieutenant. Many witnesses in the proceedings accused Federmann of kidnapping and abusing Indigenous women.[20] The documentation also states that Federmann was charged with massacring the men and kidnapping the women of Guayarna/Coyarna. Jimenez writes:

There's an emphasis in [the testimonies from 17 witnesses] that in his first expedition he took more than 200 Caquetíos chained and that in his expedition towards Cabo de la Vela he imprisoned more than

500, leaving the towns of Cumarebo, Huerbacoa, Tamodare, Caya-
gua, Todare, Maragina, Miraca, and Coyarna depopulated. From those
towns he took caciques and most pronouncedly their daughters and
wives. Upon his return from Cabo del la Vela he ordered Pedro Limpias
to go to Paraguaná to ask the caciques that they send him women from
each village, and preventing any resistance, he made them threaten that
if they did not comply they would take [the caciques'] wives and daughters. (1986, 235)

Once the women were gathered with those residing in Coro, they were
forced to accompany Federmann and his men on another expedition. The
crown had abandoned its policy prohibiting the enslavement of women and
children in the province in 1534, though it still maintained the provision
that they should not be taken outside of Venezuela (Jimenez 1986, 225).[21]
Furthermore, in the AGI there is a Real Cédula created in Valladolid directed to the officials at the Casa de la Contratación dated 5 June 1545 concerning the "Liberty of a Certain Indian Girl" (Libertad de Cierta India) as
Federmann had brought a young Indian girl ("yndia muchacha de poca
edad libre") and an administrator and moneychanger ("corredor de cambios"), Juan de Arbadán, intended to make her his slave over the objections
of Prince Philip II, who demanded she be freed immediately.[22]

As discussed earlier, Welser governors were involved in the Indigenous
slave trade and as with the Guaycarie and other indigenous women, Federmann participated in the sexual trafficking of native women and subjected
enslaved women to forced labor and sexual violence. Nonetheless, Federmann left most of those details out of the *Indianische Historia* for his European readers. He may not have wanted to publicize his involvement with
this kidnapping and rape and tarnish his reputation as an effective but "just"
commander. Events such as this show that the hegemonic patriarchal colonial system oppressed Indigenous women and children in large numbers and
in particular ways; the conquistador took advantage of Indigenous women
and disposed of them without remorse. For all his crimes, Federmann was
sentenced to pay 500 pesos of "good gold."

As Jimenez contends, the Welser's desire for gold outweighed any other
goal of colonization. To take on their gold-finding expeditions they needed
to exploit Indigenous labor as porters, guides, interpreters, and soldiers.

To achieve this the Germans constantly attacked and set fire to indigenous settlements, they would resort to kidnapping and abuse, and they
kept them in chains to avoid their escape, of course not paying attention to any of the regulations that were openly promulgated [against
this abuse]. (Jimenez 1986, 232)

The *Indianische Historia* reveals the accuracy of Jimenez's comments: Federmann acts as a ruthless conqueror who completed his expedition by violent means. It exhibits the many tactics of conquest that Welser governors
employed. His expedition depended on Indigenous peoples' very lives to
meet their end goal of finding gold.

While Federmann's troubles with the Welsers as well as the Spanish
crown would damage his reputation, his wanderlust, as revealed in his narrative, portrays a man equally at home in the Spanish administrative system
and the German mercantile milieu. That said, South America bears the
legacy of Federmann's name. In Bogotá, a city that he helped found on his
second expedition, there is a neighborhood called Barrio Nicolás de Federmán; in Riohacha Colombia, another city he founded, there is a Plaza Federmán. In Venezuela, the memory of Federmann is less prominent, though
the residents of Cuara claim him as a direct ancestor and therefore named
their local football team and their local pharmacy "Los Welser" (Rupprecht
2011). In short, the problematic self-portrait of Federmann drawn in the
Indianische Historia, as well as the picture that emerges of him in colonial
chronicles, sixteenth-century court records, and later Spanish as well as
Venezuelan and Colombian historiography and cultural memory offer very
different accounts of a man charged with the conquest of Tierra Firme. As
a Welser agent aiming to colonize the territory under racialized merchant
capitalism, Federmann took his main responsibilities to be the search for
gold and the south sea in costly and arduous expeditions that enslaved many
native Indians. And his writing of a *German* Indian history reveals the uneasy relationship between Germans and Spaniards in conquering and pacifying the land that had recently been claimed by Spain.

Finally, as Mauss suggests, a gift is never really free since the giver expects a reciprocal gesture. Federmann's gift exchanges resemble those of
Columbus. He depicts complicated instances of gift-giving practices he enacted and the Indian nations he encountered in South America. Federmann
and the Guaycaries, Caquetíos, and Ayamanes seek to form or reject al-

liances through gift-giving. A gift must always be repaid in time. I have focused on Federmann's conquest tactics as he narrates them; by unveiling Federmann's narrative strategies, we read through the conquistador-narrator's swagger on the page to critically decipher faulty exchanges that lead to violent subjugation. Federmann, a violent trickster and a language manipulator, takes broken oaths and turns them into opportunities to publicly shame two Indigenous leaders. He depicts these leaders as devils because they refuse the bargain he would impose on them. In other words, his conquest tactics reveal the strategy of exploitation of natural and human resources over the long-term colonization employed in Welser Venezuela. While this may not have been Bartholomäus Welser's plan in Augsburg it was certainly the strategy enacted by his agents, including Federmann and his equally infamous predecessor, Ambrosius Alfinger.

PUBLICATION HISTORY OF THE *INDIANISCHE HISTORIA*

The publication history of the *Indianische Historia* further complicates Federmann's (self-)portrait presented in the narrative. According to Hans Kiffhaber's prologue (3–4) and to María Arias López (1969, 606), the *Indianische Historia* was in reality a German embellishment of the routine expedition report that a Spanish notary in Federmann's crew wrote for the emperor. The original document has never been found in the archives, and the text was forgotten until the nineteenth century. Gauti Kristmannson (2019, 366) writes that in Germanic Europe, "the development of the vernacular through translation shows perhaps best that the Renaissance(s) were, essentially, about translations." However, also in the German lands, the advent of the printing press combined with the Reformation and its focus on biblical translation for the masses served to solidify the readership of German vernaculars (Kristmannson 2019, 368). While Kiffhaber promoted the *Indianische Historia* as a gift to a public eager to read about the exotic Americas, its publication by Sigmund Bund suggests that even in Protestant cities there was a market for such narratives of travel and conquest. Federmann astutely prepared the manuscript for this readership by translating it into German. However, Kiffhaber and Bund may have promoted the text as a Protestant production.

The work appeared in 1557, the same year as Hans Staden's best-selling narrative of captivity in Brazil, fifteen years after Federmann's death. It never had the same success as Staden's narrative, which became part of the wildly popular *Grands Voyage* travel series edited by the great Flemish-German editor Theodor de Bry or the lesser-known editor and translator of travel accounts, Levinus Hulsius. But it gained attention after the French Latin Americanist and bibliophile Henri Ternaux-Compans translated it into French in 1837 and published it in his America travel series. It subsequently reappeared in German in 1859, as part of *N. Federmanns und H. Stadens Reisen in Südamerica* (N. Federmann's and H. Staden's Voyages in South America), together with Hans Staden's canonical captivity narrative of his time as a prisoner of the Tupinambá in Brazil. The publisher, Karl Klüpfel, may have thought that bundling them together would give Federmann's narrative more status despite the fact that the printing costs incurred may have been higher. If so, it worked; the *Indianische Historia* became popular again. Arias López (1969, 610) writes that the public ignored this "very rare work until Ternaux lists it for the very first time in [nineteenth-century] France."[23] To this day, the work is not held in the collections of Haguenau or Strasbourg. In the preface to his French edition published in 1837, Ternaux-Compans also calls the the *Indianische Historia* "very rare" and states that no German bibliography has included it (Federmann 1837, 10).[24] As Arias López (1969, 606) states, "The Germans could not ignore such a novelty and twenty-two years later they published the work in a collection that appeared in Stuttgart."[25] The *Indianische Historia* would remain in the German public consciousness through the Nationalist Socialist era, when authors such as Erich Reimers would revisit the "lost colony" of Venezuela and laud Federmann and other Welser conquerors as German heroes.

The text became popular in Latin America in the twentieth century. Two Spanish translations from Ternaux-Compans's French version appeared (Pedro Manuel Arcaya, 1916; Nélida Orfila, 1945), and the anthropologist and historian Juan Friede (1901–90) translated the text in 1961 directly from the German, further popularizing the narrative in Colombia and Venezuela. Today, outside of Colombia, Venezuela, and Germany, Federmann's text remains obscure.

Given the Habsburgs' penchant for collecting exotica, the *Indianische Historia* was marketed as a travelogue, though it failed to have commercial success. Like Hernán Cortés's accounts of his conquest of Mexico—though

Federmann's narrative details the military tactics of warfare and conquest more than the marvels of the New World—the book was originally marketed as travel literature. The prologue, written by Federmann's brother-in-law, Kiffhaber, posits this audience. Kiffhaber also refers to the goodness of a gracious God who allowed the discovery of gold and spices and other fine commodities in the New World.

> Nach dem ich in erfarung kommen bin, das E. V.[26] ein sonder liebhaber und erforscher der Antiquiteten, deßgleichen auch deren dinger, so sich bei unsern zeitten durch mörschiffung, mit erfindung der newen Inseln, welchs man die New welt nennet, auß Gottes des allmächtigen schickung wunderbarlich herfür gethon, und noch für und für, mit mancherlai gaben, von Goldt, Edel gestein, und köstlichem holtz, gewürtz und anderm herfür thun, unnd eröffnet werden, darauß dann die miltigkhait, gütte und liebe Gottes gegen dem menschlichen geschlecht, ymmer dester mehr erkhant und mit lob und dancksagung billich zu hertzen sol genommen werden. (Federmann 1557, 1)[27]

> After I came to the knowledge that E.V. [Thou Almighty] is a lover and researcher of Antiquities as well as those things miraculously known in our times because of almighty God's will through sea travel and discovery of the new islands, those that are called the New World, and which continue to unfold, with manifold gifts, Gold, precious stones, fine wood, spices, and other things, so that God's charity, grace, and love for humankind will be known more and more and taken to heart with praise and thanks as it should be.

Kiffhaber frames Federmann's history as a gift to an audience hungry for tales of the discovery and conquest of the New World. By invoking God's will in supporting Federmann's conquest, he seeks to elide the destruction emphasized in Federmann's narrative and seeks to entice Johann Wilhelm von Laubenberg zu Wagegg, collector of curiosities and exotica (to whom the prologue is dedicated), to display the work along with Laubenberg's curiosities.

Strasbourg was the most prominent center of Protestant printing, and Haguenau was known more for producing Protestant pamphlets and religious emblem books than travel narratives. For example, Arias López (1969,

605) notes that Haguenau was a center of humanist and religious works.[28] However, Haguenau was the second most important town for printing in Alsace, and there was rivalry between Haguenau and Strasbourg printers (Ritter 1955, 466). Bund had been a publisher in Strasbourg between 1539 and 1545, when he abandoned the trade, but returned to it in Haguenau around 1550 (Ritter 1955, 408). According to Arias López (1969, 605), he was "second-class,"[29] and Ritter (1955, 466) describes him as being of "minor importance."[30] But he published the works of Caspar Schwenckfeld, a Protestant from Silesia who Martin Luther considered radical.

In 1553 Bund solicited a license from the council as detailed in the *Ratsprotokoll* (council minutes) to publish works of a literary rather than religious nature, which he received with the help of Jean Schwintzer, a former printer and a scribe. Arias López suspects that he did this to divert the suspicions of the Senate, which regarded Bund's friendship with the Anabaptists with mistrust. However, the welcoming attitude toward religious refugees in Alsace changed between the 1520s and the 1550s when other Protestants such as Calvinists and Anabaptists were no longer tolerated. That is perhaps why Bund, who had published Schwenckfeld's works, later tried to publish only works of literature.[31] Before the *Indianische Historia*, he published two sermons from Jean Wernher (Ritter 1955, 410).[32] According to Arias López (1969, 610), scholars had thought that most of Haguenau's printing business had declined by 1543, but the *Indianische Historia* belied that assertion.

While it is difficult to establish how Federmann's narrative fits in the context of the Reformation in sixteenth-century German lands, the Protestant publisher Bund encountered fewer hindrances in publishing Federmann's travel narrative than in continuing to publish Protestant reformation pamphlets. According to Ritter, the market forces required most printers to publish religious materials. Once they had fulfilled this duty to the clergy and educated readers, they might print instructional works and then, finally, works whose purpose was to entertain (Ritter 1955, 467).[33] In Strasbourg, for example, all printers except Jean Grüniger were Protestants, and the printing trade spread the new faith quickly throughout the city (Ritter 1955, 466).

Sandra Pott's article on the Protestant cartography of Sebastian Münster suggests that a Protestant framework involves personal interpretation and critique (2005, 12). If Federmann's text can be read as a sixteenth-century Protestant narrative—one that incorporates and encourages a subjective interpretation and critique—then we also need to consider its post-humous publication. Alfinger and Federmann were from Ulm, the center of Reformation activities in the southern Swabian region of the German lands. The city was the center of the Schmalkaldic League of Protestant princes, of which Augsburg was also a member, which rebelled against the pope and the Holy Roman Empire.[34] While the Federmann and Alfinger families supported the Reformation movement to an extent, many Spanish *cronistas* (chroniclers) such as Las Casas often portrayed the men themselves as heretics (Friede 1960, 23).[35] The Spanish characterization is predictably more extreme. Although the context of the work's publication fifteen years after Federmann's death raises important questions about the intention of both Federmann's Protestant brother-in-law (Kiffhaber) and the semiretired publisher (Bund), there is nothing in the text itself that points to Federmann as a specifically Protestant writer.[36]

A Protestant view of the New World emerged in Dutch, German, and French cartography, prints, and best-selling travel literature published in the sixteenth-century; in Hans Staden's narrative, a Protestant God delivers him, his faithful servant, from the captivity of his naked and cannibal Tupinambá oppressors in the Brazilian jungle. His work, which uses both narrative and ethnography, was very popular in Protestant Europe; it was meant to reaffirm his and his readers' Protestant faith. In addition, the Calvinist Jean de Léry's narrative includes passages where he likens cannibalism to the schism between Protestants and Catholics over transubstantiation. Moreover, Pott (2005, 12) characterizes Sebastian Münster as a Protestant cartographer, much as scholars such as Grégory Wallerick (2010) have suggested that Theodor de Bry's engravings display a Protestant view of the New World.

In Federmann's case, the intentions of the publishers warrant some consideration, but Federmann himself would seem to be primarily interested in the practicalities of conquest. Exactly what a publisher of primarily Protestant works (Sigmund Bund) and a supporter of the Anabaptists in Ulm (Federmann's brother-in-law) wanted to prove with the publication of Federmann's narrative remains a mystery. Perhaps they sought to portray the discovery of America as not only a Catholic-Spanish Habsburg enterprise but also a specifically Protestant discovery of the American lands. While I could not find any correspondence between Bund and Kiffhaber, Bund might have been eager to print *Volksbücher*, a genre that was supposed to entertain the masses, rather than religious works that might have been censored and caused the annulment of his publication permits. Bund was familiar with the successful publication of Americana and marvel literature in Strasbourg, and he may have been ready to try his hand at finding the commercial success that others had found through works relating to the New World. The following excerpt from Kiffhaber's prologue attempts to clarify the origins of Federmann's *Indianische Historia* and how he and Bund tried to market it as part of a body of adventurous travel literature that detailed the "discovery" and conquest of the New World.

> Dieweil dann etliche, so gemelte New wellt, mit vil geferlicheit, schweren raisen und uncosten erfaren, auch grosse bücher darvon haben geschriben, und solch ding ahngezaigt, deren sich wohl zuwerwundern, So hat sich unther anderm, mein Schwager Niclaus Federmann von Ulm selig, verschiner zeit, in namen und anschickung etlicher herren auch defs wöllen erkundigen, und so er zwai mal in Indien uber Mör geraiset, hat er die erste raiß und was ihm und andern mitgeferten drunder begegnet, was er auch gesehen und erfaren, von eynem tag zum andern, wie es erstlich auß befehl der Kay. Maiestaten durch ainen Notarien so mit geraiset Hispanisch in ain büchlin verzaichnet, ins Teütsch transferiert unnd nachgeschriben, welchs ganz lustig unnd kurtzweilig ist zu lesen. (Federmann 1557, 3–4)

> ―――――――

> Just as quite a few then, with many dangers, hard voyages, and many expenses experienced the mentioned New World, wrote many thick books about the subject, and [in them] mentioned such things that astound, so my now deceased brother-in-law Niclaus Federmann from Ulm also set out to explore this in different times, in the name of and engaged by several gentlemen [to complete a contract]. He traveled twice over the Ocean in India, and from the first trip he wrote about what he and his companions experienced and saw, from day to day, at first in a book in Spanish at the request of His Majesty through a notary, and then it was transferred and written into German. This is very amusing to read.

Kiffhaber places Federmann in the grace of Emperor Charles V, yet Federmann had been dead for close to fifteen years. Perhaps Kiffhaber was well aware of the Welsers' accusations against Federmann of embezzlement and was attempting to rescue his brother-in-law's reputation. Kiffhaber paints a portrait of Federmann as an adventurous man from Ulm who, with the help of a Spanish notary, described every day of their travels, collected these texts for the emperor, and, finally, translated them for a German audience. If the text functioned as a Protestant production, it is because Kiffhaber and Bund published it as such. Yet the importance of God's deliverance cannot be ignored by readers. Moreover, Federmann's "translation" of the book into German transforms the text in several ways. While the addressee of the original (lost) report was Charles V, the addressee of this second version is the German reading public.

As Arias López has written, the linguistic aspect of the *Indianische Historia* stands out because Federmann needed to explain the details of the American land so that it would be comprehensible to a German audience.

> In effect, Federmann's work was composed in Spanish by a *notario escribano público*. The author translated it into German himself and added many clarifications. As he tells us in the text, and we think he was thinking of his superiors, the Welsers of Augsburg, to whom he needed to communicate the results of his first American expedition in the province of the Terra Firme—he needed to give clarifications.[37]

Federmann then needed to explain the subtleties of the American context to a German readership if his narrative was to find success. The narrative's play on codes and manipulations demonstrates that Federmann bends the Spanish and German languages to suit the needs of his readership, but Federmann of course features as a character in his own travel narrative.

It is clear, however, that despite the lost original, Federmann inserts himself into the narrative as a first-person narrator but also as the narrative's main hero. While the time that elapsed between the text's production and publication raises questions, Bund and Kiffhaber perhaps sought to rescue the text by casting it as a validation of Federmann's experience in the New World as a citizen of Ulm, an employee of the Welser firm, and a paid agent recognized by the Habsburg Empire and the Spanish crown. Moreover, language in the book's title, such as "kurtzweilig" (entertaining), suggests that Bund and Kiffhaber promoted Federmann's narrative as a true adventure story.

I have argued that gift-giving and forced friendships show Federmann as a conquistador who conquers with words as efficiently as he kills with the sword. The conquistador makes and breaks oaths, encourages (and discourages) communication through the use of interpreters, and rewards friends but destroys his enemies. In light of postcolonial studies that often focus on the physical violence of conquest (and as I have described, the violence is real), I argue also for its social and psychological nature. Much like Michel de Certeau has argued in *The Writing of History* (1988), the Europeans' use of the written word against the Indians' orality privileges the former and essentially applauds the circulation of problematic narratives of conquest. Finally, just as faulty narrators give away counterfeit coins, Federmann presents us with his *Indianische Historia* or his faulty *Gift*. Yet, just as Federmann relies on translation and gift-giving to carry out the Welsers' project of conquest and racialized merchant capitalism, Indigenous interpreters use the same tools of "mistranslation" to fight back against Federmann's poisonous gifts. As readers of the conquest narrative, it is up for us to decide how much of the author's poison we want to drink.

Finally, the *Indianische Historia*'s publication and reception history reveals that the narrative was marketed as a travelogue, especially given its dedication to a known collector of exotica. Unfortunately, the text disappeared as quickly as it was published. During the next three hundred years, there was no mention of it in bibliographies, and hardly anything is known regarding its immediate reception. By 1895, however, the German editor, Viktor Hantzsch, provided excerpts only, noting in his introduction that while it had "interesting content," "it is written in long and tedious sentences and in a barbaric German" (Hantzsch 1895, 28). The next chapter presents how the Welsers viewed their Venezuela colony in maps, with nostalgia as a way to remember their mastery over colonized soil and racialized others.

CHAPTER 4

Blood and Soil

Welser Venezuela between Cartography and Genealogy

> Wohl dem, der seiner Väter gern gedenkt
> der froh von ihren Taten, ihrer Größe
> den Hörer unterhält und still sich freuend
> ans Ende dieser schönen Reihe sich geschlossen sieht.
>
> —Johann Wolfgang von Goethe,
> *Iphigenia in Tauris*

Sixteenth- and seventeenth-century Spanish, Venetian, and German maps continued to depict the Welsers' Venezuela colony in parts of present-day Venezuela and Colombia even after the Welsers had been forced out by the Spanish and Welser governors and agents such as Nikolaus Federmann, Philipp von Hutten, and Bartholomäus Welser VI had died or been executed. While Venetian maps made by Giacomo Gastaldi (1500–1566) and Battista Agnese (1500–1564) simply reflect the Welser possession, the Seville-based Portuguese cartographer Diogo Ribeiro (d. 1533) and the Augsburg resident Emmanuel Stenglin (1606–1676) incorporated in their maps powerful narratives about the Welser family's and company's ties to the Venezuela colony. In this chapter, I analyze how these cartographic depictions, some of which the Welsers owned or commissioned (after losing the colony in 1556), functioned as nostalgic mementos of the family's vanished prestige. As such, the cartographic commemoration of the Welser Venezuela colony is an early example of the cultural memory of German colonization. These maps and genealogical materials are meant to show hopes rather than reality as they envisage an imaginary connection between the Welsers' blood and the lost Venezuela soil.

The Welsers's nostalgic cartographic commemoration of their Venezuela colony as well as their map collection practices provide clues about the social status the Welsers held and sought. As I mentioned in the introduction, sixteenth-century Augsburg was a free imperial city led by the powerful elite, the minority patricianate class to which the Welsers belonged, which opened itself up to new members of the wealthy merchant class, such as the very wealthy Fuggers, in 1538.

Leading patrician families in southern Germany who were anxious about their elite status created genealogical illustrated manuscripts and prints that sometimes depicted the family's territorial possessions. They also collected books and maps that contributed to the family's erudite legacy. The Welsers and the Fuggers were also map viewers and collectors with ties to diplomatic and trade networks between Seville, Augsburg, and Venice that included sharing of cartographic information on the New World colonies. Ultimately, family networks, political influence under Charles V and the larger Habsburg realm, and access to credit and capital influenced how elite families in Nuremberg and Augsburg collected maps, as well as how they historicized their own participation in New World colonization. These cartographic and genealogical materials exemplify the aspirational nature of Welser self-fashioning.

WELSER VENEZUELA IN MAPS: THE *WELSERKARTE* AND DIOGO RIBEIRO'S *PADRÓN GENERAL*

It is difficult to pinpoint exactly how many maps of the New World the Welsers had access to as most of the Welser company's records were lost after the bankruptcy of the firm in 1614. Considered worthless except as extra paper, company records were split, recycled, and bound within other books. Archivists and preservationists have restored and edited these fragments, published under the title *Rechnungsfragmente der Augsberger Welser-Gesellschaft* (2014), edited by Peter Geffcken and Mark Häberlein. In the 1960s a preservationist found the manuscript map now known as the *Welserkarte* among the company's account fragments in the rival Fuggers' Dillingen an der Donau library. Diogo Ribeiro (also known as Diego Ribeiro), the official cartographer for the Spanish monarchy under Charles V, had authored the map in 1530; it may have served the Welsers in their plans to navigate and administer their Venezuela colony. The *Welserkarte* was certainly one of the maps of the Americas the Welsers owned that depicted their possession of Venezuela.

Ribeiro's map promoted Spain's imperial vision as an optimistic projection and the Welsers relied on this vision to produce their own imaginary visualization of colonial possession. Ribeiro was a Portuguese-born mapmaker who worked at the legendary Casa de Contratación in Seville and guarded Spain's cartographic secrets. He became one of the most important cartographers there, working alongside both Ferdinand Columbus and Sebastian Cabot, both of whom had held the post of pilot major for the Spanish crown.[1] Ribeiro was the sole cartographer for the Spanish monarchy in the early 1500s and was trusted to make notes of all the discoveries made on Spanish voyages of exploration. These notes were incorporated into the secret *Padrón General* (General Map), which was the official map expected to be used by all official navigators who had the authorization to do so. The history of the Casa de Contratación and the *Padrón General* are intertwined: King Ferdinand ordered Pilot Major Amerigo Vespucci to make the *Padrón General*, which in 1508 would be called the *Padrón Real* (Cuesta Domingo 2010, 27). There was a master copy at the Casa de Contratación in Seville, and copies were made for pilot navigators. The Casa had been established by order of Queen Isabel I in 1503, and it would grow to have power over the training of pilots, the licensing of emigrants (permitting them to leave Spain for the Indies), the collections of taxes and customs, and the maintenance of secret maritime and political knowledge. Navigators and captains were expected to report any new discoveries as well as location information to the Casa under oath. The Casa employed cosmographers, cartographers, and instrument makers who responded to the empire's expansionist desire (Sánchez Martínez 2013, 123–25). It was also one of the first scientific centers in Spain, with a major role in analyzing and manipulating information that came from the colonies to serve the monarchy's imperial purposes (Sánchez Martínez 2013, 127).[2] While no copy of the complete *Padrón General* has been located, copies that Ribeiro authorized still exist. All pilots had to purchase these copies and take them on their voyages or risk a fine. The *Padrón* was revised in 1518, 1527, and in 1535 in an ongoing effort to clarify the Tordesillas line, which had been drawn in 1494 to divide newly discovered possessions between the Portuguese Empire (east) and Spain (west) (Sánchez Martínez 2013, 115). The Welsers gained access to Spain's secret geographic information via Ribeiro's copy of the *Padrón General*. That copy, the 1530 *Welserkarte*, is one of a few Ribeiro copies of the *Padrón General*.

In the following paragraphs I present a chronology of copies of the Ribeiro map made between 1527 and 1530. These maps depict South America and the area labeled "Castilla del Oro," which included the province of Venezuela, which the Welsers would colonize beginning in 1528. The change between Ribeiro's 1527 to 1529 copies confirms what Antonio Sánchez Martínez (2013, 92, 103) has claimed: in this time period there was a shift from maps as astronomical and navigational tools to political instruments that showed the governance information for each territory, and the Welser inscription on Venezuela exemplifies this. The first, Ribeiro's world map of 1527, a copy of the 1527 *Padrón*, does not have any of the political governance information included in later map copies of the *Padrón* (figs. 4.1, 4.2). The 1527 copy of the map, located in Weimar, authored *before* the granting of colonization rights in Venezuela to the Welsers, looks and reads more like a portolan chart.[3] Drawn around the continent are ships, wind roses, and uncolored crests. For such an early date, the map shows a surprisingly accurate depiction of the Moluccas in Southeast Asia and the eastern coast of the American continent.[4] South America has only textual inscriptions that refer to the territory's perceived natural resources: "Castilla del Oro" (with gold paint around it), "Brasil" (in larger font), and "Mar del Sur" designating the Pacific Ocean. Hence the 1527 map highlights gold, brazilwood, and maritime passage to Asia.

A 1529 map signed by Ribeiro called the *Propaganda* or the *Second Borgian Map* has scant geographic or political textual descriptions for Castilla del Oro, the name Spanish settlers usually used for territories in northern South America, from the Gulf of Urabá (near the Colombian-Panamanian border) to the Belén River. Now in the Vatican Library after years at the Museo Borgia of the Propaganda Fide, the *Propaganda* also exists in a copy by W. Griggs, made in 1887, held at the US Library of Congress (fig. 4.3). The map resembles similar maps of the New World from the period that filled in the area of South America with mythical fauna and flora. In the area of South America, labeled "Mundus Novus," there are toponyms such as "Castilla del Oro," "Peru," "Tera Brasilis," "Tiera de Solis," and "Tiera de Patagones." While Ribeiro depicts Indigenous people cutting down brazil-wood trees in "Tera Brasilis," in "Castilla del Oro" Ribeiro drew mythical American fauna, including a winged dragon, and a South American ostrich or rhea. Other than the "Mar del Sur" marker for the Pacific Ocean, the focus is on the mythical natural resources to be found in the New World, a golden "Castilla," rather than political organization.

The first map to show Castilla del Oro as a Welser possession, one surrounded by warlike Indians, is a second 1529 map copy, *Carta Vniversal*, signed by Ribeiro. It is currently in the Herzogin Amalia Library in Weimar (fig. 4.4). Compared to the earlier maps, it contains less flora and fauna and more text concerning each territory along with its natural resources and its political governance. The map's inscription for Castilla del Oro reads (fig. 4.5):

> It is so called because much gold is found there. The Indians are more warlike than those of Santo Domingo and other parts, because they used poisoned arrows. Here there is a locality called Sta. Martha where large quantities of gold are found in the soil. Within it, *the Germans have their territory*, from Cabo de la Vela to Cumana, from 140 to 150 leagues. (My emphasis.)[5]

This 1529 map specifically delineated the eastern and western limits of the Welsers' colony, warns pilots about the rebellious Indians there, and invites its viewers to exploit the gold to be found in areas of present-day Colombia and Venezuela. The map refers to the Germans' Venezuela possession without highlighting the Welsers' prestigious commercial company and the nobility of their name, as highlighted in a subsequent *Welserkarte* that Ribeiro probably created a year later.

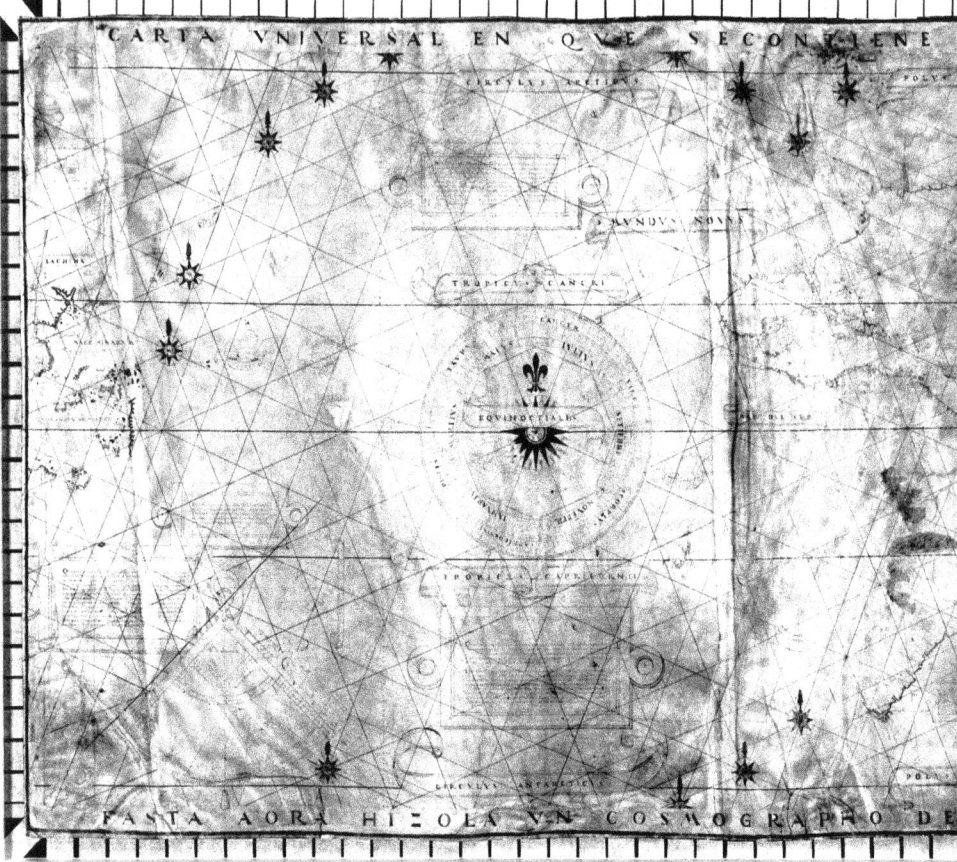

CARTA VNIVERSAL EN QVE SE CONTIENE

CIRCVLVS ARTICVS

MVNDVS NOVVS

TROPICVS CANCRI

EQVINOCTIALIS

TROPICVS CAPRICORNI

CIRCVLVS ANTARCTICVS

FASTA AORA HI ZOLA VN COSMOGRAPHO DE

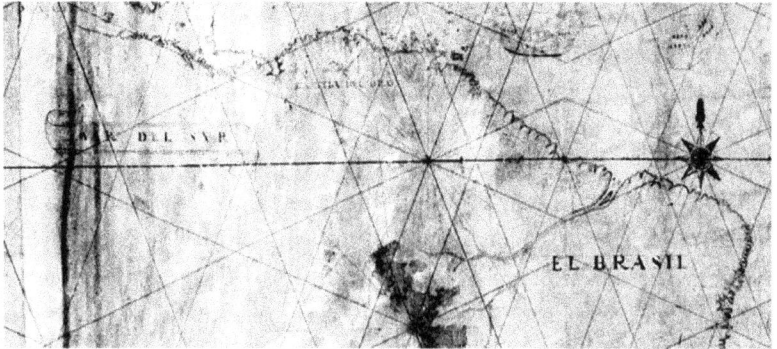

MAR DEL SVR

EL BRASIL

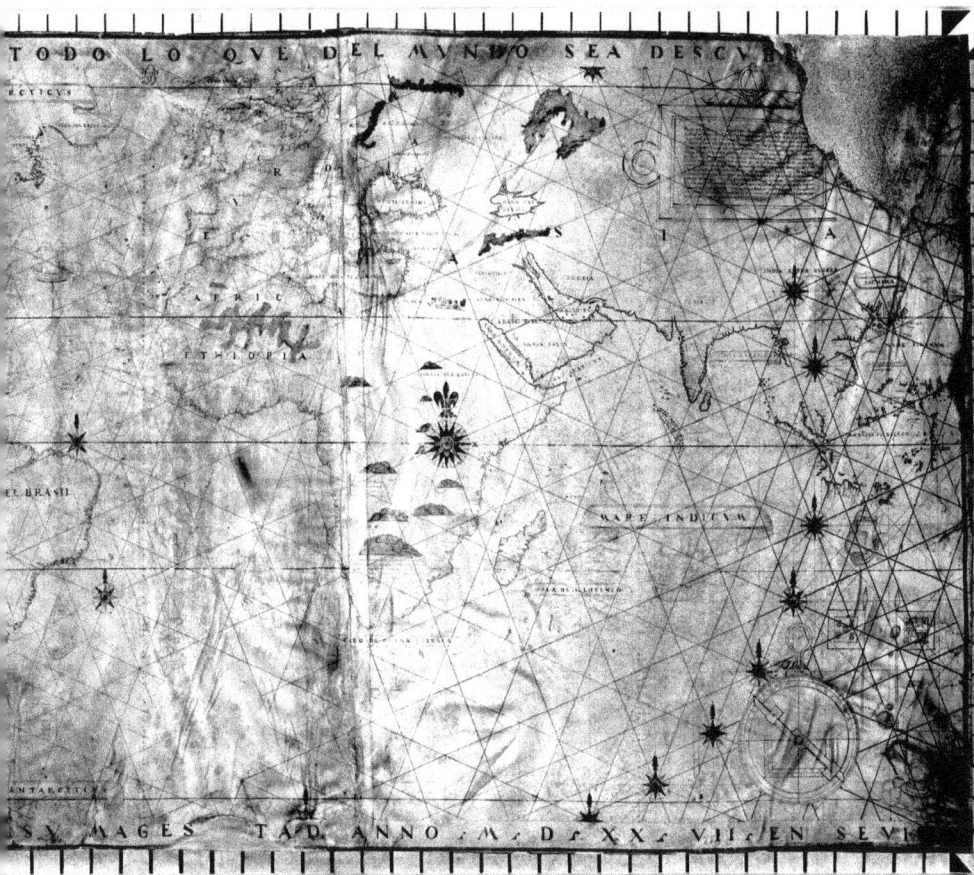

FIGURES 4.1 and 4.2 (detail). Diego Ribeiro, *Carta Vniversal En Qve Se Contiene Todo Lo Qve Del Mvndo Se A Descubi[erto] Fasta Aora Hizola Vn Cosmographo De Sv Magestad Anno M.D.XX.VII.* (1527). Herzogin Anna Amalia Bibliothek. Source: Klassik Stiftung Weimar. http://haab-digital.klassik-stiftung.de/viewer/epnresolver?id=1664127518.

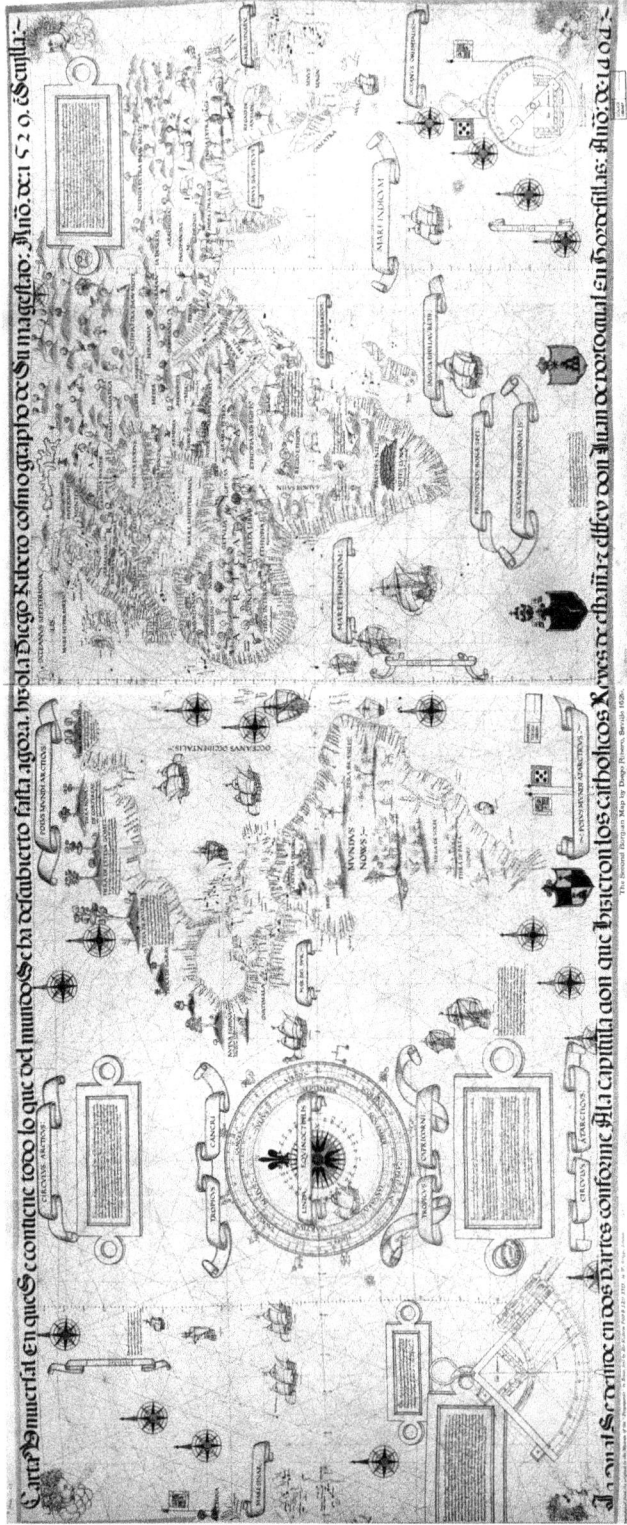

FIGURE 4.3. Diogo Ribeiro, *Carta universal en que se contiene todo lo que del mundo se ha descubierto fasta agora* (1529). Copied by W. Griggs in 1887; Library of Congress. http://hdl.loc.gov/loc.gmd/g3200.ct002450.

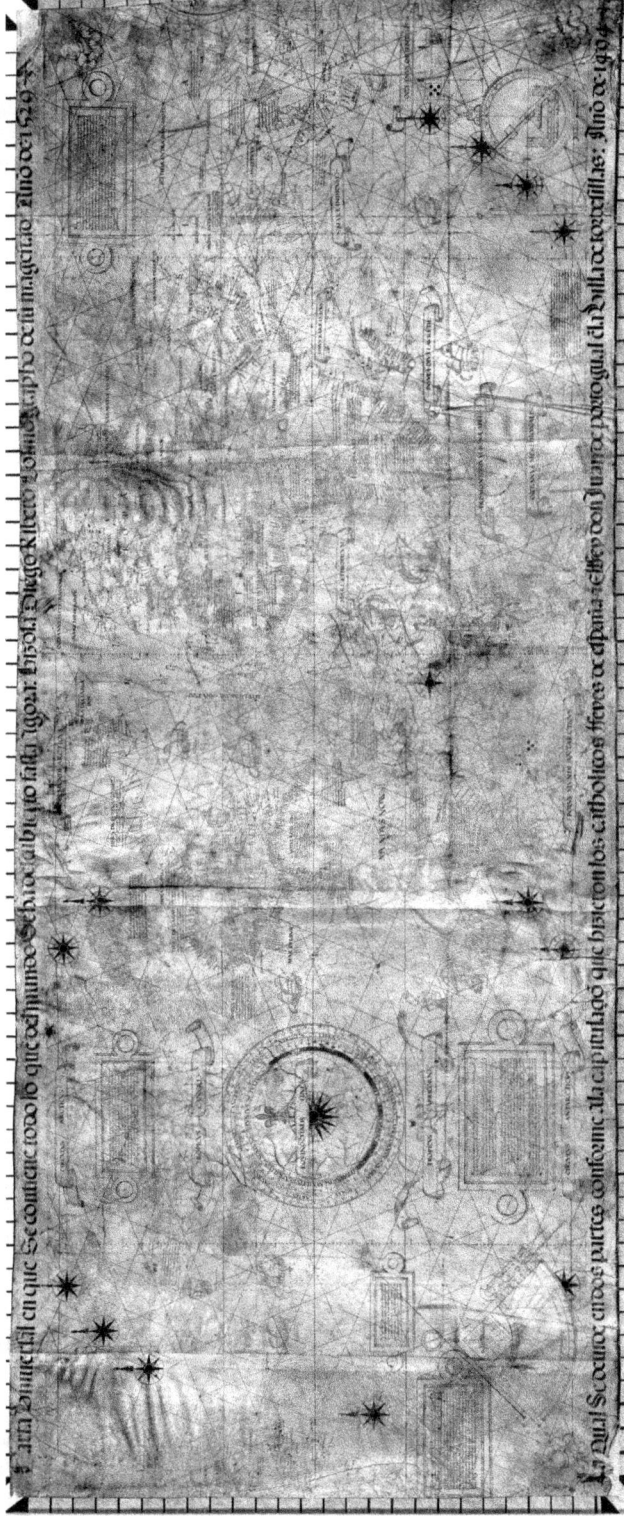

FIGURE 4.4. Diogo Ribeiro, *Carta Universal en que se contiene todo lo que del mundo se ha descubierto fasta agora: Hizola Diego Ribero Cosmographo de su Magestad An[n]o de 1529: La qual se deuide en dos partes conforme a la capitulaçio[n] que hizieron los catholicos reyes de españa y el Rey don Juan de portugual e[n] la Villa de tordesillas: An[n]o de 1494* (1529). Colored manuscript map, 88 x 212 cm. Herzogin Anna Amalia Bibliothek. Source Klassik Stiftung Weimar. Shelfmark: Kt 020 - 58 S. http://haab-digital.klassik-stiftung.de/viewer/epnresolver?id=1664181814.

FIGURE 4.5. Detail, *Carta Universal* (1529). Herzogin Anna Amalia Bibliothek. Source Klassik Stiftung Weimar. Shelfmark: Kt 020 - 58 S.

The 1530 *Welserkarte* confirms the cartographic portrayal of the Welsers' status claim over the colony; it is meant to show company affiliates, family members, and possible competitors that the Welsers' lineage would be forever associated with the colony of Venezuela (figs. 4.6, 4.7). The *Welserkarte* is probably a fragment of a *Padrón Real* copy made by Ribeiro,[6] and the 1530 date makes it likely that the Welsers actually used this map when they governed the province from 1528 to 1556. According to Wolfgang Wüst (2011) the attribution came mainly from toponyms within the map. Moreover, the area of Venezuela was represented simply as Castilla del Oro, a golden El Dorado under Spanish rule that affected the early capitalist vision of navigators and merchants of the New World.[7] On the map, the inscription below "Castilla de Oro" states: "This is the governance of the great and noble Welser company up to the strait of Magallanes" (fig. 4.8).[8] The fragment, an early cartographic example that describes the Venezuelan territory in South America as a possession of the Welser Company, documents the Welsers' political activities in South America at the time of the map's production. The richly illustrated America fragment contains American flora and fauna, including ducks, birds, pumas, lions, a variety of trees, and, on the southern margin of South America, an ovine-looking llama (figs. 4.8–4.10). It is part of a larger world map that includes Africa and India (now in fragments) decorated with flora and fauna such as a number of elephants, monkeys, and birds. However, many questions remain, such as whether the Welsers themselves or Charles commissioned Ribeiro to make the map. Given that Ribeiro was the Spanish king's official cartographer, the latter seems more likely. Surekha Davies (2003, 109) suggests that Charles presented important state dignitaries with the planispheres, which implies that the maps were used for important diplomatic purposes. If this was the case, the presence of the Welsers on the map would have shown European sovereigns how the family and company that had helped finance the conquest and colonization of Venezuela were rewarded, thus securing the family's status as "noble" conquerors on par with Europe's leading monarchs.

That an *official* Spanish map from the Casa made by Spain's official cartographer, Ribeiro, was in the Welser Company's possession suggests that as the de facto governors of the province, the Welsers had gained access to Spain's guarded cartographic information and were agents in creating their geographic expansion in South America. Ribeiro's text on the map demonstrates that Venezuela's status as a "governacion" legitimates the Welsers'

SCYTHIA EXTRA IMAVM MONT

INDIA EXTRA GANGEM

SINVS GANGETICVS

GEDROSIA

INDIA INTRA GANGEM

ARACOSIA

CARMANIA DESERTA

PERSIA

SCYTHIA INTRA IMAVM MONTEM

SARMATIA AS

MESOPO

BABIL

ARABIA DESERTA

ARABIA DE SIRA

ARABIA FELIX

PROVINCIA

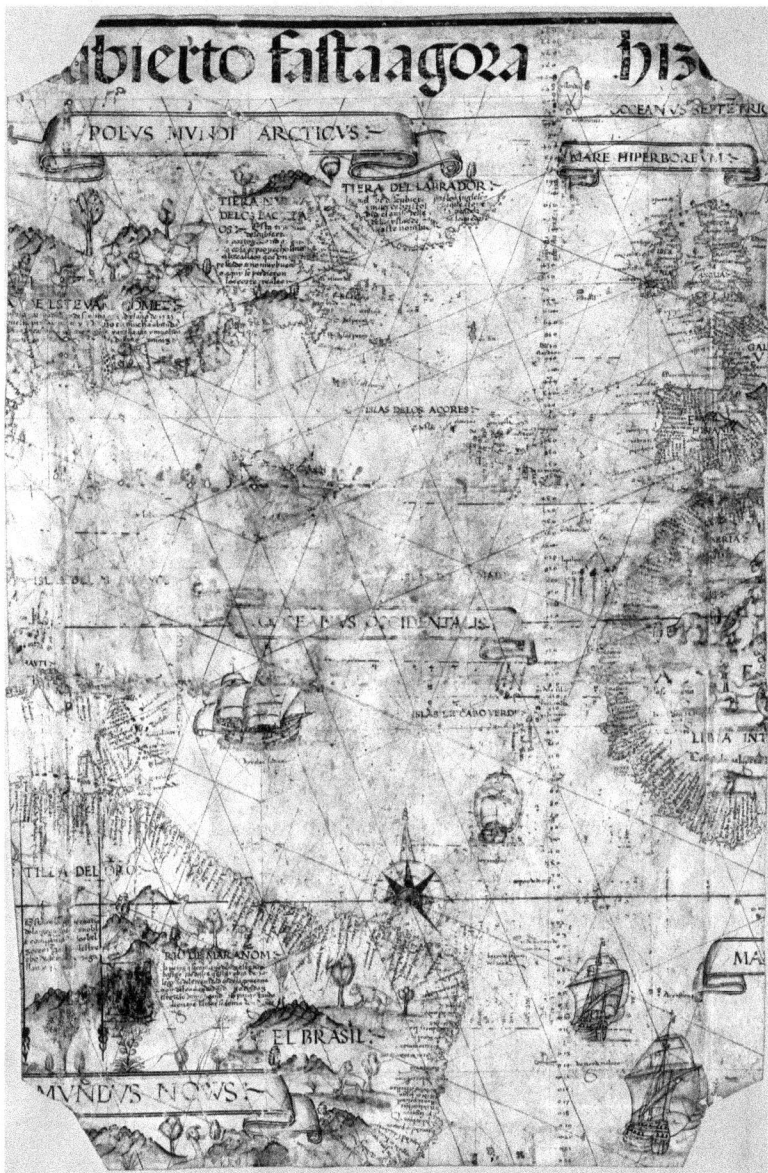

FIGURES 4.6 and 4.7. Diogo Ribeiro, *Welserkarte*, Seville, 1530. Two fragments of manuscript map on parchment, 37 x 54 cm and 60 x 41 cm. Dillingen, Studienbibliothek, Mapp. 1. SDL-Hss Mapp 1. urn:nbn:de:bvb:12-bsb00105879-5. Creative Commons. The first image shows Africa, Europe, and Asia, and the second image, on this page, depicts the Mundus Novus, or New World.

FIGURE 4.8. Detail from Ribeiro's *Welserkarte*. The text reads, "This is the governance of the great and noble Welser company until the strait of Magallanes" (Esta es la governació[n] de la gran casa & noble compañía de los Bezares hasta el estrecho de Magallanes). Creative Commons.

FIGURE 4.9. Detail of Ribeiro's *Welserkarte* of South America showing a llama.

FIGURE 4.10. Detail of Ribeiro's *Welserkarte* showing New World fauna.

sovereignty over the possession. It also recognizes both the dynastic and economic importance of the Welser family and company, calling them "the great house & noble company" (*La gran casa & noble compañia*) (fig. 4.8). Most daringly, the map lacks a southern limit for the Welsers, showing that their contract encouraged them to take over the South American continent southward "until the strait of Magallanes." This is the only known cartographic evidence that the Spanish crown had given the Welsers the right to colonize the land that extended south from Castilla del Oro. That the map was probably made by Spain's official cartographer suggests that Spain officially recognized the Welser governance and its claim to southern expansion a mere two years after the Welsers arrived in Venezuela in 1528.

The header "Discovered Until Now" (*[des]cubierto fasta agora*) at the top of the *Welserkarte* highlights the discoveries of the New World, as well as new political realities attached to those discoveries. The titles of Ribeiro's other five planispheres suggest the full title would have been Universal Map Which Contains All That Has Been Discovered Until Now" (*Carta Universal en que se contiene todo lo que del mundo se ha descubierto fasta agora*). The planisphere labels areas in North America "Tierra Nueva de los Bacalaos" (New Land of Cod [Newfoundland]), "Tierra del Labrador" (Labrador),[9] and "[Tierra] de Estevan Gómez" (America's northeastern region; Gómez [1483–1538] was a Portuguese explorer). In South America, in addition to the aforementioned Welser inscription below "Castilla de Oro," there is one below "Brazil" called "Rio de Maranom" (Amazon River) (see fig. 4.8). The various toponyms suggest either descriptive names linked to the resources rumored to be found there or to the explorers or governors of the area.

The 1532 copy attributed to Ribeiro held in the the Herzog August Bibliothek in Wolfenbüttel resembles the *Welserkarte* copy in its political depiction (figs. 4.11, 4.12). It has a similar inscription under "Castilla del Oro"; it is labeled "esta es la gobernation de la gran casa compania de los Belzares" (this is the governance of the great Welser company). From 1527 to 1532 Diego Ribeiro's official maps, made for the Casa de Contratación, and the copies of the maps, which were sold to all departing ships' pilots, held increasingly more information about the Welsers' political authority in Venezuela and its eastern, western, and southern limits. In his official capacity as cartographer for Charles, Ribeiro put the Welser colony on the map; in tune with the political and mercantile realities of his day, the maps show the reputation of the Welsers as an important force to be reckoned with, either in the

FIGURES 4.11 (full map) and 4.12 (detail of northern South America). *Zwei zu einander gehörige Karten von der neuen Welt und dem grossen Ocean, westlich bis zu den hinterindischen Inseln reichend.* Ca. 1525. Manuscript map on parchment, 85 x 65 cm. Herzog August Bibliothek, Wolfenbüttel, Cod. Guelf. 104a Aug. 2°.

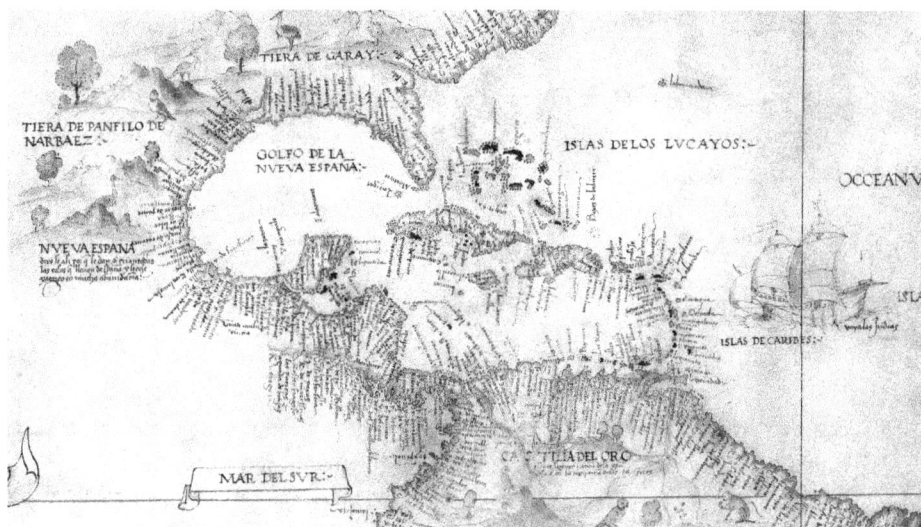

ports of Seville or as political leaders in charge of ruling a *Spanish* territory. The map serves as prescriptive in that its author intended that those monarchs who viewed the map should recognize the Welsers' possession, but it also had a proscriptive function in that those interested in exploring the area or conducting trade were forbidden to do so unless they had the authority of the Welsers.

VENETIAN MAPMAKERS' INCLUSION OF
THE WELSER GOVERNANCE

Maps with information originating in the *Casa* ended up in Italian and German collections, reflecting German, Venetian, and Florentine interest in the exploration of the New World.[10] Two Venetian mapmakers in the sixteenth century who included the Welser Venezuela polity in the *mappamondi* and maps of the New World were Giacomo Gastaldi (1500–1566) and Battista Agnese (1500–1564). Both cartographers produced maps that included Tierra Firme and depicted the Venezuela territory as governed by the "Compagnia de los Belzares" (Welser Company), which meant they were aware of the commercial and geopolitical realities at the time.[11] Geographic information from Spain and Portugal made its way to Venice and Florence very quickly during the era of European exploration of the Americas. If Ribeiro's imperial cartography contributed to an early modern geopolitical imaginary that suggested openness to colonization and trade (Padrón 2020, 68), Venetian and German merchants were invested in taking advantage of the bounty represented in those maps.

Venice's close mercantile connection to Augsburg was also likely responsible: Augsburg-based merchants had been active since Johannes Apothecarius in the fourteenth century in the Fondaco dei Tedeschi, the headquarters and mandatory residence of German merchants conducting business in Venice.[12] The Welsers and the Fuggers were among the Augsburg German merchants involved in northern Italian business, especially in Venice. The structure of the Fondaco dei Tedeschi gave the Augsburg-based German merchants a place to conduct trade but of course under the direct control of the Venetians (Kellenbenz 1984, 270). German families there included the Gossembrots, Herwarts, Paumgartners, Welsers, Hoechstetters, and Rehlingers. For example, Jakob Rehlinger from Augsburg became involved in a Venetian enterprise to Constantinople. The brothers Ulrich, Georg, and Jakob Fugger traded in spices and other goods from the South (*Südwaren*) and in fine textiles. They found a good market for their Tirolean copper and silver in Venice, as well as the opportunity to collect manuscripts and texts for the *Stadtbibliothek* (City Library) founded in Augsburg in 1537 (Kellenbenz 1984, 270).

German merchants' representatives also bought maps, including manuscript atlases made by the Venetian mapmaker Battista Agnese. Henry R. Wagner (1862–1957), a collector and bibliographer who wrote *The Atlases of Battista Agnese* in 1931, remarked on how little was known about Agnese, except for what was demonstrated in his atlases and maps; he calls Agnese, active between 1536 and 1564, "one of the most prolific map-makers of the sixteenth century" (Wagner 1931, 2). About eighty manuscript atlases with about ten maps per atlas were either made by Agnese or attributed to him (Wolff 1992b, 139). Wagner estimates that Agnese must have produced at least one hundred during his lifetime. Agnese marketed his manuscript atlases to wealthy collectors. He used a portolan style with colorful details such as wind roses that make them beautiful pieces. Because his buyers included wealthy collectors such as dukes, barons, and those who may have had business interests in the larger New World, it was important for Agnese to show the political denominations of territories in his manuscript atlases. Augustus the Younger, Duke of Brunswick-Lüneburg, paid the handsome sum of 200 ducats for a copy for his library, now the Herzog August Bibliothek (Haase and Jantz 1976, 51). The Augsburg merchant Johann Jacob Fugger had an atlas cover made for him in red morocco with gilded edges by a "Venetian Fugger Master" around 1550 that is very similar to the Bavarian State Library exemplar (Wolff 1992b, 139).

Agnese's portolan-style atlases usually have a wind rose, a diagram showing the relative frequency of wind directions at a place, yet the parchment on which they are made makes it clear they would have never been intended for navigational purposes. This differentiates them from Ribeiro's map copies of the *Padrón General*, even though they include much of the same geographic information. Agnese's maps were meant to be admired and collected as beautiful objects. Indeed, his artistry in depicting landmasses, wind roses, and unusual details is remarkable. His portolan-style maps in the atlases usually use a thick blue line for depicting the coastlines, and the uncolored continental masses are not filled in, except for a topographic feature, such as mountains drawn with gold paint to represent the gold found in the Andes of Peru (fig. 4.13).[13] In other maps, Agnese fills in the continental landmasses with green and uses red dots for cities. Topographic features are kept to a minimum, except for mountains (in gray and gold) and rivers (in blue). Wagner (1931, 8) has suggested that Ribeiro's planisphere of 1529 (the copy of the Propaganda Fide, Rome) or one like it may have been the source for Agnese's maps as they include numerous "discoveries" of explorers such Lucas Vázquez de Ayllon, Esteban Gomez, Hernán Cortés, and Francisco Pizarro. And while Wagner remarks on the shared features of Agnese's and Ribeiro's maps, including their endpoints at the same places east and west, many copies of maps made in Seville, themselves copied from Ribeiro's *Padrón General*, had similar features.

While Agnese made a series of atlases in which most maps appear in the same order, an incomplete atlas includes a map of South America that is distinct. It has the text "Gober de la nobile compagnia de los Belzeres" close to northern South America and depicts the area of Peru as belonging to "Gober' de Diebo [*sic*] de Almagro" (Newberry Ayer Ms 12) (figs. 4.13, 4.14).[14] Like his emphasis on the holdings of Pizarro, Cortés, Almagro, and the Welser Company, this signifies the greater importance of political information over

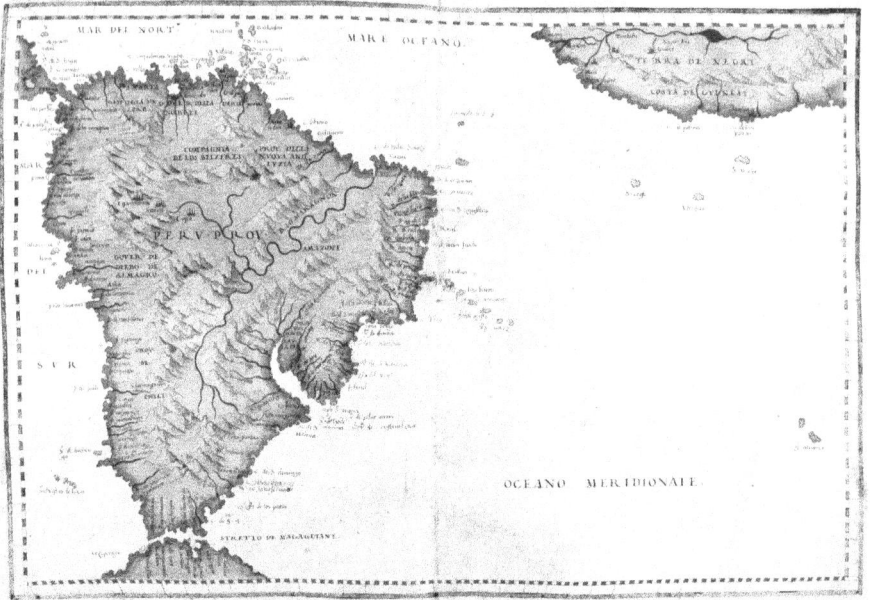

FIGURE 4.13. Battista Agnese, Manuscript portolan atlas of the world (1550). Manuscript on parchment, 28 cm. Newberry Library, Ayer, MS map 12, p. 4.

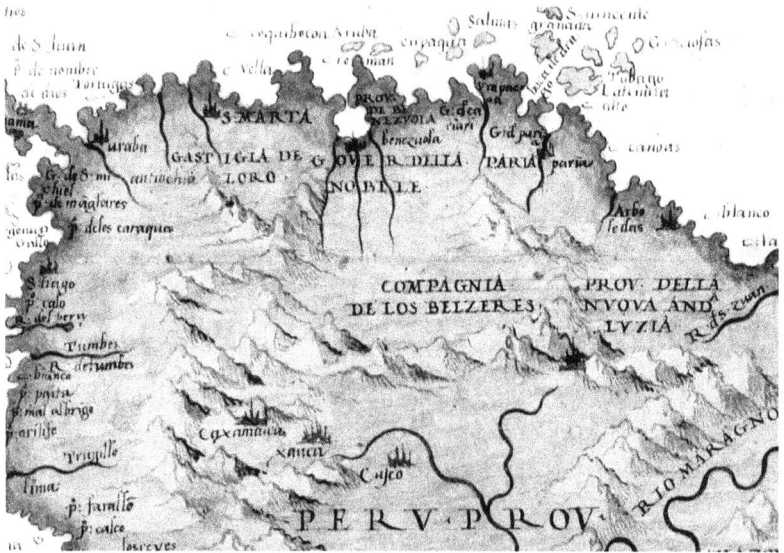

FIGURE 4.14. Battista Agnese, Manuscript portolan atlas of the world (1550). Manuscript on parchment, 28 cm, Newberry Library, Ayer, MS map 12, p. 6.

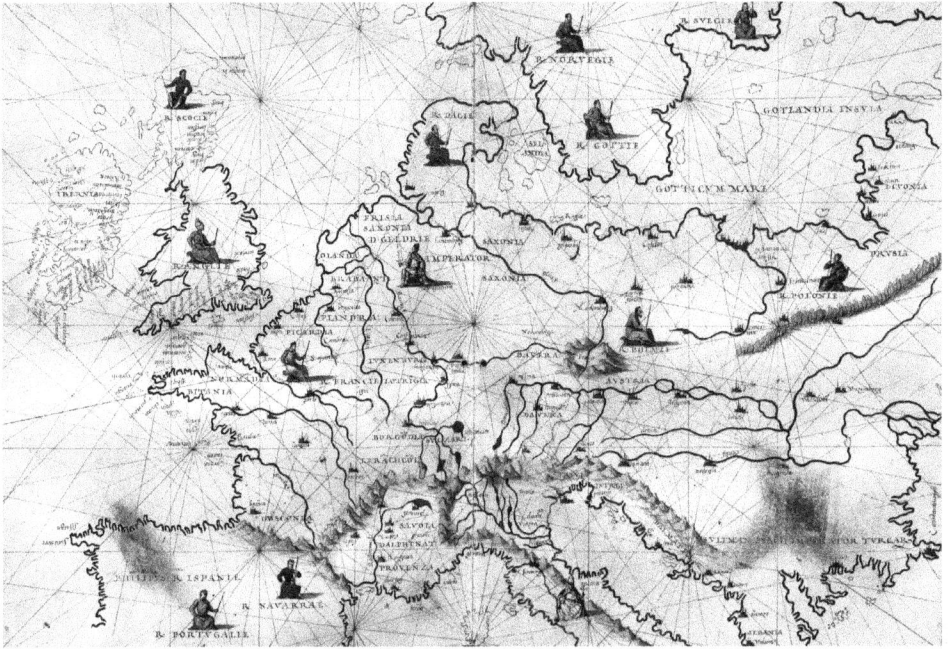

FIGURE 4.15. Battista Agnese, Manuscript portolan atlas of the world (1550). Chart of Europe and the British Isles, with miniature portraits of European rulers. Manuscript on parchment, 28 cm. Newberry Library, Ayer, MS 13, p. 10.

environmental and topographic data. The Welsers' Venezuela territory was a unique and important merchant polity. One of the most impressive details about Agnese's atlases is how the physical and political landscapes come together. In the map of Europe, Agnese goes one step further. Instead of only representing who is in power over what territory in map legends, he includes miniature figures such as Queen Elizabeth I of England. By doing so, he was following the portolan chart tradition, which often included beautiful decorative flags and sometimes figures of rulers meant to mark territorial possession (Wolff 1992a, 130). In one version (fig. 4.15), Philip II of Spain and Suleiman of the Ottomans, who looks toward the European rulers in most of the versions, have been erased from the political landscape. The line drawings are still present below the smudges representing Philip and Suleiman.

Venice had become a center for the map, manuscript, and book trade of New World media in the sixteenth century. Collectors such as the Augsburg Fuggers collected items that were both produced and traded in Venice,

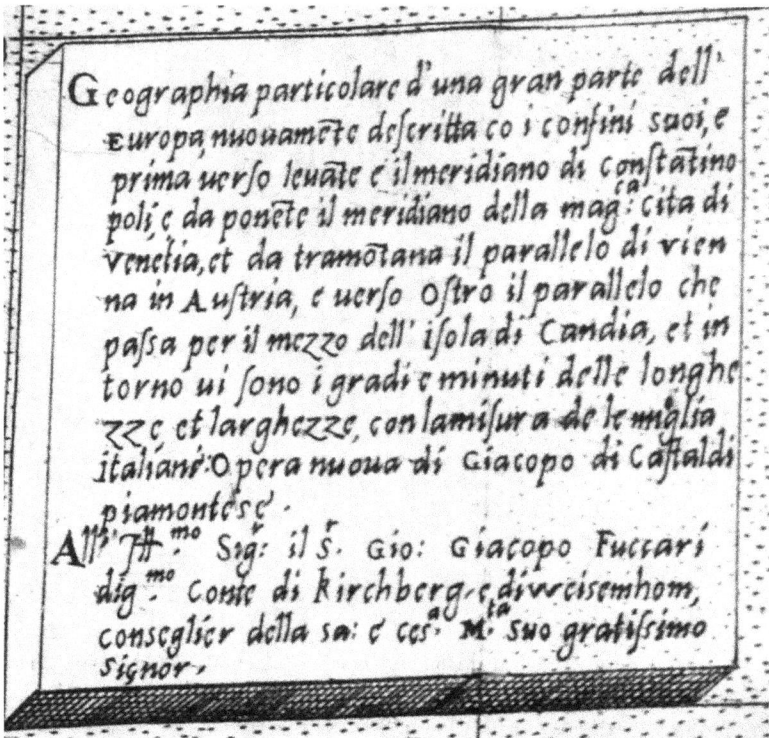

FIGURE 4.16. Giacomo Gastaldi, *Geographia particolare d'una gran parte dell'Europa* (Rome: Anton. Lafrerj, 1560). Map, 837 x 1,063 mm. Newberry Library, Novacco 6F35. The cartouche shows a dedication to Giovanni Giacomo Fuccari digmo. Conte di Kirchberg et di Weissenhorn, conseglier della sa. cesa. mta. suo gratissimo Signor.

to the point that they appear on cartographic commissions. Venetian cartographers such as Giacomo Gastaldi also included patronage and political information on their maps. Giacomo Gastaldi's *Geographic particolare d'una gran parte dell'Europa* has a dedication in the lower left cartouche to "Gio. Giacopo Fuccari digmo. Conte di Kirchberg" (Dignified Count of Kirchberg Johann Jacob Fugger) (fig. 4.16).[15] This would be the aforementioned Jakob Fugger, book collector, whose library would be sold when the Fuggers went bankrupt some years later. These map inscriptions and dedications to the Fuggers and the Welsers disappear in 1565; the *Vniversale descrittione di tvtta la terra conoscivta fin qvi* has no such designation.[16]

Giacomo Gastaldi (or Gastaldo, Castaldi, Castaldo) made a series of printed maps that include Tierra Firme as a Welser colony that also replicated the Spanish imperial imaginary from Ribeiro's map. Originally from Villa-franca in the Piedmont, Gastaldi signed his maps as "Piemontese," though he lived and worked in Venice from 1539 on. The first map he signed was a map of Spain, *La Spaña* (1544), and two years later, in 1546, he would complete his first world map (*Vniversale*), which includes Venezuela as a Welser territory. David Woodward (2007b, 781–82) locates similarities to Agnese's maps in Gastaldi's depiction of North America. Given that Agnese's maps resemble Ribeiro's, it is no wonder that Gastaldi's maps include information originating in Spanish cartographic sources and advertise Venezuela as a territory of the Welser Company. Just as Ribeiro's map was used to legitimate Spain's claim over the Spice Islands, so too would it be used to legitimate the Welsers' claim over Venezuela.

Gastaldi's 1546 *Vniversale* splits the territory of Tierra Firme according to the then-governors; however, it shows that in the case of Venezuela, it was the merchants who held sway, unlike other parts of South America that were governed by individual representatives of the Spanish crown (fig. 4.17). Gastaldi names part of Venezuela (south of its actual location) as "Governation de la Compagnia de los Belzares" (fig. 4.18). "Castilla de Oro" appears as the "Governation de Bastidas," after the founder of Santa Marta, Rodrigo de Bastidas (1465–1527).[17] The area of present-day Ecuador is under the "Gobernation de P. de Heredia," after the conquistador Pablo de Heredía y Fernández (1505–54). Peru appears as part of "Gov. de Francesco de Piçaro," after the famous conquistador of Peru (1471–1541). The actual territory under the governance of the "Belzares" pertains not to the part of northwestern Venezuela around the gulf of Lake Maracaibo and the city of Coro where the colony was actually located. Instead the map depicts that territory as part of Bastidas's Castilla del Oro; this may have just been a geographic imprecision by mapmakers who did not have to navigate particular political realities.

Gastaldi's later maps show the common practice of recycling old cartographic information in later reprints; despite the fact that the Welsers had ceased governing the province in the 1550s, some maps showed they still did. The *Vniversale descrittione di tvtta la terra conoscivta fin qvi* (1565) was printed almost twenty years after the original *Vniversale* and is held at the US Library of Congress (figs. 4.19, 4.20).[18] The title is almost the direct translation of Ribeiro's world map: "Universal Map Which Contains All That Has Been Discovered Until Now." The oval projection map is based on the earlier, 1546 Gastaldi *Universale* world map and omits political demarcations altogether in favor of decoration (ships, a mermaid, but also

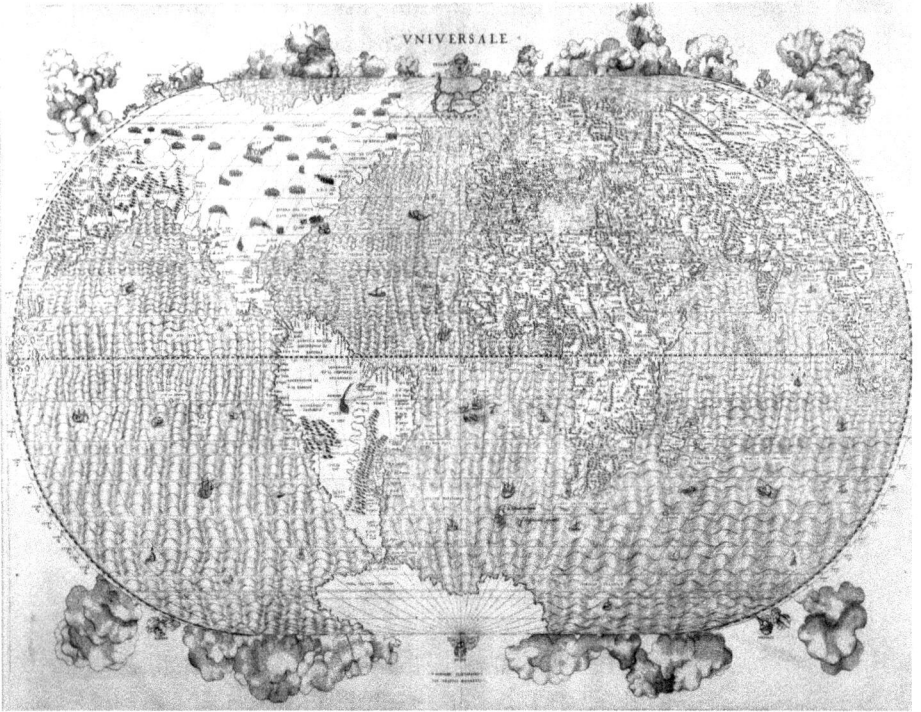

FIGURE 4.17. Giacomo Gastaldi, *Vniversale* (Venice: n.p. [1546]). Printed map (engraving), 373 x 529 mm. Newberry Library, Novacco 4f_04.

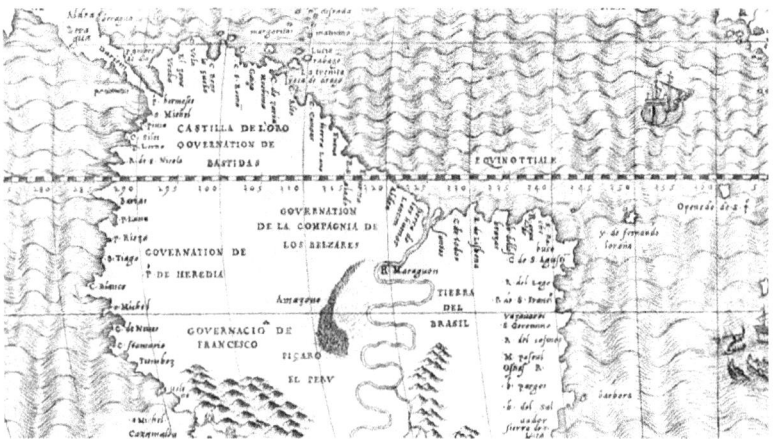

FIGURE 4.18. Detail of Gastaldi's 1546 *Vniversale*, showing Welser Venezuela as Governation de la Compagnia de los Belzares.

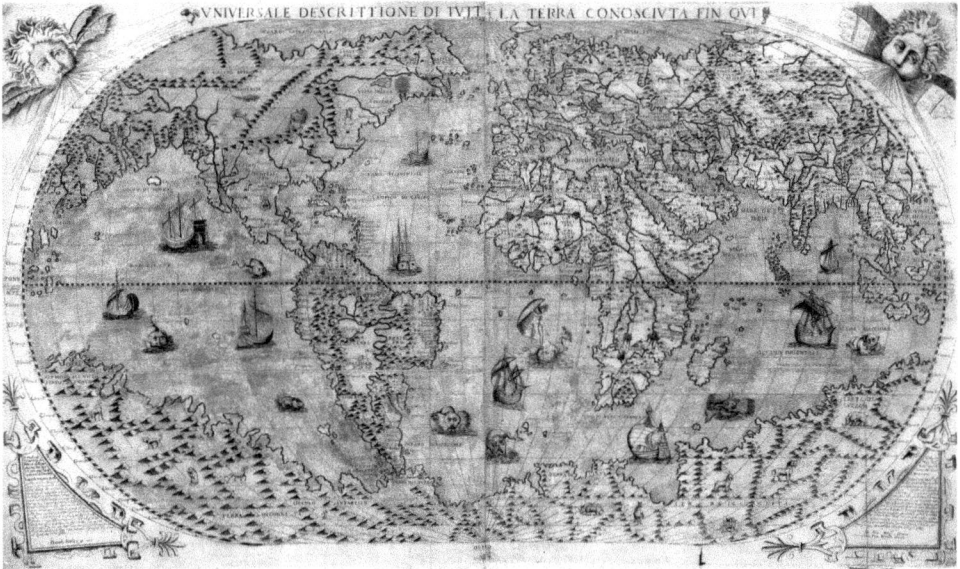

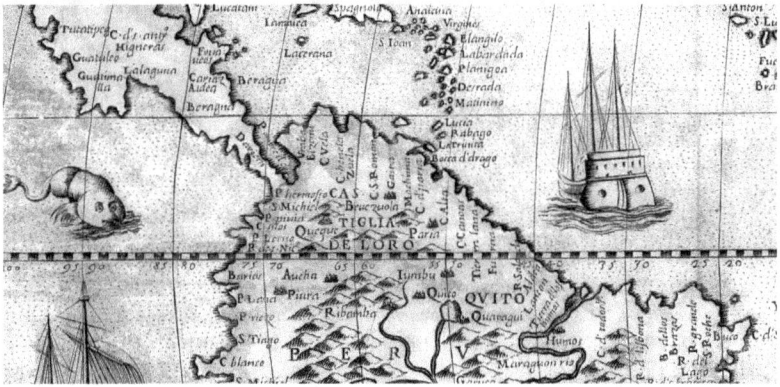

FIGURES 4.19 (full map) and 4.20 (detail showing South America). Paolo Forlani and Giacomo Gastaldi, *Vniversale descrittione di tvtta la terra conoscivta fin qvi* ([Venezia]: F. Berteli, 1565). Hand-colored engraved map, 41 x 75 cm. Library of Congress, Geography and Map Division, Washington, DC, G3200 1565.F6.

fauna such as an elephant, a leopard, and a lion) (Wolff 1992a, 79). "Castiglia de l' Oro" makes up present-day Venezuela and Colombia, and the name "Benezuola" appears twice. There is no mention of the Welser Company or any of the aforementioned governors. However, the Welsers appear in the *Geografia tavole moderne di geografia* (ca. 1565), created by Giacomo Gastaldi and Paolo Forlani for the Antoine Lafréry atlas (Rome, 1575) (figs. 4.21,

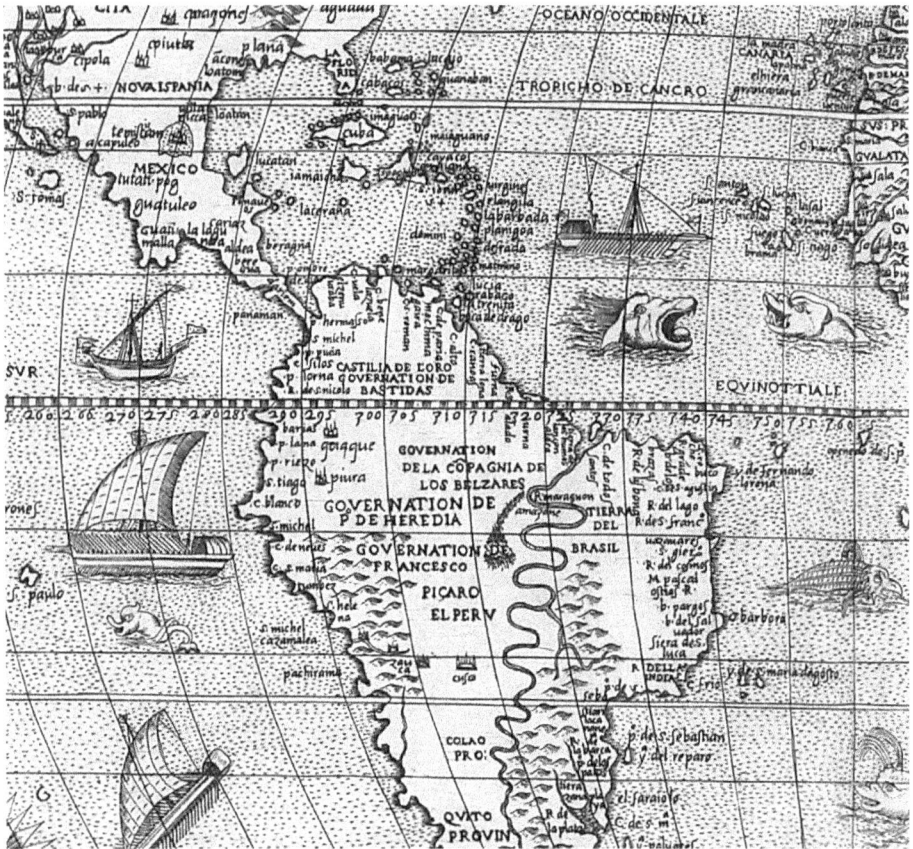

FIGURE 4.21. Paolo Forlani and Giacomo Gastaldi, [*Weltkarte*] *Paulus de furlanis Veronensis opus hoc . . . Jacobi gastaldi Pedemontani instauravit . . .* (Venetiis: Camotius, 1560). 53.1 x 29.3 cm. Herzog August Bibliothek, T 45.2° Helmst. (4). Detail showing South America.

4.22). This map also uses the 1546 *Vniversale*'s political markers such as the Governation de la Compagnia de los Belzares (depicted erroneously below the equator) and for Castilia de l'Oro the Governation de Bastidas. Gastaldi's and Forlani's practice of copying each other's maps, as well as the successful Lafréry atlas printing project in Rome (1575), suggests that Italian cartographers in Venice and Rome recycled maps of South America even after the Welser Company ceased governing Venezuela in 1556. However, the Welsers would continue to visualize their colonial speculations in genealogical and cartographic materials.

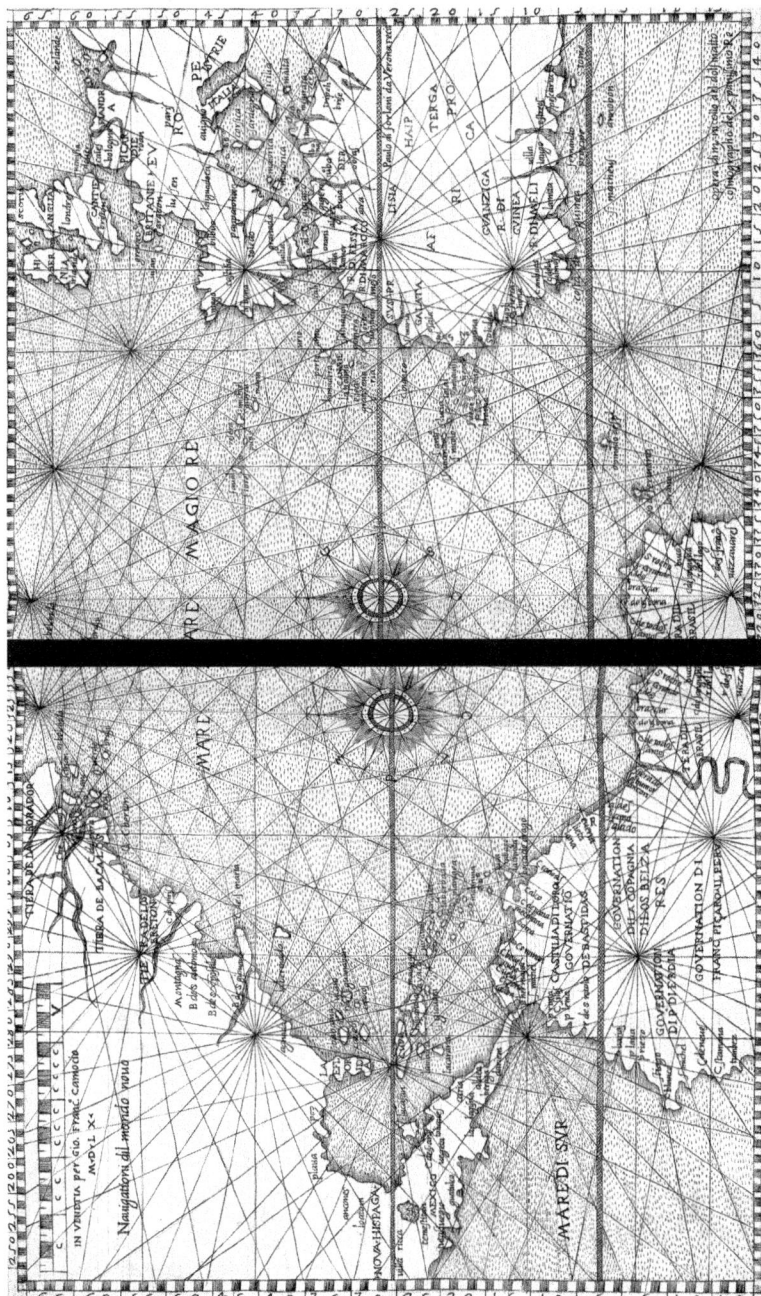

FIGURE 4.22. Nicollo M. Dolfinatto, [Atlantischer Ozean] (Mare Magiore) opera di m. nicollo del dolfnatto (Venetia: Camocio, 1560). – 34.7 x 23 cm. Also known as "Navigationi dil mondo novo" in venetia per Gio. Franco Camocio MDLX. Opera di m. Nicollo del Dolfinatto; cosmografo del Cristianissimo Re. Herzog August Bibliothek Wolfenbüttel, T 45.2° Helmst. (48).

GENEALOGY AND MAPS IN AUGSBURG
AND NUREMBERG

A map made in the 1680s in Augsburg historicizes the Welser colony. It was commissioned by the Welsers more than 120 years after they lost the colony in order to safeguard their genealogical history (see fig. I.4). This was a common practice among patrician families in the free imperial cities, copied from the Habsburg's tracing of their supposed mythical or biblical pedigree.

Genealogy, or the study of family history, was instrumental in distinguishing the Habsburgs' and later ruling patrician families' exclusive lineage from that of commoners. Through the diffusion of genealogical materials families could claim ties to biblical and mythological figures such as Adam or Noah and Aeneas of Troy, though they had to be careful in doing so. Nobles thought of ways to integrate "local" history with "biblical" or mythical time, such as in the example of a 1700 genealogical tree of the Habsburgs that stems from Rudolf I's corpse. In an inventive twist the artist has the roots of Rudolf I extending into the ground (Bauer 2013, 23) (fig. 4.23). Emperor Maximilian's own preoccupation with the direct transmission of power from Rome to the Germanophone empire through Charlemagne sparked his interest in genealogy, prefiguring Augsburg patricians' desire to distinguish their bloodlines, as demonstrated in Paul Hector Mair and Christoph Weiditz's *Bericht und Antzaigen der loblichen Statt Augspurg aller Herren Geschlecht* (Jecmen and Spira 2012, 32) (fig. 4.24). An extensive imperial genealogy was commissioned and overseen by the antiquarian, jurist, and city secretary of Augsburg, Conrad Peutinger, between 1509 and 1512. Though the genealogy was left unfinished, the printmaker Hans Burgkmair (1473–1531) completed seventy-seven of ninety-two planned woodcuts (Jecmen and Spira 2012, 32). These books of nobles also have a correlation to the chronicles published on the Habsburgs such as Jakob Mennel's *Fürstliche Chronik genant Kayser Maximilians geburt spiegel* (Mirror of Birth; 1518). Mennel's chronicle was intended to legitimate Emperor Maximilian's power. As he was no longer crowned by the pope, he had to show commoners how he, as a member of the House of Habsburg, was the "Holy" Roman Emperor. Therefore Mennel's illustrations depict members of the Habsburg clan climbing up a ladder and being blessed by the moon,

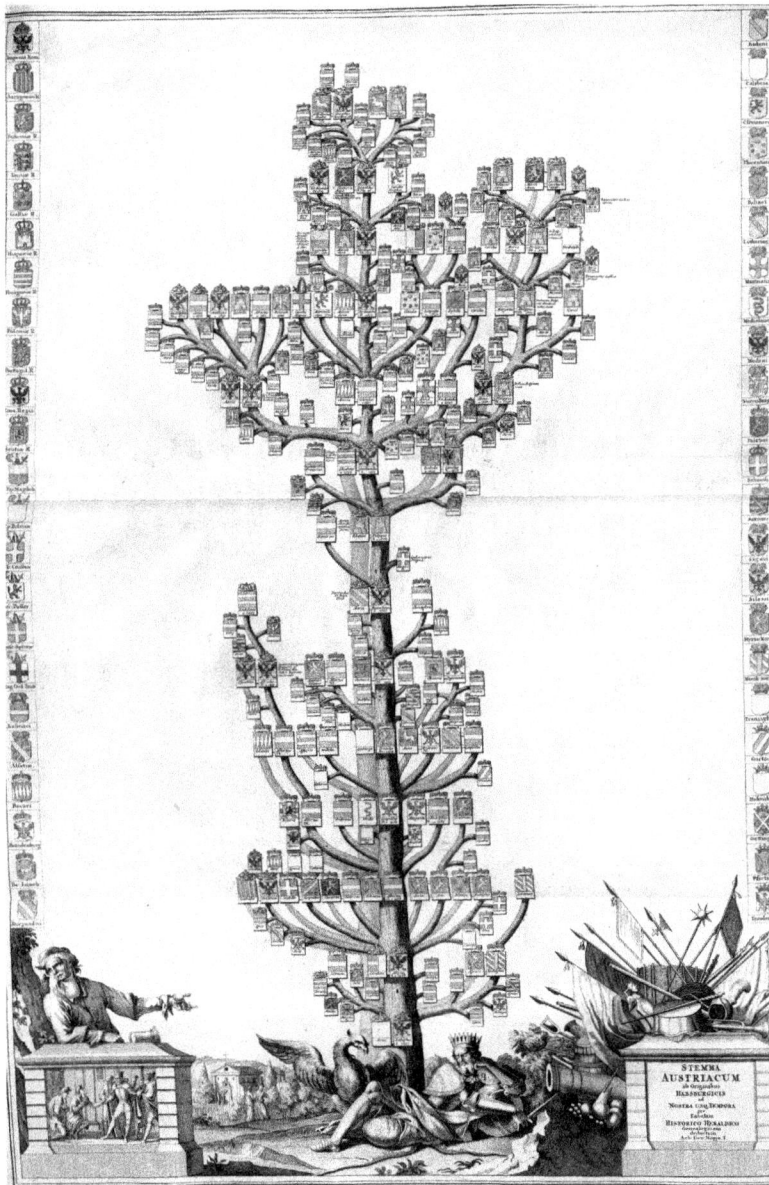

FIGURES 4.23. Johann Wilhelm Schele, "Stemma Austriacum." In *Sammelband mit 12 genealogischen Tafeln Europäischer Herrscherhäuser* (n.p.: n.p. [between 1700 and 1710]). Copper engraving. Katholische Universität Eichstätt-Ingolstadt Universitäts-bibliothek, 183/1 Rs 237, urn:nbn:de:bvb:824-dtl-0000145731. The tree starts with the roots of Albert IV, Count of Habsburg, and proceeds with Rudolf IV, Count of Habsburg and King of Germany (d. 1291).

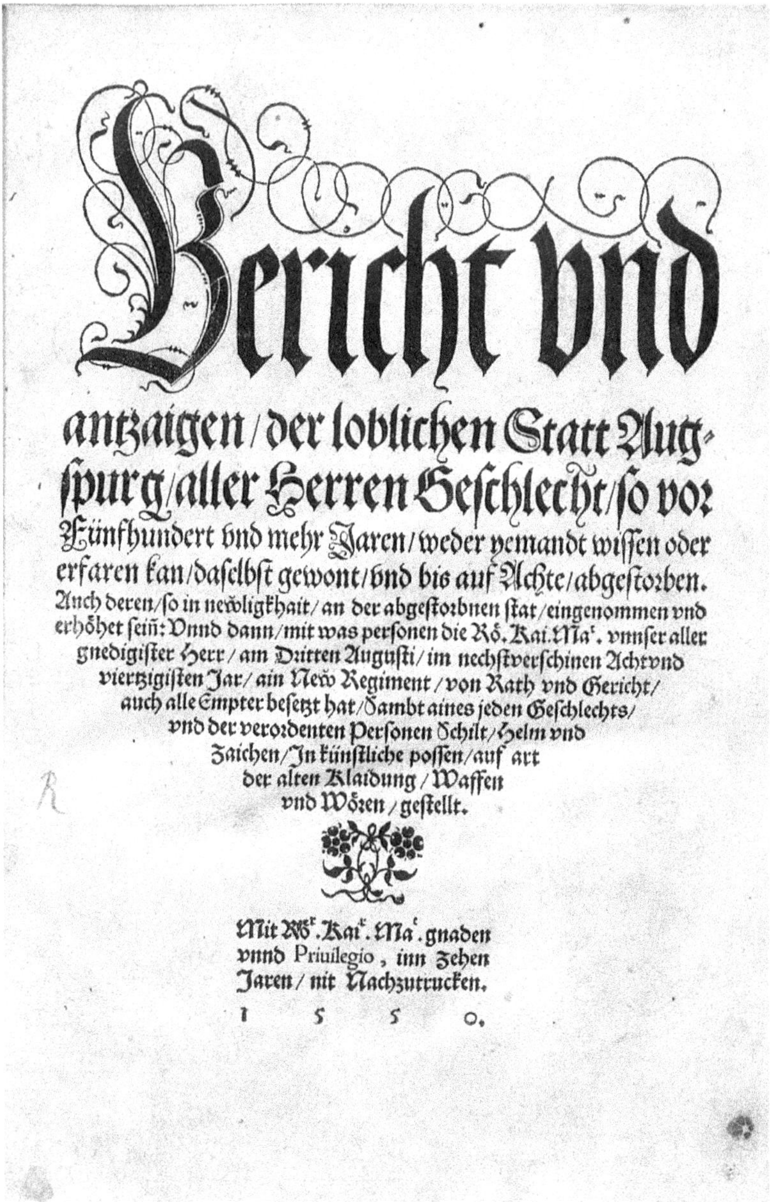
Bericht vnd
antzaigen/der loblichen Statt Aug-
spurg/aller Herren Geschlecht/so vor
Fünfhundert vnd mehr Jaren/weder yemandt wissen oder
erfaren kan/daselbst gewont/vnd bis auf Achte/abgestorben.
Auch deren/so in newligkhait/an der abgestorbnen stat/eingenommen vnd
erhöhet sein: Vnnd dann/mit was personen die Rö. Kai. Ma. vnnser aller
gnedigister Herr/am Dritten Augusti/im nechstverschinen Achtvnd
viertzigisten Jar/ain New Regiment/von Rath vnd Gericht/
auch alle Empter besetzt hat/Sambt aines jeden Geschlechts/
vnd der verordenten Personen Schilt/Helm vnd
Zaichen/In künstliche possen/auf art
der alten Klaidung/Waffen
vnd Wören/gestellt.

Mit Rö. Kai. Ma. gnaden
vnnd Priuilegio, inn Zehen
Jaren/nit Nachzutrucken.
1 5 5 0.

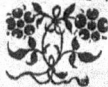

FIGURE 4.24. Paul Hector Mair, *Bericht vnd antzaigen der loblichen Statt Augspurg aller Herren Geschlecht so vor Fünfhundert vnd mehr Jaren weder yemandt wissen oder erfaren kan daselbst gewont vnd bis auf Achte abgestorben* (Augsburg: Melchior Kriegstein, 1550). Munich, Bayerische Staatsbibliothek, Rar. 641. urn:nbn:de:bvb:12-bsb00071015-6. Cover page.

the sun, and, of course, God. The leading patrician families of Augsburg and Nuremberg were no different from the royals; they too wanted to illustrate their noble family history and their claim to power through hereditary titles.

Just as they had done with the nobility, artists began depicting Augsburg's patrician class with their corresponding coats of arms in illustrated manuscripts in the fifteenth century in commissions meant to promote the patricians' elite social status. First, the *Augsburger Chronik* manuscript from 1457, written by Sigismund Meisterlin and illustrated by the Augsburg merchant Hektor Mühlich, includes fifty-six crests of Augsburg's patrician families.[19] Second, the first hand-colored *Wappen und Familienbuch* of Augsburg was made by Hans Gossembrot around 1468/69 and includes the hand-painted crests of fifty-one patricians. For seventy years, until in 1538 Augsburg's patrician class opened to new families such as the Fuggers, this was the only manuscript of its type.

The arrival of the printing press only deepened Augsburg patricians' need to fashion themselves as knighted nobility in full armor, like Emperor Maximilian I had done.[20] The Welsers were no exception. The book planned by Hans Burgkmair the Younger (1500–1559) and Heinrich Vogtherr the Younger (1513–68) would replicate the "old patrician class" that was illustrated by Gossembrot with minor changes. Burgkmair the Younger and Vogtherr the Younger prepared their "Augsburg Book of Peerage" (*Augsburger Geschlechterbuch*) for publication, but it was never completed and printed in its entirety (figs. 4.25, 4.26). Their goal was to represent the old patrician families as well as some of the more recent families that joined the patriciate in costly armor along with their crests, for example, the Fuggers, Baumgartners, Vöhlins, and Peutingers. As in the humanist and city historian Conrad Peutinger's case, these families already belonged to the city's elite merchant and political circles (Zäh 2012, 12). The Burgkmair and Vogtherr volume of the *Augsburg Book of Nobles* (held by the Staatsgalerie in Stuttgart) of 1545–47 consists of 43 drawings and 53 etchings that were planned for a version that was not published, though an abridged edition created by Wilhelm Peter Zimmermann was published in 1618. The drawings show ink and red chalk corrections, sometimes on the coats of arms. Usually, one male member of the patrician family is represented in Italian Renaissance style, dressed in imaginary expensive armor and accompanied by their family crests. Burgkmair the Younger had actually decorated armor for some of Augsburg's most distinguished armor makers, who often supplied Emperor

FIGURE 4.25.
Hans Burgkmair der Jüngere
and Heinrich Vogtherr,
"Welser." Red chalk, ink,
and watercolor. From
Augsburger Geschlechterbuch,
1545. Ins. Nr. D 2010/777,
92 (KK). Staatsgalerie
Stuttgart, Graphische
Sammlung.

Maximilian's luxury tastes. In figure 4.25, the Welser family is represented by a man in such grandiose, fictitious armor, completed with a helmet with feathers, and sporting a flowing mustache, accompanied by the Welser crest, which would have been colored white and red, as seen in figure 4.26. The drawing is meant to depict the assumed grandiosity of the Welser male hereditary line.

Mair and Christoph Weiditz's *Bericht und Antzaigen der loblichen Statt Augspurg aller Herren Geschlecht*, published in 1550, is similar to Burgkmair and Vogtherr's *Augsburg Book of Nobles* (see fig. 4.24). Both projects resulted from the city's elites' need to be pictorially represented as a sign of their newfound prestige after they were accepted into Augsburg's patrician class (39 families with 80 individuals; no women, of course, as the patriciate re-

FIGURE 4.26.
Hans Burgkmair der Jüngere
and Heinrich Vogtherr,
"Welser," *Augsburger Ge-
schlechterbuch*, ca. 1545–47.
One of forty-five prints
showing coats of arms of
Augsburg families; full-
length male figure in armor
turned to the left, holding a
short lance with his left
hand, with shield showing a
red and white fleur-de-lis for
the Welser family. Etching
with hand-coloring on the
shield and feather on helmet.
British Museum, 1848,
1209.67. © Trustees of the
British Museum.

mained male-inherited).[21] The imaginary armor was of course part of the
way artists represented their prestige and claim to their status. Mair and
Weiditz's *Bericht* celebrates Augsburg's innovation in drawing, printmaking,
and armor production. Like Burgkmair and Vogtherr's *Augsburg Book of
Nobles*, Christoph Weiditz's woodcuts represent Augsburg's illustrious patrician families by depicting a male member of each family in costly imaginary
dress armor. Mair's is a printed coloring book for adults and a guide to Augsburg's prominent families and crests that includes a legend in the back that
explains how to color each crest. However, already in Gossembrot's manuscript there were instructions to the readers on the hand-coloring of the
shields, so that addition is hardly unique to the later print edition from Mair
and Burgkmair (Zäh 2012, 13). Mair and Weiditz's book also ranks the

FIGURE 4.27.
Paul Hector Mair,
*Bericht und Antzaigen,
der löblichen Staat Aug-
spurg, aller Herren Ges-
chlecht* (Augsburg:
Melchior Kriegstein,
1550). Munich, Bayeri-
sche Staatsbibliothek,
Rar. 641 (p. 19, Welser
clan and crest in
idealized armor).
urn:nbn:de:bvb:12-
bsb00071015-6.

FIGURE 4.27.
Paul Hector Mair,
*Bericht und Antzaigen,
der löblichen Staat Aug-
spurg, aller Herren Ges-
chlecht* (Augsburg:
Melchior Kriegstein,
1550). Munich, Bayeri-
sche Staatsbibliothek,
Rar. 641 (p. 19, Welser
clan and crest in
idealized armor).
urn:nbn:de:bvb:12-
bsb00071015-6.

patricians according to the oldest. First, the Welsers appear in the first most honorable registry (Mair 1550, 19), represented in the figure of a bearded man in armor with the Welser lily crest at his feet (fig. 4.27). Second, the Welsers also appear in the following part, which depicts the eight remaining patrician families (second registry; Mair 1550, 57), as well as those who joined the patriciate after it opened to wider membership in 1538 (Mair 1550, 82), whose crest appears along with the others. Third, individuals appear who were confirmed present when Emperor Charles V came to Augsburg in August of 1548. Here individual members of each family are drawn, including Bartholomäus Welser (fig. 4.28) and Anton Fugger, both part of *Des gehaimen Raths*, or privy council, along with indicated positions of pres-

Herr Bartholme Welser/
Deß gehaimen Raths.

3

FIGURE 4.28.
Paul Hector Mair, *Bericht und Antzaigen, der löblichen Staat Augspurg, aller Herren Geschlecht* (Augsburg: Melchior Kriegstein, 1550). Munich, Bayerische Staatsbiblio-thek, Rar. 641 (p. 106, Bartholomäus Welser). urn:nbn:de:bvb:12-bsb00071015-6

tige because of their close relationship to the emperor (Mair 1550, 106, 109). All in all, the editions by these renowned artists and editors show that each new and old patrician family wanted to represent their status and claims over Augsburg's society in a way similar to the Habsburgs.

Beyond the printed works meant to illustrate Augsburg's upper social caste, each family usually produced its own set of manuscript and printed genealogical materials meant to display their power and hereditary claims. The Augsburg patrician families traced their genealogical history in media such as *Geheim Ehrenbücher* (Secret Books of Honor), *Geschlechterbücher* (Books of Nobles or Peerage), *Stammesbeschreibungen* (Descriptions of Genealogy), and *Cronica* (Chronicles). According to Hartmut Bock (2008), the illustrated genealogical books, which often feature costumed family members, show the aspirations of patrician families to the nobility in the free imperial cities of Augsburg, Nuremberg, and Frankfurt. They are fascinating material objects in that they incorporate elements of history, art, and literature. There were more of these books produced in Augsburg than Nuremberg, however (Zäh 2012, 12). The genealogical books show a connection between Augsburg's city life, family genealogy, and the aspirations of the patrician class to the nobility, and they exist as a bridge between the Holy Roman Imperial Court and each city's ruling class. For example, the rival Fuggers' *Ehrenbuch* was distinctive among these as a book that also relied on family portraiture, colorful crests, and beautiful calligraphy to display family history (Rohmann 2004, 26). In addition to displaying past honor and nobility, the family book secured the family name for the future. Georg Strauch, who printed genealogical materials for the Welser family, also hand-painted a genealogy of the Nuremberg Derrer family (Ms. Ludwig XIII 12, Getty Museum), which meant to memorialize generations of an illustrious Nuremberg family along with the city's history. Many family members are depicted wearing jewels and furs and other expensive clothes in a manner common to the manuscript genealogy books (*Geschlechtbücher*) circulating around the free imperial cities. The portrayal of the family's wealth would confirm their status according to sumptuary laws. In the Derrer genealogy, Strauch also included architectural depictions of the impressive Derrer residence in Nuremberg, as well as "The Garden of Magdalena Pairin." Descriptions of rich gardens and palaces commemorated the Derrer's possessions (fig. 4.29).

The Welsers produced manuscripts and printed genealogical media similar to other family books produced in Augsburg, Nuremberg, and Frankfurt in the early modern period that were meant to record the family's claim to hereditary titles as a way to legitimate their social power.[22] Bock has written about the *Geschlechtsbücher* commissioned by the Welsers, which is held in the Welser family archive. The Welser family's search for noble origins began in 1536 when Jakob Welser I, the patrician from Nuremberg, began writing to his family members in Augsburg about editing a genealogical history (Bock 2008, 97). Soon after, Bartholomäus Welser VIII (1557–1628) edited a *Geschlechtbuch*, which narrated the family history from 1241 to 1560. The search intensified in the sixteenth century, when Jakob convinced his son Hans (1497–1559) in Augsburg as well as his friend

FIGURE 4.29. Unknown, Georg Strauch (German, 1613–75), Genealogy of the Derrer family, ca. 1626–1711. Tempera colors with gold and silver highlights on parchment bound between original wood boards covered with original dark brown velvet. Leaf: 37.6 x 26 cm (14 13/16 x 10 1/4 in.). The J. Paul Getty Museum, Los Angeles, Ms. Ludwig XIII 12 (83.MP.155). Digital image courtesy of the Getty's Open Content Program.

Conrad Halle to bring the project to Conrad Peutinger, the famous Augsburg humanist, who was married to Margarete Welser, Jacob I's niece.
Jacob I's plan was to try to prove the noble origins of the family (Bock 2008,
103). They did so by taking advantage of the Latinized form of their last
name, "Belzares," as they were known for their business in Iberia. Based on
this they traced their origins to a Roman warrior known as "Belizar." Like
the Habsburgs and other elite families, the Welsers sought to justify their
claim to their hereditary status and power in the patrician class by linking
their family's pedigree to the ancient Romans. However, in the seventeenth
century they also claimed noble status from medieval knights.

The *Genealogical Table of the Family von Welser* made by the Nuremberg
printmaker Georg Strauch (1613–75) in 1666, depicts the legendary pater-
familias Philipp Welser (d. 839) dressed in armor.[23] His corpse forms the
root of the family tree, which grows from his loins and sprouts multiple
branches that contain no less than 950 hand-painted coats of arms (see
fig. I.7). The tree, like most genealogical tree designs, favors the representation of primogeniture and is agnate in style.[24] That is, the male descendants
of Herr Philipp Welser are depicted on the trunk. For example, the first lines
describe Julius Welser knighted by Emperor Frederick II in 1225.[25] The
family's genealogical documents from the early modern era show illustrious
Welsers from the Middle Ages such as Philipp Welser (d. 839), who report-
edly served Charlemagne, and Emanuel Welser (d. 1076), who was canon of
the Basel cathedral and the brother of Octavianus. Emanuel, Julius Welser's
son, they claimed, served Emperor Otto I. The use of these knights, nobles,
and persons of important birth may have been part of the larger trend to tie
the family's origin to someone of noble birth from the Middle Ages rather
than a biblical or mythical figure. Royal families had recognized that claiming a biblical ancestor such as Noah or Adam would imply that any common
Christian was of their same caste. However, noble ancestors within the Holy
Roman Empire formed a stronger basis for recognition of nobility.

Moreover, the genealogical tree significantly shows the many mater-
familias, the women the Welser men marry; departing from the custom of
leaving the women out, the wives also contribute their own coats of arms.
The tree shows how the wives readily add to the family's noble history
through strategic marriages and alliances. In the fifteenth and sixteenth centuries German genealogical trees and tables sought to represent not only the
reproduction of the family's blood purity but also how marriage confirms
the family's untainted status.[26]

The Welsers, like the Habsburgs, were aware of how print's power to disseminate media could promote the family name after the Welser Company had gone bankrupt. Generally speaking, only dynastic noble houses used copper engravings to illustrate genealogical trees, but the Welsers spared no expense. The *Genealogical Table of the Family von Welser* was engraved copper, more than two meters wide, made from twelve hand-colored copper plates.[27] There are three assembled copies, one in the Library of Congress and the other two in the Welser family archives at the Welser Castle in Neunhof, close to Nuremberg, where the original copper plates are still located.[28] The three extant copies of Strauch's[29] printed genealogical tree of the Welser family, which have the hand-colored cut copper engravings pasted together on a roll of canvas, are more than two meters in length when complete (266 x 91 cm in the case of the Neunhof display copy). The Neunhof display copy (fig. 4.30), which has faded colors and wooden rollers used as a hanging mechanism, suggests that it was displayed in the Welser family castle. Family crests and dates were added, and some were in the process of being pasted in the 1700s, implying that these family documents were a work in progress (fig. 4.31). Yet, while the Neunhof copies served as the family's collage of genealogical material, the Welser genealogical tree held at the Library of Congress stands out because it also contains a printed map of the Venezuelan province made by the Augsburg engraver Emmanuel Stenglin (ca. 1682) (fig. 4.32), which establishes that the possession of these lands was an important part of the Welser family legacy.[30]

THE STENGLIN VENEZUELA MAP

Stenglin's seventeenth-century map is a southern German nostalgic view of the province that the Welsers had lost more than one hundred years before. While we do not know for sure who added the map to the copy of the Welser family tree held at the Library of Congress or their reasons for doing so, we can hypothesize that someone decided to embellish this copy with the map because of the Welser's historical association with Venezuela.[31] Stenglin's Venezuela map is framed in a rectangle. It shows the compass directions as well as the mostly correct latitudes.[32] It also includes the title banner and the legend given in German miles (Milliaria Germanica). The creator's name, Em. Stenglin D., appears at the lower right. The region depicted is an inset of northwestern and eastern Venezuela at the time. The title of the map

FIGURE 4.30. The Welser genealogical table. Freiherrlich von Welsersche Familienstiftung (Shelfmark WFA AK).

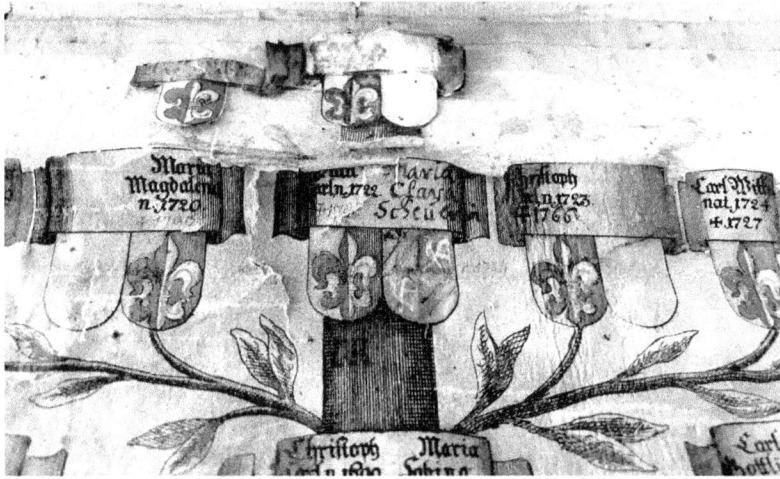

FIGURE 4.31. Detail of the Welser genealogical table. Freiherrlich von Welsersche Familienstiftung (Shelfmark WFA AK).

FIGURE 4.32. Detail of the Welser genealogical table. Library of Congress, Rare Book and Special Collections, CS629.W4.

refers to its political past. Visually striking, it is a text banner held by two cherubs that announces "VENEZUELA Provincia in America Occidentali. Quam olim Dni. Velseri Patricij Augustani pofsidebant a CAROLO V Imperatore ipsis Consignata" (Venezuela—Province in Western America that in past times the Patrician Welsers of Augsburg possessed as authorized by Emperor Charles V) (see fig. I.4). This commemorative statement suggests the basis for the German nostalgia for the colony in later centuries.

Beyond the commemorative statement, at first glance there is not much in the map that shows traces of the Welser's presence on the land. The Indigenous populations are shown in certain territories by Lake Maracaibo. There is also the Xirijara povince (which shows the town of Torquillo, present-day Trujillo), the Bariquicimeto province, and south, close to the plains region, the Cuyca province. Indigenous nations are labeled in a different font as Pocabuies Populi, Achoholados Populi (to the west of the lake), and the Bobures Populi (close to the Valle de Ambrosio south of the lake). The valley was named for the first Welser governor, Ambrosius Alfinger, after he died from being struck by an arrow there in 1533. Gonzalo Fernández de Oviedo also mentions these Indigenous nations as well as topographic features in his manuscript map of Maracaibo, featured in his *Historia general y natural de las Indias*, with the exception of the Achoholados (fig. 4.33). For example, south of Lake Maracaibo, Fernández de Oviedo wrote, "Here is the place where Gov. Ambrosio was killed."[33] In short, Stenglin's and Férnandez de Oviedo's maps depict the presence of the Welsers and their conflicts with Indigenous peoples around Lake Maracaibo.

Not only is Welser blood commemorated in the Stenglin Venezuela map, but so are the settlements they founded. There are a total of ten settlements marked by red churches. These include the Welser colony of Coro, as well as Rio della Hacha and La Rancheria, northwest of Lake Maracaibo in the Guajira peninsula. The latter two settlements were founded by the Welser lieutenant governor Nikolaus Federmann. Other settlements are Laguno, south of Lake Maracaibo, Portilla de Carora, Nueva Segovia, Tucuyo, Nueva Xerces, Nueva Valentia, Santiago de Leon, and Nuestra Señora de Carvalledo (in the province of Caracas). The most important water sources depicted are Lake Maracaibo (its mouth is called Golfo de Venezuela) and of course the Caribbean Sea, which borders Venezuela and includes four ships sailing the seas (with first the Windward Islands, Aruba, Quaracao,

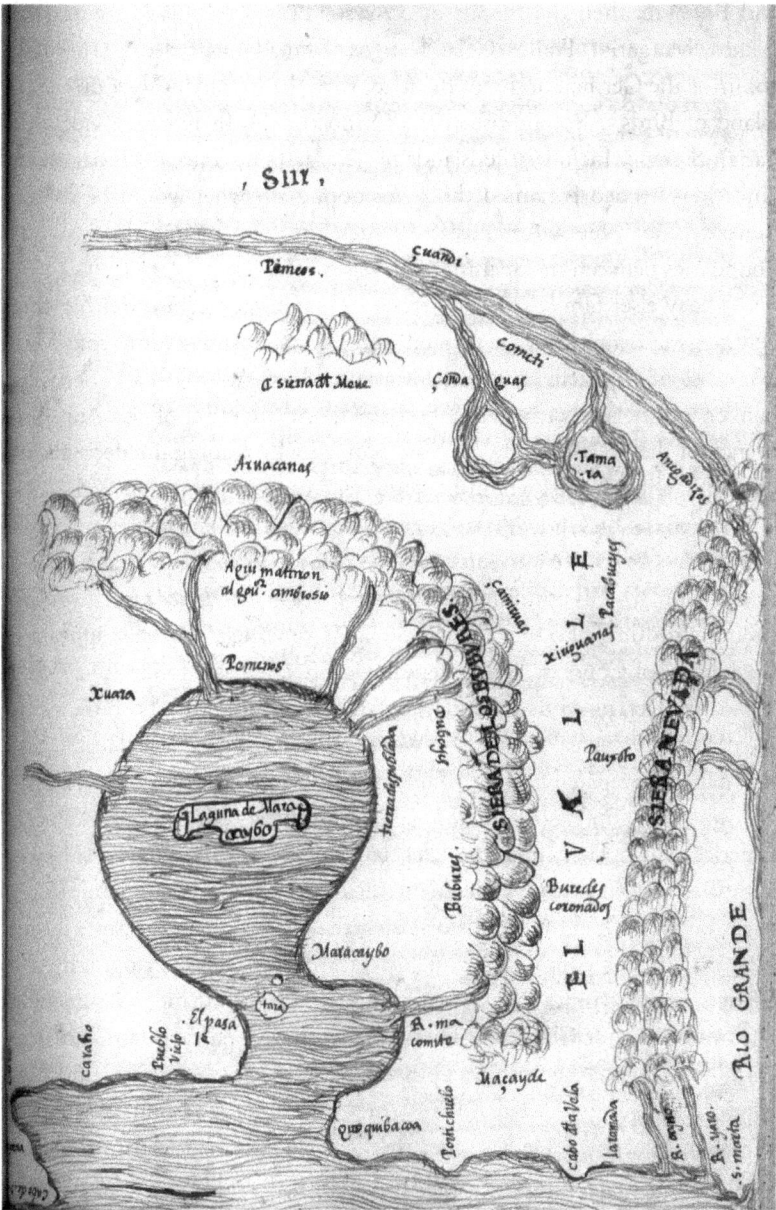

FIGURE 4.33. *Mapa de Laguna de Maracaibo,* from Gonzalo Férnadez de Oviedo's *Historia general y natural de las Indias.* Manuscript, Palacio Real, Madrid, PR MS.11/3041, 241–42. © Patrimonio Nacional

and Bonayre; then the islands of d'Aves, Rocca, Orchilla, Torguta [*sic*], Blanca, Margarita, Frailos/Cola, Testigos, Granada, and Beckia). Stenglin confirms the German origin of the map, with the toponym *Vogel Eyland*, or Island of Birds. Also, almost in the Orinoco delta (here called Golfo del Paria), Stenglin includes the islands of Trinidad and Tabaco (Tobago). Inland the Orinoco is named the "Worinoque" in what would be eastern Venezuela, or Nueva Andalusia. As such the map retains the east-west boundaries between the Spanish and Welser colonies.

The Welser family's own interests in mapping and historicizing their genealogy also appear in the printed works of its most illustrious son: Mark Welser (1558–1614; also known as Markus, Marx, and Marcus Velserus). A banker, politician, astronomer, humanist, and member of the Augsburg branch of the Welser family, he corresponded with leading intellectuals, including Galileo Galilei whom he wrote regarding sunspots. M. Welser was also one of the first individual scholars who began making copies and replicas of maps from late antiquity and the Middle Ages (Kupčík and Kuntsmann 2000, 6). His posthumous *Opera historica et philologica sacra et profana* (Nürnberg, 1682) also includes the Stenglin Venezuela map that appears in the Library of Congress Welser genealogical tree (Welser 1682, 26–27) (fig. 4.34).[34] In fact, given that the map's creation coincides with both the printing of the genealogical tree and M. Welser's *Opera historica*, it is plausible that the map was prepared for that volume seventy years after his death.

The Stenglin map with the title, "Venezuela—Province in Western America that in past times the Patrician Welsers of Augsburg possessed as authorized by Emperor Charles V," in the *Opera historica* accompanies a few pages of Welser's chronicle historicizing the Welser's Venezuela possession (26–27). In this combination of historical writing and cartography, the Welsers in "past times" "possessed" the Venezuelan province as a personal gift from Emperor Charles V. The Welsers intertwined their family history with the legend of the territory's possession. M. Welser cites Girolamo Benzoni's *Historia del mondo nuovo* as a "true" source of the account of what occurred in Venezuela. He also cites the German historian Martin Crusius's (1526–1607) *Annales Suevici* (Swabian Chronicle), and his own *Chronika* of Augsburg translated by Engelbert Werlich.[35] In this last text, after the dedication, there is a a poem about Augsburg that celebrates the wealth of the city and the international spirit of its merchant families, most notably, the Fuggers, thereby linking merchant capitalism and overseas expansion. It is the "Lobspruch und kurtze pöetische Beschreibung der Statt Augspurg" by

FIGURE 4.34. Emmanuel Stenglin, Map of Venezuela. In Christoph Arnoldum, *Viri Illustris, Marci Velseri. Vita, genus et mors*. In Marcus Welser, *Opera Historica et Philologica* (Norimbergae: Wolfgang Mauritii, 1682), 26–27. Accessed at CAMENA, Corpus Automatum Multiplex Electorum Neolatinitatis Auctorum, http://mateo.uni-mannheim .de/camenahtdocs/camenahist.html.

Salomonen Frenzelium von Breslau (1585). The poem portrays the Fuggers rather than the Welsers as emblematic of the city's wealth: "Ja uber diese Gantze Welt / Der Fugger Nam den Preis behelt / Ihr Helden und Heroisch muth / Hoch uber alles Schweben thut" (Over the whole world / the Fugger name retains its worth / their heroes and heroic courage / floats high). The poem describes the effect of merchants' travel and trade in Augsburg.

> Groß Kauffmanshändel und Gewerb
> Durch fremde Lanndt gar weit und fern.
> Durch Frankreich und Italien
> Durch Teutschland und Hispanien
> Mit Sumen groß und Kosten schwer

Die Bürger führen hin und her.
Auf solche weiß in schneller eill
ist Augspurg worden feist und geyl
Und uber alle Stätt beruhmpt
So hier in unsern Landen sind
Dahin hat sie das Reichtumb bracht
Wächst mehrentheils/Wie man denn
Aus Indien von fernen wirdt/ (Not paginated.)

———

Great merchants and trade
Through foreign lands far and away.
Through France and Italy
Through Germany and Spain
With great sums and great costs
The citizens lead here and there.
In such a way that they hurry
Augsburg has become more famous
than all the cities that are here in our lands.
Here Wealth has come
Which routinely grows
Like it does after returning from the Indies.

Mark Welser likely included a poem about the Fuggers' wealth and continued influence in the city because by the seventeenth century the Welser
name had been in decline and there were no such laudable global feats to
display in maps and poems. The poem was readily available and reflected the
city's glory. However, the inclusion of the "Lobspruch" is a nostalgic look
back at Augsburg at the beginning rather than the end of the sixteenth century, when the city was plagued by inflation and economic decline (Safley
1997, 98). Even the Fuggers after 1560 were said to experience a "time of
decay" (Häberlein and Burkhardt 2002, 99). Augsburg was by then known
as the site of the Peace of Augsburg (1555), which was a direct response to
the religious conflict that arose from the Reformation. This temporary
agreement ratified by Charles V and the Catholic Holy Roman Empire
allowed each German prince to determine which confession (Roman
Catholicism or Lutheranism) would be practiced in his territory. The genealogical and geographic preoccupations of the Welser and Fugger families

were entrenched in a difficult reality that penetrated the German realms; literary and geographic nostalgia was a way to overcome the reality of economic and cultural strife and decline. Furthermore, the genealogical and geographic preoccupations of both families signaled their attempts to mark their place within the nobility, outside of the dynamics of Augsburg.[36]

In his introduction to *Monarchs, Ministers, and Maps* David Buisseret aims to decipher why a new map consciousness that started with the diffusion of Ptolemy's work and was driven by the print revolution continued to influence the way Europeans "saw" their geopolitical realities. Buisseret (1992, 2) asks, "For what purposes were these maps commissioned? How accurate and useful did they actually prove to be? How did the new cartographic knowledge strengthen the hand of central governments in dealing with provincial autonomies?" His arguments apply even to maps in manuscript form. Among the maps that I have referred to here, only about half were part of the "print revolution": those by Gastaldi and, later, by Stenglin that were included in printed histories. Ribeiro's maps were manuscripts replicated from the *Padrón General.* They were meant to be used specifically by political entities, including the Welser Company. Agnese's manuscript atlases were meant for a lettered political elite who also would have been aware of the political realities of the then-rulers of the Old and New World. That is why the Agnese manuscript atlas, which depicts the figures of Suleiman and Phillip II over the territories they possess, coexists with one of the New World, which labels the governors of the New World province. Agnese played with the visual and textual hierarchy on maps, and despite his decoration of the Andes Mountains and some environmental features, the political information is salient.

Gastaldi probably received information on the *Padrón General* from his Spanish contacts in Venice. It was actually Gastaldi himself who published the first standalone map of Spain, *La Spaña*, in 1544. It contained information on the interior provided by the Spanish ambassador to Venice, don Diego de Hurtado de Mendoza (Parker 1992, 126). Information on New World discoveries crossed political entities, for example, from Seville to Augsburg and Venice, despite the relatively high demand for "secrets" by the Spanish. In sum, Gastaldi's and Agnese's successful print and handcrafted manuscript ventures reveals that there was a thriving market for cartographic material that answered the geopolitical questions of the day, such as the natural and human resources found in the New World and whether Spain, Portugal, or the Welsers governed them.

In the case of the Stenglin map that appears both in a Welser gene- alogical tree and in Mark Welser's *Opera historica*, the map was commis- sioned on behalf of a patrician family to commemorate its historical (yet lost) political power. It shows the Welser family's eagerness to make its mark on its local community of Nuremberg through a diffusion of their family accomplishments and genealogical history. As for the Welsers, their descen- dants continued to use exotica in imagery of their family alliances, as in the print made for the marriage celebrations and processions of Johann von Kolowrat, nephew of Philipp Welser and Katharina von Payrsberg (fig. 4.35). It depicts the white bride riding on top of a lizard and accompanied

FIGURE 4.35. Sigmund Elsässer (1579–87), *Hans Bauer*, imp. (1580). Hand-colored engraving mounted on parchment. Illustration for a publication (untitled [Innsbruck: Hans Bauer, 1580]) of the procession celebrating the marriage on 15 February 1580 of Johann von Kolowrat, nephew of Philip Welser (1527–80), and Katharina von Payrs- berg. Fol. 7. In this print two Black men accompany a woman riding a lizard. 1580. Kunsthistorisches Museum Wien, Sammlungen Schloss Ambras., PS-5269, Innsbruck.

by two black porters.[37] Exotic men and exotic beasts served to reinforce the wealth and caste of the young Katharina Payrsberg and the strategic Welser family alliance. Like the Welser genealogical tree, this codified visual media consecrated blood alliances through the conquest of "Other" racialized humans, animals, and territories. The Welser family's status was elevated because of their dominion over these racialized beings and the beasts, all meant to work for the capital accumulation of an elite Augsburg family.

Whereas many of the maps discussed here were used to indicate Venezuela as a possession not just of the Welser Company but of the Welser family as well, Spanish crónicas, as textual productions, critiqued the Welser colony as an intrusion on Spanish sovereignty. The next chapter investigates how Spanish historiographers saw the Welser governance as an affront to the "Spanish" nature of Habsburg conquest.

CHAPTER 5

"Foreign" Governance

The Welser Colony Remembered in Latin American
Colonial Literature

> Estos son los daños temporales del Rey; sería bien considerar qué tales
> y qué tantos son los daños, deshonras, blasfemias, infamias de Dios y de
> su ley, y con qué se recompensarán tan innumerables ánimas como
> están ardiendo en los infiernos por la cudicia y inmanidad de aquestos
> tiranos animales o alemanes.
>
> —Bartolomé de Las Casas, *Brevísima*
> *relación de la destrucción de las Indias*

My analysis of the first attempts by Spanish chronicle writers to historicize
the Welser period in the colonial era shows the anti-German stance of the
authors, some of whom critiqued the "foreign" governance as not only
strange and unfamiliar, but antithetical to Spanish loyalism. The same xenophobic critiques that Charles endured when he first became the Spanish
king were directed at the Welsers, especially because of the anti-Lutheranism
permeating Spain during the Reformation. Crónica writers who were con-
temporaries of Federmann and Ambrosius Alfinger such as Bartolomé de
Las Casas, Gonzalo Fernández de Oviedo, Juan de Castellanos, fray Pedro
Aguado, and José de Oviedo y Baños wrote about what they had seen.

164

Gonzalo Fernández de Oviedo's *Historia general y natural de las Indias, islas y tierra firme del mar océano* (1535) (Natural History of the Indies, Islands and Tierra Firme of the Ocean Sea) is a (mostly) benevolent depiction of the German conquistadors. This account remains neutral, except when it comes to Nikolaus Federmann, who Fernández de Oviedo charges was disloyal to both the Welsers and the Spanish crown. His account differs from the scathing critique of the Welser conquest of Venezuela in Las Casas's *Brevísima relación* (1555), which connected the Germans' heretical Lutheranism to their penchant for butchery. Las Casas, while critical of all conquistadors' violence, displays anti-German sentiment. In contrast, Castellanos used the epic poetic genre to eulogize those same men, including Federmann and the other Welsers. Castellanos's epic poem, *Elegías de varones ilustres de Indias* (written 1578–1601), lauds the German conquerors and treats them like heroes. Conversely, Aguado's moral history, *Recopilación historial de Venezuela* (written at the end of the 1570s), insists on the duty of the Spanish nation and the Catholic Church to save souls; to Aguado, the Germans are merely agents of a larger imperial project of conquest that uses both Spanish and German actors. Aguado certainly added a religious tone to his moral history; his belief that Spanish nationalist sentiment drives the conquest affects his treatment of the Welsers. Finally, Oviedo y Baños intertextually weaves the crónicas already written about the region, but he does so highlighting the bourgeoning creole national identity characteristic of pre-independence Venezuelan literature. Oviedo y Baños's eighteenth-century account employs the trope of the romance of conquest that criticizes the German conquerors for raping the land of Venezuela rather than treating her like a bride and colonizing her.

In a now-canonical 1982 essay, Walter Mignolo lists crónicas as one of the central genres of the corpus of colonial Latin American literature.[1] "Seeing," or witnessing, is central to the crónica and the historia; however, since the word *historia* did not include the temporal aspect with which we imbue it today, writers use *crónica* to refer to texts that detail past or present events using a temporal structure.[2] The crónica originated in a list of events to be preserved in cultural memory (Mignolo 1982, 75). Most authors I discuss in this chapter propagated a cultural memory of the Welser colonization of Venezuela that was anti-German and anti-Protestant. My aim is to reframe the Black Legend and historicize early modern arguments about nationhood and religion during the Habsburg Empire but also to reread the crónicas and study the conflicting depictions of Germans as "barbaric," which draw on

Roman-Barbaric antagonisms that permeated Europe in the early Christian era. These works had an intertextual nature. Yet they differed in their portrayal of the Welsers. Most Spanish cronistas depict the Welser governance as flawed, continuing a Latin, anti-German perception of German cruelty and greed. By contrast, cronistas in general admire Federmann as a warrior but despise the German nature of Welser governance.

GONZALO FERNÁNDEZ DE OVIEDO'S *HISTORIA GENERAL Y NATURAL DE LAS INDIAS, ISLAS Y TIERRA FIRME DEL MAR OCÉANO*

Gonzalo Fernández de Oviedo wrote about the then very recent events and the Spanish presence in the Americas from 1492 to 1549 based on firsthand accounts by many of the conquistadors.[3] Mignolo (1982) describes a general, moral, and natural epistemological triad that emerged in the sixteenth-century notion of "history" and describes Fernández de Oviedo as its first practitioner. The chronicler's ties to the royal family, previous travels in Italy, and erudition led the Spanish authorities to entrust this office to him; they also valued his firsthand knowledge of the conquistadors' character (78).

Fernández de Oviedo describes the Welsers in mostly genteel terms. He writes that Ambrosius Alfinger,[4] the first German governor sent by the Welser Company, is a "a German gentleman; a good and well-spoken man."[5] He refers to the whole German venture in the Indies as Emperor Charles V's concession given to the Welsers and views the Welser expedition mainly as serving the emperor. He points out that the authorization to govern included many limitations.[6] Specifically, the Welsers had the right to *serve* the crown through governance of the province inasmuch as doing so served Castilian interests. He saw the Welsers as the fortunate beneficiaries of a favorable business opportunity from the Spanish monarch.

Most of Fernández de Oviedo's observations on the Welsers' actions in Venezuela are detailed in the twenty-two chapters that make up book XXV of volume 3 of the *Historia general*. He begins with the arrival of the Germans in Tierra Firme (ch. I), discusses Ambrosius Alfinger's and Georg Hohermuth von Speyer's (Jorge Spira's) expeditions into the interior, analyzes Federmann's rebelliousness and conflicts with other Welser governors, and ends with Bishop Rodrigo de Bastidas, labeled an "eyewitness and person of great authority,"[7] who gave a personal account of the events that happened in the Welser colony of Coro to the chronicler (ch. XXII).

While earlier chapters depict Federmann in a more positive light, in chapters XVII and XVIII, Fernández de Oviedo begins to portray him as disobedient to the emperor. Speyer orders Federmann to found a town on Cabo de la Vela, but Federmann disobeys in order to embark on an expedition to find gold in Venezuela's interior. Fernández de Oviedo also states that Federmann was given the title of governor of Venezuela before Alfinger's death but was stripped of it before he could return to Tierra Firme due to accusations by an hidalgo, Alonso de la Llana, *procurador de la cibdad de Coro*, at court. This same testimony would have a significant impact concerning Germans in the colony.

> And after hearing the prosecutor, De La Llana, those gentlemen, so they say, were in no position to permit any German individual to govern in those parts. The Welsers were then offended to the point that Governor Jorge Espira [Georg von Hohermuth von Speyer] was permitted to take over [in Coro]. Those gentlemen also thought that Federmann should not return to Venezuela.[8]

In addition to being stripped of his title, Federmann was not trusted by either the Welsers or the Spanish crown. Yet Federmann apparently found a way to return to America, first to Santo Domingo, then to Coro, where Speyer made him his lieutenant (*teniente de capitán general*).

Fernández de Oviedo's account shows Federmann critical of both the Spanish administrators in Venezuela and his German superiors. He summarizes a letter Federmann sent from Oristan, Jamaica, that criticized Alfinger's and Speyer's actions. Federmann nonetheless sought the court's favor when discussing his conquest efforts in land he argued was under the jurisdiction of the Venezuelan governance rather than Sancta Marta. Francisco Davila, councilor, or *regidor*, of Santo Domingo, showed Fernández de Oviedo an emerald Federmann sent, along with his letter (3:52).

Fernández de Oviedo includes an account authored by the conquistadors Joan de Sanct Martin (dates unknown) and Antonio de Lebrija (1507–40) of Gonzalo Jiménez de Quesada (from Santa Marta), Sebastián Benalcazar (from Peru), and Nikolaus Federmann (from Venezuela) that sheds further light on Federmann's struggle for recognition. All three men arrived in Bogotá and laid claim to the conquest of New Granada and then agreed to personally appear before the emperor to claim the riches they found there.[9] Among them, Jiménez de Quesada received the highest reward: recognition of his conquest of Nuevo Granada on behalf of the crown. He received the title Marshal (*mariscal*) of Nuevo Granada, as well as Mayor of Sancta Fé (with a salary of 400 ducats per year), a repartimiento of indios, 2,000 ducats from the crown, and a *mayorazgo* (an entailed estate) for his descendants (3:93).

Fernández de Oviedo wrote that Sebastián de Belalcázar would also do well because "he brought to Castilla many emeralds and money; he negotiated better than did Federmann."[10] In fact, "Nikolaus had believed that [the emperor] would give him the governorship of Venezuela (as Georg Hohermuth von Speyer had received it from the German Welsers) in return for having left many Spaniards and even more Indians dead." The chronicler notes that of the three conquistadors "Federmann has the most souls on his conscience" and that the Welsers discredited him because, given how much they had spent on the initial contract, they took umbrage at him "going around as if he were a rich man." Férnandez de Oviedo suggests that Federmann abused his power and stole gold, emeralds, and other commodities that would have belonged to the Welser Company. He implies that this umbrage is no better than Federmann deserves because "he was never esteemed as someone loyal to his employers, as he was known to keep tabs on everything and everyone, and *even then had a reputation for being a Lutheran* [my emphasis]."[11] For Fernández de Oviedo, Federmann epitomizes excess in conquest, but his concern over Federmann's assumed Lutheranism is meant to be a warning to his readers.

BARTOLOMÉ DE LAS CASAS'S *BREVÍSIMA RELACIÓN DE LA DESTRUCCIÓN DE LAS INDIAS* (1555)

Bartolomé de Las Casas tells a different story about the Germans in his *Brevísima relación*, a summary of his larger *Historia de la destrucción de las Indias*, which would not be published completely until 1821. While Férnandez de Oviedo focused on Federmann's misbehavior, in Las Casas's account the Welser governor most notably accused is Ambrosius Alfinger. Written as a warning to the Spanish monarch, Las Casas's chronicle was the first internal critique of the conquest of the New World. It is preoccupied with

Amerindian history. Las Casas's scathing account of the conquest of the Indies finds fault with all the actors involved, Spanish and German, although
the Germans are the most severely criticized. In the end, he makes a pun,
calling them "tiranos animales o alemanes" (tyrant animals or Germans). He
states that the Welser governors arrived with three hundred men and are
incomparable in their methodical destruction, torturous treatment, and
wholesale annihilation of Indigenous peoples. Like Fernández de Oviedo,
Las Casas included eyewitness accounts of the many violent incidents that
the Spanish conquistadors perpetrated on the Indigenous populations of the
New World. He details the inhumane treatment Indigenous people endured
and the atrocious nature of conquest. The pages of his books are filled with
depictions of conquistadors who use swords and dogs to rip Indian bodies
apart limb by limb in order to subjugate their people. Las Casas, of course,
fought for the rights of Amerindians and in 1550–51 engaged in the famous
Valladolid debate with Juan Ginés de Sepúlveda to discuss the human rights
of the colonized Amerindians. While Sepúlveda doubted whether Amerindians deserved human rights, Las Casas was adamant that they did.

Las Casas's *Relación* is ordered geographically. He writes of the horrors
perpetrated on the native peoples of Hispaniola, Cuba, Nicaragua, New
Spain, Guatimala (Guatemala), Yucatán, Santa Marta, Cartagena, the París
coast of Venezuela, the island of Trinidad, and the kingdom of Venezuela
(among others). He describes the Welsers as using "deceit and certain malicious persuasions" on the king such that he would give the "entire rule and
governance and jurisdiction" of Venezuela to them. "Men of evil intentions
have always worked to conceal from [the king] the harms and perditions that
God and the people's souls and the king's estate suffer in those lands of the
Indies," he laments (Las Casas 2003, 64).

To be fair, Las Casas also sees most Spanish conquistadors as deceitful
in their efforts to gain the king's favor so that they may continue their mas-
sacres in the Indies without intervention from the royal authorities. Yet Las
Casas's bold critique of the king's political trade that resulted in the transfer
of the Venezuelan territory to the Welsers underscores the perceived threat
that hidden Protestantism posed for Spain. Of the Welsers he writes:

These men entered into those lands, then, with more, I do think, incomparable cruelty than any of the other tyrants that we have spoken
of, and more unreasonably and furiously than the most bloodthirsty
tigers and ravening wolves and lions. (Las Casas 2003, 64–65)[12]

Indigenous nations, in contrast, are "as gentle and meek as lambs" (64).[13] Las Casas also likens the German governors to "demons incarnate," suggesting that supernatural evil played a role in their evildoing (65).[14]

Las Casas does not give names, but the first German governor he refers to is most likely Alfinger. He relates an anecdote in which Alfinger orders his soldiers to trap Indians in a corral and only release those who can muster ransom before they starve to death. Las Casas's representation of the Welsers as predatory demons with supernatural powers also appears in his tale of how the Welsers tricked the king into giving them the original capitulación to govern the land; it is most prominent, however, in his retelling of the conquest of Venezuela as an act of German butchery.

> For with more eagerness and more blind and wrathful avarice, and with much more exquisite skillfulness and ingenuity in obtaining and *robbing silver and gold* than all those who went before, and putting aside all fear of God and the king and the shame of humankind, and forgetting that they were mortal men, and with more freedom and brazenness and daring than any others, they took possession of all the jurisdiction of the land. (65; my emphasis)[15]

The Germans employ the same cunning and trickery in obtaining the original capitulation to govern Venezuela from the emperor to extract precious metals and gems, *plata y oro* (silver and gold), from the Venezuelan province. Las Casas notes the significance of Welser bullion in financing the emperor's European wars. But it is the Germans' unquenchable thirst for precious metals that makes them monsters.

Las Casas calls the first German governor a tyrant and a "heretic, for he neither heard mass nor allowed many others to hear it neither, with other signs of Lutheranism" (67).[16] His antiforeign sentiments blur with his anti-Protestant sentiments. In his telling, many Indians died from wounds inflicted by "this foreign and pestilential knife" (64),[17] emphasizing the alien nature of the perpetrators of such wicked and ungodly violence in the Spanish project of Indian conquest.

Las Casas asserts that the Germans stole a large quantity of gold from the king; hence money becomes a polemical point, along with suspected Lutheranism. He laments that the king had never burned "any of these vile and execrable tyrants" alive, as heretics were punished in Spain (67). They are, he writes, "the enemies of God and the king"[18] who stole three million *castellanos* and depopulated "the richest land and the most prosperous in gold, and was likewise in population, that there is in the world" (68).[19]

As early as 1535, royal administrators had deemed the Welsers danger-ous to the project of Catholic conversion of all natives, and Las Casas may have been influenced by this attitude that emerged twenty years before he published his work. For example, in the cedulario of 11 May 1535, Empress Isabella ordered that no Germans be allowed to enter the province of Vene-zuela without permission, because if this took place

> it would disturb the habitants of the land and the conversion of its na-tives to our Holy Catholic faith, and, hence our Lord, which would be a disservice to Him, so I command you and charge you that from now on not to consent or allow any naturals from Germany to enter this land without our specific permission.[20]

The threat of Protestantism produced an anti-German stance on the part of the Spanish monarch, as all Germans had to request special permission to enter the Venezuelan province. The empress charged the bishop with the task of policing the Germans who were already in the province for signs of any Lutheran activities; their lifestyle was to be scrutinized, and at any signs of heresy they were to be expelled from the territory.[21] Given the policy from the royals that flip-flopped on Germans in the Americas, even while the Welsers technically ruled Venezuela, it is unsurprising that Las Casas's history would be uncritical of the Germans. However, Las Casas's writings on the Welser conquest of Venezuela depict a "pestilential" foreign nature that dared to threaten Spanish Christian solutions to the conversion of the Amerindians to the Catholic faith.

JUAN DE CASTELLANOS'S HEROIC PORTRAYAL OF FEDERMANN

Juan de Castellanos's *Elegías de varones ilustres de Indias* (Elegies of Famous Gentlemen of the Indies), which comprises more than 110,000 verses in octave Tuscan rhyme, celebrates different conquest expeditions in the Americas from around the 1490s to the 1590s (Pardo 1962, LXXIV).

According to Elizabeth Davis's *Myth and Identity in the Epic of Imperial Spain*, most epic poems in Spain were written in *octavas reales* (eight hendecasyllables ending with a rhymed couplet ABABABCC) and divided into books or cantos (2000, 4).[22]

According to Mignolo (1982, 104), the Golden Age of Spanish literature (early sixteenth century to late seventeenth century) had a strong influence on historiography from 1543 to 1592 that led to playing with literary genres, as well as an emphasis on truthfulness. These debates and literary expressions would influence Castellanos's use of verse to narrate the conquest of Venezuela. Canonical poems such as Alonso de Ercilla's *La Araucana* (1569) show this use of lyrical verse, which was influenced by the lyric poetry of Francesco Petrarch (1304–74) and the sonnets of the Spanish poet Garcilaso de la Vega (1501–36), to depict the Spanish conquest of Amerindians. As Davis (2000, 1) writes, the epic was a "major site of early nationalism and Golden Age cultural identities." Influenced by debates in Italy about the functions of an epic poem, Spanish poets followed the models of either Ariosto's *Orlando Furioso*, which offered a radical alternative to the epic canon, or Tasso, who "insisted on the superiority of historical (or historico-religious epic)" (4). Ercilla, a court poet, in *La Araucana* detailed the conquest of the Patagons in Chile (1569). He based the work on his experiences as a veteran of the military campaigns of Patagonia's Arauco and saw himself as a creator of historic epic: *La Araucana* was a "narration taken from truth," yet even Ercilla tired of narrating the boring yet violent truth and added some amorous episodes in his poem (4).

In contrast to Ercilla, Castellanos's poem subscribes to this renewed interest in the poetic genre's power to convey the imagery of the conquest. Yet the reception of Castellanos's work was characterized by a debate about narrating history through verse. Many contemporary critics, including Jiménéz de Espada, objected to Castellanos's choice of poetry, stating that the forced rhyme was responsible for the confusion of reading history in verse. María de Lourdes de Peguero Mills (2008, 16) describes Castellanos as adhering to a providential and teleological interpretation of history. Luis Fernández Restrepo (1999, 37, 39) describes the *Elegies* as representing Castellanos's defensive pro-conquest and pro-encomienda views during a time of crisis in Spain in the late sixteenth century. Moreover, Emiro Martínez-Osorio (2016, 21) writes that Castellanos may have chosen verse because it allowed him more freedom from the censors, despite the fact that he was pro-conquest (xiv).

Castellanos wrote from the periphery of the empire. Historical and political messianism and belief in the divine providence of the Spanish imperial
project imbues Castellanos's verse with the religious and political aspirations
of the Spanish Empire and its right to conquest of the New World (1962,
29–30). However, he lauds the German conquistadors Federmann, Alfinger,
Bartholomäus Welser VI, and Philipp von Hutten.

> Cuando vinieron por los alemanes.
> Lucidos y valientes capitanes.
> Fueron soldados mas de setecientos.
> En militares artes instruidos,
> Copia de belicosos instrumentos
> De que todos venían proveidos;
> Lucian varïados ornamentos
> De las bizarras ropas y vestidos;
> De las bélicas trompetas dan clamores,
> Suenan incitativos atambores. (177)[23]

———

> When they came for the Germans
> Lucid and valiant captains.
> They were more than seven hundred soldiers
> Instructed in military arts
> Abundance of bellicose instruments
> With which they were armed;
> They wore varied ornaments
> With their bizarre costumes
> From the bellicose trumpets they clamored
> pounded the inciting drums.

Castellanos claims there were seven hundred soldiers (Las Casas's estimate of
three hundred was probably closer to the truth) and emphasizes their military power. He depicts Ambrosius Alfinger thus: "Micer Ambrosio Alfinger
los regia, / Persona bien nacida y eminente, / Y cuya discrecion y cortesia, /
Se puede bien decir ser escelente" (Mister Alfinger guided them / A well-
born and eminent person / and whose discretion and courtesy / could be
said to be excellent) (177). The "good" Philipp von Hutten sheds his blood
on Venezuelan soil along with Bartholomé Berzar (Bartholomäus Welser VI)

whom Castellanos calls "pujante" (powerful) but also, referring to his and Hutten's execution on Venezuelan soil, "falto y ajeno de ventura" (lacking good fortune) (177).

Castellanos offers a commendable description of Federmann as well: "Hombre de entendimiento peregrino, / Capitán admirable y escelente; / Pues en cualquier rigor de este camino / Ninguno mas sagaz y diligente: Del valor de los cuales, Dios mediante, / Diremos grandes cosas adelante" (A man of exceptional nature / Admirable and excellent captain / For in whatever obstacles offered by this road / there is no one more wise and diligent: From the valor about which we will say grand things later) (177). In fact, later in the text, Federmann is called "brioso / Y ambicioso varon de su cosecha" (determined / and ambitious gentleman of his creation) (191), especially when he fights for the title of lieutenant. Castellanos writes that Federmann was passed over for promotion to lieutenant but that Alfinger promotes him, giving a speech to his men calling Federmann his "fiel amigo" (faithful friend) and "llano capitán y compañero" (modest captain and companion) (192), who will now guide them on an inland expedition as lieutenant.

Castellanos relates the events that Federmann published in his *Indianische Historia*; he cites among his sources the Spanish friar Vicente Requejada, who tells him of the expedition in Federmann's text—"y él me dió relacion desta jornada" (and he told me about this expedition)—and the captain Martin de Arteaga, who supposedly "escrita me ladio mas largamente" (gave me a longer written version) (192). Hence, Requejada provided an eyewitness account, while Arteaga gave him a mysterious written account. Castellanos details the route taken by Federmann: "caminaron al sur por barlovento" (they walked towards the south through the windward route), "atravesaron sierras" (they crossed mountains), and "ameno valle ven y tierra llana, / Fertíl y pobladísima ribera" (they arrived in a flat land / a fertile and populated land [the valley of Barriquicimeto]). In fact, as Restrepo (2002, 85) mentions, "through the narrative of pilgrimage, the *Elegías* inscribe Amerindian territories within Christian teleology and imperial aegis."[24] Perhaps that is why Castellanos portrays Federmann as a peaceful explorer who aims to pacify rather than conquer. For example, when he encounters a group of armed Indians, Federmann "con paz les ruega, / loando su pacífica venida" (asks with peace / praising his peaceful arrival) and is received by all in peace. In Hitiabana, Federmann begs for peace, even though the Guaycaries receive him with a threat of war.

La cual de populosas poblaciones
Estaba por allí no menos llena :
En los vecinos hay alteraciones,
Y todos ellos recibieron pena
De ver que sus labranzas y riberas
Se hollasen de gentes estranjeras,
Amenazan con bélicos pertrechos
Diciéndoles: 'volved á esotra mano',
Que son señales de furor insano;
Pero con pretension de sus provechos
Ruégales con la paz el Fedrimano. (Castellanos 1962, 193)

Of which from populous dwellings
was there no less full
In the dwellings there are altercations
and all of them were disgruntled
to see in their land and riverbanks
there were foreign peoples
they threatened with bellicose arms
which are signs of an insane fury
but hoping to get their provisions.
Federmann begged them for peace.[25]

In this depiction, as in Federmann's text, the Guaycaries are "fieros escua-drones de desnudos" (brave troops of naked men) who stand quietly while their leader speaks. However, unlike Federmann's narrative, Castellanos's text casts Federmann as a "buen alemán, que sagaz era" (good wise German) who escapes the armed and furious Indians. That said, he asks to make peace with them because he has an ulterior motive: "Pero con pretension de sus provechos / Ruégales con la paz el Fedrimano" (but hoping to get their provisions / Federmann begged them for peace). Later, Federmann's at-tempts at peacekeeping fail and the "good Nicholas" (*buen Nicolao*) tells his men that the day has come to show the infidels the glory of God. Castella-nos's Federmann tells his men: "¡Ea, señores, que la gloria es nuestra, / Y este de que gozamos es el dia/ Para que deis á indios clara muestra / De la fuerza, vigor y valentía / De que Dios ha dotado vuestra diestra" (Hail, gentlemen, the glory is ours! / and this which we enjoy is the day / so that you will clearly show the Indians / the force, vigor, and courage / which God has given you) (194). We see that Castellanos's portrayal of Federmann and other German leaders foregrounds a belief in divine providence: the Spanish imperial project of conquest is the will of God. The battle ends with many "bárbaras gentes" (barbarous peoples) killed and many Spaniards hurt. They again encounter "indios de mal arte" (bad Indians) whom they fight. In an instructive passage Castellanos describes Federmann's tactics.

> A los restantes hacen los peones
> Que viesen luego miserables fines,
> Pues el cacique solo quedó vivo,
> El cual del Arteaga fué captivo. (195)

> From the rest of the Indians, porters they make,
> Who would see miserable ends.
> As such only the cacique remained alive
> Who became the prisoner of Arteaga.

Here Castellanos sheds light on the treatment of the enslaved Indian porters. None of the men taken survived, with the exception of the cacique, who became Arteaga's prisoner. Again, there is no distinction between the German and Spanish troops: whereas Castellanos recognizes Federmann's work as captain, the Spanish Arteaga will have the cacique as a prisoner. Castellanos's representation of the Indian porters suggests that their death is certain under Federmann, but the poet does not lament Federmann's ruthlessness. He exculpates Federmann by claiming he initially offered peace and only unleashed violence on the tribes that do not accept his offer. He also states that Federmann pillages and attacks so that he may continue to discover new lands, just as Federmann had described his own actions in the *Indianische Historia*.

> Después de los encuentros sucedidos,
> A Haricagua guian sus pisadas,
> Adonde fueron todos recebidos
> Como de gentes atemorizadas;
> Y de aquella provincia despedidos,
> Apaciguando gentes alteradas,

Procuran ya por paz, ó ya por guerra,
Descubrir mas secretos de la tierra. (195)

———

After the encounters that have been recounted
their footsteps led to Haricagua
and from that province they were expelled
pacifying angry peoples,
procuring through peace or through war
to discover more secrets of the land.

Natives are collateral damage and Federmann's goals reasonable. Castellanos uses vocabulary such as "caudillo de salvajes" (caudillo of savages) and
"bárbaros compuestos" (composed barbarians) that reveal his view of their
inferiority (195). In one of the most interesting passages, Federmann and his
men encounter a town of *chipas*; they are "gente brava, feroz y carnicera" (a
ferocious and bloodthirsty people) and invite them to eat meat they have
just roasted. In a chilling passage, Castellanos explains how they realize that
they have eaten human flesh.

Carne hallan asada los cristianos:
Comieron sin que sepan de quién era;
Mas ojos propios los hicieron ciertos,
Hallando piés y manos de hombres muertos.
Luego vereis estar imaginando:
Unos que ven y no quieren creello,
Otros en otra parte basqueando,
Otros para bosar mover el cuello,
Otros meter los dedos para ello,
Otros quisieran con aquellas sañas
Abrirse con sus manos las entrañas. (196)

———

Meat the Christians found roasted
Without knowing from whom it came
But their eyes made it a fact
Finding the feet and hands of dead men.
Afterwards you think you are imagining.
Some see it and do not want to believe it

Others in another part heaving,
Others moving their necks to vomit
Others inserting their fingers for that purpose
Others would wish with such exasperation to
Open with their hands their entrails.

Federmann's narrative does not mention this sensationalist cannibalistic episode that conveys the inherent disgust and taboo of eating human flesh to Christians, a trope of conquest narratives. Castellanos uses this episode to universalize the experience of the European Christian in light of the Amerindian Other. Federmann participates in the project of conquest: he makes peace and war, experiences hunger, and feels the ultimate disgust at their own consumption of human flesh. Ultimately, Castellanos was one of the few chroniclers who saw the Germans not as Lutherans but as united with their Spanish comrades, eager to gain glory for the Spanish crown.[26]

In Castellanos's crónica, the Germans and Spaniards suffered together and reaped the benefits of their conquest together. This perspective, which favors the unity of the imperial European force against the barbaric Other, underscores the European, civilized nature of the Conquest. Perhaps it was Castellanos's dynastic impulse that allowed him to embrace a pan-European perspective. As I show below, this account in rhyme is a eulogy for the Spanish Habsburgs and the Welsers, unlike the ecclesiastical crónica authored by fray Pedro de Aguado.

FRAY PEDRO DE AGUADO'S MORAL HISTORY

Pedro de Aguado (1513 or 1538–ca. 1600), a Franciscan friar, has been called the forgotten cronista of Venezuela and Nueva Granada. Around 1581, after spending fifteen years in the region, he produced a manuscript called the *Recopilación Historial de Venezuela* (Historical Anthology of Venezuela and Nueva Granada). The *Recopilación* is divided into two volumes, one on Nueva Granada, the other on Venezuela. Evidence suggests that fray Antonio Medrano, who accompanied Gonzalo Jiménez de Quesada on his search for El Dorado, compiled the dates and facts for this historical project, and Friede (1964, 180) suggests Medrano may have written the complete manuscript.[27] In any case, after Medrano's death during Quesada's expedition, around 1569, Aguado continued the project, as he states in his introduction (1987, 8). Aguado did not find a publisher for the volume after he returned to Spain, though he received permission to publish it in 1582 (Friede 1964, 196). The manuscript remained "lost" for many years; however, many crónistas apparently read parts of it, including El Inca, Garcilaso de la Vega, who saw it at a printer's shop in Córdoba, and Antonio León Pinelo, who lists the manuscript as part of his library in 1629. The manuscript was recovered, albeit with words blotted out, in the nineteenth century by the Spanish historian Joaquín Acosta in the Real Academia de Historia in Madrid; it would not be published until about fifty years later (Friede 1964, 197). The Nueva Granada volume was first published in Bogotá in 1906 (ed. Posada and Ibañez). The volume devoted to Venezuela appeared in 1913, published under the government of the dictator Juan Vicente Gómez.[28] Between 1916 and 1918 the Spanish historian Jerónimo Bécker published the complete manuscript in four volumes.[29]

The structure of the *Recopilación* follows that of other crónicas: there is a prologue, a dedication to King Philip II, a notice to the reader, and the king's publishing license. The dedication states that Aguado's goal was not to seek fame but rather to explain what he had "seen with his eyes and touched with his hands."[30] He also calls himself a Christian and faithful servant of His Majesty

> because in the course of fifteen years—the best of my life, that I was employed in the preaching and conversion of the idolaters, who lived like beasts in the New Kingdom of those Indies in the service of the devil, I understood through the decrees issued by His Majesty the Catholic zeal of the benefit/profit and conversion of those souls.[31]

Aguado's intention to convert Indians fit ideologically with the aims of King Philip II, who ruled Spain from 1556 to 1598, after his father, Charles, had abdicated, and of the ecclesiastical authorities, as it would end in the "the multiplication of the Christians and the growth of the Church."[32] Aguado interpreted and critiqued the colonization of the province of Venezuela, the administration of the Welsers, and the barbarity of the Indians from a Catholic Franciscan perspective. According to Jaime Humberto Borja Gómez (2002, 16), Aguado exemplifies both a Franciscan tradition that promoted the evangelization of the world's peoples and the written description of these places and peoples. Yet, just as the influence of classical rhetoric and scripture informed the Franciscan view of the world, so did medieval notions of the Other when Franciscans considered the "savagery" of native Amerindians (31–34).

Aguado describes Charles V's concession of the province of Venezuela to the Welser Company amid the ferment of the Reformation and the Diet of Worms in 1521 in a negative light. His depiction of the Welser administration relates to his criticisms of the policies of Emperor Charles V, in his role as Charles I, king of Spain, because they favored European rather than pressing Spanish problems. The emperor addressed the followers of Martin Luther and the fermenting Reformation movement at the Diet. As Aguado explained, Charles had come back from Germany

> where he had been for a few days procuring and extinguishing the harmful sparks and broiling flames that Luther, the year before 1521, had spilled and planted among those peoples, and his arrival [in Spain] took to matter all of the administrative tasks of the Spanish, who had been uneasy, because of the Communities and the conflicts that in the same year of 21 had been engendered within them, because of the oppressions and harm that certain foreign governors appointed by the Emperor had done.[33]

After applauding the emperor for labeling Martin Luther a heretic, forbidding public support for Luther, and putting a bounty on Luther's head, Aguado criticized the emperor's policy in regard to national affairs and the Guerra de Comunidades, known also as the Revolt of the Comuneros, which began in 1519 and ended in April 1521. The first modern rebellion in European history, it protested, among many things, foreign rule.[34]

Aguado, writing soon after the Welsers had been expelled from Venezuela, explains that the emperor conceded the territory of Venezuela to the Welsers due to Spain's "lack of funds" (Aguado 1987, 30). He describes the Welsers as famous because of "the important trade contracts that they had in many parts of the world."[35] According to Aguado, they proposed their plan to govern the Venezuelan territory to Charles after they heard about the legendary riches of the land; like Fernández de Oviedo and Las Casas, he emphasized Welser greed. Aguado's status as a Franciscan made him especially sensitive to the possible heresy of the Germans. In hindsight, he also suggested that Charles should have been more cautious about backing foreign governance. To Aguado, foreign governance was harmful to a specifically *Spanish* Habsburg dynastic hegemony *and* to Catholic dominance over the souls of all Spain's subjects. The threat of heresy and of Luther's beliefs fully took shape in Aguado's recommendation regarding the future spiritual and tactical conquest and colonization of the Indies.

German greed is dangerous, but in the preface Aguado suggests that Spanish Castilian greed is not. Hoping to recruit possible colonists, he advertises the riches found in the New World (precious stones, emeralds, gold), concluding, "I have said all of this for those that I will not be able to convince to go to those lands with the desire to convert the infidels, and so that they may go because of a desire for riches."[36] Castilian greed, for lack of a better word, is good because it will attract colonists who will convert the Indians. Aguado's loyalties are clear in his prologue as he emphasizes the importance of the heroic work of so many Spaniards in the Indies: "the very heroic deeds and works of our Spaniards that should not be forgotten" and "the hard work, hunger and deaths that our Spaniards suffered."[37]

Aguado's motivations for writing this history, as he explains in the dedication, are his love for his nation and empire, his willingness to become part of a canon of moral history writing, and to save souls from the grasp of the devil (Aguado 1987, 6–7). Anticipating critiques of his ecclesiastical authority, he states that it is precisely his cleric's habit and his daily work saving souls in a land of idolatry that grants him the license to write. Aguado's personification of the nation (*patria*) that, like a mother (*como madre*), attempts to save America's Indigenous peoples' souls, fuels his writing (6). Aguado also uses the metaphor of the Church as Mother when he refers to Medrano, whom he describes as his coeditor of the *Recopilaciones*, stating that Medrano had accompanied Jiménez de Quesada through the Nuevo Reyno to El Dorado to convert souls "and give our Church, our mother, new children."[38] Like Medrano, Aguado casts himself as the son of Spain and the church who procures more "children" for the church and fights for Spanish interests and categorizes anything that harms these institutions as a threat to his two mothers; unsurprisingly, the Welsers, or Belzares, upset this hegemony.

In the abstract of the Venezuela volume, Aguado discusses Nikolaus Federmann, "from whom the permits were revoked because of complaints made about him."[39] The first chapter of this volume depicts Federmann as calculating, albeit well spoken and well mannered, saying that he gave the Welsers some gold pieces to convince them to allow him to govern the province of Venezuela for them.[40] He writes that "Federmann's speech and luck" impressed the Welsers, "as he was great and from their own nation, and the good order and appearance that he gave in the government of that land."[41] Aguado writes that Federmann had competitors who described him as "rowdy and uncongenial," charging that he "mistreated his soldiers with abusive words, and that all of the people in the governance abhorred him because of his strange and insufferable words, and that the same thing would occur to those he took with him."[42] Yet Aguado appears sympathetic to Federmann, portraying his detractors as unfair. He highlights Federmann's camaraderie with Jorge Espira (Georg Hohermuth von Speyer), the German leader whom the Spanish authorities ultimately appointed to govern the province, with Federmann as his lieutenant governor. Given his approval of the Spanish authorities' decision, the statement that "there was never any type of discord between them" suggests this approval extends to Federmann, although he attributes their accord to the fact that the length of the western Venezuelan coast meant they could make inland expeditions without encountering each other.[43]

Though Aguado is partial to the Spanish Catholic empire, he sees the Germans as devout leaders rather than heretics. This becomes evident when he attributes the near-destruction of the ships on Federmann's second voyage in 1533, with Georg Hohermuth von Speyer (here referred to as Speyer or Spire), to one of the ship's passenger's sin of sodomy, which had invoked the wrath of God. Here Aguado's biblical textual support firmly roots him as a cleric and crónica author who views history through the prism of Christian morality; he writes about what he sees and hears following the tradition of the chronicle writer, but he also includes judgments about what is right and wrong in the eyes of a Christian God. The captains—Federmann and Speyer—find out after the crew lands at Cadiz that there are queer sexual practices among the crew.[44] In stating that they are "punished and burned in concordance with the laws of the Kingdom for their homosexuality," Aguado depicts the Germans as orthodox.[45] His Federmann acts as any model Spaniard would. Thus, while the episode could be read as suggesting a moral taint on the expedition, it actually depicts Federmann in a positive light and confirms the judgment and mercy of God.

The first chapter ends with Aguado explicitly acknowledging that the incident involving the sexual transgressions of the sodomite was a digression. It is his goal to write the history of the discovery and settlement of the Indies and not history outside the empire of the Indies, but as his next book will recount Speyer's and Federmann's respective expeditions "it seemed to me that I should consider [the history's] beginnings, to have more clarity than I have now, to write in this history about those who are travelers to the Indies."[46] This is the first crónica to elucidate why it is important to discuss the history of the charter with the Welsers as well as Spanish portrayals of the German expeditions. He devotes much of the two volumes to the Welser period.

Speyer's and Federmann's expeditions are of interest to Aguado primarily as ways to remember the illustrious origins of the *Spanish* gentlemen who accompanied them, and this genealogy would be spotlighted in the twentieth century. A footnote by Jerónimo Bécker in his 1916 edition of Aguado expounds on what the Welser colonization of Venezuela means for Spanish and, perhaps, Venezuelan historiographers in the twentieth century with a list of the illustrious Spaniards who took part in the Welser expeditions and their noble descendants who went on to become the elite of Venezuelan Spanish creole society.[47] For example, Francisco de Graterol literally was the "tronco de ilustres familias" (tree trunk of good families). There is no mention here of German conquerors who were the illustrious forefathers from which elite Venezuelan families originated.

Interestingly, in his early twentieth-century reading, Bécker depicts the original Spanish colonizers as soldiers who participated in a worthy expansionist Habsburg imperial project. He writes:

> Damián del Barrio, natural from the Kingdom of Granada, whose services in America corresponded to those that he had performed beforehand, having found himself in the memorable battle of Pavia, in the sacking of Rome with the duke of Bourbon, and other famous events of the utmost importance in that time; the Parras and Castillos from Barquicimeto; the Silvas from this city of Santiago [Caracas], and other illustrious families in the province descend from this gentleman.[48]

In this passage Damián del Barrio's past exploits in the business of the Habsburg Empire, including the battle of Pavia (in which the French were defeated) and the sacking of Rome (by underpaid imperial troops that included many Germans) point to a strategic conceptualization of conquest, one in line with imperial modes of conquest in Europe and abroad; from this "illustrious" man descended the very best Venezuelan families. Del Barrio's famous deeds define him as a subject and warrior for the Holy Roman Empire and not just as a Castilian or *extremeño* from the Spanish kingdom.

JOSÉ DE OVIEDO Y BAÑOS: CRIOLLO
CONSCIOUSNESS AND THE TROPE OF
ROMANTIC CONQUEST

While Férnandez de Oviedo, Las Casas, Castellanos, and Aguado wrote under the shadow of Habsburg and Welser power, in the eighteenth century, overlapping with the War of the Spanish Succession (1701–14), which would lead to the takeover of Spain by the French Bourbons, José de Oviedo y Baños would expound a Venezuelan *criollo* (creole) national consciousness against Bourbon Spain. Oviedo y Baños can be credited with planting the roots of a Venezuelan national consciousness in his *Historia de la conquista y población de la provincia de Venezuela*, which he wrote between 1705 and 1723 and which historicized the colonization of the province of Venezuela from its conquest to 1600. Oviedo y Baños remains a crucial *crónista* because he frames the history of the province of Venezuela, where he was born and lived, through a perspective both peninsular and European.

The text, with its singular geographic subject, also remains rooted in an incipient Venezuelan national consciousness. As a Spanish criollo (born in the Indies to Spanish parents), Oviedo y Baños raises the question of the social struggle between the peninsular Spaniards born in Spain and the members of the creole class born and raised in the Indies who considered themselves to be, at the beginning, as Spanish as the former. Yet the favoring of peninsular Spaniards over Spanish creoles for posts in the colonial administration would lead to a criollo identity crisis, which, in turn, was the germ of a growing national consciousness and ultimately of the battle for independence. In fact, a second part of the *Historia* leading up to the 1700s was supposed to have been written but has never appeared and has become a legend. As the late Argentinian Venezuelan writers and critics Tomás Eloy Martínez and Susanna Rotker suggested in their introduction to the 1987 edition, Spanish creoles could not escape the identity of the continent where they lived: "The place that engendered them ends up condemning them, canceling any privileges gained by conquest or inheritance. 'Climate' becomes more important than 'race,' or, as it was said in the nineteenth century, geography comes before history."[49] That is, being born in the Indies transformed the colonial master into a weaker copy of his peninsular European self. This in Venezuela, a colonial provincial backwater of Spain subject to illicit trade and covert commerce, as Jesse Cromwell (2018) has argued.

Perhaps seeking to dispute the claim that the tropics forced Europeans such as himself to go native, Oviedo y Baños portrays examples of subversion, such as accounts of the Welsers, the tyrant Aguirre, and the rebellion of the *cimarrón* (maroon) Negro Miguel, in a narrative style that pictures them as "imaginary" (Oviedo y Baños 1987, xxvii).[50] This constitutes an attempt to construct a genealogy free of foreigners and subversive individuals: the Welsers, with their problematic German and Lutheran origins, threatened Spanish hegemony in the colonies. Subversive slaves such as Miguel, who escaped his master and founded a community of fugitives modeled on the Spanish monarchical system, directly contested the Spanish monarchy and the system of slavery. Declaring himself king along with his black queen in the Buria Mountains, he ruled a community of 150 Amerindians and fugitive African slaves before colonial forces killed him. His reign began in 1552 and lasted until sometime between 1553 and 1555. The Tyrant, or *Tirano*, Aguirre overthrew his captain, don Pedro de Ursúa, on an expedition on the Amazon River, then wrote to Philip II, declaring war on Spain and claiming to be prince of Peru, Tierra Firme, and the Indies. Aguirre was finally killed and quartered outside of El Tocuyo in the province of Venezuela, the same site where the Welser agents Bartholomäus Welser VI and Philipp von Hutten, as well as the Spaniard Juan Carvajal, would lose their heads. These three subversive acts marked Venezuela as a place of lawlessness in need of control.

According to Martínez and Rotker, not only did subversive agents meet their death on Venezuelan soil, but the narration of those events conformed with an antisubversive stance; hence they argue that Oviedo y Baños wrote about Miguel and Aguirre "from the viewpoint of bloody madness and farce."

It would not be credible [to his readers] (or admissible to the censors who could have vetoed all stories about the colonists' subversions in America if the narration of these had not immediately condemned such actions) that a kingdom would be created parallel to the Spanish model and less so under the rule of a slave or a heretic.[51]

In addition, Oviedo y Baños had to demonstrate that white creoles came from the best peninsular white genealogies without any trace of Moorish, Jewish, or subversive blood (Martínez and Rotker 1992, xxviii). Whitewashing a "criollo" Venezuelan history meant that Afro-Venezuelan discourses were silenced.[52] Attributing excesses and bad behavior to the Welsers in the first part of his history advances that project. Martínez and Rotker contend that Oviedo y Baños describes the contract signed between the Welsers and Emperor Charles V as a transaction that results in senseless destruction of the province.

> The matter concerns a loan or a purchase, not an inherited or contested fact. Because the origin is only a trace, the end cannot be anything other than destruction: the Germans who arrive in the Venezuelan province do not settle anywhere and decide, rather, to pillage and plunder. They disembark, plunder, and leave (without piety or compassion to stop them). That is, they plundered without settlement, marking the origin of the province with the sign of the foreigner, of the nomad, the one who does not love.[53]

In Martínez and Rotker's (1992) critique of the *The Conquest and Settlement of Venezuela*, the Germans shape the conquest of the country; Venezuela is a place to be plundered and pillaged but not settled. While the very act of conquest leaves the foreign mark of the conqueror on the conquered people and land, the dual Spanish-German venture makes the Venezuelan province a unique example of unhinged violence.

In Oviedo y Baños's leisurely writing style, failures and victories appear as one and the same. Paradise is never reached, even when the German explorers can almost see it: "It is what occurs with Alfinger, Speyer, with Federmann: their infinite delay of the conquest of El Dorado, in what seems to be an unusual preconception of Kafka's nightmares."[54]

To Oviedo y Baños, the Germans, who thought of colonization as a "mercantile" project, were never meant to settle the Venezuelan province.

> Enrique de Alfinger and Jerónimo Sailler, German agents of the Welsers, were at that time present at the Court of our Emperor Charles V. The Welsers were esteemed everywhere in Europe as members of a famous company that several merchants had formed in order to trade in large volume and to engage in enterprises throughout the world. Learning of the considerable profits which Coriana and its coasts were enjoying through trade, Alfinger and Sailler surmised that it would be advantageous to their company to acquire the region for its sole benefit. They therefore asked the emperor to lease it to them. (1987, 15)[55]

Oviedo y Baños sees greed as the reason the Welsers actively sought the Venezuela governance. His emphasis on the Welsers' mercantilism underscored the political and economic interplay of powerful entities negotiating the exploitation of the New World. The narrative continues: "as the emperor had benefitted from the Welsers' money through loans for military purposes, it was not difficult for them to attain their aspirations" (1987, 15).[56]

Oviedo y Baños's narration of the Welser exploits follows a chronological order, highlighting Alfinger's and Federmann's "foreignness." Yet while Alfinger is the perpetrator of violent conquest on the territory and its people, Federmann is represented as a victim of libel. For example, he portrays the first German governor, Alfinger, as an opportunist, thus paving the way for his recurring critique of the Germans as exploiters: "Alfinger took office as governor, but his concern and those of the Germans who succeeded him were never directed toward the development of the province but rather toward reaping benefits from it while the opportunity lasted" (1987, 16).[57] Oviedo y Baños emphasizes that during his rule and on his expedition, Alfinger's men plundered the land, to the distress of the Amerindians living on the banks of Lake Maracaibo.[58] He focuses on the Germans' sacking and pillaging in a corner of the empire that could not appeal for help to the administration. Alfinger's conquest of Lake Maracaibo fails: "From this ill-conceived plan, perpetuated by the Germans who succeeded him, his own perdition and the total ruin of this province resulted" (1987, 18).[59] Oviedo y Baños highlights the futility of conquest in the sixteenth century and the destruction wrought by Alfinger's soldiers.

His soldiers now realized that there was no intention of settling any-
where, that they had nothing to hope for as the fruits of their labors,
and that they were to have only what they could seize. *Undeterred by
compassion*, they laid waste to delightful provinces, destroying the benefits that might have made them secure in the possession of fertile lands
for themselves and their descendants if they had settled along the routes
they explored. However, the Germans, as foreigners, foresaw that control of the province could not long endure for them, and thus they gave
more heed to immediate gains than to future benefits that might be
obtained by initial moderation. (1987, 18; my emphasis)[60]

The emphasis on "foreignness" and lack of compassion, along with an appetite for destruction, characterizes Oviedo y Baños's account of the first expedition by the Welser governors. The Spaniards became "natives" compared
to the German foreigners. "Like unhinged furies," he writes, "they razed and
destroyed [everything]," including the fertile land.[61] As Karen Stolley has
related in *Domesticating Empire: Enlightenment in Spanish America* (2013),
Oviedo y Baños used the Welsers as a way to exemplify the tension between
conquest and settlement that is at the center of Venezuelan historiography's recounting of the Welser episode. Stolley ponders, "Perhaps a nascent
sense of local, or criollo, identity leads to his rejection of the Welsers as
'foreign'" (18).

Oviedo y Baños portrays the Germans as fiery in their passion for de-
struction. There is an intertextual element that also references Las Casas, as
Stolley (2013, 24) has also noted. Oviedo y Baños's portrayals of Alfinger,
Federmann, Speyer, and Hutten reveal that he admires individual qualities
of each respective commander but ultimately despises the whole German
venture. For Stolley (2013, 20), Oviedo y Baños is "ambiguous" concerning
Philipp von Hutten but labels Georg Hohermuth von Speyer an "anti-hero";
Oviedo y Baños gives Hutten's failed El Dorado expedition as an example of
how "the Welsers squandered human resources in their heedless pursuit of
El Dorado" (Stolley 2013, 23).

The Germans' greed and ravenous nature here resembles Las Casas's
account of them. Alfinger, for example, has a "harsh nature" and an impa-
tient desire for profit: "he still had ardent ambitions to gain riches as quickly
as possible without considering whether the methods used were just or
unjust" (Oviedo y Baños 1987, 16–18).[62] But, similarly to Aguado, he writes
kindly of Federmann.

A man of high ideals and a German by birth, Federmann, who was wealthy, had a close friendship with the Welsers, which encouraged him to seek the position of governor. He therefore embarked for Spain on the first passage available, well provided with money of his own and with some friends. He presented his position at Court with such skill that the Welsers' agents readily agreed to confer the office on him. (Oviedo y Baños 1987, 28)[63]

Oviedo y Baños makes less than Aguado does of the attacks on Federmann's character that followed but is equally unequivocal, writing that Federmann's detractors "imputed to him a harsh character, bellicose spirit, haughty nature and arrogant heart. On the contrary, these were the attributes most alien to him, he being endowed with an affable nature, affectionate speech, compassionate heart and calm spirit" (1987, 28).[64] Diverging from Aguado's treatment of Federmann, Oviedo y Baños's narrative turns Federmann from perpetrator into a victim: the Spaniards are jealous of his power and seek to impede his progress in Coro. Oviedo y Baños presents Federmann as a model conqueror, whose ability to impress the Spanish court absolves him of any taint of being German.

Oviedo y Baños again mentions Federmann's benevolent spirit when he recounts his 1538 entrada through the provinces. Federmann arrived in a town whose inhabitants fled despite initially showing him friendship and hospitality. As I discussed in chapter 3, Federmann at best practiced thinly veiled extortion in this case; his demands of gifts of gold, food, slaves, and women from his supposed friends were premeditated ruses. Oviedo y Baños sees it differently, however; he writes that Federmann was "sentido" (offended) at the Indians' deceptions and orders his soldiers to follow them, but his men turn to pillaging the abandoned huts. Thus Oviedo y Baños masterfully contrasts the soldier's shameful actions to their commander's modest and well-intended nature.

On observing their actions, Federmann, gazing steadily at them, shouted wrathfully: "Oh, soldiers, how little shame you have!" Since in the *affable* nature of that man his troops *had never detected any anger,* those words astonished them to such a degree that they named the town Poca-Vergüenza (Little Shame). (1987, 53; my emphasis)[65]

Federmann remains calm and composed, even in his legitimate wrath. His speech is performative in various ways. First, Federmann's command is disobeyed, and instead of pursuing the Indians, his soldiers pursue material goods. Second, Federmann's anger at the soldiers' (in)action results in his didactic words. And third, these words brand the soldiers and the episode as an embarassing local memory as the town is named Poca-Vergüenza, or Little Shame.

Oviedo y Baños gives Federmann an honorable elegy.

> Federmann, who deserves to be remembered among the most laudable heroes of his time reached the end of his life. Born in the Swabian circle in Upper Germany, the red-haired, fair-skinned general was handsome and affable, and his brave deeds and singular bravery brought him much fame in only a few years. Although the malice of his rivals led them to attribute his generosity of spirit to pride, his military inclination to anxiety, and his courtly behavior to exaggerated caution, there is no doubt that the gifts with which nature endowed him were singular. Had he not allowed himself to be deluded by an excessive desire for independent command, even the most prying could not have found any defect to record him. (1987, 59)[66]

Oviedo y Baños approves of Federmann's actions, but he finds problems with Federmann's antiauthoritarian nature. His elegy focuses on physical presence, skill as a warrior and commander, and character: the observations on Federmann's fair skin and red hair would suggest that Oviedo y Baños prizes Federmann's German ethnicity. However, Federmann's rebellious character becomes problematic and ultimately endangers the success of the Welsers.

Oviedo y Baños presents Hutten in a far different way. He introduces him as "a relative of the Welsers, Felipe de Utre, a prudent young German" (1987, 64).[67] Hutten (Utre) was "so mild and artless" (1987, 80) that Carvajal led him astray.[68] Oviedo y Baños declares solemnly of Hutten's execution by Carvajal that he is "certainly worthy of a better fate. This native of the city of [Speyer], Germany, carried away by youthful ardor, had crossed to America where he constantly manifested his prudence and courage" (1987, 82).[69] While Federmann was subject to slanderous gossip, Hutten's youth, prudence, and modesty result in his own murder. Oviedo y Baños clearly applauds Hutten's desire for fame, praising him, stating he was certainly worthy of a better fate (1987, 82). Oviedo y Baños's account characterizes Hutten as the kindest, least war-minded of the Welser rulers: "Desire for approbation, more than a longing for riches, impelled him to search for El Dorado. . . . No captain of all those who served in the Indies bloodied his sword less (1987, 82).[70] But this is not praise: whereas Alfinger used his sword too much and Federmann used it just the right amount, Hutten used it too little. According to Oviedo y Baños, he was the conquistador who traversed the most provinces and who waged war the least (1987, 82). He lacked Federmann's acumen for the business of conquest.

In spite of his praise for the personal qualities of Federmann and Hutten, Oviedo y Baños, like Las Casas, is adamant about the destructive effect of German rule on the Venezuelan province. In his telling, Juan Pérez de Tolosa's arrival marks the end of a rather unpleasant period in Venezuelan history, a history marred by the effect of foreign (German) rule.

> The Welsers had been divested of their administration because of re-peated complaints that reached His Majesty of irreparable abuses by the Germans. These grievances were so numerous that Friar Bartolomé de las Casas, in his book *Destrucción de las Indias*, justly describes this province as miserable and hapless. If it had not been subject to foreign domination for eighteen years, it would have been one of the most opulent in America. Its vast extent, fertile land, benign climate, abun-dant waters, convenient port, and multitude of Indian inhabitants as-sured that it would have had no equal. Still, the Germans looked upon it without love, considering it simply a thing on lease. Nor did they try to preserve measures they were taking that might destroy it. Without settling the beautiful country they discovered, they took all with blood and fire; and there was nothing to which they did not lay waste. As the enslavement of the wretched Indians was the principal source of their profit, they captured the natives by the thousands to sell to merchants who flocked to Coro, drawn by the enticement of this enterprise. The result of this trade was that most of the province was depopulated because the Indians deserted their towns for the interior of the Llanos. There they have remained until this day, resulting in the loss to the Crown of many vassals and to the Church, many souls. (1987, 85)[71]

I quote this passage at length because it is a rich diatribe, bordering on xenophobic complaint, on the many faults that the Spanish found with the Welser governance. It is a condemnation of the Germans' nomadism and ethnicity. The use of phrases such as "por haber privado" (for having divested) the administration of their possession suggests that Oviedo y Baños sees the Welsers as depriving the Spanish colonists of their profits. In his view Welser rule ends with "irreparables daños, tiranías y desordenes" (irreparable destruction, tyrannies, and disorder) that color the scene as one of political and physical chaos. In addition, here Oviedo y Baños *directly* references Las Casas's portrayal of the German impact on the "infeliz y desgraciada" (unhappy and disgraced) province, which would have been extremely opulent if it had not been subjected to the "desdicha" (misfortune) of "dominio extranjero" (foreign rule). His charge that the Germans saw the land without love suggests an almost romantic notion of what possession should mean for a conquistador. It is the whoredom of the land that bothers Oviedo y Baños. Not only did the Welsers' see the land "sin amor," but they considered it "una cosa prestada" (a borrowed thing). They showed no respect for their bride and her reproduction ("aumento"); rather, they used her: "pues sólo tiraron a aprovecharse mientras duraba la ocasión" (they only took advantage of her while the opportunity lasted). The land, raped and ravaged under the Germans, who, like "fieras desatadas" (unhinged beasts), destroyed everything in "sangre y fuego" (blood and fire). Within this violence, they seek to extend their benefit of the land by selling her children in the slave market: "el interés principal de su ganacia lo tenía afianzado su codicia en la esclavitud de los miserables indios" (the principal benefit of their profits were secured in their avarice in the slavery of the miserable Indians). For the author, it is ultimately the Welsers who are guilty of a racialized merchant capitalism at the expense of Spanish settlement. Finally, Oviedo y Baños argues that despite good leaders such as Federmann, the Welser period compromised the "Spanish" nature of the conquest and destroys Spanish colonization and evangelization efforts.

Historical colonial texts recount the exploits of Welser governors through the chronicle and poetic genres. All writers mentioned here recycle themes, facts, histories, and motifs. Fray Pedro Simón copied fray Pedro Aguado (who may have taken credit for Antonio Medrano); Oviedo y Baños uses Las Casas's conquest tropes as well as his incendiary language; Castellanos receives poetic inspiration from the Italian Renaissance. The crónicas that I analyzed in this chapter convey diverging viewpoints on the Welser governance of Venezuela: Fernández de Oviedo and Castellanos elegize individual leaders to the point of including the Germans in Spanish history. Ecclesiastical accounts such as those of Pedro de Aguado do not take the Welsers for Lutherans, despite evidence in royal cedularios that mandate the policing of possible Lutheran activities in the Indies. Although separated by a few hundred years, Las Casas and Oviedo y Baños are the most vehement critics of the Germans. Following Las Casas, Oviedo y Baños desired to build a genealogy free of "foreigners" and as such portrays the Welsers as the most vicious group of colonizers. Still his work planted an incipient seed of a Venezuelan criollo national consciousness that he saw as at odds with a Venezuelan German colonial history.

In different historical genres the works studied in this chapter portray the anxieties that surround foreign governance of Spanish lands in the sixteenth century. Not only do they show diverging views of the value and required treatment of Amerindian labor and slaves, but, even more pointedly and prescriptively, they ostracize the Welser governors as Lutherans. As we shall see in the next chapters, these interpretations resurface in subsequent historical readings of this period. Latin Americans tend to critique the Germans until the 1970s, though Las Casas continues to stand out for the harshness of his critique. Many side with the "Conquest-Settlement" debate in the title of Oviedo y Baños's work. That is, they believe that the Welsers were only there to conquer and plunder the land rather than settle it. The crónica as both a literary and a historical genre serves to cement the idea of a national literary and historical culture before the independent nation of Venezuela was created. The Welsers were remembered as the most "foreign" of conquerors in Spanish colonial literature. The next chapter shows instead how Germans forgot and remembered the Welser colony through a convenient cultural memory meant to serve the interest of empire or nationalism.

PART III

Cultural Memory of the Welser Colony
in Germany and Latin America,
Nineteenth to Twenty-First Century

CHAPTER 6

The Ghost of Welser Venezuela in
German Cultural Memory

As far as the position of the [colonial] government toward the natives
is concerned, the spirit of German humanity would certainly prevail.
The Nicobar Islanders are the legitimate but incompetent owners of
the land. They have to be protected to all intents and purposes. Their
physical and spiritual well-being has to be cared for sufficiently.

> —Franz Maurer, "Outline for the Foundation
> of a German Colony and Naval Station of the
> Nicobar Islands, April 1867"

In 1867, Franz Maurer spoke to the recently founded North German Federa-
tion about the plan to establish a permanent German colony in the Bay of
Bengal. He explained that the German government would respect Nicobar
Islanders' claim to sovereignty over their territory while providing needed
"protection" and instilling the "spirit of German humanity" in the islanders
(Maurer 2010, 9). His perspective is representative of nascent German imperial desires for a share in Europe's colonial projects before the establishment
of the German Reich in 1871. Maurer's rhetoric reveals how Enlightenment
ideology and the desire to possess colonies were conflated in the push for

German colonialism in the nineteenth century. Nostalgia for the Welser Venezuela colony would be part of that imperial impetus.

The Welser period of governance in Venezuela remained largely absent from German cultural memory for two centuries, until the nineteenth-century German Empire exhumed the memory of this long-lost Venezuelan colony. During the nineteenth century, the Welser episode became a model to emulate and was lauded as the first German colony. It served as an example of Germany's right to colonize territories not yet claimed by France and England, providing a counterargument to the idea that Germany's arrival on the colonial scene was late.

The specter of the Welser colony haunted German imperialists as they undertook colonial projects in Africa and the South Pacific, and in the Nazi State, it again became a model to emulate. The Welser colony was resurrected first to serve imperialist aims, to rectify the Spanish-driven "smear" campaign against the Welsers, and to racialize German colonization. After exploring how German colonialism has been linked to the Holocaust, and specifically how the Welser episode was historicized during the Nazi State, I argue that young Germans' attempts to decolonize streets and museums are new forms of engaging with Germany's colonial past and combating contemporary racism and anti-Semitism. They are intent on creating a new cultural memory of Germany's colonial exploits, including the place of the colonization of Venezuela by the Welsers.

Places, monuments, and media all exhibit cultural memory. Pierre Nora (1997) describes realms of memory (*lieux de mémoire*) as any ritual, institution, celebration, monument, or material that becomes entrenched as part of the memorial heritage of a community; he includes street names, La Marseillaise, the Louvre, the Colonial Exposition of 1931, the cathedral, and the *coq gaulois* as diverse creations that collectively display French cultural memory. In contrast, Aleida Assmann, in her *Shadows of Trauma*, has distinguished collective memory as being divided into individual, social, political, and cultural memory; whereas political memory relies on history, cultural memory draws from media and material culture (2016, 41). The cultural memory of the Welser colony in German literature, newspapers, parades, and street names manifests a collective desire to claim a German colonial narrative.

On the one hand, the Welser episode was used to justify the idea that imperial Germany had a legitimate right to projects of colonization. On the other hand, the failure of the Welser colony became the context for racialized proposals for the German colonization of Africa, and eventual genocide, including that of the Herero people.[1] For some Germans, the Welser colony in Venezuela became a hopeful symbol for their own utopian colonial desires. Later, after the loss of its colonies at the end of World War I, Germany continued to try to make sense of its colonial past while paving the way for the transition between the short-lived German Empire, the democratic Weimar Republic, and the Nationalist Socialist state.

After Germany's defeat in World War I, the 1919 Treaty of Versailles imposed significant territorial restrictions on Germany, including the return of Alsace-Lorraine to France and the allocation of parts of its European and African territories to Belgium, Denmark, Lithuania, Poland, and Czechoslovakia. Germany lost 13 percent of its European territory and one-tenth of its population.[2] This national loss led postwar writers to continue the project of remembering the Welser period as part of an ethnic German national identity.[3] Historians and novelists writing in Nazi Germany from 1938 to 1944 interpreted the Welser period in a manner that facilitated the image of Aryan conquistadors planting the seed of German nationhood on the American continent. The Welser governors and lieutenant governors who reappeared in German literary and historical works were the same characters that many Spanish works reviled: Ambrosius Alfinger (also referred to as Dalfinger in Spanish sources), Nikolaus Federmann, Bartholomäus Sailer, Georg von Speyer (Jorge de Spira), Heinrich Rembolt, Philipp von Hutten, and Bartholomäus Welser VI (the Younger). Their Spanish "antagonists" also reappear, including Las Casas, whose negative account of the Welsers was seen as a smear job.

EMPIRE, ENLIGHTENMENT, AND RACISM

Anxiety around empire, magnified by the failure of the Welser colony, fueled German nostalgia for the Welser colony in Venezuela. Some eager imperialists even reinterpreted the colony as a successful German colonial venture. The Welser colony is among several imperial colonial projects in the early modern period by small German states and merchants, all of which historians of German colonialism have understudied. I am not the first to identify this lacuna. Arthur J. Knoll and Hermann Hiery (2010, 155) insist that no description of German imperialism can begin without mentioning the Welsers and the rulers of Courland. Nineteenth-century German imperialists celebrated the Courland colonization of Tobago in the Caribbean (1654–59, 1669–89) and the "Brandenburger Gold Coast" (Groß Friedrichsburg) (1683–1717) colony in present-day Ghana.[4] Most of the material interest in the German colonies in the nineteenth century emanated from revolutionaries and intellectuals such as the Follen brothers, Julius Fröbel, and Ferdinand Lasalle. Their thirst for unity and pan-Germanness drove their desire for a workers' solution to colonial expansion (Knoll and Hiery 2010, 157). In a sense the 1848 revolutions, which called for a spirit of pan-Germanness and unity, were predecessors of the establishment of German empire (159). Yet after the 1848 March Revolution, the question of "expansion" was first relegated to the unification of a German nation and then expansion within the European continent.[5] As Knoll and Hiery suggest, the aggressive gesture to build empire through the Austro-Prussian War might have reflected a German inferiority complex resulting from the delay of Germany's globalization (159).

Writing at the end of the nineteenth century, the German geographer, historian, and map cataloger for the Royal Library of Dresden, Viktor Hantzsch, retraced the steps of adventurers, travelers, and conquerors in a popular volume, *Deutsche Reisende des XVI Jahrhunderts* (1895). With Germany's age of expansion under way, he wrote from an imperialist and nationalist framework. Of the Welsers he wrote, "Doch bleibt ihnen der Ruhm, dass sie die ersten Deutschen waren, die nach großsartig angelegten Plänen und unter bedeutenden Opfern versuchten, unserm Volke den ihm gebührenden Anteil an den Schätzen der neuen Welt zu sichern" (Nevertheless, they retain the glory that they were the first Germans who—after magnificent planning and through significant sacrifice—sought to secure for our people their due share of the treasures of the New World) (Hantzsch 1895, 9). Hantzsch emphasizes the Welsers' "German" identity by connecting their sacrifices to his own contemporary readers, "unserm Volke." Moreover, he emphasizes that colonial Portuguese and Spanish projects benefited from "deutschem Fleiss" (German industriousness) and "deutschem Kapital" (German capital) (10). Hantzsch's attitude reflected an aggrandizement of the Welser Venezuela colony that embodied the zeal with which Germany thought about its colonial possessions during the Second Reich.

The Second Reich came to fruition after the unification of Germany in a nation-state in 1871 and the election of Wilhelm of Prussia as German emperor in 1884 (his reign ended in 1914). Colonialism reemerged during this period and lasted until the Treaty of Versailles stripped Germany of its colonies. The idea that Germany should establish colonies and that it would be different from its European predecessors held sway among Germans (Zimmerer and Perraudin 2011, 5). The fact that Germany lost its colonies soon thereafter disrupted its sense of self.

The thirst for imperial expansion occurred simultaneously with German immigration to Latin America. Venezuela's Colonia Tovar was founded in 1843 by Swabian residents. More than thirty thousand people of German ethnicity immigrated to Chile. Many Germans started to arrive in Guatemala in the mid-nineteenth century, and some would go on to form a small group of coffee barons who held large parcels of land worked by exploited Indigenous people.[6]

Analyzing the way in which Germans remembered the Welser Venezuela colony in the nineteenth century against the questions that Hannah Arendt poses in her *Origins of Totalitarianism* (1966) reveals European imperialism's ties to the Enlightenment. According to Arendt, German imperialism and race thinking became a "nationalist enterprise" after 1870, as German nationalists promoted the idea of a "common origin" as well as a Romantic notion of "natural nobility" (170). She describes racism as "the main ideological weapon of imperialistic politics" (160). In making this point, she references the Boers in South Africa and British imperialism rather than German colonialism. She explains that racism was instrumental to maintaining white rule over Blacks in South African society and that the Boers used "messianism," or the idea that they were chosen to rule, in their conflict with the Zulus. Similarly, in the resurrection of the Welsers in the nineteenth century, this "messianism," which presents Germans as innate colonizers, emerges.

During the Enlightenment, naturalists and philosophers had tried to neatly categorize everything found in the world, including peoples in the tropics.[7] Early Enlightenment thinkers such as Johann Joachim Becher (1635–82) fantasized about the benefits of colonial possession.[8] Becher was a chemist, the councillor of commerce at Vienna under Emperor Leopold I, and the acquirer of Guiana on behalf of the count of Hanau. In his book *Politischer Diskurs* (1669), he expressed his interest in uniting his humanist bent with his work with traders and merchants to found a civil society based on German mercantile interests in Brazil. Later, unification of the nation and growing prosperity would allow imperial Germany to turn those colonial fantasies into realities.

As Russell Berman (1986, 6) wrote, "Enlightenment thought is the ve-
hicle through which empire establishes domination." The efforts of German
imperialists would demonstrate civilizatory projects in action. Arguments
such as Becher's and Mauer's for the empire's expansion into colonial realms
were accompanied by debates on the world's "races,"[9] which Immanuel Kant
(1724–1804, in Prussian Königsberg) heavily influenced. Kant's 1775 work,
Of the Different Human Races (*An Announcement of Lectures in Physical
Geography in the Summer Semester 1775*), promoted the new field of anthropology to potential students at Königsberg University (known as the Alber-
tina). Kant described the "Negro" race as a "base" race and the "Amerindians"
as a "Hunnish" race that has either acclimated to its environment or actually
degenerated. Two years later, in his essay "Of the Different Human Races"
(1777), Kant expanded his theories on "manifold diversity": his race scheme
emphasizes skin color more prominently; for example, the Hunnish and the
Hinduish race now belong to an "olive-yellow race" and the "copper red"
are Amerindians living in North America (Mikkelsen 2013, 57). In short,
the legacy of the Enlightenment's universal but racist ideals was used by
empire's thirst for expansion. Ideas on "national character," "aesthetics," and
"race," originating in Enlightenment thought, permeate the racial discourse
later exploited by nineteenth-century imperialists eager to once again reap
the benefits of racialized capitalism in new colonies in Africa and the Pacific.

GERMAN NINETEENTH-CENTURY SOURCES: THE FAILURE OF THE WELSERS AND THE GERMAN EMPIRE'S COLONIAL SUCCESS

Writers of both history and historical fiction in nineteenth-century imperial
Germany looked to the strength of the Holy Roman Empire of the Middle
Ages, which they read as the first ethnically German Reich, as a model for
building an empire for the Second Reich. To do so they sought to reinvent
the history of the Welsers' Venezuela colony as a bridge to new colonial
projects and ignored other early colonial ventures. While they often had to
rely on non-German sources, including Las Casas's account, they took a
very specific, pro-German stance. Suzanne Zantop (1997, 29) describes
these reimaginings as "almost obsessive revisitings and reworkings" to create
a "foundational fiction of Germany's colonial origins. . . . In fact, the retell-

ing of the Welser story helped to circumscribe German national identity by creating a national self as colonizer." The figure of the sixteenth-century Swabian conquistador functioned as a model to emulate in future colonial enterprises, with the caveat that if the Germans had failed in Venezuela, they would not do so again in Africa.

As Hayden White (2014) acknowledges in his investigation of the philosophy of history and metahistory, history is not about the fight between "fact" and "fiction." Rather, historians wish for the discourse of history "[to] be faithful to its referent," even though it has "inherited conventions of representation that produced meaning in excess of what it literally asserted" (51). The excess of meaning in historical narrative developed into the florid literary style that became part of nineteenth-century positivist historiographical convention. To analyze this "excess" in the context of historical narrative, it is necessary to examine just how historians depicted the sixteenth-century Welser Venezuelan colony in nineteenth-century Germany.

Hantzsch was the first nineteenth-century historian who looked critically at Spanish historiography of the Welser Venezuela governance, although he was hardly impartial.[10] He writes that fin-de-siècle Germans should look back on their colonial history with pride.

> Erst neuerdings hat eine vorurteilsfreie Geschichtsschreibung, welche die vorgekommenen Grausamkeiten weder leugnet, noch beschönigen will, aber als durch die Umstände erklärt betrachtet, es dem Deutschen ermöglicht, mit Freude und Stolz auf die Pläne jener Pioniere deutscher Kultur im Lande von Klein-Venedig hinzublicken. (Hantzsch 1895, 17)

> Impartial writing of history which neither seeks to deny the atrocities that occurred nor sugarcoat them, but to view and explain them in context, has only recently made it possible for Germans to look back at the plans of those pioneers of German culture in the land of Little Venice [Venezuela] with happiness and pride.

Similarly, Hantzsch points out that the Spanish and Portuguese used practices similar to the Welsers in their conquest. Las Casas and the other cronistas, he charged, had misrepresented the Welser enterprise as "eine lange Reihe von Greuelthaten" (a long list of atrocities) (17). Focusing on Las Casas's account and arguing that most cronistas followed him, he pointed out that the Spanish crónicas portray Alfinger "als ein roher Kriegsknecht von unerhörter Grausamkeit" (as a rough mercenary of unprecedented cruelty), Federmann "als ein gewissenloser Abenteurer von grenzenloser Habsucht" (as an unscrupulous adventurer with boundless avarice), and Hohermuth "als ein gewalthätiger Landverwüster und Sklavenjäger" (as a violent destroyer of land and slave hunter). Only the mild and "gerechten" (just) Juan Aleman and the "liebenswürdigen und leutseligen" (gentle and affable) Philipp von Hutten escape Las Casas's judgment (47). Hantzsch highlights that Las Casas supported the African slave trade, suggesting that Las Casas's opposition to Amerindian slavery did not put him on the moral high ground, omitting the fact that Las Casas eventually renounced his support for any form of slavery. Hantzsch tries to contextualize the Germans' mistreatment of the natives in a new light.

> Auch lassen sich ihre Ausschreitungen wenn auch nicht entschuldigen, so doch sehr wohl erklären. Die Indianer waren keineswegs jene friedlichen Naturkinder, als welche sie Las Casas zu schildern versucht, sondern sie erschwerten den deutschen Entdeckern durch hinterlistige Überfälle, durch Wegschaffung und Vernichtung der Lebensmittel und durch den Gebrauch ihrer vergifteten Pfeile das Vordringen nach dem Innern ungemein. (48)

> Although their excesses cannot be excused, they can be explained. The Indians were not the peaceful children of nature that Las Casas portrayed; rather they greatly hindered the German discoverers' progress into the interior through deceitful attacks, through removal and destruction of food supplies, and through their use of poisoned arrows.

Hantzsch justifies German violence against the indigenous population by relabeling their resistance as malicious; hence the trope of the rebellious Indian reemerges. Their poisoned arrows, their misinformation, and their denial of food to the colonizers were justifiable grounds for their repression. Hantzsch views conquest "gegen die Heiden" (against the heathens) as "ein gottwohlgefälliges Werk" (a god-ordained work) and the slave raids as "ein berechtigter Zweig des Handelsgewerbes" (a legitimate branch of commerce) (48). He concludes that although the facts could not be excused, they could be criticized and placed in perspective. In his version, the Welser agents, including Federmann, were not conquerors intent on plundering but rather colonists favoring settler colonialism and determined to work the land and reap the benefits of "Little Venice" (or "Little Germany"). Hantzsch's underlying message is that through pride in their history of colonialism, Germans would be able to remake history in their favor.

Hantszch's account followed a spate of nineteenth-century cultural expressions in which the emphasis on a German ethnic and cultural group identity, which would become nationalist in scope, permeated accounts of the Welser Venezuela colony. Poets, historians, and novelists eulogized Welser agents. As the first German colony, the province of Venezuela became a touchstone as Germany attempted to expand its empire. For some writers, the Welser Venezuela colony became the lost paradise that nineteenth-century German colonialists sought to reconstruct in their new grand colonial ventures. The Welser colony became a colonial ur-narrative.

Adolph Seubert's 1887 poem, "Ambrosius Alfinger," is representative of this larger trend. Seubert (1819–80), himself a military colonel and commander, wrote plays and poems, including an anthology of sonnets dedicated to the heroes of Swabia, combining his love for history with imperial-colonial wanderlust and nostalgia. In "Ambrosius Alfinger" natives kill the first Welser governor, but in dying he fertilizes the virgin South American soil with his own spear and blood.

Wem haben Cortez' und Pizarro's Thaten
Die junge Seele feurig nicht bewegt?
An Abenteuern ward die Luft erregt,
Es flog der Geist nach jenen Goldkorn staaten
Der Rühmsten Einer, der sie einst durchfegt
Ein Schwabe war's! Er und die Seinen traten
Zuerst den Grund vom Reiche der Granaten;
mit seinem Herzblut hat er ihn belegt.
Er kämpfte dort mit wilder Schwabenkraft,
War er sich gleich des Zieles nicht bewusst,
Für Deutschlands Sache—ein vergess'ner Held.
Doch wo er pflanzte seiner Lanze Schaft,
Wo ausgeblutet seine tapfre Brust,
Erwuchs ein Recht uns an die neue Welt.
(Seubert 1856, 82)

———

Whose young fiery souls were unmoved
by the exploits of Pizarro and Cortés?
The air was alight with adventure
The spirit flew after those places full of gold.
The awesome one, that once came through
It was a Swabian! He and his men marched
first the Kingdom of [New] Granada
with his blood, sweat, and tears was occupied
He battled there with truly Swabian strength,
Though himself unconscious of the goal,
For Germany's cause—a forgotten hero.
Yet where he planted deep his spear,
And where his valorous breast did bleed its last,
In the New World we planted a rightful claim.

Alfinger's blood stains the virgin land but also, through the act of blood-shed, renders Venezuela German (21). Retellings of the beheadings of the Welser agents Philipp von Hutten and Bartholomäus Welser VI at the hands of Juan de Carvajal likewise describe their sacrifice as the legitimization of the German possession of Venezuela. Seubert presents Alfinger as a forgotten hero in need of remembrance; tales from popular culture did the same with von Hutten and Bartholomäus Welser VI. These poems and tales suggest that Welser blood ran through American lands, staining it and planting it with German roots. In a footnote, Seubert writes that a valley "wo sich besonders häufig mit den Indianern schlug trägt noch seinen Namen" (where [Alfinger] fought particularly often with the Indians still bears his name) (82). This is confirmed in the cartographic record; there is a "Valle de Ambrosio" under Lake Maracaibo which probably denotes the valley of Chinácota where Alfinger was killed by an arrow shot by a member of the Chitarero nation.[11]

Seubert adopts a historical tone in his footnote, citing a Spanish source who had been the official royal chronicler for Philip II of Spain. He acknowledges that Alfinger "gegen die Indianer mit große harte verfuhr" (led against the Indians with severity) and also that Federmann continued Alfinger's tradition of inland expeditions that are documented in his travel narrative, *Indianische Historia* (1557). Seubert does not admit to actually reading the *Indianische Historia*; his main source was the royal Spanish crónista Antonio de Herrera y Tordesilla's *Historia general de los hechos de los castellanos en las Islas y Tierra Firme del mar Océano que llaman Indias Occidentales* (1601–15; General History of the Deeds of the Castilians on the Islands and Mainland of the Ocean Sea Known as the West Indies]. Herrera y Tordesillas (1525–1626) would later be accused of plagiarizing entire unedited works, even though in the seventeenth century such copied compilations were widely circulated.

In 1892 the four hundredth anniversary of Columbus's encounter was celebrated throughout Europe. The *Hamburgische Festschrift zür Erinnerung an die Entdeckung Amerikas* (Hamburg Commemorative Publication on the Remembrance of the Discovery of America) (Wissenschaftlichen 1892) published two handsome volumes meant to commemorate the German presence in the Americas, particularly the Hanseatic cities and northern Germany's important commercial role in the Americas. In the first volume, Dr. G. Neumayer's introduction positions the book as a corrective to Abbé Raynal's *Histoire philosophique et politique des deux Indes*: "Ein Vergleich der Darstellungen Raynal's mit den geschichtlich getreuen Schilderungen in den Werke Schumacher's . . . belehrt uns ohne Weiteres über die Bedeutung des letzteren, vom nationalen Standpunkte betrachten" (A comparison of Raynal's representation with those true historical depictions in Schumacher's work . . . teaches us about the significance of the latter, especially considered from a national perspective) (Wissenschaftlichen 1892, xxxix). Abbé Raynal's popular work examined colonization in the East and West Indies and the Americas and was emblematic of the French Enlightenment; it was translated into many European languages despite being banned in France. The second volume, written by Hermann A. Schumacher (a former ambassador from the German Empire to Bogotá and Lima, as well as the former general consul in New York), includes a history of the Welser Venezuela colony and translates parts of an epic poem on the conquest of Venezuela. That is, it includes parts of the full text of *Nueva Granada* written by Juan de Castellanos (*Elegías de Varones Ilustres de Indias*), which had been published for the first time in 1847, after languishing for centuries after the publication of the first of its three volumes in 1589.[12] Schumacher's son, Hermann Albert Schumacher,[13] prepared the manuscript lauding the Welser governors after his father's death; in his introduction to both texts the son writes, "Castellanos der einzige spanische Dichter ist, welcher deutsche Thaten verherrlicht, welcher die Welser-Unternehmungen in Venezuela mit eifrigem Interesse verfolgt und in ruhiger Würdigung niedergeschrieben hat" (Castellanos was the only Spanish poet who glorified German deeds, who traced the Welser Venezuela colony with interest, and who wrote about it with quiet appreciation) (21).

Nineteenth-century imperialists were interested in the history of the Welser Venezuela colony, as they made clear in the *Deutsche Kolonialzeitung* (*DKZ*), the newspaper of the Deutsche Kolonialverein (later the Deutsche Kolonialgesellschaft, German Colonial Society). The issue includes Paul Dehn's statement.

> Wenn heute mit den Geistern der Welser und Fugger und der kühnen Hansaführer der Genius der deutschen Überlieferung herniedersteigen würde, um das Thun und das Wollen seines Volkes zu prüfen—was würde er empfinden und urteilen? Wohlbekannt sind ihm die beiden weltgeschichtlichen Thatsachen der jüngsten Zeit: wie im den deutschen Volk das nationale Bewusstsein endlich feste Form angenommen, wie nunmehr auch ein wirtschaftliches Nationalbewusstsein zum Durchbruch zu kommen begonnen hat. (Dehn 1886, 231)
>
> ———
>
> If the genius of German tradition would descend today, along with the spirits of the Welsers, Fuggers, and the bold Hanseatic leaders, to assay the deeds and will of the people, how would he judge them? Well known to him are the historical facts of the recent past: how national consciousness has finally taken a specific form in the German people, how we have begun to have a breakthrough also in the economic realm.[14]

The Welsers' ghosts, along with those of other "bold" merchants and leaders, he suggests, would judge the nineteenth-century imperialists' nationalism and their colonial undertakings harshly, although then-recent efforts might have inspired hope.

On 18 February 1888, *DKZ* published an article regarding the Welsers' involvement in Francisco de Almeida's 1505 trip to India and East Africa. A Welser agent, Balthasar Springer (or Sprenger), accompanied Almeida and published his travel narrative of the trip illustrated with woodcuts by Hans Burgkmair in 1509 (Springer 1509). Lukas Rem, the Welser agent based in Lisbon (see ch. 1), wrote about Springer's experience negotiating the terms of contract between the Welsers and the Portuguese king Manuel I for this voyage in his diary (*DKZ* 1888, 52–53). The article showcased the author's pride in the history of German involvement in the Portuguese overseas trade in the Indian Ocean.

On 25 April 1891, *DKZ* published "Die öffentliche Hauptversammlung am 30 Juni" (The Public Meeting on June 30), a subarticle related to "Die Versammlung der deutschen Kolonialgesellschaft in Nürnberg am 29 und 30. Juni 1891" (The Convention of the German Colonial Society in Nuremberg on June 29–30, 1891). This article references the important events of the meeting and recalls the work of Martin Behaim, the fifteenth-century Nuremberg merchant, cartographer, and creator of the famous globe, or *Erdapfel* (1492), which incorporated knowledge of the West African coast. The author refers to the Welser colony of Venezuela as inspiration for the members of the German colonial society: "Denn in unserer Gesellschaft ist auch ein Teil jener Idealen und praktischen Kraft verkörpert welche im Mittelalter neue Wege einschlug und den Augsburger Welser nach Venezuela führte" (In our association, we embody the ideals and practice that also opened up new roads in the Middle Ages that would lead the Welsers from Augsburg to Venezuela) (*DKZ* 1891, 104). The author cites Philipp von Hutten's wanderlust. It concludes by describing how great it was for the colonial assembly to be presented with a version of Germany's past involvement in colonial endeavors, which even included an exhibit of nautical and scientific instruments at the German National Museum "der das Alte mit dem Neuen verbindet" (that connects the old with the new). The article then glorified the German Empire's recent colonial adventures: "Aus dem Schutt der Jahrhunderte heraus, wo er versteckt wie des Reiches Krone lag, hat der deutsche Geist sich wieder emporgerungen und will noch—in letzter Stunde—eine der Zeit entsprechende Bethätigung [sic] in den deutschen Kolonien erstreben" (From the rubble of the century, where it was hidden like the Holy Roman Empire's crown, the German spirit wrestled itself up, and in this final hour, wants to strive in the German colonies for the actions corresponding to the time) (*DKZ* 1891, 104). Here the Welser colonial past was invoked at an important meeting of colonists who would dictate Germany's colonial future.

In a later issue, of 12 January 1905, a commemorative chronology titled "Kalender 12 bis 18 Januar" remembered the day when "Georg Ehinger von Konstanz . . . landet in der Nähe von Paraguana mit 147 Ansiedlern (Spanier und 24 deutsche Bergleute aus Joachimsthal)" (George Ehinger from

Constance landed close to Paraguana with 147 colonists including Spaniards and 24 German miners from Joachimsthal (*DKZ* 1905a, 13). The same issue's section titled "Aus den Abteilungen" (From the Branch Offices) contains announcements for previous lectures, including those from "Privat Dozent Dr. Passarge am 9. Dezember in Breslau über Venezuela und am 8. und 10. Dezember in Forst i.L. und Lissa über Deutsch-Südwestafrika und den Hereroaufstand" (Independent Researcher Dr. Passarge on 9 December concerning Venezuela and on 8 and 10 December in Forst Lausitz and Lezno on German Southwest Africa and the Herero rebellion) (*DKZ* 1905b, 60). Thus it is clear that Dr. Otto Karl Siegfried Passarge (1866–1958), who had been a prominent German geographer working in East Prussia and later the Colonial Institute in Hamburg, delivered a lecture about the Welser colony. According to Holger Herwig's *Germany's Vision of Empire in Venezuela 1871–1914* (1986), Passarge had visited Venezuela in 1901–2 and believed the "land was backward and in a state of moral and physical decay; only through an infusion of German influence could it ever hope to aspire to progress and prosperity." Perhaps, Herwig stipulates, that is why Passarge purchased a large estate in Venezuela's Caura (49).[15]

Many nineteenth-century German colonizers took colonial history more broadly as their inspiration. Wolfgang Struck (2010) describes this dynamic with respect to Carl Peters (1856–1918), who founded the German–East African Society and began German colonization there. In his *Im Goldland des Altertums: Forschungen zwischen Zambesi und Sabi* (1902; English translation, *The El Dorado of the Ancients* [New York, 1902]), Peters recalls how he was inspired by a map of Africa he found in an atlas.[16] Invoking Portuguese conquerors, he fantasizes about the continent's natural resources, including mythical gold deposits.[17] When Peters wrote this narrative he had already been discharged at the request of the German Empire because of his brutal treatment of the native Tanzanian population. Dubbed "hangman Peters" by the critical press, he made the case for his innocence through tropes of conquest: maps and conquerors. Through these references he creates a narrative of history in which his personal role as perpetrator of violence plays out in a never-ending colonial narrative. Peters's references suggest the growing appetite for reclamation among the reading public. Peters himself likely read the *Deutsche Kolonialzeitung* and was in all probability aware of the Welser episodes, yet he may have wanted to see himself as an unorthodox colonizer who made his own history. By 1900, Peters's successors—as seen in the frequent references to the Welsers in the *Deutsche Kolonialzeitung*—had come to view the Welsers as their forefathers.[18]

Konrad Haebler, for example, published his 1903 book on the Welsers, *Die überseeischen Unternehmungen der Welser und ihrer Gesellschafter* (The Overseas Ventures of the Welsers and Their Partners), which narrates the Welser enterprise as an early colonial undertaking, highlighting the problems between Alfinger and his predecessor as governor of the colony, the Spanish governor Juan Martínez de Ampiés.[19] At the time that Haebler's book was released, Germans had a new economic interest in Venezuela driven by its emigré communities. As Holger Herwig (1986, 48) states, at the end of the nineteenth century, German writers began demanding that the Reich support Germans overseas and thereby *Deutschtum* (Germanhood). The hope was that the Reich would overcome its lack of overseas colonies by drawing upon its emigrés who, because of their German ethnicity, would look to the Reich to establish commercial ties, instill German culture, and serve as point persons for arms sales. However, the hope for financial profit was mired in racist and nationalist rhetoric. Visitors such as Wilhelm Sievers, a professor of geography at Giessen University who made two trips to Venezuela around the turn of the century, were distressed at the racial miscegenation and saw Venezuela's stagnant development as a result of the "Romance element" (i.e., Latin or Hispanic heritage) which, in his mind, could not be compared to superior Germanic ethnicity (Herwig 1986, 48). This overreliance on German ethnicity, nationhood, and race was key to dominating the continent and continue racialized capitalism. According to Sievers, South America "is the only part of the world whose future has not yet been decided" (quoted in Herwig 1986, 48). Hence, all hope for development, and thereby domination, hinged on the emigré community.

For a short time, it looked like the Reich succeeded where the Welsers had not. Wilhelm Wintzer points out in *Der Kampf um das Deutschtum: Die Deutschen im Tropischen Amerika* (1900; The Fight over Germanness: Germans in Tropical America) that although the Welser episode had an "unglückliche[n] Ausgang" (unlucky ending), the current German émigrés in Venezuela take the number one spot in trade (47, 48) (fig. 6.1). As Erik Grimmer-Solem (2019, 152) attests, Hanseatic merchants dominated the Venezuelan economy as exporters of coffee and served as moneylenders. To Grimmer-Solem, Venezuela in the fin-de siècle was more or less "part of an informal German overseas Empire" (310). In 1902 the Second Venezuelan

FIGURE 6.1.
Cover of Wilhelm Wintzer's *Der Kampf um das Deutschtum: Die Deutschen im Tropischen Amerika* (The Fight for Germanness: Germans in Tropical America) (Munich: T. F. Lebmann, 1900).

Crisis began due to a blockade of Venezuelan ports in which German state-owned ships took part. Venezuelan president Cipriano Castro had refused to pay off debts owed to foreign-owned companies (such as Krupp's Great Venezuela Railway) during the Venezuelan Civil War, and Germany joined Italy and Britain in blocking the ports to demand payment (324–25). This interest in the Welser period persisted even after Germany lost her colonies in the Treaty of Versailles in 1919 and in theory had no reason to glorify a colonial past.

THE TWENTIETH CENTURY: IDEALIZATIONS OF
GERMAN CONQUISTADORS DURING THE WEIMAR
REPUBLIC AND THE NAZI ERA

Historical narratives that sought to re-create the Welsers' colonization of
Venezuela appeared throughout the period of the Weimar Republic. In his
1929 historical account for young adult audiences, *Auf der Jagd nach dem
goldenen Kaziken: Die erste deutsche Kolonie der Welser in Venezuela 1527 bis
1555* (On the Hunt for the Golden Cacique: The First German Colony of
the Welsers in Venezuela 1527–1555), Otfried von Hanstein (1869–1959) describes Las Casas's life and works and discusses his project to convert, rather
than exploit, the natives (Hanstein 1929, 116). Yet he also notes that Las
Casas did not present the Welsers fairly. He writes that Las Casas "war . . .
ein Spanier, und jede[r] Grausamkeit, die ein Mann, der einer Anderen Nation angehörte, erschien in umso Schwärzeren Lichte" (was a Spaniard, and
any cruelties committed by a man who belonged to another nation, appeared in a worse light) (116). With respect to Las Casas's depiction of the
Welsers in the *Brevísima relación*, he exclaims, "Armer Ambrosius Dolfinger[20] und arme Welser! Dieser sonst so gerechte Richter hat ihnen Unrecht
getan" (Poor Ambrosius Dolfinger and poor Welsers! This otherwise just
Judge has done them wrong) (118). While praising Las Casas for his respect
for human rights and his recognition of Indians as human subjects, Hanstein
writes that Las Casas's fierce Spanish nationalism and fervent faith left him
blind in his judgment of the Germans. He acknowledges that the venture
was economic in nature but points out that Spanish undertakings were
equally profit driven. While mentioning that some of the Welsers had converted to Lutheranism, he protests Las Casas's reading of all Germans as
Lutherans: "Dolfinger, der wie die Welser und Fugger der katholischen
Religion auch nach der Reformation treugeblieben war, sei ein verstedter
Lutheraner" (Dolfinger, who like the Welsers and the Fuggers, had remained
faithful to the Catholic Religion, was seen as a Lutheran) (118). Hanstein
acknowledges that "Ambros Dolfinger war kein Engel" (Ambrosius Alfinger
was not an angel) and admits that Alfinger was probably as cruel as Pizarro
or Cortés) (119). After all, the Welsers undertook the project "um Gold zu
machen" (to make money) (119). Hanstein nonetheless valorizes the Welsers

for a Weimar audience. Yet he also departs from most accounts of the day, emphasizing the similarity of the Welsers to the Spanish instead of high-lighting the German character of the Welser colony and their colonial enterprise.[21]

Other accounts fictionalize the Welser period by expressing a nostalgia for lost territories. One such account, by Hugo von Waldeyer-Hartz,[22] *Die Welser in Venezuela: Bilder aus der Frühzeit deutscher Kolonialgeschichte* (1927; The Welsers in Venezuela: Pictures from Early Modern Colonial History), opens with the scene, "Der Kaiser in Augsburg A.D. 1530," in which the masses wait for Emperor Charles V's arrival. After he arrives, Charles spots Bartholomäus Welser V (the Elder) in the crowd.

> "Sieh da, der Herr von Venezuela!" Karl schritt lebhaft auf Bartholomä Welser zu. "Habt Ihr gute Nachrichten von drüben? Ist das Dorado von Gold und Silber endlich gefunden, das Ihr erwartet? Oder ist es noch immer die Ware von Schwarzen und brauen Heidenmenschen, die den besten Gewinn abwirft." (Waldeyer-Hartz 1927, 11)
>
> ———
>
> "Look over there—the Lord of Venezuela!" Karl approached Bar-tholomäus Welser excitedly. "Do you have good news from there? Did you finally find the Dorado of gold and silver that you sought? Or is it still the trade with black and brown infidels that yields the best profit?"

In this meeting, the emperor asks Welser for news of silver and gold discoveries. Yet he acknowledges that the truly profitable trade under racialized merchant capitalism is the slave trade; after all, we remember the Welser Company received one of the first permits to import four thousand enslaved Africans to the Americas.

Welser's response describes Venezuela as a site of German Holy Roman rule. Although the reader knows that an international and ethnically mixed crowd awaits the emperor in Augsburg, the German nation dominates in this colonial narrative.

> Aus allen Nationen und Himmelstrichen. Neben Hispaniern, Flan-drensern, Burgunden, standen Deutsche der verschiedene Stämme dazu Kroaten, Griechen, Italiener, ja selbst braune Araber in Weissen Burnussen und schwarze Äthiopier fehlten nicht. Und allen, die das

Gepränge des Einzugs bestaunten, ward offenbar, das der Kaiser ein
gewaltiger Herrscher sei und Deutschland ein machtvolles Reich. (11)

From all nations and corners of the earth. Next to the Spanish, Flemish,
and Burgundians stood Germans of all tribes, Croatians, Greeks, Italians, even brown Arabs in white burnooses and black Ethiopians were
not absent. And it was obvious to all who marveled at the pomp of the
march that the Emperor was a powerful monarch and that Germany
was a powerful Empire.

The colonial anxieties manifested in Waldeyer-Hartz's account emphasize
the power of the lost German Empire and its leader, recognized by the Spanish, Flemish, Burgundians, Croatians, Greeks, and Italians. The "brown
Arabs" and "black Ethiopians" represent colonial subjects who also recognize the superiority of the empire.

World War I Allied powers at times advanced an alternate narrative of
Germany's colonial history. The German invasion of Belgium sparked a
spate of narratives presenting German colonial atrocities as more serious
than their own. The Lord Bryce "Report of the Committee on Alleged German Outrages" during the 1915 German invasion of Belgium was rapidly
translated into ten languages. British propaganda depicted the Germans as
barbaric Huns eager to rape and pillage the gendered Belgian territory.

From the 1930s on, German attention to colonialism in the Americas
played a part in Nazi Germany's politics, and authors of popular German
fiction and history promoted the myth of the greatness of the Aryan conquerors and the cruelty of the Spaniards.[23] Erich Reimers's historical novel
Die Welsern landen in Venezuela (The Welsers Land in Venezuela, 1938)
draws on archival material to tell the story of the Welsers' most famous leaders, including Ambrosius Alfinger, Nikolaus Federmann, and Philipp von
Hutten (fig. 6.2). In Venezuela, Reimers writes, Alfinger encountered "die
feindlichen Umtriebe der Spanier" (the hostile activity of the Spanish)
(1938, 33). He states that the land had been depopulated "unter dem Ein-
fluß der brutalen spanischen Kolonisationsmethoden" (under the influence
of the brutal Spanish methods of colonization) and that Spanish slave hunt-
ers terrorized the natives on the coasts of Venezuela. In regard to the Welsers,
Reimers emphasizes that Las Casas was a "frühere Sklavenhalter, spätere
Dominikanermönch und Deutschenhasser" (former slave owner, later

FIGURE 6.2.
Cover of Erich
Reimers's *Die Welser
landen in Venezuela:
Das erste deutsche
Kolonialunternehmen*
(The Welser Land in
Venezuela: The First
German Colonial
Undertaking) (Leipzig:
W. Goldmann, 1938).

Dominican monk and German hater), alleging that he advanced human rights for the Indians while demanding the importation of four thousand enslaved Africans from Emperor Charles V (41).

The *Tag der deutschen Kunst* (Day of German Art) in Munich featured a "Welser" float, complete with a silver ship and German *Landsknechten* (mercenary soldiers), in its parade in 1938 (fig. 6.3). It was the fifth year of the parade and the first when Nazi propaganda culture fully appropriated all aspects of German history to culminate in a pageant and parade performed in the presence of Chancellor Adolf Hitler. Whereas the program pamphlets from 1933 through 1937 featured an image of the goddess Athena, the 1938 pamphlet showed the head of "der Bamberger Reiter" (the Bamberger Horseman), a secular equestrian statue of an anonymous king the Nazis had adopted as a symbol of the great northern race entrenched in Germanic culture (Schweizer 2007, 198). The parade had always had floats devoted to the Germanic, Romanesque, Gothic, Renaissance, Baroque, Neoclassical, and Modern periods, as it was conceived as representative of the political and artistic history of the German people. The 1938 parade was the first to include a Welser float. The parade had much to do with the celebration of economic elitism and colonialism. It presented Nationalist Socialism as the culmination of German cultural and historical achievement that had begun in the Roman Empire (202).

The 1938 *Tag der deutschen Kunst* program gives the following background on the Welser float.

> Kaum war die Welt in all ihren Weiten erkundet, da blühte schon der überseeische Handel. Die Welser zählten mit zu den ersten, die unserer Heimat die Schätze fremdländischer Erde erschlossen. Sie liehen dem Kaiser das Gold, rüsteten Schiffe für ihn und empfingen dafür Venezuela als Pfand. Sie lebten im Wohlstand wie Prinzen, hielten sich farbige Diener, seltene exotische Tiere und reiste in eigenen Kutschen und Sänften.[24]

> ———

> Barely had the world's full extent become known when overseas trade was already thriving. The Welsers were some of the first that accessed the treasures of foreign lands for our homeland. They loaned the emperor money, equipped ships for him, and received Venezuela as collateral. The Welsers lived prosperous lives like royalty, kept colored servants, exotic pets, and traveled in their own coaches and litters.

In short, the pamphlet made no mention of any failure of the Welser colony and emphasized the emperor's dependence on the resources of these Germans, as well as their position among the first colonizers. In the excerpt above, the human slaves the Welsers kept were part of an exotic menagerie, part of a life of luxury and travel. Moreover, the pamphlet glosses over distinctions between the Welser agents and the Welser governors, some of whom were not part of the family.

FIGURE 6.3. Tag der Deutschen Kunst 10. Juli 1938 (Day of German Art, 10 July 1938, Munich). The group picture depicts the Welser float. Stereograph photograph by Heinrich Hoffmann. Courtesy of Art Resource/BPK Bildagentur, Bayerische Staatsbibliothek München Abtlg. Karten u. Bilder.

German popular literature written during Hitler's rule acknowledged the failure of the Welser colony, but generally implied that Germany's empire had been on equal footing with larger colonial powers such as the Spanish, English, Portuguese, French, and Dutch. Gustav Faber, for example, assembled a biographical catalog, *Deutsches Blut in fremder Erde* (1944),[25] that includes notable Germans involved in exploration efforts throughout the world in 1944, including Philipp von Hutten (fig. 6.4).[26]

Faber explained the failure of the Welser colony as the result of von Hutten's violent death. He describes the Tocuyo episode and Carvajal's capture of von Hutten and Bartholomäus Welser VI as trickery. He calls Carvajal a "Falscher, bübischer Spanier" (false, roguish Spaniard) (44). He charges, "Mit offenen und geheimen Mitteln arbeiten fremde Mächte, an ihrer Spitze spanische Interessenten" (Foreign powers work with both open and secretive methods, but at the top there are parties with Spanish interests) (45). This account resembles Weimar-era depictions of the German defeat in World War I as caused by trickery and foreign interests rather than the failure of the Germans. Like accounts written during the Weimar Republic, it depicts the Spaniards' claim that Germans were Lutherans and cruel to the natives as chauvinist falsehoods.[27]

FIGURE 6.4.
Cover of
Gustav Faber's
*Deutsches Blut
in Fremder Erde*
(German Blood in
Foreign Lands)
(Berlin: Junge
Generation, 1944).
Wartime edition.

Faber drew on a well-established tradition that preceded the *Tag der deutschen Kunst* parade: a *Hitlerjugend* group chose the Welser governor Georg Hohermuth von Speyer (also known as Jorge de [E]spira) as a "patron" in 1933 (Armani 1985, 105–6). They embraced the myth of the grandiose German conquistador and knight as an embodiment of the ideals of National Socialism. The Spanish cronistas Gonzalo Férnandez de Oviedo and Antonio Herrera y Tordesillas had already established his reputation as a brave and just conqueror who fell victim to Spanish nationalism, and the Nationalist Socialists drew on these sources.

Individual Germans also celebrated the Welsers. Arnold Federmann, a descendant of the Welser governor Nikolaus Federmann, chose to present his forefather heroically in a reprint of *Indianische Historia* in 1938 (fig. 6.5). The text's epigraph, Johann Filchart's "Ernstliche Vermahnung an die lieben Teutschen" (Serious Admonition to the Beloved Germans) (1573),[28] reveals the younger Federmann's agenda in republishing the travel narrative: he wished to reembed his forefather's story in the lineage of German heroes (Federmann 1938). It contains a prayer to God to strengthen "edlen deutschen Geblüt" (noble German blood) and the German "Adlersgemüt" (eagle nature). The poem's narrator "als Deutscher" (as a German) "aus deutschem Blut" (of German blood) looks back at "vielen Helden" (many heroes) when he "dies deutsche Bild blick an" (looks at this German picture). The 1938 publication uses the poem to link German identity to the rebel nature of el Libertador Simón Bolívar, a Venezuelan-born member of the criollo elite who rebelled against the Spanish royalists. Many German intellectuals of the 1930s were interested in Bolívar and Alexander von Humboldt's influence on Bolívar. For example, the epithet inscribed on the statue of Humboldt outside of the Humboldt University in Berlin, a bequest of the University of Havana, mentions Humboldt as the "second discoverer" of the Americas, a term that Bolívar purportedly employed to describe the baron.[29]

Federmann, however, claimed that his ancestor had paved the way for Simón Bolívar's campaign for independence in Venezuela, Colombia, Ecuador, Peru, and Bolivia. Without giving evidence, he states that Nikolaus Federmann's expedition through the marshes and the cordillera enabled Bolívar's eventual quest for independence from Spain.

> Und wenn man den Zug Bolívars würdig eines Livius gennant hat, so verdiente erst recht der Zug Federmanns der Vergessenheit entrissen zu werden, der als erster das Innere Venezuelas durchzog und der—hätte man ihm mehr vertraut und mehr geholfen—wohl auch schon damals den Grund gelegt hätte zu einer Vereinigung von Venezuela und Columbien, dem Traum Bolívars. (1938, 80)

> And if Bolívar's tour would have been deemed worthy of a Livy, then Federmann's expedition truly deserves to be restored from oblivion, he who was the first to explore the interior of Venezuela, and if he had been trusted more and had received more help, he would have paved the way for unification between Colombia and Venezuela—Bolívar's ultimate dream.

FIGURE 6.5.
Cover of
Arnold Federmann's
*Deutsche Konquistadoren
in Südamerika* (German
Conquistadors in
South America)
Berlin: R. Hobbing,
1938).

Federmann insists that his relative was the first European and, most important, the first German who entered the Venezuelan jungle—and more preposterously, the first politically minded conquistador who tried to unify Venezuela and Colombia. Clearly, Arnold Federmann's attempt to recast Nikolaus as Bolívar's spiritual forefather was rooted in an attempt to reestablish Bolívar's position as a hero worthy of national praise in light of the renewed German interest in him. Some individuals had a more personal stake in recovering the Welser period, just as with the Welsers' descendants' relationship to remembering this history (see ch. 4).

Beyond the imperial ambitions of the Nazi State, the refiguring of the Welser colony reflected the dogma of Nazism during this period. Antimiscegenation laws in place in the German colonies attempted to regulate the purity of the German colonizers' blood, reflecting the anxieties of unfulfilled colonial ventures; these sanctions barred Germans from having children with Black Africans or Indigenous Pacific Islanders.[30] The Nuremberg antimiscegenation laws, the *Gesetz zum Schutze des deutschen Blutes und der deutschen Ehre* (Protection of German Blood and German Honor Act), enacted on 15 September 1935, prohibited German and Jewish marriage and sexual relations, evoking prior laws enforced in Germany's colonies. Germany's late rearrival and hasty departure from the colonial scene prompted Hitler and his architects of the Final Solution to search for a colonial realization of the racial state in the homeland itself during Nationalist Socialism. The employment of racist and expansionist policies is a direct link between Germany's colonial past and its National Socialist agendas, specifically in the context of the Holocaust.

It is impossible to ignore the way works of the Nazi period reconfigured the Welser Venezuela colony through a teleological perspective. Literature of Nazi Germany portrays the Welsers as benevolent caretakers of the Venezuelan province and their engagement in the slave trade as a charitable endeavor. Ernst Wilhelm Bohle (1903–60), leader of the *NSDAP Auslandsorganization*, was one of the main Nazi propagators of the notion of colonial *Lebensraum*,[31] claiming that the Welsers took slaves in order to protect them from slave traders who would treat them badly, something they themselves would never do.[32] J. G. Lettenmair in 1939 described a German woman, a miner's wife believed to be the first to set foot in Venezuela, who came with Hans Seissenhofer in 1530, in ways that accentuated her "pure" German blood (Schmölz-Häberlein 2002, 339).[33] Similarly, Arnold Federmann's edition of the *Indianische Historia* reiterated the symbolic value of the purity of German blood on "foreign" soil vis-à-vis the racialized depictions of natives as well as other foreign powers such as the Spanish, drawing on Faber's *Deutsches Blut in fremder Erde* and Filchart's poem praising the "edlen deutschen Geblüt."

Many scholars have grappled with the continuity theory that links German colonialism to the Holocaust. These debates concern the various assumptions of a German *Sonderweg* (special path), bridging Germany's experience of colonialism and the Holocaust. Pascal Grosse contends that German colonialism was not necessarily the precursor to National Socialist racial politics but rather that it was simply in line with prevailing nineteenth-

century theories of eugenics. Fears of miscegenation and the right-wing policies of colonialists on the German mainland cannot, by themselves, account
for German policies to exterminate those deemed "undesirable" on racial
grounds. While this may be true, there is no denying that the emphasis on
eugenics along with an interest in shepherding a new type of colonialism
that was still conscious of old colonial histories guided Germany's imperial
colonial projects. This history influenced those Nationalist Socialists who
wanted to use policies centered on settler colonialism, especially *Lebensraum*.

Hannah Arendt's readings of the connections between racism and empire emphasize the fact that Germans viewed themselves as "legitimate" settlers in their conquests of Indigenous peoples. The links between colonialism
and genocide may not be unequivocal, but the racial and ethnic component
of the Herero genocide, the Holocaust, and, more recently, the Rwandan
genocide also suggests that genocidal violence was aggravated by colonialism. For example, in the Herero genocide the racial branding by German
colonizers set a group apart as an enemy and allowed bureaucrats to exterminate that group without guilt (Lee 2007, 80). During the Nazi State, Germans saw themselves as the original settlers of Europe at the expense of the
Slavs and Jews (Baranowski 2011a, 53; 64). More recent explorations of the
Rwandan genocide reveal patterns of violence enforced by Belgian colonial
authorities: for example, the Hutus considered themselves an "Indigenous"
group and the Tutsis as Rwanda's "invaders," suitable for slaughter.[34] Dirk
Moses (2002, 33) defends Arendt's project for its tracing of the roots of
modern projects of extermination; in doing so, he proposes that the period
from 1850 to 1950 can be viewed as the "racial century" in which the processes of nation building and "people-making" culminated in Auschwitz
(33). Whether or not German colonialism was linked to the Holocaust, the
prevalence during the National Socialist era of reimaginings of the Welser
colonists as pure "Germans" fighting bravely against illegitimate native
peoples to colonize a "virgin" land suggests that the Welser episode needed
to be whitewashed and rewritten for the political expansionist purposes of
Hitler's Germany.

THE IMPLICATIONS OF MEMORY

Projects of German empire building during the Prussian Empire invested in
mythical histories of German conquest, resurrecting memories of the Welser
Venezuela colony. In the Weimar era, these lost colonies would be lamented,

alongside the memories of more recent territorial losses, while during the Nazi regime authors glorified the vision of these first German conquerors. After World War II, German colonialism was remembered with anticolonial rhetoric and actions in the German Democratic Republic (East Germany) and with neocolonial cooperation in the case of the Federal Republic (West Germany), which contributed German legionnaires to the French Foreign Legion and still had some say in questions surrounding the status of a small German-speaking group in Namibia.

Similar to the ongoing debates in the United States surrounding Confederate monuments, since the turn of the twenty-first century, there have been attempts in Germany to "decolonize" the history of the Welsers and Fuggers in the Americas and re-present their legacies in a less glorifying light. The WordPress site "Fugger and Welser Street Decolonized" (2017) documents this process (fig. 6.6), following other attempts to decolonize street names in Berlin referencing colonialists such as Carl Peters. The site states:[35]

> Im Gegensatz zur Lüderitzstraße oder der Petersallee gibt es zu der Fugger- und der Welserstraße bis dato noch keine Ambitionen auf dieses Stück weißgewaschener Geschichte aufmerksam zu machen und die glorifizierte Darstellung der beiden Familien als große Kaufleute besteht fort. Dieser Blog ist nicht nur eine Intervention gegen diese Geschichtsschreibung, sondern auch gegen die Leerstellen, die wir selbst Tag für Tag durch die nicht- Auseinandersetzung mit solchen Orten des kollektiven Gedenkens produzieren und somit implizit zu der Verdeckung und Bagatellisierung der deutschen Kolonialgeschichte und ihrer selektiven Weitergabe beitragen.

> ———

> In contrast to the debate on Lüderitz Street or Peters Boulevard, there has been no attempt to do [decolonize] Fugger and Welser Streets [whose names were changed between 1957 and 1958] and draw attention to this piece of *white* washed history and the persistence of a glorified presentation of both families as great merchants. This blog is not only an intervention against this writing of history but also against the empty spaces where we ourselves on a daily basis, through the absence of debate on these places, produce collective thought and are implicit in the concealment and trivialization of German colonial history and its selective dissemination.

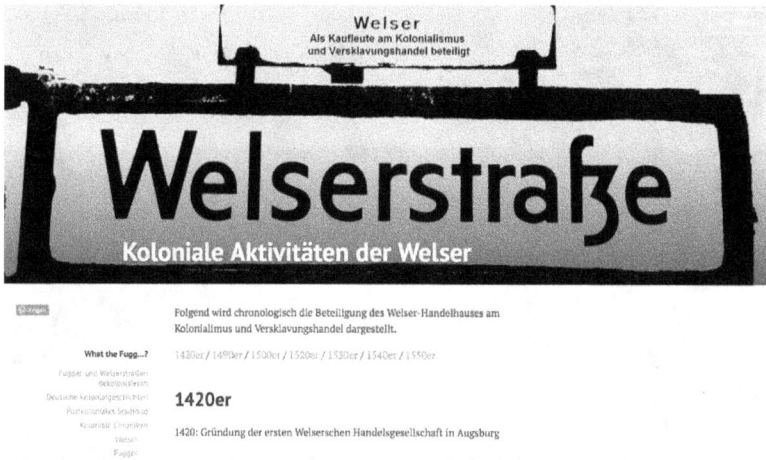

Welser
Als Kaufleute am Kolonialismus
und Versklavungshandel beteiligt

Welserstraße
Koloniale Aktivitäten der Welser

Folgend wird chronologisch die Beteiligung des Welser-Handelhauses am
Kolonialismus und Versklavungshandel dargestellt.

What the Fugg...?

1420er / 1490er / 1500er / 1520er / 1530er / 1540er / 1550er

Fugger und Welserstraße
dekolonisieren

Deutsche Kolonialgeschichten

Postkoloniales Seminar

Koloniale Chroniken

Welser

Fugger

1420er

1420: Gründung der ersten Welserschen Handelsgesellschaft in Augsburg

FIGURE 6.6. Screenshot from the WordPress website, https://fuggerandwelserstreet decolonized.wordpress.com/timeline/koloniale-aktivitaeten-der-welser/.

Recent attention to colonial figures such as Carl Peters has sparked activism to change street names that bear his name (fig. 6.7), yet the streets named for the Fuggers and the Welsers have not yet been the subject of activism. The blog's authors argue that this reflects the glorification of early venture capitalism and denies the nature of their actions in the Americas.

This whitewashing of the Fuggers and the Welsers seems unlikely to last. The turn in the past twenty years of scholarship to uncover imperial Germany's role in slavery, mass violence, and resource extraction has led to investigations of earlier colonists—particularly the forgotten Welsers and Fuggers. This research has not yet permeated mainstream secondary and postsecondary education, but a group of students from the Humboldt Universität Berlin have created the decolonize.hu WordPress site that went live in 2016 after they participated in a seminar on German colonial history and were shocked at how little the subject has been taught in the past (fig. 6.8).[36] Perhaps revisiting the Welser period in Venezuela and decolonizing German cities exemplifies a new investment in the historical record, one with potential to facilitate new conversations about Germany's most painful history.

Koloniale Straßennamen im Afrikanischen Viertel in Berlin-Wedding

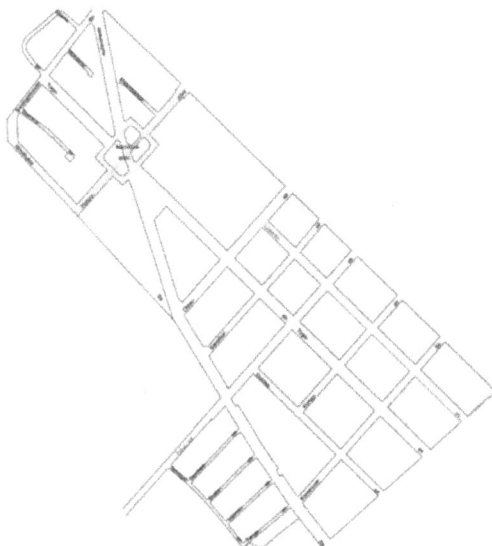

Stadtplan des Afrikanischen Viertels in Berlin-Wedding (mit freundlicher Genehmigung des Bezirksamts Mitte Berlin, Abt. Stadtentwicklung/Vermessungsamt). Zur Vergrößerung bitte auf das Bild klicken.

FIGURE 6.7. Screenshot from www.freedom-roads.de/frrd/staedte.htm showing Berlin colonial street names in the Afrikanisches Viertel (African Quarter).

FIGURE 6.8. Screenshot from Decolonize HU Berlin website, https://decolonizehu .wordpress.com.

CHAPTER 7

The Venezuelan View of German Conquest

Post-Independence Literature and History

Algún día será verdad. El progreso penetrará en la llanura y la barbarie retrocederá vencida.

—Romulo Gallegos, *Doña Barbara*

At the fin-de-siècle, Venezuelan historiography celebrated the typical Spanish heroes of the colonial era, and the Welsers were largely seen as a blemish in a primarily Spanish colonial history. However, several works of revisionist historiography and historical fiction provide some exceptions to the mostly static and unsympathetic Venezuelan cultural memory of the Welsers. Adolfo Briceño Picón's play *Ambrosio de Alfinger* (1903), influenced by positivism, celebrates the "Hispanic" conquest of Venezuela but also serves as inspiration for alternative readings. José Ignacio Cabrujas's postmodern drama *En nombre del Rey* (1963) critiques all conquest as an idiotic project. Francisco J. Herrera Luque's novel *La luna de Fausto* (1983) re-creates Welser Venezuela through mythology, specifically, the Faustian myth; and, most recently, William Ospina's novel *Ursúa* (2005) comments on contemporary

Colombian politics through his reading of the conquest that also features the Welsers. These latter works often portray the tension between civilization and barbarism prevalent in the contemporary nation-state that is central to Venezuelan cultural memory of the Welsers. In this chapter, I first investigate historiographical works before moving to historical fiction. My analysis of Venezuelan historiography demonstrates that static models influenced by Positivism read the Welser episode as antithetical to a civilizatory Spanish colonization; however, more recent Latin American historical fiction has tended to read all European conquest and its legacies of colonialism as barbaric (fig. 7.1).

The pre-positivist Rafael María Baralt, an eminent nineteenth-century Venezuelan historian, portrays Charles V as a non-Spaniard interested only in funding his wars and interfering with the civilizatory aim of Spanish colonization in Venezuela. Baralt, the first Hispanic American writer to be elected to the Real Academia Española (Royal Spanish Academy), points out that Juan de Ampiés, the first Spanish governor, incorporated the native Caquetío society into the settlement of Coro rather than enslaving them.

FIGURE 7.1. Venezuelan stamp depicting the 400th anniversary of the founding of the city of Maracaibo (1569–1969): Ambrosio Alfinger, Alfonso Pacheco, and Pedro Maldonado. Alfinger is the only Welser governor shown.

Had de Ampiés retained control, he suggests, he would have brought "European civilization" to Venezuela. Instead, the king gave control to the Welsers, "a company of merchants who want a quick return on their profits" (Baralt 1887, 194). This, he lamented, "era lo mismo que entregar éstos y aquel como presa, á la acerada é impaciente garra de la codicia" (was the same as giving them [the natives] as prey to the paws of greed) (194). Baralt replays the theme of the "foreign" nature of Charles V's Flemish advisers, and of the Welsers, decrying "the rapacity [*rapacidad*] of foreign hands" that made Venezuela essentially into a space where slavers came to conduct raids on the native populations (194). This stance that blames German colonizers for slowing the civilizing progress of the nation continues far into twentieth-century historiography.

Venezuelan positivists such as José Gil Fortoul (1861–1943), author of *Historia Constitucional de Venezuela* (1907), continued the work of writing Venezuela's history begun by Aguado and Oviedo y Baños analyzed in chapter 5, as well as Baralt, though with less emphasis on the nation's colonial period. Nonetheless, in this work, Fortoul used the crónicas of fray Pedro Simón, Oviedo y Baños, and Castellanos to recount how the Welsers along with Spanish conquistadors went on numerous expeditions without consideration of Spanish law or the conditions set out in the 1528 capitulación (Fortoul 1907, 6). Instead, he writes that the historical record mentions two harrowing events during the Welser governance. One is the first account of Spanish cannibalism in which Francisco Martín, a soldier, not wanting any meat to be wasted, ate the penis of one of the Indians he and other Spaniards had been ritually cannibalizing. The other event recounts the Spanish-German attack on the Indians in the Tamalameque lagoon, which I discuss later in this chapter (Fortoul 1907, 6).

Civilization and barbarism are central to reading Venezuelan historiography and historical fiction. The Venezuelan author Luis Britto García (1940–) in his essay "Historical and Political Fundamentals of Venezuelan Narrative" investigates the roots and effects of positivism in Venezuelan culture and literature. Positivism, under the guise of August Comte's epithet "order and progress," influenced the Venezuelan dictatorships of the Andean caudillos Cipriano Castro (1899–1908) and Juan Vicente Gómez (1908–35) (Britto García 2014, 34).[1] In Venezuela, positivism became tied to the doctrine of social determinism and the dichotomy between civilization and barbarism (35, 36), which demanded that the people infected by "barbarie" become civilized and positivist. Consequently, certain episodes in Venezuelan history were reinterpreted in a positivist fashion; for example, Lau-reano Vallenilla Lanz (1870–1936), a politician who worked with Juan Vicente Gómez, wrote *Cesarismo democratico* (1919; Democratic Caesarism). The text justified the caudillo system as the only way to keep public order in Venezuela. This is known as his theory of "the necessary gendarme." In analyzing history, Vallenilla Lanz saw in Simón Bolívar the anarchical roots of Venezuelan history as he insisted that the War of Independence was in effect a civil war (Britto García 2014, 36).

The civilization/barbarism dichotomy also informed historiographical treatment of the Welsers. In 1938 Alejandro Necker wrote a nine-page pam-phlet, "La conquista y el régimen de los Welser," for his bachelor's thesis at the Central University of Venezuela. In terms that resemble Las Casas's, he condemns Alfinger: "He didn't know how to make friends with anyone due to his ambitious and cruel personality [and] . . . he won all of the Spaniards' hatred" (Necker 1938). That said, Necker saw the Welsers differently from Las Casas or Baralt. He suggested that the quarrels between the Spanish and the Germans made colonization efforts almost impossible and that the Spanish were constantly placing German interests in danger. Of the whole twenty-eight-year Welser episode, Necker concludes that it was cruel; he acknowledges their heroism but also their cruelty, which was much like that of the Spaniards. Necker is the first to recognize that both the Spanish and the Germans were perceived by other European powers through their violent acts of conquest. He also emphasizes the Welsers' failure to colonize the land because their interests remained those of a capitalist enterprise seeking to gain a quick profit. More than forty years later, Marianela Ponce de Behrens, in her *Juicios de residencia en la provincia de Venezuela: Los Welser* (1977), agrees with Necker. She examines the 1528 capitulación stipulating that the Welsers found townships as well as the juicios de residencia taken around 1546 that recorded the Coro dwellers' reports on the Welsers' achievements. Based on the juicios de residencia, she concludes that the Welsers never founded the cities they were supposed to and that they also destroyed In-digenous townships.

Ermila Troconis de Veracoecha (1929–2018), a Venezuelan historian, in her *Historia de El Tocuyo colonial* (1984, 22–23), sees the Welsers' failure as a result of the Germans' focus on searching for gold, gems, and trade routes rather than beginning a colonization effort. In addition, she excuses Carva-jal for the execution of von Hutten and Welser VI. The Germans, preoccu-pied with the search for gold, risked their lives and the lives of Spaniards.

Moreover, they abused the Indians and used them for their expeditions, thereby limiting the agricultural production of the colony. Coro, as a result, remained stagnant, which had a negative impact on *Spanish* colonization on Tierra Firme. Troconis's study details Juan Carvajal's founding of the city of El Tocuyo while the last German governor, the Welser-appointed Philipp von Hutten, was on his expedition. Carvajal had achieved this by relocating the residents of Coro and presenting documents that verified that the Real Audiencia in Santo Domingo had named him governor to replace von Hutten. Troconis proves through various sources that the documents were legitimate, and Carvajal's governorship of Coro and subsequent founding of El Tocuyo was in good faith, but many later chroniclers such as Castellanos and Oviedo y Baños considered Carvajal a usurper.[2] In effect, Troconis argues that Carvajal's legacy serves as the true foundation of Venezuela, attributing its earlier stagnation to German interference in Spanish colonialism. To Troconis and other Venezuelan historians, Carvajal is not an assassin but rather the man who set the Spanish colonists free from the yoke of the Germans. Ambrosio Perera, another Venezuelan historian, also celebrates Carvajal for ending German interference: "It is not strange that this was what caused the tragic end of the Welsers, and that with this America would be liberated from a probable German colonization that would have settled on its holy soil" (1943, 26). In this instance terms such as "territorio patrio" (patriotic territory) and "sagrado suelo" (sacred soil) mark Venezuela as a Catholic land with Castilian antecedents that German invaders had defiled for an unfortunate but short period (26). The Welser era was but an error, and happily, Carvajal changed the course of history. Significantly, Perera was writing in Venezuela in 1943 when the threat of Nazi expansion and German world power must have had an effect on a historian writing about German conquistadors, even one who was writing from South America.

THE REVISIONISTS AND THEIR REINTERPRETATION OF THE WELSER PERIOD

Reinterpretation of the Welser period began after World War II. Guillermo Morón's 1956 *Historia de Venezuela* (1971) states of the expeditions that took place from 1530 to 1546 that while the Welser governors waged continuous war against the Indians and took them as slaves when they could, and searched for gold ardently, they also tried to gain useful knowledge of the territory. Morón writes, "All of the German actions are still controversial [to Venezuelans]" (192). If some of his predecessors charged that the Germans were the perpetrators of much of the evil of colonization, Morón does not outright defend their actions against the Spanish, but he does offer a more nuanced view of the Welser conquest. He suggests that the Welsers were not more cruel than the Spaniards, and that the Spanish juridical system failed to rein them in. As to the suggestion that they failed to leave a trace because they did not successfully colonize the area, Morón writes that the Germans succeeded in founding a few *rancherías*, or rural settlements (349). José Rafael Fortique also defied popular pro-Spanish tradition when he stated:

> This concession [of the province of Venezuela] from Charles V constitutes an exceptional event in the history of Spanish America that would never be repeated. It was a conquest and colonization contract given to a foreign firm that affected the very foundations of Venezuela, being one of the most important chapters of our historical process because it breaks, at least for a short while, the purely Spanish nationalist character of the conquest itself (1976, 4).

Fortique acknowledges that the Welser period was important because it was the only non-Castilian operation in the history of the administration of the Spanish Indies.

Juan Friede (1902–90) studied the colonization of the Americas through an ethnographic lens; he began his historical work in his investigations of Colombian Indigenous populations.[3] Fröschle (1979, 772) sees Friede's work as rectifying some of the misleading information in both Spanish and Venezuelan historiography that had been tainted by religious and nationalist attitudes. Friede writes that the cronistas, who were mostly nationalist and Catholic, considered any German or Protestant influence in the Americas with hostility. He himself conducted a thorough analysis of the Fuggers' and Welsers' economic activities, describing their pan-European banking networks and their importance as lenders to Charles V.

European historians such as Alberto Armani (1985) and Jörg Denzer (2002) mainly explored the links between merchant capitalism and the Welser Venezuela colony. Armani sees the Welser project as a stage of Euro-colonialism and describes the mutual dependency between Charles V and the Welsers as lifelong. According to Armani (1985, 53), the Welsers had three motives for undertaking the colonization of Venezuela: (1) to find a way to cross the Pacific, or the South Sea, in order to circumnavigate the world faster and thereby compete with the Portuguese, who had a monopoly on the spice trade; (2) to expand their trade and increase their business, especially with the coast of Tierra Firme (as discussed in chapter 1, this was successful); and (3) to find gold, which they believed was possible because they had heard exaggerated legends about the Chibcha people in Colombia who made refined pieces in gold. Denzer (2002, 291) ascribes similar motives to the Welsers' governance of Venezuela. He argues that the Welsers were already exporting many goods to Hispaniola, but they did not have enough materials to import to Europe. Thus they believed they could make their sea trips worthwhile if they expanded to the Venezuelan province on Tierra Firme. Friede (1961), Armani (1985), and Denzer (2003) revise the history of the Welsers in Venezuela and contextualize the project of colonization in terms of European economic and religious history. All three historians connect the demise of the Welsers in Venezuela to antiforeign sentiment on the part of Spanish explorers and the early Hispanization of both the conquest and the colonial enterprise. They write that this time was reconstructed in Spanish archives and chronicles to portray the German colony in Venezuela as bloody and violent while painting a rosier view of Spanish colonizers.

Denzer (2003, 232) critiques the positivist myth of Venezuela as a nation made up of mestizos who inherited the best qualities of their Indigenous and Spanish forefathers.[4] Historians perpetrated the myth of a Venezuelan mestizo nation that was particularly resilient in its resistance to colonizers. Rebels such as the chief Guaicaipuro, the Negro Miguel, and Simón Bolívar were representative of a multiracial nation.[5] Denzer (2003) found that Maracaibo, the second-largest city in modern-day Venezuela, which Ambrosius Alfinger founded, refuses to acknowledge him as founder, though a Venezuelan stamp depicting the 400th anniversary of the founding of the city of Maracaibo (1569–1969) depicts Ambrosio Alfinger, Alfonso Pacheco, and Pedro Maldonado. Alfinger is the only Welser governor shown (fig. 7.1). In Coro, Juan de Ampies is named as founder instead of Alfinger. However, there is a bust of Carvajal in El Tocuyo's central plaza.

In short, the primary and secondary sources reflect a historic German-Spanish tension. As I explained in chapter 6, nineteenth-century imperial

Germany used the Welser episode to prove that colonizing was Germany's destiny. Venezuelan historians also used the Welser episode to build their own national image. In doing so they specifically built their history according to the rise of the Venezuelan nation-state as independent from Spain or any other colonial dominion. In nineteenth-century Venezuela the image of the conquistador that was often promoted was tyrannical. In the early twentieth century, the influence of positivism gave rise to a history that recognized Venezuela's many origins (enslaved Africans, Indigenous peoples, Spanish and German conquistadors) to specifically underscore Venezuela's claim that it is a mestizo nation with mixed-race citizens—a place that could produce a powerful criollo revolutionary such as Bolívar.[6] Interestingly, geography would play a part in revisionist views of the Welser venture.

FROM HISTORIOGRAPHY TO FICTION: THE HISTORICAL NOVEL AND HISTORICAL DRAMA

While my analysis of Venezuelan historiography suggests that it was led by static models that celebrated the heroes of positivism, the relatively recent wave of Latin American historical fiction since the 1980s reflects an alternate reading that mostly critiques the legacy of colonization. Before analyzing the representations of the Welsers in Venezuelan and Colombian historical novels and drama, I examine how these representations of the conquest of the province of Venezuela fit into a larger trend in Latin American literature in the 1980s that gave rise to the New Latin American Novel.

María Cristina Pons, in *Memorias del olvido* (1992), describes the trend of re-creating, adapting, and reimagining history through fiction: "This re-writing uses, even more than the historical facts themselves, an explicit distrust towards historiographical models and their production of official history" (16). That is, twentieth-century fiction writers "engage with historiographical methods, but critique the methodologies of the Positivist and Romantic historians. The New Latin American Novel is characterized by its alternative approaches to understanding the past; while some novelists reflect upon the possibility and impossibility of knowing and reconstructing the past, others try to rescue the omissions and the silences in history (Pons 1992, 16). In addition, the conscious use and misuse of archival sources at times becomes part of the story. In many historical novels, the authors question or feature the historical document itself and the textual culture of the colonial archive in a way that calls attention to the privileging of Eurocentric written culture and critiques it. Magdalena Perkowska, in *Historia híbridas* (2008), has investigated how the new Latin American historical novel grew as a reaction to the "now" of postmodernism. Perkowska maintains that the Latin American historical novel reflects new practices and techniques such as fragmentation, metanarrative, intertextuality, anachronisms, parody, and humor (2008, 34). Fiction writers and playwrights employ these literary techniques in order to reconsider the past with an eye to the sociohistorical and cultural reality that the authors experience every day in Latin America. Scholars in Venezuela have also reflected on this adaptation process. For example, in 2014 the Instituto Autónomo Centro Nacional del Libro held a conference on historical fiction.[7] As the introduction to the conference proceedings states, "Writing has had a prominent place in our history. In fact, history and literature have gone hand in hand; they intertwined themselves in a dynamic that was not exempt from wrong value judgments" (López and Ardiles 2016, 10). This need to "retell ourselves" is part of the Latin American story; the conference proceedings argue that history, even in its fictionalized form, is necessary to understand Venezuelans' past.[8] After all, we have to recognize we are historical "animals" and that "sooner or later we will be history" (López and Ardiles 2016, 11).[9]

How does the Welser period function in this fictional historical model? Do authors and playwrights affirm or question the Spanish historical narrative of conquest? As the late Venezuelan anthropologist Fernando Coronil and his wife, the American anthropologist Julie Skurki, wrote, the Venezuelan nation has seen its struggle between civilization and barbarity charted in canonical works of Venezuelan literature, especially in Romulo Gallegos's *Doña Bárbara* (1929). It is "a foundational fiction that depicts the path to nation building through an allegorical romance[;] the narrative charts the domestication of unconquered nature and uncivilized humans" (Coronil and Skurki 2019, 180). Gallegos (1908–35), who briefly was president of Venezuela (1948), wrote the novel about a leader who rules the masses by consent rather than coercion (Coronil and Skurki 2019, 180). Other authors have also reflected on the conquest of the region. William Ospina's historical novel, *Ursúa* (2005), represents the Welsers' Venezuela history as one entrenched with the Spanish conquest of the Americas. Francisco J. Herrera Luque's historical novel, *La luna de Fausto* (1983), re-creates the Welser

Venezuela period in a Habsburg Renaissance context. Dramatic works also adapt this Welser history. Beginning with the Venezuelan playwright Adolfo Briceño Picón's *Ambrosio de Alfinger* (1903), which contains Romantic tropes of conquest that strike contemporary readers as sickening, José Ignacio Cabrujas's postmodern drama, *En nombre del Rey* (1963), breaks with the expectation of a linear (and Romantic) conquest narrative. Briceño Picón wrote his play in Venezuela during a time when the newly independent republican nation sought to reconcile its historical colonial past with its future development; Cabrujas, writing after Fidel Castro's Cuban revolution influenced Venezuela guerrilla movements such as the Revolutionary Left and the Armed Forces of National Liberation, comments on the madness of all conquest. The conquest trope shows how Venezuela and Colombia are always in danger of returning to barbarism, a barbarism that Cabruja already sees embodied in Venezuelan national culture and that can be traced to the trauma of conquest.

RECYCLED MYTHS: BETWEEN FICTION AND HISTORY

William Ospina (1954–), a Colombian novelist, poet, and essayist, has frequently made the conquest of territories that make up parts of present-day Colombia and Venezuela the topic of his works. While critics have looked at his novels as critical of contemporary Colombian society, his writing bears on this study as it provides a detailed look at the Welser governors in comparison to other Spanish colonial figures. Like several of the novelists and playwrights I discuss, he has used the genre of historical fiction to comment on the fate of the the current nation-state.

　Ursúa (2005) is a biographical novel on the life of the Spanish conqueror Pedro de Ursúa (1521–61). Along with *El país de la canela* (2008; The Land of Cinnamon) and *La serpiente sin ojos* (2012; The Blind Serpent), it forms a trilogy on the conquest of South America. The former, a fictional narrative about Francisco de Orellana's discovery of the Amazon River and Francisco Pizarro's conquest of Peru, won the prestigious Romulo Gallegos Prize, an international literary prize started in Venezuela in 1964 and awarded to a novelist writing in Spanish. The latter detailed Pedro de Ursúa's repetition of Orellana's journey seeking the land of the mythical Amazons.

Gabriel García Márquez called *Ursúa* the best novel of 2005. It draws on the style of the Latin American boom writers as it takes Latin American history as its primary subject matter. From the point of view of a narrator who traveled with Ursúa, it narrates the conquistador's travels through Navarra and the New World. Ursúa was one of the most polemic officials of the New Kingdom of Granada. He governed the province of Santa Marta and founded the city of Pamplona in Santander, Colombia (1 November 1549). The mestizo narrator who reveals his identity in bits and fragments throughout the novel, uses analepsis and prolepsis to insert himself in and omit himself from the story; his narrative voice, presented through a variable internal focalization in the novel, seeks to also understand his own role in the conquest (Ospina 2005, 57). For example, later in the novel, the narrator resurfaces to remind the reader that the story is also his own (206).[10] The narrator writes that in Tierra Firme, "las minas hambrientas de las Antillas devoraron por millares a los nativos" (the hungry mines of the Antilles devour natives by the thousands), and the business of pearl diving "reventaron los pulmones de los más jóvenes en las costas de Cumaná y de Cubagua, de Margarita y del Cabo de la Vela" (burst the lungs of the youngest on the coasts of Cumaná and Cubagua, Margarita, and Cabo de La Vela) (35).

While the novel focuses on Ursúa, in one of the many asides in what Yuly Paola Martínez Sánchez (2015, 49) calls its "pretension of order," the novel details episodes of conquest by other infamous conquerors, including the Welser governors. Ospina writes about Alfinger's conquest of the Guanebucanes and Caquetíos around Maracaibo: "Alfínger dejó por el Valle de Upar y las orillas del río Grande las tierras arrasadas, las familias destruidas, y un rastro de cuerpos y cabezas de indios que cebaba a las bestias y hacía correr tras su expedición una plaga de tigres (Alfinger left through the Upar valley and the banks of the Río Grande the razed lands, destroyed families, and a trail of Indian bodies and heads that fed the beasts and made a pack of tigers run after his expedition) (2005, 36).

Ospina also scathingly remarks on the treatment of Indigenous peoples by both the Welsers and the Spaniards when he relates in a gruesome and dramatic scene a surgeon saving Philipp von Hutten's life after he was shot with an arrow that pierced his heart.

Por los mismos días en que Ursúa tomó la vara, von Hutten se reponía milagrosamente de una flecha india que le atravesó el corazón, en la ciudad de muertos ilustres de El Tocuyo. Digo milagrosamente, y vacilo, porque el modo como fue curado el joven von Hutten tal vez no tiene igual en la historia de las Indias. No habiendo médico en la expedición, un soldado español se ofreció para operar al muchacho y extraerle la flecha, pero como no estaba segura de la trayectoria que el proyectil había seguido, hizo que le trajeran a un indio joven y le clavó una flecha similar en la misma dirección en que el capitán la había recibido, para después estudiar con cuidado los daños que la flecha había causado en su organismo. Varios soldados inmovilizaron al indio, mientras el aprendiz de médico le abría los músculos y le destrozaba la jaula del pecho, pero pronto ya no hubo necesidad de fuerza porque el indio se fue desangrando y murió en medio de grandes sufrimientos. Así quedó demostrado que los hombres de caoba de Venezuela y los muchachos blancos del imperio alemán tenían el pecho tejido de un modo idéntico, lo cual no quiere decir que fueran iguales ante la suerte, porque el indio murió, pero el médico, aleccionado por tan cuidadosa carnicería, logró extraer la flecha del corazón de Felipe de Hutten y rescatarlo de la muerte. La verdad es que el joven alemán no se salvó porque fuera a vivir una larga y provechosa vida, sino porque el dios de Germania y de Hispania, que es diestro en paradojas y en ironías, había mandado que no muriera por flecha de indio sino bajo el filo romo y mugriento de los machetes de sus propios hombres. (133)

———

During the days that Ursúa took up the scepter, von Hutten was miraculously recovering from an Indian arrow that pierced his heart in the city of dead celebrities, El Tocuyo. I say miraculously, and I am joking because the way the young Philipp von Hutten was cured is unmatched in the history of the Indies. As there were no doctors who accompanied the expedition, a Spanish soldier volunteered to perform surgery on the young man and extract the arrow, but because he was unsure as to the trajectory that the projectile had taken, he made the others bring him a young Indian man whom he spiked with an arrowhead in the same way that Captain von Hutten had been struck so that he could study with care the damage that the arrow had caused in his body.

Various soldiers immobilized the Indian, while the apprentice surgeon opened his muscles and destroyed his rib cage. The Indian slowly bled to death with great suffering. That is how it was proved that the mahogany men of Venezuela and the young white men from the German Empire shared the same anatomy, which does not mean they were equal in their fate because the Indian died, and the surgeon, aided by his own careful butchery, was able to extract the arrow from Philipp von Hutten's heart and save him from death. The fact of the matter is that the young German did not escape death because he was destined to live a long and fruitful life, but because the God of Germany and Spain, who is skillful in paradoxes and ironies, had ordered that he not die from an arrowhead but instead under the blunt and filthy edges of his own men's machetes.

This horrifying passage makes von Hutten's survival not, as the narrator notes, a miracle but rather a symbol of the conquest as a whole. Even as the episode provides conclusive evidence that race does not determine anatomical difference, it treats the young Indigenous man as experimental flesh, and he suffers an agonizing death. Nonetheless, bad luck and fate exist, and it comes only a few years later for von Hutten at the hands of the "blunt and filthy edges of his own men's machetes."

In addition to the massive violence enacted by Spaniards and Germans in power, Ospina's novel includes Bartolomé de Las Casas's attempt to remedy the situation through his frequent ocean crossings to plead with the emperor. However, Ospina depicts Las Casas's failure from Charles V's point of view: "No era fácil para el amo del mundo resistir la presión de sus hombres, las embajadas con cara de piedra de sus acreedores alemanes y genoveses" (It was not easy for the master of the world to resist pressure from his men, the delegations with stone faces sent by his Genoese and German creditors) (38). Ospina, then, subscribes to the narrative of Charles as a ruler beholden to his creditors, which included both the Genoese and the Welsers.

Ospina includes historical details on contested jurisdictions within the recently conquered Tierra Firme.[11] For example, Ursúa's uncle, Miguel Díaz de Armendaríz, receives an appointment as juez de residencia of four distinct regions within Tierra Firme to institute the *Nuevas Leyes* (New Laws), which were in theory designed to protect the Indigenous populations. Juxtaposing the topography of Valladolid and the Duero region to the plains of the Orinocos "given to the Welsers" as a result of their contribution to Emperor Charles V's election, Ospina labeled Charles a "child," though he was at least nineteen years old (65). He charges that the officials only imagined this land through a type of sketch map depicting a space with a few churches and a river guarded ferociously by Alfinger. Their ignorance contrasts with the narrator's direct experience and evident excitement in depicting the details.

The reader learns that when Ursúa's uncle Amendáriz begins hearing witness statements about the conquest, he situates it in stories about German conquests and desire for natural resources: "Oyó de testigos las andanzas de Pedro Martínez de Agramante, que derribó a un gigante en las serranías de Venezuela, cuando andaba con los alemanes" (He heard from witnesses who partook in Pedro Martínez de Agramante's adventures about him fighting a giant in the mountains of Venezuela when he was with the Germans) (176). German technology features in a battle between Pizarro and Atahualpa involving "167 españoles y un griego, armados de cañones de Augsburgo y Arcabuces de Ulm" (167 Spaniards and a Greek, armed with cannons from Augsburg and harquebuses [long guns] from Ulm) (167). When Ursúa is late to return, the narrator imagines that Armendáriz paces back and forth, nervous about Ursúa's absence, because, after all, "fundar en el país de los chitareros era la gran oportunidad de incorporar al Nuevo Reino las tierras que tanto codiciaron los hombres de los banqueros Welser" (to settle in the Chitareros's country was the great opportunity to incorporate into the New Kingdom of Granada the lands that so many of the Welser men desired) (298).

The Welser governors' fates are intertwined with that of the conquest of the Americas, and Ursúa follows in the steps of Ambrosius Alfínger by embarking on many expeditions to find El Dorado and the Amazons. In a dialogue between Ursúa and Armendaríz, they discuss the tale of Alfinger's bloody conquest expedition around Lake Maracaibo where "cuatrocientos hombres navegaron con él por el mar de Maracaibo, quemando rancherías y enfrentando pueblos guerreros, y entraron el el Nuevo Reino (four hundred men navigated Lake Maracaibo with him, burning towns and confronting warring peoples before entering the New Kingdom [of Granada]) (313). In the end the conquistador's troops forced the Indians to retreat and the captain sent three distinct troops to explore the Río Negro (314). The most important report, or *informe*, came from Esteban Martín, who assured the men that "era verdad que las arenas del río eran doradas, y de allá obtenían el oro hacía siglos los indios de la región" (it was true that the sand in the river was golden, and that was where all of the region's Indians got gold since centuries ago) (314). Alfinger's troops breathed sighs of relief at this news, thinking that the innumerable battles since Coro, the storms, and the plague of insects had been worth it. But as the narrator explains, Alfinger changed his mind a month later, in January, and changed the course of the expedition, ignoring his destiny.

> El mismo ignoraba cuál era el designio que lo llevaba a Chinácota: y es que allí lo estaba esperando la muerte. En esos bosques paradisíacos, llenos de guayacanes floridos, la flecha de un indio chitarero le atravesó la garganta, y de nada valieron las plegarias latinas, ni los sanadores de la tropa, ni la amistad distante de los grandes banqueros de Augsburgo, ni el recuerdo final de su hermano, el ostentoso Enrique Alfínger, quién años atrás compró en una tarde todas las especias que trajo de los confines del mundo la arriesgada expedición de Magallanes. Era el año de gracia de 1533, y muy al sur también había otro cuello en tormento, porque el verdugo estaba apretando con el torniquete una cinta de acero en torno a la garganta de caoba de Atahualpa, que había sido bautizado la noche anterior, para que no muriera sin el amparo de Dios. (315)

> He also ignored the plan that took him to Chinácota, and that's because death was waiting for him there. In those paradisiacal forests, full of flowering guaiac trees, the arrow from a Chitarero Indian traversed his throat, and neither the Latin prayers, nor the troops' healers, nor the friendship with the great bankers of Augsburg, nor the final memory of his brother the ostentatious Heinrich Alfinger, who years before had bought all of the spices that the risky Magallanes expedition brought back, could save him. This was the year of 1533, and farther to the south also there was another man's neck in torment, because the executioner was tightening with the tourniquet a steel band around the mahogany throat of Atahualpa, who had been baptized the night before, so that he would not die without the protection of God.

Ospina turns the lengthy account of the doomed Alfinger expedition into a mythological account of the power of fate. His men were not destined to mine the gold found in the sandy banks of the Río Negro but rather to follow Alfinger to his death at the hands a Chitarero. Ospina here uses literary negation to describe that at the moment of death, nothing would be of help:

not Latin prayers, not the troops' medics, not the friendship with the Welser bankers or the memory of his "ostentatious" (powerful) brother, who was one of the most influential delegates for contracts with the crown during this period.

The topography conquered by the Welsers resurfaces as a motif. On the Andes range of eastern Colombia or the Andean Cordillera Oriental, Ursúa follows the footsteps, and the butchery, or *carnicería*, of Alfinger (319). Yet despite the narrator's view that Quesada was the right man to look for the golden waters because of his unusual "thirst for gold," inopportune events prevented him from doing so. However, it was the strife between Federmann, Belacázar, and Quesada concerning the conquest of Bogotá that saved the Chitareros and Guanes from more conquests and more violence.

While all of the Europeans converged in the Bogotá savannah, they almost fought each other, but "la sagacidad del poeta Quesada y la de su hermano Hernán Pérez" (the sagacity of the poet Quesada and that of his brother Hernán Pérez) mitigated the stubbornness of Belalcázar, such that they formed an alliance (169). That alliance influenced "the German" (Federmann) who nonetheless "andaba un poco lejos de los límites que le habían asignado sus jefes" (was roaming a bit far from the borders assigned by his superiors) (169). The narrator reveals that according to Ursúa, soon after, all leaders, Jiménez de Quesada, Belalcázar, and Federmann, sailed to Spain to see to whom the Consejo de Indias would give the rights of the kingdom (170). The Consejo recognized Quesada's claim that he was the first one there, but instead of granting Quesada the title, they would give it to the man who financed the expedition, the *adelantado* Pedro Fernández de Lugo, after appeasing Federmann "con oro suficiente para que no volviera jamás a las Indias" (with sufficient gold so that he would never come back to the Indies) (170).

Ospina draws attention to both the exploitable labor and the natural resources that the Spaniards and the Germans wanted to use and destroy but also to unexplainable natural phenomena. For example, Ortún Velazqués de Velasco, who cofounded Pamplona in Santander, found gold mines close to Valle de los Locos, and Ursúa put Ortún in charge of the exploitation of the riches found in the land (327). Instead, he followed in Alfinger's footsteps to Lake Maracaibo, where he heard about the natural phenomena of the Catatumbo lightning (*relámpago del Catatumbo*), in which for about half of the year lightning storms occur for up to ten hours each night (328). While

Ospina's narrative may comment on the state of corruption in Colombia at the time the author published the work, he stays close to Adolfo Briceño Picón's meditations on Alfinger and Aguirre, historical figures of the conquest, to highlight their status as psychotic outliers among Spaniards and criticize their actions. In his review of the novel, Bernardo Pérez Salazar (2006) points out how Ospina uses his novel to critique Colombia around 2006. In an episode from the novel in which Ursúa's uncle Armendáriz ponders his future as the bearer of justice in his new post as juez de residencia in the Americas, a Spanish courtier brings Armendáriz to his senses. The secretary of the imperial treasurer assures him that his only job is to elevate and restore the names of those who have been subject to ill repute (Ospina 2005, 306). After all, "un juicio de residencia es la ocasión de rehabilitar a unos hombres sujetos al odio de nuestros enemigos y a la murmuración de sus propios soldados" (a juicio de residencia is the occasion to rehabilitate a few men who have been subjected to the hatred of our enemies and even critiques from his own soldiers) (67–68). Pérez Salazar (2006, 306) describes this as a "paralelo notable con el espíritu que hoy anima a ciertos cuerpos de justiciar" (notable parallel with the spirit that animates certain judicial bodies) in Colombia at the time, who had closed the investigation against Colombia's former president Ernesto Samper, who was accused of accepting financing for his 1994 campaign from drug cartels. The Accusation Committee of the Colombian House of Representatives, which acquitted Samper of any wrongdoing, was called by many Colombians *la comisión de absoluciones* (the commission of absolutions).

Pérez Salazar cites an interview that Ospina gave on the precariousness of the political situation and the links between Colombia's colonial past and its twenty-first-century present. Ospina told the interviewer that in Colombia the conquest of the Americas has not finished. Rather, Colombians continued to experience many episodes similar to those of many centuries earlier when rich Spaniards displaced thousands of human beings because their thirst for riches outweighed all other costs (Pérez Salazar 2006, 1).

Ospina does not directly allude to present events in *Ursúa*, but his comments clearly suggest he connects Colombia's landowning oligarchy to its colonial past and specifically the displacement the conquistadors created. Pérez Salazar (2006) sees this history of land seizure as being part of land grant patterns that evoked the "cuerpo cierto"—that is, land whose exact boundaries and contents were unknown. When colonial governors were given official permissions (privileges) to conquer and settle a specific land, certain mythical and/or chimerical places were included; for example, in *Ursúa*, El Dorado was included in Armendáriz's privilege to his nephew Ursúa to govern the province of Santa Fé (Ospina 2005, 307).

Some critics generally disparaged Ospina's novel for attempting to tell the whole history of the conquest, yet having García Márquez call it the best novel of the year offset some of those negative reviews. One review, for example, called Ospina's novel demanding, as readers must concentrate to not lose their way "in the grand labyrinth of characters and histories" (Zuleta 2006, 122). Making historical novels memorable is difficult according to some critics, yet if any of the output of Latin American boom writers such as García Márquez and Alejo Carpentier serves as a point of departure, it is precisely an engagement with history that makes fiction memorable.

While Ospina's narrative took Ursúa's life as a point of departure from which to explore the larger conquest of the Americas, others before him had done the same with a similar cast of characters. One of them was Lope de Aguirre, with whom Ursúa traveled to try to find El Dorado. When Ursúa would not allow Aguirre's lover on the expedition, Aguirre conspired with another soldier, Fernando de Guzman, who began a riot, assassinated Ursúa, and seized control of the expedition. While the madman Aguirre became the subject of Venezuelan novels, including Miguel Otero Silva's *Lope de Aguirre, Principe de la Libertad* (1979) and Arturo Uslar Pietri's *El camino de el Dorado* (1947), Briceño Picón at the turn of the century wrote and staged a successful play on Aguirre's life and death and also Alfinger's.

ADOLFO BRICEÑO PICÓN'S *AMBROSIO DE ALFINGER*: A NATIONAL AND REGIONAL DRAMA

It has not only been authors of historical novels who decided to represent figures from colonial Latin American history, Latin American playwrights have authored dramatic works that grapple with history. Scholars and critics have taken note: Verena Dolle's edited volume, *La representación de la conquista en el teatro latinoamericano de los siglos XX y XXI* (2014), takes the quincentenary of Latin American independence celebrated around 2011 to review the way the conquest was represented on the stage throughout Latin America in the twentieth and twenty-first centuries (xi).[12] In "La Conquista en el teatro venezolano contemporáneo," Luz Marina Rivas (2014) analyzes the works of the Venezuelan playwrights César Rengifo (*Carayú o el vencedor* [1947] and *Obscéneba* [1958]), Luis Britto García (*El tirano Aguirre o la conquista de El Dorado* [1975]), and José Ignacio Cabrujas (*En nombre del rey* [1963] and *Acto cultural* [1976]). She writes, "In general, the conquest theme is not [represented] frequently in Venezuelan theatre, as it has been in narrative" (Marina Rivas 2014, 149). Yet she points out that the exceptions were generally written by the most famous Venezuelan playwrights and that their dramatic works on these themes have been staged frequently in recent years (149). She attributes this to the fact that in moments of crisis the "country falls back on historical fiction to try and understand the collective identities that overwhelm us" (149).

Adolfo Briceño Picón (1846–1929) was a dramatist, novelist, and physician who lived most of his life in Mérida in the Venezuelan Andes. His most well-known dramatic work was *El tirano Aguirre* (1872) in three acts. His *Ambrosio de Alfinger* (*Los alemanes en la conquista de Venezuela*) critiques the Welser period of colonization in Venezuela. As Kim Beauchesne (2011) has explained in her article on Briceño Picón's *El tirano Aguirre*, during the period of state formation in Venezuela when Briceño Picón was writing, anticolonial rebels had a special place that was apparent on the Venezuelan stage. Fifty years after the military triumph of the Venezuelan creole nation, under the first mandate of Guzmán Blanco (1870–77), Briceño Picón presents Aguirre as an antihero (670). Similarly, Briceño Picón uses the figure of Ambrosio de Alfinger to criticize the whole Welser enterprise in Venezuela. In the prologue, Briceño Picón (1903, 8) explains that his play presents "a critique of the Germans to whom Charles V gave this land for its conquest and settlement, and who treated the Indians so badly, and whom history has also justly treated harshly, just like I do in the drama, after all I follow the history in detail."[13] As in *El tirano Aguirre*, the author proposes to study the "outsider" episodes of the conquest and colonization of Venezuela. Alfinger's Spanish wife and daughter represent a benevolent, pacifist Spanish conquest.

Critical response to *Ambrosio de Alfinger* has been minimal; it was never republished. Even Briceño Picón's better-known play, *El tirano Aguirre*, had just two stagings in Mérida, in 1872 and 1873 (Rivas 2014, 150). However, even Rivas remarks about the interesting intercultural element in *Ambrosio de Alfinger*: "Indigenous peoples are represented as dignified warriors who fight to preserve their lands and their liberty" (150).

Ambrosio de Alfinger has three acts. The first act, "El Asalto" (The Ambush), follows Alfinger, his Spanish wife, doña Elena, and their daughter, Margarita, and her suitor, Francisco Martín, one of her father's soldiers and the man described by Oviedo y Baños of engaging in phallic cannibalism. As Alfinger prepares to ambush the Tamalameques after annihilating many Indigenous populations around the valley of Upar, Margarita and Elena convince Francisco to go on a secret mission (and defy Alfinger) to convince the Tamalameques to become vassals to the Spanish crown and pay tribute to avoid Alfinger's bloodbath.

The second act, "El combate" (The Combat), takes place on the lake of Tamalameque or Zapatosa. The leader of the Tamalameque nation, the cacique Tamalameque, discusses the upcoming warfare with the prince, Guarantín. In the next scene Tamalameque dreams of the conquest and is awakened by his daughter, the princess Kairana, whom he tells she will be his heir. An adviser tells Tamalameque that Francisco Martín has come, yet Tamalameque refuses to submit to gain what Martín describes as civilization. Francisco sees Kairana and they immediately fall in love, although he at first takes her for an apparition, and he forgets about his love for Margarita. Alfinger's offensive against the Tamalameques occurs next, and he claims victory, taking Tamalameque prisoner. Tamalameque vows vengeance.

The third act is "La Venganza" (Vengeance). On the way to Chinacotá, Alfinger advances with Colonel Esteban Martín (known in the historical record as an interpreter; some say he was a German whose name was Stephan), despite the fact that he is in the jurisdiction of Santa Marta. Meanwhile Elena and Margarita reveal they believe Francisco is dead because he was never found after the battle. Indigenous informants say that Francisco survived, that he has married Kairana, who was hurt in the battle; he abandoned "civilization" to become an "Indian"—hence embracing barbarity. Margarita spies on the couple. Despite her sadness, she offers her former lover and his new Indian bride her blessings and returns to Spain to enter a convent. The play ends with Tamalameque's revenge; after escaping, he ambushes Alfinger and stabs him to death.

The play uses gendered nationalist stereotypes to display Spanish-German antagonism. For example, in act 1, scene 1, doña Elena exclaims, "No me canso de admirar esta tierra firme que llaman Venezuela" (I never get tired of admiring this tierra firme which people call Venezuela). She also admires the natural world, full of "animales de mil especies" (animals of a thousand species). Her husband, Alfinger, rebuffs her speech as "Women's Foolishness" (Niñerías de Mujeres); he instead admires "las grandes riquezas que hallamos á cada paso en este inmenso continente" (the great riches that we have found every step of the way in this immense continent). He sees nature as only valuable for the mineral wealth found within it: "¡Oh, cuanto oro . . . cuantas riquezas!" (Oh! so much gold, so much wealth) (Briceño Picón 1903, 196). Doña Elena complains that men like him only think of how to get rich. While Elena fits the stereotype of the lover of Romantic nature, Alfinger represents the cold, calculating conqueror who, as ruthless as his employers, the Welsers, seeks only profits. Alfinger tells Elena about his assignment from the Welsers.

> No puedes imaginar, mi buena esposa, la inmensa dicha que se apoderó de mi corazón, cuando fui nombrado Gobernador por la Compañía de los Belzares, esos ricos alemanes que han contratado con Carlos V—el grande Emperador—la conquista de esta parte de las Indias que llaman Venezuela. ¡Oh, mi ambición quedó satisfecha! De origen alemán, pero casado contigo de sangre española, me fue fácil unir mis alemanes á los españoles, que han querido compartir mi fortuna, como los nobles caballeros Villegas, Briceños, Guevaras, Garcías, Peñas y otros. (196)
>
> ———
>
> You cannot imagine, my dear wife, the immense happiness that took over my heart, when I was named governor by the Welsers, those rich Germans who have contracted with Charles V—the great Emperor—the conquest of these rich part of the Indies which they call Venezuela. Oh, my ambition became satisfied! Of German origin, but married to you of Spanish blood, it was easy for me to bring together my Germans to the Spaniards, who have wanted to share my fortune, such as the noblemen of the Villegas, Briceños, Guevaras, Garcías, Peñas, and others.

The reference to Briceños, the playwright's own family, seems significant. Alfinger reveals that his personal ambition complemented the Welsers' own ambitions and that his marriage allowed him to bring together both Germans and Spaniards. In naming his own family, the Briceños, among the noble Spanish families, Briceño Picón essentially excuses himself from the disapproval he reserves for the Germans while securing them a place among Venezuela's founders.

Elena is the representation of Spain. She believes it is right to conquer Indigenous peoples but only to bring them civilization and evangelize them. She warns Alfinger:

> Si empleáis medios crueles é inhumanos para estos indígenas; si no pensáis sino expropiarlos; si llevais la ferocidad hasta conquistarles la vida; si los reducís a esclavos á ellos que son tan libres como las aves que pueblan el aire, como los animales que habitan en sus bosques, no lograréis su civilización. (199)

> But if you use cruel and inhumane means for these indigenous peoples; if you only think about expropriating their goods, using rage to conquer their lives; if you reduce those men into slavery that are free like birds in the air, like the animals that live in their forests, you will not achieve their civilization.

But Alfinger is not interested in either civilization or religion; rather, he is eager to represent the Welsers and his own plans "a volver lleno de riquezas" (to return full of wealth or riches) (200).

In the end, Elena exclaims:

> ¡El oro! ¡el oro! . . . ese es el único móvil de los alemanes á quienes, en mala hora, entregó Carlos V estas tierras en arrendamiento, á fin de pagar las grandes deudas que contrajo con la compañía de los Belzares, para saciar su ambición de mando. ¡El oro! único móvil de los alemanes, hombres sin fe, sin religión; ¡materialistas que no creen en Dios! (200)

> The gold! The gold! that's the only motive of the Germans, to whom, during a bad time, Charles V leased these lands so that he could pay his great debts which he contracted with the company of the Welsers so he could fulfill his desire to rule. Gold! the only motive of the Germans, a people without faith, without religion: they are materialists who don't believe in God!

This passage highlights how Briceño Picón adapted the available Spanish historiography on the Welsers, infused with its own anti-German stereotypes, to further augment the idea that colonial Venezuela was ruled by an atheist interested only in wealth. The claim that Germans have no faith is essentially a criticism of Lutheranism as well.

Margarita comments on her father's atrocities, saying, "mi corazón se aterró" (my heart died of terror) (205), after witnessing what he and his men committed in the Upar valley area. She pleads with him not to destroy the Tamalameques. Francisco also condemns Alfinger, if not to his face, saying as he agrees to go on the secret mission that "la crueldad del gobernador Alfinger en la conquista de los indios es atroz. Recuerda lo que hizo en el valle de Upar. . . . Aquello fue horrible: la matanza, el despojo, la esclavitud, el incendio" (the cruelty of the governor Alfinger is atrocious. Remember what he did to the Indians in the Upar valley. That was horrific: the killing, the stealing, the slavery, the fire) (211). He concurs with Elena, saying,"La sed de oro de Alfinger es insaciable y, para satisfacerla, no ahorra las crueldades más grandes. En su corazón no hay otro sentimiento que la ambición de riquezas y la crueldad más refinada. Esto no podemos ya sufrirlo y es necesario que acabe" (Alfinger's thirst for gold is insatiable, and to satisfy it, he is ready to commit the worst cruelties. In his heart there is no other feeling except that of his ambition for wealth, and of course, his refined cruelty. We cannot suffer this anymore, it is necessary to stop this) (212).

Beyond these reports, act 1, scene 7, shows Alfinger's cruelty when he asks an Indigenous man, Joyogüire, for information about the best plan of attack of the Tamalameques, who have retreated to islands in the lake. Alfinger wants to know if there is a way that his men can wade or go on horseback to reach the islands and launch their offense. Joyogüire speaks in a pidgin Indigenous language that Briceño Picón invented. The scene continues as the "palmadas" (slaps) turn into "cintarazos"(strikes), as Alfinger humiliates Joyogüire, hitting, soaking, and taunting him until he reveals the desired information (220–21). The scene plays on the stereotype of the "drunken Indian." The subjugated status of Joyogüire is evident in his expression of distress. In this scene he is still able to express his frustrations in his native language: "¡Ay! ¡Ay¡ ¡yo parar . . . no poder! '¡yarfa! . . .' (diablo) '¡Mapusase taya!' (Estoy cansado)" (Ow! Ouch! Stand up . . . cannot I! "yarfa! . . ." [devil] "Mapuse taya!" [I am tired]) (221). In the end, Alfinger's violence has the intended effect of extracting information on the depth of the laguna. In giving this information, Joyogüire speaks in Spanish: "Por aquí no muy jondo . . . cuando no estar brava la Encantadora! no bramar hoy . . . estar dormida la Encantadora . . . no, cuquiarla echa majanazo" (Here not very deep . . . when the Enchantress is not mad . . . not mad today, today she sleeps, don't bother

her or give her a blow) (223).[14] Joyogüire has to reveal his perception of his Indigenous cosmology so that Alfinger will stop abusing him.

Act 2 also problematizes German greed. While Martín decries Tamalameque's refusal to submit to Spanish domination, calling him a haughty prince, he saves his disgust for Alfinger and Germans generally. Alfinger is "ese alemán sediento de oro á quien detestan sus mismos compañeros" (that German thirsty for gold, hated by his own companions) (260). He yells that Charles V gave Venezuela to the "codiciosos Belzares" (greedy Welsers), who will enslave Indigenous peoples. In general, Briceño Picón characterizes Francisco Martín as a poor Spaniard caught between the orders of a foreign despot, his own love for the despot's daughter, and his loyalty to the Spanish project of conquest. In doing so, he characterizes the Germans as unnaturally greedy.

Elena picks up the theme in act 3, scene 2, when she retells the story of how she joined her husband with the particular aim of restraining his brutality and greed. She tells her daughter, Margarita: "Los españoles descubrieron su rico Continente y fueron los primeros blancos que ellos conocieron. . . . Y vienen después estos alemanes á aprovecharse de los descubrimientos y aniquilar á los indígenas" (The Spanish discovered their rich continent and were the first whites who the Indians met. . . . And afterwards these Germans came to take advantage of the discoveries and to annihilate the Indians) (281). Then Esteban Martín warns Alfinger, whose troops are in the valley of Chinacotá, that he had crossed the limits of his governance by going into the Upar valley and would be subjected to a hearing because of the infraction (272).

Alfinger responds with confidence: "No tal; no lo creas. Carlos V no será capaz de contrariar lo que hagan los Belzares, con quienes tiene compromisos de dinero para sus guerras. Carlos V es el alma, pero los Belzares son el brazo" (No, don't believe it. Charles V would not be capable of opposing the Welsers' actions, with whom he has various agreements involving money for his wars. Charles V is the soul, but the Welsers provide the physical force) (273). Alfinger believes that Charles V himself is subject to the Welsers because they have funded his wars. Consequently, as governor for the Welsers, Alfinger believes he has the right to conquer wherever he pleases despite jurisdictional limits.

In a strange use of the trope "going native," Francisco Martín in conversation with Kairana reveals that he has become the "second chief" of the Tamalameques (act 3, scene 4): "Á no ser por su orden, no hubiera seguido á Alfinger, que ha dejado marcada su carrera con la persecución y exterminio de tu raza, á la que amo desde que te conocí, Kariana mía, y me convertiste de oficial español Francisco Martín en el segundo jefe de tu nación" (If it wasn't for his orders, I would not have followed Alfinger, who has left his career marked by the persecution and annihilation of your peoples, whom I love, since I have met you, my Kariana, and since you have changed me from Spanish official Francisco Martín and made me the second chief of your nation) (290). Martín's loyalty is transferred because of the beauty of the natives and the cruelty of the Germans. Martín thereby highlights his Spanish affinity for the natives that would later become part of the Venezuelan mestizo identity. Likewise, he highlights a certain "noble" barbarity.

Even Tamalameque condemns Alfinger and apparently distinguishes him from the Spanish. As he prepares to kill the villain, he exclaims in a monologue, "¡Ambrosio de Alfinger, maldecido conquistador, avariento alemán, que no has venido á estas Indias, sino á robar nuestros tesoros y aniquilar nuestra raza! has amontonado crímenes y atrocidades sin número" (Ambrosius Alfinger, damned conquistador, greedy German, who only came to the Indies to rob our treasures and annihilate our race! You have accumulated multiple crimes and atrocities on your record!) (301). Stabbing him, Tamaleque calls him a monster and orders him to die, as other tribe members scream, "Muere, miserable Ambrosio" (Die, miserable Ambrosius) (305). Briceño Picón interprets Alfinger's death as due vengeance on the Welsers.

FRANCISCO HERRERA LUQUE'S *LA LUNA DE FAUSTO*: PHILIPP VON HUTTEN AND FAUST'S PROPHECY

Ospina, discussed above, and Francisco J. Herrera Luque (1927–91) used narrative and the historical novel as a way to examine the dissatisfaction with the postcolonial present in both nations. While Herrera Luque wrote his novel during the boom years of Venezuela, which allowed him to travel to Germany and conduct historical research for his novel, for Ospina, it was dissatisfaction with political corruption that made him look back at the dark beginnings of the Kingdom of New Granada. Herrera Luque's historical novel on the Welsers extends to the Germanophone realm and includes the archetypical and mythical Faustian pact with the devil. *La luna de Fausto* (1983; Faust's Moon centers on von Hutten).[15] The novel differs from other representations we have seen of the Welser agents in that it also spends a significant amount of time (about a hundred pages) to describe the political, cultural, and religious life during the Holy Roman Empire from Vienna to Seville through Ulm and Augsburg, where the young von Hutten travels. While well received initially, Hererra Luque's novels became best-sellers in Venezuela later in his life and posthumously.

Unlike any of the novelists and dramatists discussed so far in this chapter, Herrera Luque begins with an intertextual reference to the legendary alchemist of the German Renaissance, Johann Georg Faust (1480–1541), immortalized in works such as *The Tragical History of the Life and Death of Dr. Faustus* (1604) and Johann Wolfgang von Goethe's drama *Faust* (1808). Márquez Rodríguez comments on Herrera Luque's use of the universal myths of Faust and Parcival in the novel (after all, von Hutten is searching for El Dorado just like Parcival searches for the Holy Grail). However, most interestingly, Herrera Luque combines these myths with local Venezuelan myths that include legendary figures from Venezuelan folklore and religion such as Maria Lionza and La Sayona (Herrera Luque 1983, 238). The novel, narrated by an omniscient narrator most common to historical novels, opens with the scene when Faust, aided by Mephistopheles, has a vision of von Hutten's death in the land of El Dorado on the night of a blood moon.

Faust reappears at the von Hutten's family castle, where von Hutten's elder brother, the bishop of Wurzburg, calls him nothing less than "a drunk and a trickster" hated by Joachim Camerarius the Elder, Joachim Cornelius Agrippa von Nettesheim, and Philip Melanchthon: "Todos los grandes sabios y ocultistas de Alemania hablan pestes de su persona" (All of the great wise men of Germany have bad things to say about him) (65). Faust hears that von Hutten plans a voyage to Venezuela; after consulting the young man's horoscope, he warns him against going. Then Joachim Camerarius the Elder contradicts Faust, calls him a charlatan, and accuses him of using witchcraft. He's accused of appearing to young men in the shape of a beautiful young woman who seduces them and convinces them to engage in acts of sodomy whereupon Faust appears in his own shape (67–68). One of Philipp von Hutten's own friends, Franz Weiger, appears to have been "corrupted" by Faust in the manner Camerarius described.

Crude jokes aside, Herrera Luque includes a "letter" from Daniel Stevar to Philipp von Hutten dated 19 March 1534 from Werneck. It details the events of the day before when he was having drinks at a local tavern with Faust and his dog, Mephistopheles, and Joaquín Camerarius came in to threaten Faust and call him a liar: "Fausto sin mostrar turbación le respondió con su habitual ironía: '¿Qué preocupa al gran Camerarius? ¿La suerte de ese joven que encontrará en Venezuela un trágico final o las codiciosas miras de emperadores y banqueros?'" (Faust without demonstrating any embarrassment responded with his habitual irony: "What worries the great Camerarius? The luck of this young man who will in Venezuela meet a tragic end? Or the covetous looks from emperors and bankers?") (69). The exchange did not end well, Daniel Stevar writes. Camerarius jumped on Faust, and then Mephistopheles the dog jumped on Camerarius, biting off a chunk of the man's left buttock. Faust ran out into the street with his devil dog, screaming that "la expedición de los Welser terminará en desastre. Y de ir Felipe von Hutten, escúchenlo bien, encontrará cruel muerte en aquellas tierras. Os lo dice Fausto, el hombre que vendió su alma al diablo y no se arrepiente" (the Welser expedition will end in disaster. And if he goes, Philipp von Hutten, he will find a cruel death in those lands. I say it, Faust, the man who sold his soul to the devil and who does not regret it) (69). After describing Faust's prophecy and warning, Daniel Stevar pleads with von Hutten not to go on the Welser expedition (69); however Stevar's pleas fall on deaf ears.

Herrera Luque devotes himself in this novel to explaining life in the German lands, including the free imperial cities of Ulm and Augsburg. For example, the omniscient narrator names prominent followers or sympathizers of Luther such as Nikolaus Federmann's father, von Hutten's own cousin Ulrich, and Bartholomäus Welser's brother Anton. In addition, the witchhunts that plagued the German lands in the sixteenth century come up in a conversation between the Danube sailor, Andreas Goldenfingen, and von Hutten. Goldenfingen tells von Hutten about a witch burning nearby, and von Hutten recalls how a witch appeared to him in the woods near his family's estate in Franken, beckoned to him, and then rubbed him down in a hallucinogenic ointment (35). He fainted when he saw her burned at the stake. Soon after the conversation with Goldenfingen, von Hutten encounters his wife, Berta, who resembles the alluring witch both in her appearance and in her actions, as she also attempts to seduce von Hutten. She too is punished and burned at the stake. The witch resurfaces several more times in the story as a motif, though across the Atlantic, she appears in the guise of a sexually promiscuous Indigenous woman, La Sayona, a Venezuelan female legendary spirit known for her revenge on womanizers, and as María Lionza, a deity worshipped to this day in a Venezuelan syncretist religion. María Lionza, usually depicted bare-breasted, holding a female pelvis, and riding a tapir, rules over a mountain in the state of Yaracuy where thousands of worshippers pay her honor every October.[16] However, María Lionza's dangerous sexuality contrasted to Philipp von Hutten's own repressed sexual desire and failure to remain chaste reinforces the novel's madonna/whore dichotomy; von Hutten prays to the Virgin Maria Sondheim (Unsere Liebe Frau vom Rosenkratz, or Our Lady of the Holy Rosary), but he yearns for the witch women of Germany and the Indigenous women of the New World to fulfill his lust.

Philipp von Hutten, characterized as a pious man, dreams of entering the clergy. His brother, the bishop of Wurzburg, reprimands him and tells Philipp to forget this as he has another destiny because he is poor: "no te queda más alternativa que tomar el vellocino de oro que en bandeja de plata te ofrecen los Welser y el emperador. ¡Déjate de tonterías, Felipe!" (you do not have a choice but to take the golden fleece that the Welsers and the Emperor offer on a silver tray. Don't be so foolish [as to aspire to the clergy], Philipp!) (64). Von Hutten does forget this plan and follows the "golden fleece" offered by the Welsers to go to Venezuela. Yet this idea of men's double occupations or desires for self-realization is also expressed with the character of Nikolaus Federmann.

The narrator depicts Federmann as a problematic yet ambitious man of his era by representing Federmann's own attempts to write the *Indianische Historia*. The mythical von Hutten and the modern Federmann collide in the halls of the Welsers' palace in Augsburg, where they were conducting business, and Federmann's manuscript pages scatter. As both men gather them on the floor, von Hutten recognizes Federmann. He says, "Termino un libro por encargo de mis señores, los Welser. Allí narro mis aventuras y todas las posibilidades que encierra esa rica provincia. ¡Helo aquí! ¡Se llamará *La Historia Indiana*! ¡Ábrelo! ¡Pálpalo sin miedo! Mira lo que aquí digo (I am finishing a book commissioned by my bosses, the Welsers. There I talk about my adventures and about all the great opportunities confined in this rich province. Here it is! It will be called an Indian History! Open it! Take a look at it! Look here at what I say) (43).

In this intertextual moment, Herrera Luque introduces Federmann as author of the *Indianische Historia* and as a boisterous employee of the Welsers who knew where El Dorado was located.

It is von Hutten's later "cursed" expedition to find El Dorado that becomes the main theme of Herrera Luque's book. The tension between Spaniards and Germans on the expeditions appear when the hungry and sick soldiers split off in search of food. The next day, the soldier Velasco is found with the cadaver of the soldier Ceballos on whom he took revenge to settle old conflicts. The other party comes back with Murcía de Rondon in chains after he had not only killed but also eaten another soldier. The Spaniards blame the augur of their own homicidal and cannibalistic acts on the Welsers (184). Georg Hohermuth von Speyer explodes in anger and sends Velasco back in chains; he throws the Spanish cannibal, Murcía de Rondón, out of the expedition after gathering what was left of the half-eaten remains of his comrade Leoncio. Murcía de Rondón responds by damning the Welsers a thousand times—"¡Malditos, mil veces, sean los Welser!"—as he attempts to run into the bushes, but a shot from Goldenfingen's harquebus kills him. This passage exemplifies the ways that Herrera Luque shows the tension between the Germans and the Spaniards as disease and hunger ravage the troops and no signs of riches are to be found. Herrera Luque's historical novel of the Welser period re-creates the environments of the southern German lands, Seville, and Venezuela in a mythical form that experiments with the Faustian myth. According to an interview that Herrera Luque gave in 1983 before he published the novel and before embarking on a trip to Germany and Spain (the article was reprinted in *El Nacional* in 2018), he wrote, "Escribo del pasado porque le rehúyo al presente. Si escribiera sobre el presente tendría que irme del país" (I write about the past because I avoid the present. If I wrote about the present I would have to leave the country) (Pulido 1983). The historical novel becomes a way to write about a historical episode in Venezuela's history that fascinated him (the Welsers and specifically Philipp von Hutten); but he did not have the thematic thread to begin writing until he heard that Johann Georg Faust may have warned von Hutten against the Venezuela journey, portending his death.[17]

Through the Faustian myth, Herrera Luque portrays the project of conquest as one where barbarie wins over civilization. Spaniards eat and kill each other, but it is the influence of the German Welsers that Spaniards read as a bad omen. The author sometimes draws on the xenophobic attitude of Spanish soldiers to comment on the conquistadors' own inhumane behavior.

JOSÉ IGNACIO CABRUJAS, *EN NOMBRE DEL REY*

José Ignacio Cabrujas (1937–95) is described in the *Oxford Encyclopedia of Theatre and Performance* as one of the most important Latin American playwrights (Chesney-Lawrence and Crowe Serrano 2005).[18] His postmodern play, *En nombre del Rey* (In the King's Name) (1967), provides another unsettling look at the Welser period: he reads the entire conquest as not only barbaric, but idiotic. It premiered on 24 July 1963 under the direction of Eduardo Mancera by the Teatro Nacional Popular in the Theater of the Ministry of Education in Caracas. The play deals with the conquistador Gonzalo Jiménez de Quesada y Rivera, who along with Nikolaus Federmann and Sebastián de Belalcázar had fought for the right to govern the Kingdom of New Granada. In the play, a mentally ill Jiménez de Quesada hides out in the jungle along with his concubine, Mariana, and a character named "the Idiot" after the last of his men have deserted him. Jimenéz de Quesada clings to the terrain that remains of his "kingdom" as he waits for the envoy that the crown should have sent to confirm his title. Cabrujas calls attention in the play to the idiocy of the conquest and the European civilizing project, which is emblematic of the debate between civilization and barbarie in the nation.

In act 1, scene 1, "Don Gonzalo" and "El Indio," an Indigenous man to whom he tries to teach Spanish, have a conversation that conveys the farcical project of conquest and colonization, which depends on rhetorical possession.

DON GONZALO.—Yo soy más importante que tú.
EL INDIO.—Tú.
DON GONZALO—Escucha. Toda esta tierra es mía y se llama Gonzalia. Gon-za-lia. Mías son tus cosas, tus mujeres, tus hijos, tus animales. Mío.
EL INDIO.—Mío. (Cabrujas 2011, 94)

———

DON GONZALO.— I am more important than you.
EL INDIO.—You.
DON GONZALO—Listen. All of this land is mine and it is called Gonzalia. Gon-za-lia. Mine are your things, your women, your children, your animals. Mine.
EL INDIO.—Mine.

Don Gonzalo descends into madness in the course of the scene. He kills one of his men, the "Indian" flees, and he is left with Mariana and the Idiot. Sebastián de Belálcazar and Nikolaus Federmann haphazardly encounter the Idiot in the woods. Federmann expresses his confusion in both German and Spanish: "*¡Zum Spiegel!* ¿Qué ocurre? ¿Quién es ese? (What is happening? Who is that?). Federmann wonders whether the group they find is a lost expedition party, and he questions the Idiot: "¿Qué lugar es este?" (What is this place?). The Idiot responds: "Un reino . . . estáis en la ciudad de Gonzalia. El emperador duerme en sus habitaciones. Yo soy el Ministro de Estado. . . . Hay aquí también aquí una mujer, que es la emperatriz" (A Kingdom . . . you are in the city of Gonzalia. The emperor sleeps in his quarters. I am the State Minister. There is also a woman here who is Empress) (113). Federmann asks about the parody of Spanish political rule: "¿hacéis mofa de nosotros?" (are you mocking us?) (113). The Idiot responds, "Os juro que no, señor. Cuando los demás se marcharon, don Gonzalo se echó a dormir como hacen los osos en los largos meses de nevada. De allí no se ha movido, esperando al enviado de la Real Audiencia. Encerrado en los tablones ha vivido un sueño" (I promise you that no, sir. When the other left, Don Gonzalo went to sleep like bears do during winter. He has not stirred since while waiting for the envoy from the Royal Audience. Shut up within the walls he has lived a dream) (113–14).

Cabrujas's commentary on rhetorical conquest is on display here when Federmann asks soldiers to take out their weapons so they can force the doors of don Gonzalo's hut open. Belalcázar and Federmann try to convince don Gonzalo that he is suffering from madness perhaps because of an "insect bite" or the "heat" and that his party needs to follow Federmann to receive "natural rest" (118, 119). Don Gonzalo asks who they are to give orders: "¿En nombre de quién habláis?" (In whose name do you speak?) (119). Federmann responds, "Habla una cultura. Por mi boca salen palabras cultas. (*Don Gonzalo ríe*) Vuestra risa comprueba lo que decimos" (A culture speaks. Through my mouth educated works exit [*Don Gonzalo laughs*] Your laugh confirms what we say) (119). The farcical conversation between Federmann, the "civilized" conquistador, and Gonzalo continues.

DON GONZALO—¡De modo que sois cultos? ¿ Sabéis latín?
FEDERMANN—Doce años de estudio
DON GONZALO—¿y el griego?
FEDERMANN—Ocho años. (119)

———

DON GONZALO—-So you are educated? Do you know Latin?
FEDERMANN—Twelve years I studied it.
DON GONZALO—and Greek?
FEDERMANN—Eight years.

Still it is the "cultured" Federmann who orders the lost party's annihilation; while don Gonzalo, Mariana, and the Idiot make their own myths concerning Arcadia, Atlantis, and the Garden of Eden, Federmann tries to force them out of the hut. At the end, when the three have shut themselves in their hut, Federmann gives his last ignored order to come out before he sets fire to their hut, presumably burning them alive (132).

As depicted in Cabrujas's tragedy, Federmann uses violence to dissolve madness. Federmann becomes the barbaric conqueror who destroys everything, he obliterates those who have lost their sanity and their use for the crown. As such, while critiquing the idiotic project of the conquest on the whole, Cabrujas's play depicts the levels of madness and idiocy that determine the characters of the most renowned historical conquistadors. While Gonzalo Jiménez de Quesada literally loses his mind, Federmann becomes a perpetrator and Belacázar a bystander in the madness of violence. In Cabrujas's depiction of the conquest, then, only the idiot has any humanity at all.

It was Venezuela's colonial history that allowed Briceño Picón to claim an Iberian colonial history that would critique the Welsers as barbaric Lutherans. His play used the figure of the mythical Indian and the trope of the Spaniard gone native (either as the benevolent chief or the malevolent cannibal) to show the Welsers as barbaric conquerors. Comparatively, Cabrujas's eerie postmodern look back at the conquest of the Kingdom of New Granada shows the unraveling of a conqueror whose aim was to take over a New World territory. In the novel *La luna de Fausto*, Herrera Luque travels to Germany to conduct research on the Welsers and Philipp von Hutten's family before writing a novel that links the fate of the Venezuelan colonization project to the legendary Faustian myth. In a more recent turn, Ospina, in the novel *Ursúa*, shows us that the episode of the Welser governance in Venezuela can be used to explore contemporary themes such as the abuse of power and a bloated bureaucracy—all problems that plague Venezuela and Colombia to this day. The Welser episode, in historical fiction and drama, serves as a reminder of the region's foreign influence but also of the corruption affecting the region's governance. It remains a convenient episode to unearth when there is a need to look inward and backward, to unearth the roots of capitalism in the continent, or when there is a need to remember the country's conquest history and debate the nation's forces that drive civilization and barbarism.

Conclusion

As scholars, even as we may aid in particular situations, our privilege is to be able to respond to social suffering by producing knowledge that shows that isolated acts of assistance cannot undo the structures of domination that produce it. Our gift, our responsibility is to work to produce forms of understanding that make intolerable the conditions that maintain injustice in any form, including our use of the privilege of science itself.

—Fernando Coronil, "Perspectives on *Darkness in El Dorado*"

Cultural memory emerges in response to particular circumstances, and the story of the Welser Venezuela colony continues to resonate in divergent ways within Venezuela and Germany. In this book, I have grappled with the history and effects of early modern racialized merchant capitalism by tracing the impact of the Welser Venezuela colony (1528–56) on both nations' cultural memory. Using travel literature, the canonical works of colonial Latin American literature authored by Spanish cronistas, maps and photographs, archival materials such as legal records, and novels and plays written by Venezuelan and Colombian authors, I have analyzed the Welsers' activities as emblematic of the Augsburg merchants involved in the business of lending money and trading wares in the Habsburg Empire. From Madeira to La Palma (Canary Islands), to Santo Domingo (Hispaniola), and, finally, to Venezuela, the Welsers sought to maximize quick profits, first in the trade of commodities such as spices and sugar and then finally in the Indigenous and African slave markets. All the while, Welser agents such as Ambrosius

Alfinger, Nikolaus Federmann, and Philipp von Hutten sought the golden kingdom of El Dorado that would ensure their wealth and status back home in Augsburg and Ulm but never located it. The conflict between the colony's Spanish administrators and its German governors that plagued the Venezuela colony shows that Europe's religious strife following the Reformation extended across the Atlantic. Bartolomé de Las Casas's claim that Germans were "animal/aleman" (animal/German) reveals the xenophobia prevalent during the colonial era when Habsburg Spain ruled Venezuela; it also determined the way the colony was remembered in Venezuela both during Bourbon Spain and after Simón Bolívar led the nation to independence. Germany, however, apart from the Welser family, would remember this episode when it sought to establish its colonies during the nineteenth-century imperial era, again during the Nationalist Socialist period, and now in discussions about decolonizing monuments and cultural patrimony.

Foundational fictions of conquest have guided the way Venezuelans view the nation's struggle between civilization and barbarism. Violence affected 1980s Venezuela particularly through the Caracazo (Caracas hit), the name given to a wave of popular protests, looting, and massive repression that began on 27 February 1989 after President Carlos Andres Pérez announced he would implement an International Monetary Fund–backed austerity plan that resulted in bus fare hikes and massive discontent. Hundreds if not thousands of Venezuelans were killed, and many were buried in unmarked mass graves. A year before, on 29 October 1988, in what was labeled the massacre of El Amparo, Venezuelan military and paramilitary forces killed sixteen rural Venezuelan men, accused of being armed members of Colombia's guerrilla force, the ELN (National Liberation Army); later it was revealed that these men had been victimized (shot in the back, their bodies mutilated, and faces and tattoos burned with acid) and dressed in ELN uniforms in what Fermando Coronil and Julie Skurski (2019, 185) call "a simulacrum of subversion" that traces violence to the nation's violent colonial past. Both of these crucial events in the nation's history revealed the tensions between the country's elite and the marginalized, darker, masses in both rural and urban contexts. The Venezuelan state continued colonial injustices in the 1980s. Many of these injustices were politicized by the leftist Venezuelan president Hugo Chávez, who ruled from 1999 to 2013, and later by his successor, Nicolás Maduro, as well as many opposition candidates who use the discourse of barbarism and civilization along with narratives of conquest to discuss the dire present and future economic and political realities of Venezuelans both at home and in the increasing diaspora. I hope this book has continued the questioning of the nation's colonial legacy amid the polarization of Venezuelan society.

To conclude my engagement with the theme of cultural memory as a long-term memory produced in a variety of media and monuments, as explored in the latter part of the book, here I want to revisit the German press's reexamination of the Welser period since 1992, the absence of attention to the Welser period on the Venezuelan side, and a debate that centers on Germany's commemoration of colonial-era figures and restitution of looted art from former colonies. In this analysis, the importance of blood, toponyms, and genealogy emerges just as it did when the Welsers decided to justify their claims to nobility by their possession of the province of Venezuela.

As the five-hundred-year anniversary of Columbus's arrival on the American continent approached in 1992, the German media capitalized on interest in Germans' role in the conquest and colonization of the Americas. Many journalists wrote articles on Nikolaus Federmann and Ambrosius Alfinger and on the Welsers' involvement in the conquest and colonization of Venezuela. In 1991, a popular travel show, *Terra X*, on the network ZDF (Zweites Deutsches Fernsehen) ran an episode titled "Der Todeszug der Lanzenreiter" (The Death Trip of the Lance-Bearing Knight) that details Federmann's second entrada into present-day Colombia (Kirchner 1991). The *Südwest Presse*, Ulm's daily newspaper, described the *Federmannomanie*, or Federmann mania, in southern Germany, detailing Ulm's fascination with the city's infamous native son (Petershagen 1992).[1]

In the 1990s, the public no longer sought gold and treasures in recovering Germany's role in the conquest but rather archival and literary manifestations of Germans involved in the conquest of the Americas. This suggests a growing need for a discourse of "national" identity that not only focused on individuals such as Federmann and Alfinger, but allows twentieth-century Germans to fashion a "Columbus" figure made out of German, perhaps particularly Swabian, stock. In Federmann's and Alfinger's hometown of Ulm, Hennig Petershagen (1992) explored the "manic interest" in the two figures that had occurred after 1992. Library materials on the two conquistadors had been "checked out for months." Petershagen explained that we know more about Federmann than Alfinger because of his *Indianische Historia*. He noted that it had languished in the library's collection for many years but that it was now in "high demand" and was unavailable until further notice. Federmann had became a local hero in the early 1990s. An exhibition, *500 Jahre Eroberung und Kolonialisierung—mit dabei Schwaben, Bayern und Franken in Handel, Banken und Versicherungen* (500 years Conquest and Colonization—with Swabians, Bavarians, and Franks in Trade, Banking, and Securities), which opened in January 1993, highlighted Federmann. This is not to say that the treatment of Federmann was uncritical; a review of the exhibition titled "'El Dorado' brachte kein Glück'" (El Dorado Did Not Bring Any Luck) describes Federmann's and Alfinger's destinies as "unlucky" but those of the conquered "Vielfaches tragischer" (tragic many times over) (Dehner 1993, 277). A 1992 article in the *Neu-Ulmer Zeitung*, a regional newspaper for Ulm, explained the reasons for the Welsers' involvement in Venezuela.

> Venezuela wollten die Welser zum Absatzmarkt für Ihren Warenhandel machen und dort Plantagen aufbauen; es sollte Sklaven für den kolonialen Handel liefern. Ganz besonderes hoffte man jedoch auf den Bergbau, der Edelmetalle wie Gold und Silber erbringen sollte. (Kreikle 1992)
>
> ———
>
> The Welsers wanted to turn Venezuela into a market for the trade of their merchandise. They wanted to build plantations there; it should have supplied slaves for the colonial trade. However, they particularly placed their hope on mining, which should have provided precious metals such as gold and silver.

The article's author, the historian Christian Kreikle, presented the colony's capacity for resource extraction and production as the grounds for conquest. The slave market (which may or may not have included Africans) would contribute to building a plantation economy that would further expand the Welsers' merchant trade (Kreikle 1992). The reference to *mining* gold and precious metals rather than the *taking* of these resources acts as a fig leaf. It would have been enslaved Amerindians or Africans who did the mining.

Nonetheless, Kreikle quotes Las Casas's *Brevísima relación* at length and indicts the Welsers for cruel treatment of the Indians. He characterizes Federmann as one of the worst agents: "Federmanns erster Zug brachte ihm schon damals den Ruf der absoluten Rücksichtslosigkeit ein und den Vorwurf, Indianer und spanische Begleiter brutal mißhandelt zu haben. Sein abentuerlicher Reisebericht . . . schildert davon jedoch recht wenig" (Already at that time, Federmann's first entrada gave him the reputation of pure ruthlessness and the accusation of having brutally mistreated the native Indians and Spaniards who accompanied him. His travel narrative describes little of this) (Kreikle 1992). Kreikle's emphasis on the Welsers' project of establishing plantations and mining suggests that the Welsers meant to stay. In general, his indictment of Federmann and analysis of Las Casas's critique of the German governors presents a nuanced view of the Welser Venezuela period.

The indictment of Federmann continues in other articles in the popular media. The Welser family joined the fray, distinguishing Federmann's personal selfish interests from those of the Welser Company. In 1991 the *Schwäbische Zeitung* published an interview with Sigmund Freiherr von Welser called "Conquistadoren aus Augsburg." On Federmann, von Welser states, "Der eigensinnige Federmann war einzig darauf aus, nach Gold zu suchen" (The stubborn Federmann was solely interested in finding gold) (Frevel 1991, 279). He insists that the Welsers were "innocent" because they had no role in the discovery, conquest, and evangelization of America: "An der Entdeckung Amerikas sind wir also völlig unschüldig" (We are completely innocent on the discovery of America) (279). According to Frevel and von Welser, "Auch für die Missionierung hätten die Welser nicht viel getan" (The Welsers did not do much for the evangelization) (279). Frevel explains, "Denn die Missionare, die bei den Expeditionen dabei gewesen wären seien spanische Mönche gewesen, die Mission sei im Auftrag und im Sold des Königs von Spanien durchgeführt worden" (The missionaries on the expeditions were Spaniards, and the conversion was mandated and dictated by the Spanish Crown) (279). Further, he notes that the Spaniards on the expeditions suspected that the Welsers were likely Protestants and impeded them in conversion missions (279). Hence, Frevel's interview of Sigmund von Welser presents the descendants of the Welser family as separating their history from Federmann's.

For the twenty years after the Columbus jubilee, the media in Ulm continued to address the Welser period. For example, on 27 August 2011, Tobias Rupprecht published an article in the *Neu-Ulmer Zeitung* titled "Gier Nach Gold" (Greed for Gold): "an der Entdeckung und Eroberung Amerikas hatten schwäbische Kaufleute und Abenteurer ihren heute *oft vergessenen* wichtigen Anteil" (Swabian merchants and adventurers played an *often forgotten* important role in the conquest and discovery of America; my emphasis). Rupprecht describes the conquest that killed many natives and the beginnings of the African slave trade to supply the needed labor force in the Indies; he makes a link between the European conquest of the Americas and the birth of European capitalism.

> Auf Plantagen und in Minen erarbeiten sie den Reichtum, der den Aufstieg der europäischen Imperien ermöglichte. Geraubtes Silber und Gold der Azteken und Inka lieferten das Startkapital für den europaischen Kapitalismus. (Rupprecht 2011, 280)
>
> ———
>
> They worked and built the wealth in mines and in plantations; they were responsible for the growth of the European empires. The Incas' and Aztecs' stolen gold and silver would supply the starting capital for European capitalism.

Rupprecht sees the Welsers as purely having an interest in profit over over the foundation of towns and the evangelization of the Indians, stating, "Sie hatten aber vor allem eines im Kopf: viel Gewinn zu machen in möglichst kurzer Zeit" (They had one thing above all in mind: to make as much profit in as little time possible). Like both Frevel and von Welser, Rupprecht focused on the Welsers' use of "plantations," suggesting they actually meant to have an agricultural plantation colonial economy, even though evidence shows that at least in Venezuela the Welser agents were focused on expeditions to find gold and the Pacific. Colonization, rather than conquest, would seem to "normalize" the Welsers' actions in Venezuela.

Rupprecht (2011) acknowledges that in Venezuela the Welsers' cruel expeditions involved "Gewaltexzessen" (excesses of violence); he states that the Welsers "galten vor allem der Suche nach einer indianische Zivilisation, die bedeutend genug war, dass dort lohnenswerte Reichtümer geplündert werden konnten. Die harte Arbeit unterwegs verrichteten dabei unterworfene Einheimische und versklavte Afrikaner" (looked above all for an Indian civilization that was important enough to hold worthwhile riches that could be plundered. The hard work on the way was performed by subjugated natives and enslaved Africans). He notes that the Spanish administration "nicht mit ihnen zurechtkamen" (did not get along with them [the Welsers]). In general, Rupprecht was correct in his analysis. He notes that the history was forgotten until the mid-nineteenth century "als Deutschnationale sich nach eigenen Kolonien sehnten" (when German nationals looked toward their own colonial possessions). Today one can find the traces, or "Spuren," of the Welsers in present-day Colombia and Venezuela. He notes that Bogotá has a neighborhood called "Nicolás de Federmán" and that the central square in Riohacha is named after Federmann. His readers would have been given a general picture of the Welsers' actions in the colony as well as the importance of the colony's history for German colonists in the imperial era. But he also claims that contemporary Venezuelans want to believe that they are descended from Welser conquerors: "Im venezolanischen Städtchen Cuara leben auffällig viele hellhäutige Menschen, die ihre Wurzeln in Schwaben sehen. Das ist zwar keineswegs belegt, aber der örtliche Fußballklub und die Apotheke nennen sich trotzdem 'Los Welser'" (In the Venezuelan city of Cuara there are strikingly many light-skinned people, who trace their roots to Swabia. It is not proven, nonetheless the local soccer club and the local pharmacy call themselves *Los Welser*). In this excerpt, Rupprecht reveals a glimmer of satisfaction when Venezuelans believe the Welsers and the Germans on their expeditions are their forefathers.

I discuss these examples from the German media in the late twentieth century and the beginning of the twenty-first to show that some Germans continue to use the Welser period to self-fashion an imperial identity. The Ulm press in particular nostalgically tries to rescue their native sons. For Rupprecht (2011, 280), the very absence of imagined forefathers for the Venezuelans of Cuara establishes that imagined genealogy remains important to Venezuelans. The light-skinned residents of Cuara fashion themselves as descendants of the Welsers themselves, while the journalist wonders about the implications of the Cuarans' imagined genealogy. Toponyms and business names reflect a selective cultural memory and an imagined community. The Cuara pharmacy is called Los Welser; in this turn of events the Welsers will finally administer the medicine they extracted from the native communities. This event is not so far removed from the Welsers' own reimagining and self-fashioning of their identity as Renaissance noblemen. That identity demanded possession of other lands and subjugation of the natives. Only time will tell whether the reimaginations of the Welser period have finally ended on either side of the Atlantic.

Epilogue

Restitution and Commemoration Debates in Germany Today

In 2012, Reuters reported on a conflict between Wolfgang von Schwarzenfeld, a German stone artist, and Venezuelan Pemón natives, over a thirty-
five-ton slab of pink sandstone that he transported from the Gran Sabana
area of southeastern Venezuela to Berlin and engraved with the word *love* in
different languages (Brown 2012). The report stated that the sculpture was
"meant to promote world peace." But the Pemón natives consider the ancient pink sandstone mountains, or *tepuis*, from which the stone originates
sacred and debate the elderly artist's claim that it was a legal gift in 1998. *Der
Spiegel* reported in July 2012:

> A Pemon legend holds that the Kueka Stone was part of a pair of rocks
> formed when lightning split a giant stone block thousands of years ago.
> The two stones represent the legend of a love story between a Pemon
> man and a woman from another tribe. Their inter-tribal romance dis-
> pleased the Pemon god Makunaima, and he turned them into stone.
> The two rocks now symbolize the tribe's grandmother ("kueka") and
> grandfather. Separating them, the people believe, would cause disaster
> to strike the area. (Spiegel International 2012)

The Venezuelan president at the time, Hugo Chávez, demanded the stone's
return to Venezuela, deeming it an example of German cultural imperialism.
The stone is a fitting symbol of the culturally insensitive activities of artists,
intellectuals, and institutions that take materials and works found in the remote corners of the world and display them without any thought to their

FIGURE E.1. Wolfgang von Schwarzenfeld, "Love Stone," Global Stone Project, Tiergarten, Berlin, July 2013. Photo by author.

origin, and yet the anthropologist Bruno Illius questioned the claim that the Pemón Indians had considered the stone holy (Brown 2012). After intense debate among officials and amid increasing protests in Venezuela, Schwarzenfeld said in 2012 that he would return the stone to the Venezuelan Gran Sabana. In May 2018 members of the Pemón nation, including twelve shamans, came to the Tiergarten, where the stone was a tourist attraction, and performed a healing ritual (Fuenmayor 2018). Yet on 12 January 2020, my friend Vladimir Bourdin kindly walked to the Tiergarten in Berlin and provided proof via photographs on Whatsapp: the stone still sat where it had since 1999, behind the city's Brandenburg Gate. I was shocked when I checked the news on 21 January 2020 as I went over the manuscript of this book. Telesur and Amerika21 reported that the stone was being restituted on 20 January 2020 (Telesur 2020). The report was accompanied by a photograph of the stone, hoisted by a large crane. Kueka has been surviving Berlin's winters for twenty years and returned to Venezuela's Guayanan Highlands of moist forests in April 2020—specifically, to the community of Santa Cruz de Mapaurí.

This cultural clash suggests how uneasy German and Venezuelan relations remain, plagued by conflicts over American natural resources and cultural patrimony from developing nations. My concern is not to determine whether Schwarzenfeld acquired the stone legally or whether he stole it. The German artist paid money to the Venezuelan government for the stone and used it as part of his "Global Stone," which includes stones from five continents that, according to the *New York Times*, signify "Peace" (on a rock from Australia), "Hope" (on a rock from Africa), "Forgiveness" (on a rock from Asia), and, in a seemingly blind nod to the Enlightenment, "Awakening" (on a rock from Europe) (Eddy 2012). However well intentioned the artist, it is hard to imagine the German government giving a part of the Brandenburg Gate to stand in the remote Gran Sabana region, or even in Caracas, to promote world peace. The fact that this hypothetical reversal remains absurd speaks to the power dynamic at the heart of this cultural encounter.

Furthermore, Schwarzenfeld's claim that the stone, which holds symbolic meaning for the Pemón Indians, would universally promote world peace and love does not bear scrutiny. To begin with, Schwarzenfeld appears to have been motivated by financial considerations. In the heat of controversy, he stated that if the stone were taken away, it would ruin fifteen years of his hard work "and all the money [he] spent" (Brown 2012). Further, the

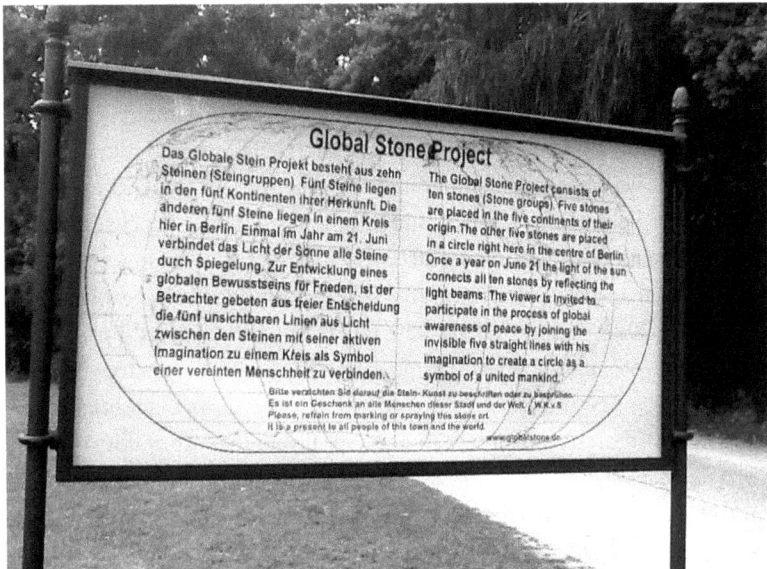

FIGURE E.2. Global Stone Project, Tiergarten, Berlin. Photo by author.

FIGURE E.3. "Love Stone," Tiergarten, Berlin, July 2013. Photo by author.

litigation over the stone reveals the changing political agendas in Venezuela: Venezuelan president Caldera supposedly gave the artist the gift of the stone, yet later President Chávez alleged that the gift had not been legal. Some said that Chávez was seeking political advantage and to distract from other problems. Meanwhile, the Pemón Indians demanded the stone's return, and the anthropologists debated the stone's sacredness. Clearly, Schwarzenfeld's choice brings up many questions: Why would the Venezuelan stone promote world peace? Would a stone from a former Soviet Bloc country be more appropriate? And how could a South American stone that does not bear any reference to its cultural origin possibly promote unity and world peace at the site of the infamous Berlin Wall? Despite the semblance of unity (one stone from each continent), it is hardly surprising that such an ill-conceived project failed in its purpose and instead caused strife. The story uncovers claims, legalities, and propaganda, as well as myths, fantasies, and delusions, about a giant slab of prehistoric stone. It mirrors the intense debate occurring in the West (including Germany) surrounding the restitution of artifacts in the collections of museums acquired during the colonial era. But it also tells another narrative about a natural object possibly valued by

Indigenous peoples and taken and molded by German hands. The stone begs us to examine its contours and see what is in the crevices. It calls us to question what occurs when individuals and institutions use exotic objects to promote universal values and when people in Schwarzenfeld's position demand a return on their investments.

Germany's recent debates over the public commemoration of its colonial past reflect similar complications. Germany began "decolonizing" its cities by changing city street names and discussing controversial colonial-era monuments in the past few years (Pelz 2018). These efforts in turn bear resemblance to debates in the United States over the memorialization of the Confederacy and its adherents, an institution founded on the preservation of chattel slavery.[1]

Activist groups demand critiques and responses. They ask, for example, how is it that one can travel from Munich to Augsburg with the Fugger express train[2] and go to the Fuggerplatz and visit the Fugger and Welser Museum[3] without any contextualization about Germany's colonial history? The Augsburg Postkolonial Group (2019) criticizes the Fuggers' use of forced labor in its endeavors in the ivory, gold, and slave trades. On 1 January 2020, the group posted a blog entry thanking the community for all their activities. In fact, the group has been active in leading "postcolonial city tours" of Augsburg that center on the colonial activities of Bartholomäus Welser and the Fuggers and that discuss—through concepts, pictures, and economic power relations—the meaning that colonial history has for Augsburg. In Berlin, the "Decolonise HU" group criticizes the streets in the district of Schöneberg that are named after the Welsers and Fuggers (Welserstraße and Fuggerstraße) (Decolonize HU 2016).

The battle in the Berlin district of Wedding that began in the 1980s to change the names of Petersallee and Lüderitzstrasse is an example of the efforts to decolonize and the resistance these efforts have met (Flakin 2012). The former was named after the notorious colonizer Carl Peters (see ch. 6), who treated native Tanzanians brutally. Yet Adolf Hitler sought to restore Peters's name by signing an act of grace in 1937 that saw Peters as a national hero; Nationalist Socialists dedicated the street in his name in 1939. The colonizer was also the subject of a 1941 Nazi propaganda film that promoted anti-British sentiment as well as Hitler's colonial fantasy of expansion. While the Wedding district council says Petersallee was technically changed to honor Hans Peters, a Nazi resistance fighter, for Christian Kopp, an anti-racism activist, this name rededication was just a convenient way to white-wash history (Rechel 2014).

Lüderitzstrasse has a similarly abhorrent past. It was named after Lüderitz, a harbor city founded in German Southwest Africa (present-day Namibia) where imperial Germany founded its first concentration camp to slaughter Indigenous Herero women, men, and children after the tribe rose up against the colonizers; 80 percent of the Hereros died in the concentration camps or from thirst after fleeing into the desert.[4] Recently, the German government returned human remains that belonged to the Herero and Nama peoples that had been stored in hospitals, museums, and universities, including the famous Charité, Berlin's largest hospital (Deutsche Welle 2018). There are scheduled changes: Lüderitzstrasse should become Cornelius-Fredericks-Straße, after a leader of the Orlam people in German Southwest Africa (Namibia) that resisted the Germans. Petersallee should be named Anna-Mungunda-Allee, after the Herero (Namibian) woman who in 1959, in the Old Location Uprising, resisted the police's violent actions against demonstrators protesting apartheid conditions in Windhoek (the South African National Party had effectively ruled Namibia since it came to power in 1948). Another strip of Petersallee should be named the Maji-Maji-Allee after the armed rebellion against German colonial rule in German East Africa. Nachtingalplatz, named after Gustav Nactingal, who colonized parts of present-day Togo and Cameroon under the German Empire, should also be renamed, as Manga-Bell-Platz, after the leader of the Duala people of southern Cameroon during the period when Germans controlled the country (Bergermann 2019). While the streets could be renamed, due to slow bureaucratic red tape in the Berlin Mitte District Office, it is not clear exactly if that will occur.

Debates surrounding the exhibition of artifacts acquired during Germany's colonial era continue to plague the opening of Berlin's newest museum, the Humboldt Forum (which opened virtually in December 2020 due to COVID-19 restrictions). It has led Jürgen Zimmerer (2017), the prominent historian of Africa and German colonialism, to remind Germans that "colonialism is not a game" in response to curators' ambivalence about the display of controversial objects. As the debate on Europe's restitution of artifacts that may have been stolen or acquired through dubious means during the colonial era deepens, Germany and the United States have been at the forefront of this controversy on cultural imperialism. For example, in a debate between the art historian Horst Bredekamp and Jürgen Zimmerer for the *Frankfurter Allgemeine Zeitung*, Zimmerer was asked whether German scientists were involved in colonialism before Germany became a colonial power itself (Zimmerer and Bredekamp 2019). Zimmerer's answer warrants consideration. In effect, he brought up the Fuggers, the Welsers, and the electors of Brandenburg (who also attempted to enter the slave trade on the African west coast). According to Zimmerer, colonialism affected politics, the economy, and even intellectual history.

Since the Welsers, there have been individuals, corporations, and state entities that have sought to profit within colonial structures. While the early merchant capitalism of the Welsers and Fuggers had specific economic goals and the Brandenburg electors sought to continue what the Welser slave traders had begun in West Africa, scientists and intellectuals also participated in the system that the bankers started. Even though we praise Alexander von Humboldt, renowned for his scientific contributions to botany, climatology, ecology, geology, and other fields, as well as his political writings in which he expressed his disdain for slavery, it was a colonial system that allowed him access to travel, collect specimens, use native labor, and meet special dignitaries such as Thomas Jefferson in the United States. Alexander von Humboldt traveled to South America because a Spanish colonial system allowed him to do so (Zimmerer and Bredekamp 2019).

Zimmerer, who is in favor of restituting the famous Benin bronzes that form part of a 580-object Benin collection housed at the Ethnological Museum of Berlin, questions how German (and Western) museum directors and curators are separating colonial history from their collections that were acquired in dubious colonial situations.[5] Germany has only recently begun to deal with its colonial history (Eligon 2018); yet the debate over the restitution of stolen art, according to a headline in Munich's *Süddeutsche Zeitung* from 18 February 2019, has become "die größte Indentitätsdebatte unserer Zeit" (the biggest identity debate of our time) (Zimmerer 2019). More recently, alliances and clubs such as Berlin Postkolonial and Decolonise Berlin have demanded that early colonial history also be contextualized. The links between early venture capitalism and colonization as well as its legacy have not been debated.

Young Germans are reengaging with their colonial history, emphasizing a postcolonial turn that critiques yet informs the larger public about Germany's colonial past. The project "Freedom Roads: koloniale straßennames postkoloniale erinnerungskultur" (Freedom Roads! 2015), started by the Berlin Postkolonial Group, aims to take street names, or at times whole neighborhoods, named after German colonial figures and provide them with new context about the legacy of the German Empire.[6] In Munich, Von Trotha Street was renamed Hererostrasse to commemorate the agents of the anticolonial rebellion. In 2006, in Bielefeld, a group performed a re-creation of the German colonial experience in East Africa at Karl-Peters Strasse. In addition, the project Afrika-Hamburg.de archived more than 5,600 votes and compiled more than 800 responses from Hamburg's citizens debating the future of the statue of German East Africa's bloody governor, Hermann von Wissmann (Afrika-Hamburg.de 2005).[7] At least 200,000 people have walked by the monument and read the information about its historical context. The statue was also shown in the German Historical Museum's exhibition on German colonialism.

As for the Berlin streets, there are changes approved by the district office. Petersallee will have two new names: one part of the street will be named after the Namibian independence fighter Anna Munguda; the other part of the street will be renamed Maji-Maji-Allee, after the German East African resistance movement. Lüderitzstrasse would be named after Cornelius Fredericks, a resistance fighter from German Southwest Africa.

Of course, this is not the first time that German cities have renamed their streets. After the Nationalist Socialist period, many officials in both the German Democratic Republic (East Germany) and the Federal Republic of Germany (West Germany) changed street names that honored fascist leaders. There were diverging models: in East Berlin, one of the widest boulevards was named Stalinallee from 1949 and 1961 and then after de-Stalinization to Karl-Marx Allee. Since reunification there have been talks about returning it to its pre–World War II name, Große Frankfurterstraße. Set after the fall of the Berlin Wall, Wolfgang Becker's 2003 film, *Goodbye Lenin!*, showed that the toppling of monuments was a political ritual aimed to usher in a new reconstruction of public memory that wove history and a new Weltanschauung into the urban fabric.

Public officials, curators, university presidents, and community leaders should pay attention to the debates started in Hamburg and Berlin. Here in the United States ongoing debates surrounding the fate of Confederate monuments such as the toppled Silent Sam monument at the University of North Carolina at Chapel Hill beg for historical contextualization and a critical debate on commemoration of symbols representative of racism and violence. However, if the slow process of changing street names in Berlin's Wedding "African" quarter is an example, it will take years before a compromise or solution is found—perhaps not before experiencing yet another bout of amnesia regarding Germany's colonial history.

Writing this book about the Welser Venezuela colony and its cultural memory is my small attempt at combating this amnesia concerning Germany's and Spain's colonial past in Venezuela that is linked by racialized capitalism. Personally, I am optimistic that colleagues in both Latin American colonial studies and German studies will rethink their perceptions of the colonization of the Americas and its cultural memory. I hope this book acts as an exposé of how individuals, states, and, institutions reclaim and distort that colonial history through various nationalist claims and commemorative projects. This is my contribution to questioning European colonial legacies in the Americas and the monuments and narratives that celebrate suspect victories.

NOTES

Introduction

1. "credit, n." *OED Online*, September 2021, www-oed-com.

2. For a study of cosmography and the Welsers' role in promoting German exploration voyages, see Johnson 2008. For Habsburg economic history as well as the Welsers' economic goals, see Armani 1985; Häberlein and Burkhardt 2002. The main monographs on the Welser Venezuela colony remain Haebler 1903; Friede 1961; Simmer 2000.

3. See Warsh 2018.

4. Anton Welser married Katharina Vöhlin (1460–1514), the daughter of Hans Vöhlin d.J. (1423–96), leader of the Memmingen Vöhlin Company that traded salt, wine, iron, and fustian cloth. Konrad Vöhlin (ca. 1455–1511), son of Hans Vöhlin d.J. and brother of Katharina Vöhlin, married his brother-in-law Anton Welser's sister Barbara (1460–1504) (Kießling 2002, 186).

5. Twenty-nine representatives of artisanal guilds selected fifteen "of the best and most important patricians" to join them on the Small Council (*Kleinen Rat*) (Blendinger 1984, 151). The guildsmen then selected one of their own and one patrician to serve as *Bürgermeister*, creating parity in government between guilds-men and patricians (Stuart 1999, 35). According to Schnith (1984, 154), even though the ratio was 29:15, the patricians held the upper hand in both the more powerful Small Council and the Large Council because at times they doubled as guild members. Moreover, in the late Middle Ages the interests of the merchants (who could be members of either the patricians or the guilds) became a unifying power between members of those classes that led to Augsburg's stability but also to its conservatism (Schnith 1984, 154). Kießling (1984b, 244) also sees, in comparison to other cities, the absence of animosity between the patricians and the merchants in the upper circles, or *Obersicht*.

6. For example, as Häberlein has recorded, the Fuggers' pattern of marriages from the late 1500s assured their entry into the most selective circles, thereby increasing their social status, their social capital, and their economic capital by their investments of their wives' fortunes.

7. To put together the information, the editors used extant tax records from Augsburg as an indicator of "taxable income" or wealth. They also followed membership in Augsburg's closed circles and their economic activity and used individuals' social standing within the various Augsburg "classes" (Reinhard and Häberlein 1996, xiv). This hierarchy includes members of the patriciate that ruled the city and later the influential guilds or exclusive social groups such as the *Herrenstuben*, or Gentlemen's Drinking Halls (xiv). Häberlein and Reinhard's study includes numerous appearances of the leading business figures of the Welser Company (*Gesellschaft*). First Anton Welser I (head of the Welser-Vöhlin Gesellschaft) and Bartholomäus V, who headed the Welser Company during its heyday (1498–1530), conducted business with other members of the patrician and the merchant class. There are records of Bartholomäus V's business contacts with his managers in Spain such as Heinrich Ehinger, Hieronymus Sailer, Heinrich Sailer, and Heinrich Geßler; his Santo Domingo managers, Anton Lauginger, Pedro de Cuebas, Peter Marcus; and his Venezuela representatives, such as Nikolaus Federmann, Hans Seißenhofer, Georg Hohermuth, Bartholomäus Sailer, Andreas Guldenfinger, Franz Lebzelter, Melchior Grubel, and Andreas Rem.

CHAPTER 1. Colonization, Commerce, Commodities, and Imperial Credit

1. "wunder schone kurtzweilige Reis mit guoter geselschaft und der Compania nutz mit einbringen der schulden."

2. "rechnong alum von unsern factoren zuo nemen."

3. "Het underwegen in fil stetten zuo schaffen, dz Ich ob 24 teg nit anheim plib."

4. "Not also krank rit ich hinein und tatt ain nuotzle anelgong mit marokan: Saffran."

5. "Hett etlich wexel gelt zuo empfachen und verwexeln."

6. "ward ich schwerlich krank am Fieber, het gros hilff und rat durch fremd, dan ich nit ain bekannt mensch da fand."

7. "primo Aug. tat wir den vertrag mit portugal king der armazion 3 schiff per Indian."

8. "Gott pehielt uns! Die pestilenz XImal in Haus hett, mir fil einkaufer, megdt, und sturben."

9. In addition to the plague, Lisbon had experienced environmental catastrophes that led to a drought in the early 1500s. While Rem made no mention of it in

his diary, thousands of Jews who had fled Spain for Portugal after 1492 were slaughtered beginning in 1506 due to scapegoating for the epidemic and drought. On 19 April 1506, the night of the Lisbon massacre, hundreds of suspected Jews, said to be guilty of heresy and deicide, were tortured and burned at the stake.

10. "Die Zeit ich in Portugal was, von 8 May 1503 bis 27 Septb. 1508, underfong mich on mas gros und fil hendel mit verkaufen kupfer, pley, zinober, Kecksilber. . . . Ich began mich gen Madera, Ilhas Dazors, Cavo Verde, Barbarien armieren. In Portugal kauffe ich fast fil Specey, und tat gros Kaufhandel mit dem King."

11. "mit vertresten und verwenen nit mer in portugal ze schicken."

12. "Ich sollte per mar oder per terra gen Lisbonna, Madera, Palma raissen des Ich mich widert, um des verwenen des Compagnia."

13. According to Peter Geffcken's "Ravensburger" entry in the *Stadtlexicon Augsburg*, Leo Ravensburger (d. 1557) was a merchant who belonged to one of the original patrician families in Augsburg (Geffcken 2021). He was a factor for the Welsers in Madeira in 1509 and after his marriage to Felizitas Herwart (1521) worked for his in-laws' firm before being elected mayor of Augsburg in 1548, a post he held until he resigned in 1553 because of his role in the 1552 Prince's Revolt. Hans Schmid was also a factor of the Welsers in Madeira, though not much is known about him.

Rem explains on 2 October 1509 from Funchal, "Jacomo and I sat and went over the accounts, and ordered them as best as I could. I left Hans Egelhoff under him" (Rem 1861, 13; "Da fand ich Leo Ravespurger, Hans Schmid in unser geselschaft haus ain ebermlichs Regement unerbens wesen. Setzt Jacomo und mich uber die Conti, het lang noch nacht ruo noch frid, tatt boest ich vermocht, verordnet als ding, boest ich mocht").

14. As usual, the names in Spanish or Portuguese transcription suffer, but we have records of a Jacome Olizpoq (Jacob Holzbock), Lleam Ravenspurgher (Leo Ravensburger), and Joam Schmidt (Hans Schmid). A Juan Agusto also appears in the Spanish records; it is probable that it was the Spanish version of Hans Egelhoff, as the Egelhoff family appears in Augsburg's city records in the sixteenth century. In her article "Los Flamencos en Canarias," Viña Brito says that Hans Egelhoff was a Flemish trader, though in all likelihood he came from Augsburg and was known as Juan Augusto (2012, 180). In general, to discuss nationalities, even Carande used the term "flamenco" to refer to bankers whose primary residence and place of business was Antwerp, despite their original place of birth.

15. The period 1450–1506 was one of growth for the sugar industry in the Atlantic islands. Growth was 13 percent a year between 1451 and 1472 and a striking 68 percent between 1472 and 1493. A two-year decrease followed, but the industry recovered, and there was another high point of returns in 1506 (Vieira 2004, 61).

16. The arroba was a unit of measurement used in Spain, Portugal, and Latin America, equal to one-fourth of a quintal or 25 *libras castellanas*. In Spain, the Canary Islands, and Spanish America, the arroba was normally about 25 pounds. In Madeira, it was 28 pounds until 1504, when it was increased to 32 pounds (Schwartz 2004, 16–17).

17. Juan Augusto, a Genoese citizen, would later be involved in a legal dispute with the Casa de Contratación (House of Trade) for having gone to the Indies without permission as he was an "extranjero," or foreigner. The process was started around 11 January 1566. See AGI, "Pleito fiscal: Juan Augusto" JUSTICIA, 875, no. 1.

18. "Tierras 1 fajana y aguas y 5 cahices."

19. "Adi 25 fruo nt gen Taza Cortt (Tassacorte) das verfluocht land genannter Egelhoff unser geselschafft Kaft het." On the "damned land," see also Viña Brito and Kur 2010.

20. "Plib ich bis am 30 Septbro. Da solt ich lang pliben sein, gros [und] vil gut ordnung tan haben. Aber ich erfandt, daz got geb, was ich befelch nach mein abschid nit flostreckt wurd. Zuom wasserleiten, land bauen, etlich Jar gehoret, die ich nit pleiben wolt, gleich eylett, bei tag das land, leit, fich, die gantz nacht rechnongen (und) biecherbesach, on al ruo. Eylet on mas, um den winter aus den Insseln zuo komen. Liess Hans Egelhoff Obersten mit sonst fil leiten dar" (Rem 1861, 13).

21. "Wasen meist mein hendel rechten widern King der Amazon d'India, librong etlich zucker, und gehederischen recht von Madera, Ilhas d'Azores etc, etc. das alles fil und schwer handel wasen" (Rem 1861, 14).

22. Groenenberg, Tazacorte's new owner, was a merchant from Cologne who represented his uncle Johann Byse in the sugar export business to Antwerp and Cologne (Kellenbenz 1984, 134–35). He became well known as a sugar baron in Antwerp at the time when the city was the primary center for sugar imports; Antwerp would have twenty-eight sugar refineries by 1575 (Puttevils 2016, 39). Ultimately, the Canaries Inquisition office imprisoned Groenenberg (1528–29), in part because of to his "foreign" status and rumored Protestantism. Groenenberg's descendants in La Palma would have better luck with a series of strategic marriages to families who belonged to the Spanish oligarchy there (Viña Brito 2012, 184).

23. "todos los hombres negros de cualquier sexo."

24. Florentine Juan Sonderini would ascend to La Española's high-ranking social class after he married the daughter of Alonso Hernandez de las Varas, proprietor of the Santa Barbara sugar mill. Rolf Walter remarks that Sonderini must have been very young when he started to work for the Welsers (Kellenbenz and Walter 2001, 37). For more on the early sugar mills and their effect on Hispaniola's colonial society, see Ratekin 1954.

The first Welser managers in Hispaniola were Ambrosius Alfinger (also known as Dalfinger) and Georg Ehinger. While Alfinger ended up becoming the first governor of Venezuela, Ehinger stayed behind in Hispaniola. Ehinger's replacement there was Sebastian Rantz, who managed the branch for the Welsers until 1532. Thereafter, the Milanese Pedro Jácome Gacio served until 1537, when Sonderini became the last Welser factor there (Simmer 2000, 36).

25. According to Moore (2016b), "One could conquer the globe only if one could see it. Here the early forms of external nature, abstract space, and abstract time enabled capitalists and empires to construct global webs of exploitation and appropriation, calculation and credit, property and profit, on an unprecedented scale."

26. See "Asiento con Enrique Ehinger y Jerónimo Sayler," AGI Indiferente, 421, L.12.F.296R-297R (digitized); also transcribed in Otte 1963, 241–42. This asiento for 4,000 slaves was given to Ehinger and Sayler *before* the Welsers' capitulación; it was signed on 12 February 1528 in Burgos, and the capitulación was signed on 27 March 1528. The asiento reads, "vos damos liçençia para que vosotros o quien vuestro poder oviere podáis llevar con nuestra liçençia, que para ello vos daremos, quatro mil esclavos negros, en que a lo menos aya la terçia parte hembras, repartidos por las dichas islas e Tierra Firme conforme a la provisión que para ello vos damos, lo quales ayáis de pasar e paséis dentro de quatro años contados del día de la fecha desta" (we give you permission so that you or to whom you grant power with our license, which we will give to you, you may take 4,000 black slaves, and that at least a third of these be women, taken to the islands and Tierra Firme, conforming to the provision that you have to bring them [the slaves] in within 4 years time from this date).

According to Otte (1963), the conditions Charles V required were as follows:

1. The Welsers would pay the crown 20,000 ducats in eight payments (242).
2. Slaves were to be sold in the Indias and Tierra firme at the price of 55 ducats (243).
3. They could take the slaves from Castile or the Portuguese kingdom or "de qualesquier navíos de nuestro súbditos o de Portugal" (from whichever ship of our subjects or those of Portugal); however, if they used Portuguese ships, they could have no more than three Portuguese sailors on each ship, and the ship on its return leg from the Indies had to go directly to Seville without making any stops (242).

27. For more on foreign venture capitalists and the Spanish crown, see Legnani 2020, 45.

28. The "Capitulación con Enrique Einguer y Jerónimo Sayller," signed on 27 March 1528 in Madrid, was also clear that they could take Indigenous slaves at

this point as long as they were "rebellious": "Otrosí vos doy liçençia e facultad e vos y a los dichos pobladores para que a los indios que fueran rebeldes, siendo amonestados y requeridos, los podáis tomar por esclavos" (I give you permission that you and said settlers can take rebel indians as slaves, after they have been warned and read the *requerimiento*). See AGI Indiferente, 415, L.1, F.63R–66R.

29. See Alvar 1997. From 1518's Ordenamiento de las Cortes de Valladolid (1518), the courts demanded that Charles V learn the Castilian language, which he promised to do, and that "castellanos and españoles" be employed at court so that the court's representatives would be understood. This tradition of the anti-Hispanism associated with Charles continued until the twentieth century. For example, Luis Aznar (1945, 7) wrote an anti-German and anti-empire text that criticized Charles's lack of Iberian customs. He also stated that Charles relied on the Welsers because he was incapable of organizing his own affairs (10).

30. Tracy (2002, 99) clarified the terms of Charles's election to Holy Roman Emperor in 1519 against Francis I of France: "The total required to persuade the empire's seven electoral princes to vote for the right candidate—France's Francis I was offering almost equally generous terms—was reckoned at 851,918 Rhine gulden (about 602,026 ducats), of which the Fugger provided 543,585, the Welser 143,383, and three Italian firms 55,000 each."

31. Maestrazgos were Spanish knightly orders of Santiago, Alcántara, and Calatrava. The Catholic monarchs, Isabel and Ferdinand, had received the property rights of the three orders since they had taken on the cost of religious conquest that the old orders had previously funded as their support for the crusades. Emperor Charles V inherited this right. In a sense, as Carande (1967, 2:367) sees it, the pope transferred to the state the use of certain goods and properties that the state (and Charles as monarch) could not have demanded himself. Charles played an important role as "head" of the Santiago, Alcántara, and Calatrava orders, which had many properties. The Fuggers first, then the Genoese Grimaldi, then Enrique Ehinger (the wealthy Heinrich Ehinger, agent of the Welsers), and finally the Welsers would extend credit at interest in exchange for the income of the maestrazgos. While Jakob Fugger would be the first of the Augsburg bankers to use this system, he would tire of waiting for payment on his returns, reminding Emperor Charles V on more than one occasion that he had voted for his imperial election, ignoring his own personal interest. From 1532 to 1537, Bartholomäus Welser would extend credit of 307,000 Rheinish florins (gulden) or about 200,000 ducats (Carande 1967, 2:386–87). The term of the contract would be for five years and the interest around 10 percent, and the Welsers could recoup their losses from gains established by the contract or lease. The tax levy or tribute would also be in place at a rate of 152,000 ducats. Charles would change the timing of these contracts and would allow the Fuggers to replace the Welsers with a new contract on 5 July 1535 (Carande 1967, 2:389–90).

32. Juros were interest-bearing state bonds for public debt that were sold at fixed interest rates and guaranteed by the royal revenues, or the *hacienda real*. They were available in different forms: in trust, for life, in perpetuity, and so on. However, Spain's public debt was such that by the beginning of the 1600s the country had already accounted its revenues as paying back debts; nevertheless, it took on the unsustainable practice of selling more juros.

33. See Carretero Zamora 2000.

34. These were also the years of Charles's expensive Schmalkadic War (1546–47) with the Lutheran Schmalkadic League, an alliance of Lutheran princes that included Philip of Hesse and the duke of Saxony, Johann Frederick I (also known as Johann the Magnanimous).

35. Excerpt from Doña Juana of Austria, princess regent: "acerca de los excesivos intereses que llevan los mercaderes, vienen los cambios de Italia a 26 por 100 del primer cambio y además de esto se paga acá cucado por escudo, que son otro 7 por 100, en la diferencia de moneda y además, se pone con ella otro 10 por 100, de manera que viene a costar el dinero a 43 por 100, y después corre el interés de la dilación de la paga a 14 por 100, y como las consignaciones son de hoy a tres, cuatro, cinco y aun seis años, todo viene a montar tanto que los 339,000 escudos que ha tomado el embajador de Génova, en estos postreros asientos, cuestan 898,000 poco más o menos, y con este desorden y exceso *se pierde tanto que no hay hacienda para sufrirlo*" (quoted in Carande 1967, 3:22; my emphasis). See "Instrucción y carta que llevó el contador Antonio de Eguino, de parte de la princesa para su Magestad, en materias de hacienda," Valladolid, 20 December 1554, Archivo de Simancas, Secretaría de Estado, legajo 103, fol. 380.

36. "que la arte de mercadear es licita si el fin es ganancia moderada, para mantenerse a sí y a su casa, y la arte de cambiar trae algunos provechos a la republica: Dezimos que si ella se exercita como se deve, y el fin de la ganancia, que por ella se pretendiese ordena para honesta y moderadamente mantenerse a si y a su casa, es licita. Ni es verdad que el uso de dinero, para ganar con el cambiandolo, sea contra su naturaleza" (Azpilcueta 1965, 22–23).

37. Azpilcueta's text reached a wide audience in the sixteenth century eager to discuss the ethics of merchants' business and lending practices. The Spanish version was republished in Salamanca, Antwerp, and Medina del Campo in 1557 within one year of its publication. Subsequent Spanish editions followed in Estella (1565), Valladolid (1565, 1569), and Barcelona and Antwerp (1568). There were also many translations, one in Portuguese (Coimbra, 1569), one in Italian that appeared in at least five editions all published in the mercantile capital of Venice (1568, then republished in 1572, 1578, 1584, and 1592), and one in Latin (1569; reedited in 1594 and 1616). A French edition was published in Paris (1601).

38. "Lo tercero, que (siendolo al ygual en las tierras do ay gran falta de dinero, todas las otras cosas vendibles, y aun las manos y trabajos de los hombres se dan por

menos dinero que do ay abundancia del; como por la experiencia se vee que en Francia, do ay menos dinero que en España, valen mucho menos el pan, vino, paños, manos, y trabajos; y aun en España, el tiempo que avia menos dinero, por muchos menos se davan las cosas vendibles, las manos y trabajos de los hombres, que despues que las Indias descubiertas la cubrieron de oro y plata. La causa de lo qual es, que el dinero vale mas donde y quando ay falta del, que donde, y quando ay abundancia, y lo que algunos dizen que la falta de dinero abate lo al, nasce de que su sobrada subida haze parecerlo al mas baxo, como un hombre baxo cabe un muy alto paresce menor que cabe su ygual" (Azpilcueta 1965, 74–75). See also Jeannine Emery's translation (Azpilcueta 2014).

39. This is also known also as the balance of payment.

40. See Escudero 2000. In the Consejo de Estado (State Council) that Charles V started in Granada, there were other non-Castilians, including one named "Juan el Aleman," who might have been Hans Seissenhoffer, but the crown ultimately withdrew support from him: after first being celebrated for his hard work, in 1527 he was accused of espionage and maintaining a secret relationship with the French (Escudero 2000, 93). This episode sheds light on the inner workings of the court under a non-Castilian monarch in Spain. The Welsers were perhaps viewed as possible traitors to the state, even though they governed with the crown's consent.

41. As the Venezuelan historian Marianela Ponce de Behrens (1990, 3–4) writes, "The crown did not possess enough funds to realize conquest and so asks certain companies to carry out conquest and fund these activities themselves."

42. "La desdichada actuación de los Bélzares en Venezuela bien probaría que había sobreestimado sus dotes; por otra parte, los mismos extranjeros que, a pesar de tantos pronunciamientos adversos, comerciaron en las Indias, no tardarían en convencerse de que podían obtener provechos en ellas sin aparecer en persona" (Carande 1967, 1:457).

43. Farías (1997) describes the currency as New World pesos, at the exchange of 450 maravedís for one peso.

CHAPTER 2.   The Welsers in Venezuela

1. I use the "Capitulación del los Belzares con la Corona de Castilla," digitized at www.cervantesvirtual.com/obra/capitulacion-de-los-belzares-con-la-corona -de-castilla-madrid-27-de-marzo-de-1528--0/. The original document is located at AGI, Seville, Justicia, legajo 56, fol. 1, p. 1.

2. "indios naturales de ella son belicosos flecheros."

3. "para pacificar la dicha tierra y reducirla a nuestro servicio de manera que se haya en provecho de ella."

4. Montserrat Cachero Vinuesa's project description, "The Economy of Privilege," https://histecon.fas.harvard.edu/visualizing/privileges/.

5. "vosotros os ofrecéis a pacificar y poblar."

6. "me suplicasteis y pedisteis por merced vos hiciese merced de la conquista."

7. "descubrir y conquistar y poblar."

8. The cedulario from Madrid dated 8 October 1529 discusses the capitulación made with "Enrrique Eynguer [*sic*]" and Gerónimo Sayler and explicitly orders that Germans involved in the conquest and colonization of the lands of Cabo de la Vela and the gulf of Venezuela "carry the notification and the requirement that is to be made on the Indians of the stated lands and in obedience to us, and carry out other things contained in it" ("lleven la notificación y rrequerimiento que se a de hazer a los yndios de las dichas tierras a obediençia nuestra y hagan otras cosas en é contenydas") (Otte 1959, 7).

9. "Provisión general de capítulos sobre que vos habéis de guardar en la dicha población y descubrimiento."

10. "por el mal tratamiento que hicieron a los Indios."

11. "gana de ser nuestros vasallos súbditos y naturales."

12. "vicios especial del delito nefando de comer carne humana."

13. For example, as Juanita Sundberg (2008, 35) has demonstrated in the case of Mexico, "elite conceptions of appropriate resource management informed processes of racialization and vice versa. . . . The colonial system clearly privileged Spaniards who assumed rightful ownership of the bodies and labor of 'Indians' as well as natural resources."

14. "Sepades que nos somos informados quel año pasado de myll e quynientos e treynta años çiertas personas desde la ysla de Cubagua fueron a la costa de Veneçuela de la governaçión de los alemanes e se llevaron un caçique con todos sus indios e indias cabtivos a la dicha ysla de Cubagua y ahorcaron un yndio de un árbol, y que désto se hizo ynformaçión en la dicha prouynçia de Veneçuela y se os enbió, para que hiziéredes justiçia; y que muchas vezes van a alborotar la dicha costa y que los indios que están de paz y en nuestro servicio se alborotan y tornan de guerra y los prenden y los matan y roban y hazen muchos escándalos y alborotos en deserviçio de Dios y nuestro y daño de la dicha tierra, y nos fué suplicado e pedido por merçed çerca dello mandásemos proveer del remedio con justiçia, mandando tornar dicha tierra a los dichos indios, castigando a las personas que los truxeren, y que de aquí adelante nynguna persona fuese a alborotar los dichos indios ny a hazer daño en ella, o como la my merçed fuese."

15. "por ende yo vos mando que pagueys y hagays pagar a los dichos nuestros offiçiales del dicho nuestro quynto de los esclavos que hasta agora se han tomado y nos ha pertenesçido, syn poner en ello escusa ny ynpedimento alguno."

16. "nynguna persona sea osada de tomar en guerra ny fuera della nyngunos yndios por esclauos ny tenerle por tal."

17. "pero considerando los muchos grandes e yntolerables daños que en deserviçio de Dios, Nuestro Señor, e nuestro se an seguydo e siguen de cada día por la desordenada cobdiçia de los conquistadores e otras personas que an procurado de hazer guerra e cabtivar los dichos yndios ynjusta e ynmoderadamente, *an rescatado, comprado e avido de los dichos yndios muchos esclavos que en la verdad no lo son.*" (My emphasis.)

18. Miguel de las Damas (Testimonio de Bartolomé Rodriguez de 17 Junio 1546) in the *Juicios de Residencia del Lic. Juan Pérez de Tolosa contra los Welser* (1546/47). AGI, Justicia, 996, Pieza 6 a, fols. 31–36v, Ed. *Juicios*, Bd. 1, s. 394–401. Here pp. 400–401.

19. "çinquenta y çinco ducados cada *pieça*" (Otte 1984, 323). The empress was insistent that each ducat was valued at 375 maravedís, not the 336 maravedís per ducat that Española's residents were proposing as the exchange rate in the purchase of these slaves.

20. "y que algunas personas y veçinos de esa isla y otras partes los an querido escoger, y ansí los quieren tomar y no de otra manera, en lo cual si ansí pasase, ellos reçibirían mucho agravio y daño y no podrían conplir lo que están obligados ni pueden llevar los dichos esclavos escogidos . . . las personas que los oviesen de comprar los tomasen buenos y malos como los llevasen, pues todos no podían ser iguales, y a precio de çincuenta y çinco ducados cada uno . . . porque harto daño reçiben en los que se les morían por la mar y en la tierra antes que los vendan, o como la mi merced fuese."

21. "si no vos comprasen los dichos esclavos dentro de un breve término que los desenbarcásedes en qualquiera isla o tierra que los llevásedes, los pudiéses vosotros tomar y echallos en las mina del oro o serviros dellos en otras cosas, porque si mucho tiempo los toviésedes aguardando a los vender, sería más la costa que hiziesen que lo que valiesen, o como la mi merçed fuese; por ende por la presente vos doy liçençia y facultad para que, si no vos compraren los dichos esclavos que ansí lleváredes dentro de quinze días que fuere pregonado en qualquier puerto que se desembarcaren cómo son allí llegados y los lleváis para los vender, los podáis echar a las minas y tener en otras grangerías o llevallos a otras islas e tierras que quisiéredes, y los vender al preçio que pudiéredes y hazer dellos lo que quisiéredes y por bien toviéredes."

22. "muchos mercaderes e otras personas, sin liçençia e voluntad nuestra e contra la dicha capitulación e asiento, an pasado muchos esclavos, a cuya causa ellos no pueden vender los esclavos que an pasado."

23. See "Consulta del Consejo de Indias," AGI, Indiferente, 737, no. 30, 5 September 1533 in Madrid. The text erroneously refers to the "Compañía de los

Fucares" (Fuggers) when the the Belzares (Welsers) were intended; this text was to be a clarification of where the enslaved Africans should be sold: 300 in Hispaniola, 300 in Cuba, and 200 in Tierra Firme. Instead of the customs duties and 2 ducats that should be paid for each, Charles would be paid a total sum of 3,000 ducats.

24. Another cedulario from 31 July 1529 asked the Welsers to bring 400 Black slaves (a third women) to the Island of Fernandina (Cuba). AGI, SANTO_ DOMINGO, 1121, L.1, F.191V-193R. A year later, on 10 August 1530, a cedulario issued to the governor of San Juan (Puerto Rico) asked that any African slaves brought to San Juan by the Welsers should be sent directly to be sold in Cuba given the great need for their labor in the mines and in agriculture until the quota of 400 slaves destined for Cuba was filled. AGI, SANTO_DOMINGO, 2280, L.1, F.42V-43R.

25. Already on 21 August 1529 there was a cédula that allowed Juan de Sámaro to import 100 slaves given that the license with Sailer and Ehinger had expired. AGI, Indiferente, 422, L.14. F.6V–7R.

26. Michiel van Groesen (2008) writes that De Bry's collection of voyages published in Frankfurt between 1590 and 1634 has usually been seen as presenting a Protestant New World view that further promotes the Spanish Black Legend and Catholic cruelty. Van Groesen examines the Latin and German versions, which differ in their editorial pursuits. The German version of the voyages adheres to a more Protestant worldview, while the Latin version was edited for a Catholic and humanist readership. De Bry published his German version of Las Casas separate from the *Grand Voyages* collection. On De Bry's Las Casas, see also Conley 1992.

27. Bartolomé Casas, *Newe Welt. Warhafftige Anzeigung Der Hispanier grewlichen abschewlichen vnd vnmenschlichen Tyranney von jhnen inn den Jndianischen Laendern . . . begangen. Erstlich Castilianisch durch Bischoff Bartholomeum de las Casas oder Casaus, gebornen Hispaniern Prediger Ordens beschrieben: Vnd jm Jahr 1552 in der Koeniglichen Statt . . . Sevilia in Spanien gedruckt: Hernacher in die Frantzoesische Sprach durch Jacoben von Miggrode . . . gebracht: Jetzt aber erst ins Hochteutsch . . . vbergesetzt* (1597). There is an edition at the National Library of France (BNF). It contains seventeen engravings.

28. Anselm Maler (1992, 67) discusses the German reception of Las Casas after the eighteenth century; in his view, the French Enlightenment contributed to the reception of Las Casas in Germany as a figure who continued the Spanish Black Legend. In the eighteenth century the French Enlightenment represents Las Casas as a defender of the Indians; that influence can be seen when Las Casas appears on the German stage in August von Kotzebue's 1796 *Die Spanier in Peru oder Rollas Tod.*

29. Las Casas, *Newe Welt. Warhafftige Anzeigung Der Hispanier* (Frankfurt, 1597). I consulted the Newberry Library's copy: VAULT Ayer 108 .C3 1597.

30. See Zantop's (1997, 23–24) reading of this pro-Protestant anti-Spanish translation. She holds that its anonymous translator omits Las Casas's anti-Protestant sentiment when classifying the Welsers as possible heretics. Moreover, the translator supports a Dutch rebellion against Spain in the preface.

31. Benjamin Schmidt in his book *Innocence Abroad* (2006) traces how political events in the Netherlands contributed to the perception of Spanish and Habsburg tyranny in the Americas. The translation of Las Casas's *Brevissima relación* aided anti-Habsburg sentiment. See in particular ch. 2 of *Innocence Abroad*.

32. "avía descubierto con gran travajo suyo y costa de los dichos Vélçares."

33. This would influence the way the episode was read in Spanish colonial historiography, as I discuss in chapter 5; for example, José de Oviedo y Baños's very title of his work, *Historia de la conquista y población de Venezuela* (History of the Conquest and Settlement of Venezuela), emphasizes the tension between conquest and settlement in representing Venezuela's colonial history while it was still a Spanish colony. The work underscores the focus on encomienda and repartimiento as a Spanish administrative outlook alien to the Welsers' focus on expansion.

CHAPTER 3. Nikolaus Federmann's *Indianische Historia*

1. I am using B. W. Warmister Ife's bilingual edition of Columbus's *Journal of the First Voyage* (Diario del primer viaje).

2. A Claus Federmann signed under the "Kaufleutezunft" (merchant guild) of the Abstimmungslisten from November 1530. He signed specifically under List B: "Abstimmung mit Vorbehalt" (Vote with Reservation); see Specker and Weig 1981.

3. "conscientes de su valor personal, arrogantes e independientes por vivir en un ambiente en que no jugó papel transcendental la tradicional dominación de la nobleza. Buen ejemplo de esto nos los ofrece Nicolás Federmann, cuando valerosamente se rebela contra los patricios de Augsburgo, sus patronos Welser."

4. Federmann, who had been appointed governor by Charles V in Alfinger's absence, may have been the most polemical Welser governor for the Spaniards. The order appointing him governor on 19 July 1533 states, "que myrareis bien y fielmente las cosas del serviçio de Dios, Nuestro Señor, y nuestro y a la execución de nuestra justiçia y paz ys sosiego y buena governaçión y población de la dicha tierra y acreçentamiento della y conversyon de los naturales a nuestra sancta fee cathólica y que hareis todo lo demas que por nos fuere mandado" (that you should faithfully see to the service of God, our Lord, and the execution of Justice and peace and quiet and good governance and settlement on the said land and the growth of it and the conversion of the natives to our Catholic faith and that you will do all other things that were asked) (Otte 1959, 1:134–35).

5. On 12 August 1534 there was a prohibition against Federmann's passage to America issued by the Consejo de Indias to the officials at the Casa de Contratación. However, on 28 September 1534 Charles issued a cedulario confirming the governorship of Georg Hohermuth von Speyer, or Jorge de Spira. The reasons Federmann was replaced were probably in part due to his exile from the province (after Alfinger had appointed Federmann interim governor in 1530 and Federmann abandoned his post to go on his treasure-finding expedition) and many protests over his leadership as he later attempted to clear his name. Still, on 9 November 1534 there was a Real Cédula issued to Nicolás Federman, "governor of Venezuela," appointed as a result of Heinrich Ehinger's and Hieronymus Sailer's intercession. Yet on 12 November 1534 a letter was authored by the Consejo de Indias to the officials of the Casa de Contratación seeking information about "Jorge Espira de Espira," whom Nicolás Federmann had proposed as governor (AGI, Indiferente, 1961, L. 3, F. 159R–159V). On 10 May 1535 a Royal Provisión named Federmann governor on the Welsers' behalf ("Real Provisión por la que se nombra a Nicolás Federman, gobernador y capitán general de Venezuela," AGI, Caracas, 1, L. 1, F. 2V–6R). The Welsers must have pressured the Spanish crown to maintain their right to name governors during a chaotic administrative period.

6. "Méritos y servicios: Nicolao Federmann," AGI, Patronato, 1535, L. 153, N. 2, R. 1 (Transcription: "Probanza de los meritos y servicios de Nicolás Federmann que hizo en la conquista y pacificación de la Provincia de Venezuela," Tomo VII, Archivo de la Nación, Caracas, Venezuela). Santo Domingo de la Isla de Española, 11 de enero de 1535. The document explains that it contains "information made at the bequest of Nicolas Federmann German about the services made to His Majesty." It petitions the monarch for the governorship of the province of Venezuela after Alfinger's death. Federmann writes, "Yo serví a Vuestra Majestad con toda fidelidad y dilegençia y la Conquista y pacificaçion de la provinçia de Veneçuela hasiendo todo buen tratamiento . . . a los naturales de la tierra que venian en servicio de vuestra magestad y paz y amistad de los christianos como a los mismos españoles" (I served your majesty with all of the fidelity and diligence of the conquest and pacification of the Province of Venezuela, always treating the natives the same as Spaniards) (3).

7. "Probanza de los meritos y servicios de Nicolas Federmann que hizo en la conquista y pacificación de la Provincia de Venezuela."

8. "a Vuestra Majestad fue hecha siniestra relaçion de mis servicios."

9. "abia usado bien y fyel y diligentemente como conbenia al servicio de su majestad e al bien e pro de la tierra e de la población e paçificaçion della e al buen tratamiento de los naturales . . . e que desian todos en comun que quando el dicho Fedreman fue a una entrada con çiertos españoles a bueltas de muchas buenas particularidades que del dezian era que si algund enfermo en la compañia yba y el dicho fedreman tenía algo bueno lo dexaba de comer para lo dar al dicho enfermo e sino podia andar por no le dexar le azia dar un caballo en que fuese."

10. Viktor Hantzsch criticized Federmann's use of Spanish in the nineteenth century. I return to this later in the chapter.

11. Lido Nieto and Manuel Alvar Ezquerra's *Nuevo tesoro lexicográfico del español* (s. *XIV–1726*) (2007) defines the term "Morisco/a." The editors examine and extract excerpts from various sixteenth-century sources, for example, Elio Antonio de Nebrija's *Dictionarium ex hispaniense in latinum sermonem* (1495?); Fray Pedro de Alcalá's *Vocabulista aráuigo en letra castellana* (1505). The latter reflects the development of linguistic/cultural nuances in Granada after the *reconquista*: "La finalidad de Fray Pedro de Alcalá al redactar sus obras no era otra que facilitar la comunicación de los cristianos viejos con los conversos, una vez reconquistado el reino de Granada. Y más que para enseñar a los moriscos, la intención era la de dar a conocer el árabe a los clérigos que debían adoctrinarlos" (XXXVI; Fray Pedro de Alcalá's goal in editing his works was none other than to facilitate communication between old Christians and new Christians as soon as the Kingdom of Granada was reconquered. Also, rather than teach the moriscos, the intention was to teach Arabic to the clerics who were to be responsible for the moriscos' religious indoctrination). John Mensheu's multilingual dictionary *Dvctor in Linguas* is also a source: "Morisca/o": morisco/a (morisco, Morisco) NEBR. 1495?: morisco, cosa de moro, *mauritanus,a, um.* ll ALCALÁ 1505: morisco, cosa de moro, *xéi mitá muzlim*, morisco assí, *Izlemí, ín*; v. moruno ll JARAVA 1557: morisca, v. ajedrea ll GUADIX 1593: morisco v. mozárabe.II MINSHEU 1599: morisca . . . , *a woman Moore that has become a Christian*; morisco . . . , *a blacke Moore made or become a Christian*" (Nieto and Ezquerra 2007, 6842).

12. Many scholars have criticized Mauss's work for his lack of field research and his reliance on the fieldwork of other researchers to develop his thesis. Anthropologists particularly object.

13. See Arellano's *Una introducción a la Venezuela prehispánica* (1987).

14. For an example of Hernán Cortés's rhetorical strategies of conquest as employed in the conquest of Mexico, see Carman 2006.

15. Morella A. Jimenez (1986, 65) confirms that the Ayamanes ate shellfish even though they settled far from the coast.

16. Using Mauss, Derrida states that a specific contract with a due date defines the gift when he refers to Charles Baudelaire's story "Counterfeit Money" (Derrida 1992, 40).

17. Derrida traces idiomatic expressions such as *donner sa parole* (to give one's word) linguistically: "In the style of analytic philosophy or of ordinary language analysis, one could ask oneself: What are the conditions (conditional, contextual, intentional, and so forth) for the functioning of, for example, an expression or a speech act that consists in, let us say it in French, *donner sa parole*, giving one's word (to promise or to swear) or *donner un ordre* (jussive act) and what is going on with

giving in general. On what conditions does it take place? What is a 'donating consciousness'?" (1992, 50–51). Giving "one's word" here implies a performance of solidarity, especially in the absence of the written contract. The legality of orality is construed by "giving one's word."

18. According to Morella Jimenez (1986, 64), the Caquetíos (Arawak) were known for being traders; they exchanged foodstuffs with other groups such as the Jirajaras, Curiraguas, Achaguas, and Guaiqueríes. They established a corridor described by Federmann along the Turbio and Yaracuy Rivers, where they could exchange salt and fish for agricultural products (64).

19. The *juicio de residencia* was a legal process and an institutional practice that began in the peninsula before the discovery of America. In it, public officials had to give an account of their actions to a judge delegated by the crown. The judge would generally investigate whether the accused had completed his public administration obligation, whether he respected the authority of the crown, and whether he treated his governed subjects well (Friede 1960, 137).

20. The charge appears in a document on the juicio de residencia in AGI, Justicia, Leg. 56, "Relación de los cargos que hizo el doctor Antonio Navarro, juez de residencia, a Nicolás Féderman" (Relation of the charges that Dr. Antonio Navarro, judge of residency, made on Nikolaus Federmann).

21. Real provisión al gobernador y al obispo de Venezuela, Toledo, 20 February 1534 (Otte 1959, 132–34).

22. AGI, Indiferente, 1963, L. 9, F. 232R–232V (Digitized).

23. "ouvrage rarissime . . . ignorée pendant des siècles jusqu'à ce que Ternaux la signale pour la première fois en France."

24. "relation . . . très rare."

25. "les allemands ne pouvaient ignorer pareille nouveauté et, vingt-deux ans plus tard, ils publièrent l'ouvrage dans une collection parue à Stuttgart."

26. "E.V." (Eure Veste) is an honorific emphasizing that the addressee is mighty and strong. The prologue was addressed to Herr Johann[sen] Wilhelm von Loubenberg, vom Loubenberger Stein zu Bogeck [Wagegg]. This was Johann Wilhelm von Laubenberg zu Wagegg (1511–63) from the Öberallgau region of Swabia who in a letter written on 22 April 1562 offered his collection for sale to Albert V, Duke of Bavaria, who, apparently "for a sum of earnest money," was ready to sell his "heathen earthly treasure, chests, silver books, shells, and similar antiquities" because "his sons had no appreciation of these heathen mysteries." See Janssen 1896, 11:200; see also Diemer 2010.

27. The original text is published on 63 quarto sheets. The pagination here is my own, and it is from the direct facsimile of Federmann's text produced in 1938. Hence page 1 is the prologue. I consulted the original edition in Stuttgart; a librarian also numbered the pages in pencil in this manner. See Peter Hess's *Violent First Contact in Venezuela: Nikolaus Federmann's Indian History* (2021).

28. "ce centre d'édition, très important au XVe et XVIe siècles n'avait publié que des ouvrages humanistes et pieux."

29. "imprimeur de second catégorie."

30. "de mondre importance."

31. See Schwenckfeld 1922. It refers to Bund (listed as Bun) as using similar type in his publication of Spreter's pamphlets and Schwenkfeld's treatise.

32. According to François Ritter (1955), Jean Schwintzer (printer in Strasbourg, 1529–31) helped Sigmund Bund open his printer's shop in Haguenau after he had been refused a permit. Schwintzer, originally from Silesia, was a fervent admirer of the Reformation and of Kaspar Schwenkfeld whom he had met in Liegnitz in Silesia (320). His ideas led him to leave his city and head to Strasbourg "ou les réfugiés affluent de toute part" (where the refugees pour in from everywhere) (320). He learned the printer's trade and married Apollonia Nubling, which allowed him to become a citizen of Strasbourg (320–21). In 1529 he printed theology treatises from his former theology professors and Schwenkfeld. According to Ritter, "On admet généralement que Schwintzer et Schöffer se sont brouillés à la suite de ces ouvrages anabaptistes et que c'est pour cette raison qu'ils se sont séparés" (One generally admits that Schwintzer and Schöffer had argued after the [publication] of these Anabaptist works and that was the reason as to why they parted ways) (321). Schwintzer retired from printing and became a "second scribe" for the city, then for the tribunal, then for Count Albert from Mansfeld (322). Schwintzer was very influential, even outside of Strasbourg, and hence when Sigmund Bund was denied authorization to open a printer's shop in Haguenau, Schwintzer's intervention with the magistrate of Haguenau allowed for annulment of the ban (322). In 1555, when Strasbourg tried to take severe measures against the Anabaptists, Schwintzer was named as a culprit, but on 23 March 1556 he testified that he did not belong to the sect (322). Bund started printing in Haguenau around 1550. According to Hanauer and Ritter, Bund submitted manuscripts in Latin and German to the censorship authorities for review. On 10 July he addressed himself to the Senate to obtain his printing permits or have his manuscripts returned. The Haguenau authorities told him that it would be better for him to leave printing as the city did not need a business of that kind. Ritter attributes this to printers' loss of influence in Haguenau (409). Schwintzer intervened to protect Bund's livelihood (410): "Bund cependeant s'engageait à ne publier que des textes littéraires" (Bund, nonetheless, engaged in publishing only literary works) (410).

33. Ritter (1955, 212) states that he did not find any documents that revealed that Bund succeeded Weiditz and Kandel in the printer's shop of Knobloch "comme l'indique Benzing dans son Lexicon" (as Benzing indicates in his lexicon). Ritter's book contains a useful chart at the end (Annex 1) labeled, "Tableaux Chronologique et synoptique des imprimeurs alsaciens des XVe et XVIe siècles avec

une table alphabétique" (Chronological Table of Alsatian Printers in the Fifteenth and Sixteenth Centuries with an Alphabetical Table). It lists Bund as an active printer in Strasbourg from 1539 to 1545 and in Haguenau from 1551 to 1557.

34. See Specker and Weig 1981.

35. According to Friede, the Ulm city archives mention the Federmann family of merchants and indicate that some of the family members belonged to an intellectual circle. Thus Friede hypothesizes that Federmann would have had a good education (Friede 1965, VIII).

36. According to Friede (1960, 31), Kiffhaber was a fan of Schwenckfeld, who had spent some years in Ulm before he was ousted from the city. Schwenckfeld may have been the only link between Kiffhaber and Bund. While I could not find any specific mention of Kiffhaber in Schwenckfeld's correspondence or the history of Schwenckfeld in Ulm, it is safe to hypothesize that as a sympathizer of Schwenckfeld, Kiffhaber had access to Bund's religious publications and may have approached him. Ulm's censor in 1538–39 was too careful to let Schwenckfeld's works be published there (they were published in Strasbourg, for example, by Protestant publishers like Bund). See Julius Endriss's *Kaspar Schwenkfelds Ulmer Kämpfe*, which discusses the reformer's theology as based on inner experience and on the Apostolic church as a model for the contemporary German church (1936, 11). According to Endriss, to be born again and spiritualism were at the heart of his theology (12–13).

37. "En effet, l'ouvrage de Federmann fut rédigé d'abord en langue espagnole par un "notario scribano público." L'auteur lui-même le traduisit ensuite en allemant [*sic*] en y ajoutant de nombreux éclaircissements. Comme il nous le dit dans son texte—et nous croyons qu'il le fait en pensant tout spécialement à ses maîtres, les Welser d'Augsbourg, à qui il devait communiquer les résultats de sa première expédition américaine à la province de la Terre Ferme—il luit fallait donner des précisions" (Arias López 1969, 606).

CHAPTER 4. Blood and Soil

1. Amerigo Vespucci (1508–12), Juan Díaz de Solís (1512–16), Francisco Cotos (1516–18), Sebastian Cabot (1518–50), and Alonso de Chaves (1552–87) were other pilot majors in the Casa de Contratación. The appointment was made by royal decree (*cédula real*) and the men who held it were expected to be experienced navigators and, if foreign, married to Spanish women as the fear of betrayal was great (Sánchez Martínez 2013, 134).

2. Ricardo Padrón (2020, 26) discusses Ribeiro's map as depicting a unique imperial geopolitical imaginary when it became evidence of Spain's claim to the

Spice Islands. Though Ribeiro would have been aware that Spain's claim to the South Sea was mostly an optimistic fantasy (212), the map suggested that the South Sea route was open to commercial and colonial endeavors (207).

3. Portolan charts, which had been used mostly in the Middle Ages for navigating around the Mediterranean, were characterized by thirty-two rhumb lines, which originated from one or more points, representing the thirty-two points of the compass for the use of pilots drawing their course around the coastlines (Wagner 1931, 3).

4. See Wolff 1992a, 49. In 1529 Ribeiro produced the Weimar and Rome maps, and Charles V ceded the spice-rich Moluccan archipelago to the Portuguese crown.

5. "dixo se asi por que aqui de alla mucho oro los indios son mas belicosos de lo q todos los de Santo Domingo ni de las otras partes porque las flechas y hierva. Aqui esta un pueblo que se dize S. Marta donde se alla mucha cantidad de oro por la tierra. Aquí tienen los alemanes su governación desde Cabo de la Vela hasta Cumana que seran 140 a 150 leguas."

6. "'Welserkarte'" des Diogo Ribeiro–Studienbibliothek Dillingen Mapp. 1" 2 fragments on parchment. The two fragments were bound in two works, Gylmanni's *Supplicationes* and Cardinalis Mantica's *De Tacitis et conventionibus* (1723), that had belonged to the Augsburg family Ilsung and Granz Ludwig de Bally (d. 1740). 37 x 54 and 60 x 41 cm. Digitized at http://daten.digitale-sammlungen.de/~db /0010/bsb00105879/images/.

7. "Die Provinienzzuschreibung ergab sich unter anderem durch die Kartenaufschrift für das Gebiet Venezuelas, das in der frühkapitalistischen Vision vieler Seefahrer und Handels beauftragter des 16. Jahrhunderts schlicht als Castilla del Oro, als goldenes El Dorado unter spanischer Hoheit, bezeichnet wurde. Der weitere Text verwies dann aber auf die seit von 1528 von Karl V. besiegelten Land- und Nutzungsrechte für das kapitalkräftige oberdeutsche Handelshaus der Welser, dessen Firmenzentrale Augsburg war: Esta es la governacio[n] de la gran casa & noble compañia de los Belzares hasta el estrecho de Fernâo de Magallanes."

8. "Esta es la governacio[n] de la gran casa & noble compañia de los Belzares hasta el estrecho de Fernâo de Magallanes."

9. Labrador may have been named after João Fernandes Lavrador, a Portuguese explorer who explored the coasts of the peninsula in 1498–99, or Gaspar Corte-Real, who enslaved Indigenous people from the region and associated the place with the term *lavrador*, which in Portuguese means "laborer."

10. See the 1525 Castiglioni version (Archivio Marchesi Castiglioni, Mantua); 1527–29 copies at the Thüringische Landesbibliothek in Weimar. For example, Lia Markey's *Imagining the Americas in Medici Florence* (2016) traces the Medicis' interest in collecting New World objects, including maps and feathered

items. Murals in the Uffizi Palace depicting Amerindians were tied iconographi-
cally to the Florentine Codex, the illustrated Mexican codex by Bernardino Sa-
hagún, which entered the Medici's collection in the sixteenth century (93). The
grand dukes used art patronage and the European network of gift-giving to claim
the city's unique role in the New World encounter from Vespucci's role in the exploration of the New World to the various gifts exchanged by the Medicis with
monarchs and popes.

11. See Robert W. Karrow's *Mapmakers of the Sixteenth Century and Their
Maps* (1993), Henry R. Wagner's "The Manuscript Atlases of Battista Agnese"
(1931), and K. Kretschmer's "Die Atlanten des Battista Agnese" (1970).

12. Apothecarius brought spices and textile goods, namely, silk and brocade,
back to Augsburg (Kießling 1984a, 171).

13. Herzog August Bibliothek Wolfenbüttel copy 4.1 Aug. 4°.

14. Wagner (1931) writes of Newberry Ayer Ms 12 that it resembles Agnese's
atlas found in Bologna, Biblioteca Universitaria, Cod. No. 997 (Ex. Bib. Benedict
XIV), which I have not consulted, in that they contain a special series of maps (nos.
4–7). Number 4 details North America from 65°E to 135°W and from 5°S to
55°N; number 5 details the Atlantic and parts of South America north of the equator to 45°N and extending from the prime meridian to 70°W; number 6 shows
northeastern America from about 45°N to nearly 70°N latitude and extending
westward to 43°W longitude; number 7 shows South America with part of Africa
extending from the prime meridian to about 72°W and 32°E. Wagner labels the
Bologna and the Newberry Ayer Ms 12 as "doubtful" true Agnese atlases. The Bologna atlas has the coat of arms of the duke of Este, Alfonso II, who had been
married to Lucrezia di Cosimo Medici and later to Habsburg royal Barbara of
Austria. Both the Medicis' and Habsburgs' involvements in overseas possessions
may have prompted the detailed map. On map 7 Wagner writes, "There is a large
legend in Peru 'Gover de Diego de Almagro,' and others about Pizarro and of the
company of the Belzers (? Welsers)" (101). Newberry Ayer Ms 12 is incomplete as it
does not include a world map.

15. Giacomo Gastaldi's *Geographia particolare d'una gran parte dell'Europa . . . / opera nuoua di Giacopo di Castaldi Piamontese*: Fabius Licinius [1560].

16. *Vniversale*, Giacomo cosmografo in Venetia MDXXXXVI, Newberry Library, Novacco 4F 4.

17. Not to be confused with his son, also named Rodrigo de Bastidas (1497–
1570), who would become bishop and interim governor of Venezuela (1540–42)
and Puerto Rico (named in 1541).

18. Paolo Forlani collaborated with Gastaldi on a number of his *Vniversale*
maps: Paolo Forlani et al, *Vniversale descrittione di tvtta la terra conoscivta fin qvi*
(Venice: F. Berteli, 1565). Retrieved from the Library of Congress, www.loc.gov

/item/85690919/>. The shelf mark is G3200 1565.F6. http://hdl.loc.gov/loc.gmd /g3200.mf000070.

19. In 1457 Mühlich also made a hand-painted chronicle on the Benedictine monk Sigmund Meisterlin known as the *Meisterlin-Chronik* of Augsburg. Staats- und Stadtbibliothek Augsburg, Cim 69 (2° Cod H 1). Blatt 117v.

20. For more on Emperor Maximilian's taste for armor as well as com- memorative print media for self-promotion, see the Metropolitan Museum of Art exhibit catalog, *The Last Knight: The Art, Armor, and Ambition of Maximilian I* (Terjanian et al. 2019).

21. See Zäh 2012.

22. See Bock 2008. See also Bock's webpage on the genealogical books of the Renaissance produced in towns such as Nuremberg, Augsburg, and Frankfurt: www.hartmut-bock.de/Gattung/gattung.html.

23. There are several copies of loose prints that are part of this genealogical table in various states of completion.

24. See Bouquet 1996. The article looks at examples of eighteenth-century Dutch domestic and biblical genealogical trees, including "Jesse" trees. Bouquet argues that currently all ethnographic practice on kinship studies still draws on this approach—which is essentially a patriarchal, masculine practice that elevates the male "seed."

25. The text reads, "Julius von Kayßer Friderich II. A° 1225 zum Ritter ge- schlagen, von Landgraven zu Hessen, Großmeister A °1243 zum Teutschen Orden- sherrn nach Preußen Stabilirt."

26. Bouquet's (1996, 61) readings of Dutch genealogical trees is useful here: she describes them as deeply gendered and reflecting a (patriarchal) vision of the present projected onto (and struggling with the vestiges of) a (matriarchal) past.

27. Each sheet measures about 32.8 x 42.5 cm.

28. I was only able to see one of them, but the Welser archivist Herr Edwald Glueckert believes they are still there. Loose prints from the series can also be found at the British Museum and the German National Museum. The copy at the Ger- man National Museum is hand-colored. See Beaujean and Turner 2016, 30–31.

29. Beaujean and Turner (2016) see the printer Georg Strauch's oeuvre as sig- nificant "in terms of portraiture in Nuremberg" because numerous engravers repro- duced his prints. The year 1660 stands out in that a flurry of printed Welser family histories was commissioned from Neunhof. For example, Strauch was also the artist (along with Jacob von Sandrart) and the engraver who made a portrait in 1660 of Sebaldus Welser (1609–60) from Neunhof, who had been the mayor (*Bür- germeister*) of Nürnberg. The oil portrait, the preparatory drawings, and the copper plate of this portrait are in the collection of the Welser family (Beaujean and Turner 2016, 159).

30. Stenglin 1682. The publisher, Wolfgang Moritz Endter (1653–1723), was a book handler and printer in Nuremberg who came from a line of Nuremberg printers. He also published other volumes, including the *Sacri Romani Imperii Circuli Franconici Geographica Delineatio*, which has sixty-four maps of the Franconia region, in 1692. See Bosl 1983, 176.

31. It is uncertain who commissioned Emmanuel Stenglin's map. *Hollstein's Engravings* calls Stenglin (1606–76) an architect, draftsman, and printer based in Augsburg. Stenglin was most active between 1640 and 1660. He drew and printed chorographic city views. Chorography is the study of local place. While such works also existed in textual form, they were often panoramas, or elevated town and city views that featured one angle of the city wall along with its church spires, or sometimes even a bird's-eye view perspective. It was common practice for publishers to juxtapose these to the popular chronicle genre, which charted past events. Stenglin's chorographic works include *Chorographia Marchionatus Burgoviae* (Chorography of the Town of Burgau) and other town views such as "View of Hurla" and "View of Augsburg with City Tower and Perlach Tower" (1682). He also created intricate drawings and prints of spaces such as "Interior of the Fürstensaal in Augsburg, 1657" and "View of the Arsenal in Augsburg, 1659" (Beaujean and Turner 2010, 203–11). Genealogy and chorography, cartography, and landscape and city drawings were a family business; he also had a son who was active in Augsburg around 1650 who made architectural drawings and maps (including one of Italy) and may have been known as an etcher of family crests (Beaujean and Turner 2010, 193).

32. A copy of "Venezuela, provincia in America occidentali. Quam olim Dni. Velseri Patricij Augustani possidebant, a Carolo V. Imperatore ipsis consignata" is digitized at the Yale University Beinecke Rare Book Library.

33. "Aquí mataron al Gov. Ambrosio." Kathleen A. Myers and Nina M. Scott, in *Fernández de Oviedo's Chronicle of America*, trace and compare the various manuscript and print copies of the author's *Historia* and states that the map had been missing by 1780, though it was included in the Palacio Real copy (Shelf mark: PRII/ 3041, 241–242 Bk. 25, chap I) (Myers and Scott 2008, 184, 245).

34. The Library of Congress also owns a copy of the work.

35. Marx Welser, *Chronika der weltberühmten reichsstadt Augspurg. Aus dem lateinisch verteutscht durch Engelbert Werlichium* (Frankfurt am Main, 1595).

36. The Welser's Venezuela colony was edited into German-authored comprehensive modern geographies. For example, Philipp Clüver (1582–1622) wrote important works of geography such as *Introductionis in Universam Geographiam* (Leiden, 1624; Paris, 1630, 1635, 1642; Wolfenbüttel, 1667; Amsterdam, 1629, 1683, 1729). The Prussian Clüver, recognized as an editor of antique geography, including Ptolemy, barely mentioned Venezuela in the posthumous first edition of

his *Introductionis in Universam Geographiam* (1624). However, later editions would add information on the Welsers and Venezuela. For example, the 1729 Amsterdam edition has a footnote explaining that Charles V pawned the territory off to the Welsers: "*Benezuola*; Welsers, patriciis Augustanis, a Carlos V. olim oppignorata" (Benezuola given to the Welsers, patricians of Augsburg from Charles V in past times) and "*Venetuarian* urbe corono, & Velserianis aut Germanicis coloniis" (*Venetuarian* the crown's city & Welser or German colony) (Clüver 1729, 680, 679). Clüver's later edition depicts the Welser bankers as effectively having possessed and colonized the New World.

37. See Lowe 2005, 20, which discusses stereotypes of black skin color in the Renaissance period. Even manumission could not free Black Africans from slavery as European society equated black skin color in all its variations with slavery and many free Black Africans were apprehended as fugitives.

CHPATER 5.   "Foreign" Governance

1. Rolena Adorno (2011, 1–2) has called the term "Colonial Latin American Literature" "a useful misnomer" for three reasons. First, "colonial" refers to more than three hundred centuries of Iberian domination on the American continent; second, "Latin America" appeared as a term *after independence* to refer to the area of independent nations that derived from Romance language traditions; and third, the genres within it include dubiously "true histories," "fictive romances of chivalry," travel narratives, letters, and legal documents. "Literature" came into use in the eighteenth century and thus is attributed backward. I find Adorno's distinctions important as many of the works we currently study were never meant to fulfill the function that today we attribute to literature.

2. Although the sixteenth-century "histories" were often divided by their writers into various categories, including general, moral, and natural, these categories often overlapped. The general history was usually limited geographically. Moral and natural histories on the Indies might address subjects such as botany, zoology, sociology, and psychology, topics that were separated into various fields during the eighteenth century and the push for the categorization of knowledge during the Enlightenment.

3. The dates discussed in Fernández de Oviedo's work are 1478–1557. The first part was published in 1535, and the first completed multivolume edition was published between 1851 and 1855.

4. German names are often turned into Spanish names: Alfinger is sometimes referred to as Ambrosio de Alfinger or Dalfinger; Las Casas refers to him as Ehinger. I have referred to him as Ehinger at times.

5. "gentil hombre alemán" and "hombre bien hablado y buena persona" (Fernández de Oviedo 1959, 3:7). In early modern Spain, there were various categories of gentil hombres. It is hard to figure out exactly to which type Férnandez de Oviedo refers in his estimation of Alfinger.

6. "La Cesárea Majestad del Emperador Rey don Carlos, nuestro señor, teniéndose por servido de la gran compañia que llaman de los alemanes Velzares, les concedió el cargo de la gobernación de la provincia e golfo de Venezuela, en la Tierra Firme, so ciertos límites e condiciones" (Fernández de Oviedo 1959, 3:7).

7. "como testigo de vista y tanta autoridad."

8. "Y aun estuvieron aquellos señores, segun se dijo, para no consentir que alemán alguno por su persona gobernase en estas partes, después que oyeron al procurador Alonso de la Llana. E agraviándose desto los Velzares, tovieron forma cómo fué admitido el gobernador Jorge Espira. E no creyeron aquellos señores que el dicho Fedreman había de volver a Venezuela" (Fernández de Oviedo 1959, 3:48).

9. "Relación," reproduced in Fernández de Oviedo 1959, 3:83–92.

10. "llevó a Castilla muchas esmeraldas y dineros; negoció mejor que Fedreman" (Fernández de Oviedo 1959, 3:92).

11. "El Nicolao Fedreman creyó que le darian la gobernación de Venezuela como la tenía Jorge Espira por la compañia de los alemanes Velzares, en pago de haber dejado muchos españoles e muchos más indios muertos, aunque en este caso, por determinar está cuál de los capitanes que han conquistado o seguido la guerra en Indias, tiene más animas a cuestas. Y como aquellos sus señores Velzares vieron que el Fedreman iba rico y que hellos han gastado muchos dineros en la negociación, no solamente quitaron el credito a Fedreman, mas hiciéronle estar a cuenta e justicia con ellos; y si ésta se le guarda, saldrá el litigio muy al revés que este capitán lo pensó, porque, en la verdad, nunca él estuvo por acá estimado por hombre fiel a sus amo, sino por de larga conciencia, y aun estaba en fama de luterano" (Fernández de Oviedo 1959, 3:92).

12. "Entraron en ellas, más pienso sin comparación cruelmente que ningunos de los otros tiranos que hemos dicho y más irracional y furiosamente crudelísimos tigres que rabiosos lobos y leones" (Las Casas 2005, 142).

13. "gentes mansísimas ovejas" (Las Casas 2005, 142).

14. "demones incarnados"(Las Casas 2005, 142).

15. "Porque con mayor ansia y ceguedad rabiosa de avaricia, y más exquisitas maneras e industrias para haber y *robar plata y oro* que todos los de antes, prospuesto todo temor a Dios y al rey y vergüenza de las gentes, olvidados que eran hombres mortales, como más libertados, poseyendo toda la jurisdicción de la tierra, tuvieron" (Las Casas 2005, 142; my emphasis).

16. "hereje, porque ni oía misa ni la dejaba de oír a muchos, con otros indicios de luterano que se le conocieron" (Las Casas 2005, 144).

17. "tan extraño y pestilencial cuchillo" (Las Casas 2005, 142).

18. "nunca quemaron vivos a ningunos destos tan nefandos tiranos"; "enemigos de Dios y el Rey" (Las Casas 2005, 146).

19. "más rica y más próspera de oro y era de población que hay en el mundo" (Las Casas 2005, 147).

20. "sería gran estorvo a la población desa tierra y conservaçión de los naturales della a nuestra santa fe cathólica, de que Dios, Nuestro Señor, sería deservido, por ende yo vos encargo e mando *que de aquí en adelante no dexeis ni consyntais entrar en esa provinçia persona alguna que sea natural de Alemania syn liçençia nuestra*" (Otte 1982, 254; my emphasis).

21. "ynformaros heys de los alemanes . . . presente en eska provincya como biven . . . sospechosos en la fee e sy h . . . lo es provereeys que salgan" (Otte 1982, 254).

22. The first part of the *Elegías* was published in Madrid in 1589 by the widow of the printer Alonso Gómez (official printer for the crown) while Castellanos was still alive (Martínez-Osorio 2016, xviii). It was censored by Agustín de Zarate. Volume 2, approved by Alonso de Ercilla, and volume 3, approved by Pedro Sarmiento de Gamboa, were written around 1584 and around 1601, respectively, and although accepted for publication, never reached their publisher. They would not be published until 1847 in Madrid as part of the Biblioteca de autores españoles series. Volume 4, edited by Antonio Páz y Melía, was also published posthumously as *Historia del Nuevo Reino de Granada* in 1886 (Martínez-Osorio 2016, xviii).

23. For Castellanos, I also cite the original Spanish in the verse to supplement my free verse translation. I do give the original as well as the English version to give readers a sense of the verse in the original Spanish. The spelling and accent marks in the Spanish are copied exactly from the printed edition.

24. In fact, Federmann's and other conquerors' inland expeditions featured in Castellanos's poem inspired Marco Aurelio Vila to study the Venezuelan geography recounted in *Elegías*; see Vila 1998. Vila writes that Federmann journeyed from Coro to Barquisimeto (Barraquicimeto), then into the fertile valley of Yaracuy (Depresión de Yaracuy) before continuing to Acarigua and (Hacarigua) crossing the Morador River (Amoradores), a tributary of the Portuguesa River (119–20). Also see Restrepo (1999), who covers the spatial integration of Amerindian spaces into Spanish cosmography in Castellanos. Restrepo draws on Michel de Certeau's premise of two forms of spatial projection: the tour and the map.

25. Vila sees "Hitibana, Provincia buena" as the area of Turén in the state of Portuguesa. Hitibana was the name of a cacique. It is because of Federmann's judgment that he prefers to leave and decides to cross a river, perhaps the Acarigua, which flows into the Portuguesa River (1998, 121). Vila also mentions Georg Hohermuth von Speyer (Jorge de Spira) who also crossed the Acarigua, as mentioned

in Castellanos, and found a fertile valley populated by Cuibas, Caquetíos, Coyones, and Guaraharas, all of which were mentioned in Federmann's *Indianische Historia*.

26. German scholars such as Hermann Schumacher (1892) also recognized this. He wrote that Castellanos saw the whole events of the Welser colony as sad and disappointing but could not intervene (173).

27. See Friede 1964.

28. See the book cover of *Historia de Venezuela escrita en 1581*, vol. 1, by fray Pedro de Aguado (1913).

29. For more information on the various editions of Aguado, see Guillermo Morón's prologue to fray Pedro Simón's *Noticias historiales de Venezuela*, vol. 1 (1992, xxix). Though I could also have included Simón's work published in Cuenca, 1627 (the second and third parts would remain unedited and would not be published until the nineteenth century), Simón took great liberties copying the manuscript from Aguado, as Acosta Saignes has stipulated in his study, *Historiografía de Venezuela: Aguado y Simón* (1949).

30. "visto con los ojos y tocado con las manos" (Aguado 1987, 3).

31. "porque en el discurso de quince años, los mejores de mi vida, que me empleé en la predicación y conversión de los idólatras, que como bestias vivían en el Nuevo Reyno de aquellas Indias en servicio del demonio, entendí por muchas cédulas que vi de V. M. el celo que tiene tan católico del aprovechamiento y conversión de aquellas animas" (Aguado 1987, 3–4).

32. "multiplicación de los cristianos y aumento de la Iglesia" (Aguado 1987, 9).

33. "donde había estado algunos días procurando mitigar y apagar las perniciosas centellas y aun abrasadoras llamas que Lutero, el año atrás de veinte y uno derramaba y sembraba entre aquellas gentes, y su venida fue a dar asiento de todo punto a las cosas del gobierno de los españoles, los cuales habían estado fuéra de tranquilidad y asiento que aquel reino suele tener, por causa de las Comunidades y alteraciones que el mismo año de veinte y uno se habían engendrado entre ellos, por las opresiones y molestias que ciertos gobernadores extranjeros que el emperador había dejado les hacían (Aguado 1987, 29–30).

34. See Haliczer 1981. Haliczer contends that some of the problems arose already in Isabel and Ferdinand's reign, before Charles came to Castile with a mostly Flemish court.

35. "las gran contrataciones de mercaduría que en muchas partes del mundo tenían" (Aguado 1987, 30).

36. "Todo esto he dicho para que a los que no llevare en aquella tierra el deseo de ocuparse en la conversión de los infieles, los lleve la codicia de los bienes" (Aguado 1987, 9–10).

37. "los hechos y obras tan heroicas de nuestros naturales españoles"; "los muchos trabajos, hambres y muertes que nuestros españoles pasaron" (Aguado 1987, 17).

38. "y dar a la Iglesia nuestra madre nuevos hijos" (Aguado 1987, 8).

39. "al cual revocaron las conduta por quejas que de él hubo" (Aguado 1987, 111).

40. "procuró aplacer y contentar para ganarles la voluntad, dándoles algunas dádivas de oro del que había llevado" (Aguado 1987, 113).

41. "viendo la plática y suerte de Federmann, que era muy principal y de su propia nación, y la buena orden y traza que daba en los negocios del gobierno de aquella tierra" (Aguado 1987, 113).

42. "porque era de ánimo bullicioso y soberbio e intolerable de sufrir, y que con sus pesadas palabras maltrataba los soldados, y con otros términos muy extraños e insufribles de que usaba era muy aborrecido de toda la gente en que la gobernación había, y que lo mismo sería de los que llevase" (Aguado 1987, 114).

43. "ni hubo entre ellos ningún género de discordia" (Aguado 1987, 114).

44. See Tortorici 2018. Tortirici draws on archival material to discuss how nonheteronormative sexual desires and practices are labeled *contra natura*, or against nature.

45. "fueron castigados y quemados conforme a las leyes del Reyno" (Aguado 1987, 115). In a footnote to Morón's edition of Aguado (1987), Acosta Saignes states that this is an example of intertextuality or the way in which different chroniclers copied or commented on each other's works. Specifically, he discusses how much fray Pedro Simón used Aguado, mostly copying him and just barely adding commentary (Aguado 1987, 130). Similarly, Stolley (2013, 183) and Ingrid Galster (2011, 192–93) discuss the plagiarism charge against Oviedo y Baños, who relied on Simón (who in turn relied on Aguado). Acosta Saignes also called for a biography of Federmann. He proposes such a biography as a solution for the problem of intertextuality and historical inconsistencies, such as when different accounts place Federmann in different places. See also Acosta Saignes 1949.

46. "pareciome que también era razón tratar de sus principios, para más claridad de lo que de ellos tengo de escribir esta Historia que sea peregrino de las Indias" (Aguado 1987, 116–17).

47. Jerónimo Bécker (1857–1925) was a Spanish historian and librarian of the Spanish Real Academia de Historia who revisited the Black Legend and Spanish colonization in the Indies with his books, *La tradición colonial española* (The Spanish Colonial Tradition) (Madrid, 1913) and *La política española en Indias: Rectificaciones históricas* (Spanish Policy in the Indies: Historical Corrections) (Madrid: Jaimer Rates, 1920). Perhaps this goal drives him to emphasize the illustrious backgrounds of the Spaniards who accompanied Speyer and Federmann. In his pro-

logue to Aguado, he follows what I call the Spanish version of the German Black Legend, i.e., that the government of the Germans was too cruel and too many Spanish and Indigenous lives were lost due to their governance. He explains that the colonization of Venezuela began only after the Welsers left: "These governors— if they really deserve that name, since after all, they were no more than adventurers with idle souls and medium fortunes" (Aguado 1916, x).

48. "Damián del Barrio, natural del reino del Granada, cuyos servicios en la América correspondieron á los que antes tenía obrados en la Europa, habiéndose hallado en la memorable batalla de Pavía, en el saco de Roma con el duque de Borbón, y en otras célebres funciones de las de más importancia en aquel tiempo: descienden de este caballero los Parras, y Castillos de Barquisimeto; los Silvas de esta ciudad de Santiago, y otras ilustres familias que tienen su asistencia en la provincia" (Aguado 1916, 124–25).

49. "La tierra que los ha engendrado termina siendo para éstos una condena, que cancela todo privilegio, aún los conquistados o heredados. El «clima» resulta así un valor más fuerte que el de la «raza» o, como se dirá en el siglo XIX, la geografía se antepone a la historia" (Oviedo y Baños 1987, xv).

50. All English translations of José de Oviedo y Baños by Jeannette Johnson; see Oviedo y Baños 1987.

51. "Episodios como los del negro Miguel y el Tirano Aguirre son narrados desde la farsa y desde la locura sanguinaria: no sería creíble (ni tampoco admisible para los censores, quienes hubieran podido vetar todo relato sobre las sublevaciones de colonos en América si la narración de esas sublevaciones no llevara implícita una condena) que se creara un reino paralelo al de España, y menos bajo la majestad de un esclavo o de un hereje" (Martínez and Rotker 1992, xxvii).

52. See García 2001.

53. "Se trata, pues, de un préstamo o de una compra, no de un hecho conquistado o heredado. Como el origen es espurio, el fin no puede ser sino la destrucción: los alemanes que llegan a la provincia de Venezuela no hacen «asiento en parte alguna» y se entregan al pillaje. Desembarcan, saquean y se marchan, «. . . sin que los detuviese la piedad ni los atajase la compasión». Es decir arrebatan sin poblar, marcando el origen de la provincia con la señal del extranjero, del nómade, del que no ama." (Martínez and Rotker 1992, xxviii).

54. "Es lo que sucede con Alfinger, con Spira, con Fedreman: la infinita postergación de la conquista de El Dorado, en lo que pareciera una insólita prefiguración de las pesadillas de Kafka" (Martínez and Rotker 1992, x).

55. "caballeros alemanes, a quienes llamaban en la Europa los de la famosa compañía, por una muy célebre que tenían hecha con diferentes mercaderes, traficando caudales muy crecidos en todos los puertos y contrataciones del mundo; y sabiendo las utilidades tan considerables, que producía el trato y comercio de

Coriana y toda su costa, les pareció sería de conveniencia a los intereses de su compañía el tomarla por su cuenta, para disfrutarla solos, pidiéndosela al Emperador en arrendamiento" (Oviedo y Baños 2004, 19).

56. "el Emperador se hallaba beneficiado de los Belzares, por las cantidades de dinero, que en diferentes ocasiones le habían prestado para sus expediciones militares, fueles fácil conseguir su pretensión" (Oviedo y Baños 2004, 19).

57. "su ánimo y el de los demás alemanes que le sucedieron, nunca fue de atender al aumento ni conservación de la provincia, sino disfrutarla, logrando el tiempo de aprovecharse, mientras durase la ocasión" (Oviedo y Baños 2004, 21).

58. Fernández de Oviedo (1959, 3:15–19) lists these groups (also drawn on his map of Maracaibo): Zongaguas/Pemeos/Pemenos; Pacabuyes; Xiriguaras; Sierra del Mene; Corbaguas; Aruacas/Arucanas.

59. "sin hacer asiento en parte alguna, de cuyo errado dictamen (seguido también después de los demás alemanes, que le sucedieron en el gobierno) resultó su perdición y la ruina total de esta provincia" (Oviedo y Baños 2004, 23).

60. "pues conociendo sus soldados que no llevaban intención de poblar en nada de lo que conquistasen, y que así no tenían que esperar por fruto de sus trabajos, ni los repartimientos de encomiendas para la convivencia, ni las posesiones de tierras para el descanso, pués sólo habían de tener de utilidad lo que cogiesen de encuentro; *sin que los detuviese la piedad, ni los atajase la compasión* como furias desatadas, talaron y destruyeron amenísimas provincias y deleitosos países, malogrando los provechos que pudieran haber afianzado en la posesión de su fertilidad, para sí y sus descendientes, si como les aconsejaban los más prácticos y prudentes hubieran ido poblando en lo que iban descubriendo; pero como los alemanes, considerandose extranjeros, siempre se recelaron de que el dominio de la provincia no les podía durar por mucho tiempo, más atendieron a los intereses presentes, aunque fuese destruyendo, que a las conveniencias futuras, conservando" (Oviedo y Baños 2004, 23; emphasis added).

61. "Como furias desatadas, talaron y destruyeron amenísimas provincias y deleitosos países" (Oviedo y Baños 2004, 34).

62. "como se hallase con aquellos ardientes deseos a que les incitaba la codicia de procurar y adquirir riquezas, sin reparar en que fuesen o no justos los medios para poder conseguirlas" (Oviedo y Baños 2004, 22).

63. "alemán de nacimiento, hombre de elevados espíritus; hallabase rico y con amistad estrecha con los Belzares: circunstancias, que lo animaban a pretender el gobierno para sí; y dejándose llevar de este deseo, en la primera ocasión que se ofreció de pasaje, se embarco bien proveído de dineros para España, . . . llegó a la Corte, y se dio tan buena maña, disponiendo su pretensión, con tal destreza, que con facilidad vinieron los agentes de los Belzares en conferirle el gobierno" (Oviedo y Baños 2004, 35).

64. "imputándole de ser de áspera condición, de espiritú bullicioso, de natural altivo y corazón soberbio; y aunque fueron las propiedades de que siempre estuvo más ajeno, por haberlo dotado el cielo de una naturaleza afable, conversación cariñosa, corazón muy piadoso y ánimo reposado" (Oviedo y Baños 2004, 35).

65. "viendólos Fedreman les dijo con alguna alteración: ¡Oh, que poca vergüenza de soldados! Y como en la afable condición y modesta compostura de aquel hombre jamás habían experimentado enojo alguno, extrañaron tanto estas palabras, que por memoria de cosa tan singular, llamaron a aquel pueblo el de la Poca-Vergüenza" (Oviedo y Baños 2004, 67).

66. "cuya memoria merece ser celebrada entre la de los héroes más plausibles de su tiempo; su naturaleza fue de un lugar del círculo de Suavia en Alemania la Alta; su presencia hermosa y agraciada; el rostro blanco y el pelo rojo: afable con liberalidad y apacible con agrado: sus hazañas y singular valor le adquirieron mucha fama en pocos años; y aunque el desafecto de sus émulos atribuyó su generosidad de ánimo a soberbia, su inclinación a las armas, a inquietud; y su cortesano trato a máxima cautelosa; no hay duda que fueron muy singulares las prendas con que lo adornó la naturaleza; y a no haberse dejado llevar con tanto exceso del deseo inmoderado de mandar independientemente, no hubiera hallado defecto que notarle la más curiosa atención" (Oviedo y Baños 2004, 74).

67. "caballero alemán, parente muy cercano de los Belzares, mancebo de poca edad, pero de mucha prudencia" (Oviedo y Baños 2004, 80). Oviedo y Baños refers to Hutten by his Hispanicized name, Felipe de Utre.

68. "de un natural tan dócil y sencillo" (Oviedo y Baños 2004, 103).

69. "digno por cierto de mejor fortuna . . . en la ciudad de Spira, en las provincias de Alemania, tuvo su nacimiento, y llevado del ardor de sus juveniles años pasó a la América, donde manifestó siempre los quilates de su prudencia y valor" (Oviedo y Baños 2004, 105).

70. "los deseos del aplauso más que el ansia de las riquezas lo empeñaron en el descubrimiento del Dorado. . . . Ningún capitán de cuantos militaron en las Indias ensangrentó menos la espada" (Oviedo y Baños 2004, 105).

71. "por haber privado de la administración de ella a los Belzares, mediante las repetidas quejas y noticias con que su Majestad se hallaba de los irreparables daños, tiranías y desórdenes, introducidos con el gobierno alemán, que fueron tantos que con justa razón dieron motivo para que el Señor Don Fray Bartolomé de las Casas en su libro la *Destrucción de las Indias*, llamase a esta provincia infeliz y desgraciada; y lo fue sin duda, pues si no hubiera padecido la desdicha de haber estado aquellos dieciocho años sujeta al dominio extranjero, fuera una de las más opulentas que tuviera la América; porque en lo dilatado de su distrito, lo fértil de su terreno, lo benigno de su clima, lo abundante de sus aguas, ni en la conveniencia de sus puertos hay otra que la iguale, y en la multitud innumerable de indios que la

habitaban hizo ventaja a muchas, aún de las más pobladas, pero como los alemanes la vieron sin amor, considerándola como una cosa prestada, ni atendieron a su conservación, ni procuraron su aumento, pues sólo tiraron a aprovecharse mientras duraba la ocasión, sin reparar en que los medios de que se valían para disfrutarla fuesen o no, los más eficaces para destruirla; pues sin hacer asiento en parte alguna, ni poblar en tan hermosos países como descubrieron, llevándolo todo a sangre y fuego, no dejaron cosas que como fieras desatadas no asolaron; y como el interés principal de su ganancia lo tenía afianzado su codicia en la esclavitud de los miserables indios, fueron por millares los que sacaron para vender a los mercaderes que ocurrían a Coro, con el cebo de tan infame trato; de que resulto despoblarse lo más de la provincia, porque los indios huyendo de padecer las violencias que experimentaban en semejantes tiranías, por asegurar la vida y la libertad, desampararon sus pueblos y se fueron retirando a lo interior de los Llanos, donde se han quedado hasta el día de hoy; perdiendo por esta causa tantos vasallos el rey y tantas almas la iglesia" (Oviedo y Baños 2004, 108–9).

CHAPTER 6. The Ghost of Welser Venezuela in German Cultural Memory

A version of this chapter appeared as "'The Welser Phantom': Apparitions of the Welser Venezuela Colony in Nineteenth and Twentieth-Century German Cultural Memory," *Transit: A Journal of Travel, Migration, and Multiculturalism in the German-speaking World* 11, no. 2 (2018): 21–53, http://transit.berkeley.edu/2018 /montenegro/. I want to thank *Transit*'s anonymous peer reviewers for their comments.

1. The Herero genocide, 1904–7 is referred to as the first genocide of the twentieth century, and it took place in German-occupied Southwest Africa (modern-day Namibia). The Herero people rebelled against German colonial rule, and the colonists responded by driving them into the desert, where approximately 100,000 people died.

2. The colonial possessions of the German Empire from 1884 to 1919 included the African colonies of German East Africa (present-day Tanzania, Rwanda, Burundi, and Kenya), German Southwest Africa (Namibia and parts of Botswana), and German West Africa (Cameroon and Togo), as well as the Pacific colonies of German New Guinea, Micronesia, German Samoa, and the Marshall Islands.

3. See Knoll and Gann 1987. While pre-Weimar-era materials were readily available, scant attention was paid to post–World War II literature. Yet, as these authors—writing in 1987—remind us, the Federal German Republic and the German Democratic Republic shared the characteristic of being "ruled by the successors of German parties that the Wilhelminian Establishment had been wont to

stigmatize as *reichsfeindliche Elemente* (elements hostile to the Reich) and that now [in 1987] look upon the *Kaiserreich* with hostility" (xiv).

4. Duke Jakob Kettler from Courland, the smallest European state in present-day Latvia, founded both of these failed colonies despite Dutch and Spanish interests in the area, and he was of Baltic German origin. He lost the colony to the Dutch after five years, although settlers had built a Lutheran evangelical church there, and the British took over the Courland trading post on Kuntah Kinteh island (formerly known as James Island—off the coast of present-day Gambia) seven years after its establishment. See Sooman et al. 2018. Kettler embraced the mercantile theories of his age. While acknowledging the "limited scope and success" of his imperial ventures, the article argues that they had a strong impact on the historical imagination within Tobago and Latvia (Sooman et al. 2018, 503).

5. It included the debate on how to unify German-speaking territories, what became known as the "German question." Catholic Austrians led the *Grossdeutschland*, "Great Germany," side of the debate, which favored unity across a large swath of the Germanophone world, while Protestant Prussians led the *Kleindeutschland*, "Lesser Germany," movement, which favored only unification of the northern German states. Imperial Austria did not want to give up Hungary, Czechoslovakia, Bosnia, Romania, and Croatia, none of which were eager to join a German-centric state or spoke German. "Lesser Germany" was established in 1866 and then expanded in the 1866 Austro-Prussian War, which ended in the expulsion of Austria from the disputed territories. Prussians and Catholic Bavarians ruled the new German Empire.

6. Ulrich Stelzner and Thomas Walter's 1998 *The Civilizers* (*Die Zivilisationsbringer*) has interviews with some of the German coffee, indigo, and cardamom plantation owners in Guatemala, who reminisce about Hitler—as well as their descendants: young entrepreneurs who have continued their family businesses or now work for multinational German corporations such as Mercedes-Benz. This film is an important contribution to the discussion of the connections between Nationalist Socialism's expansionist politics and German settler colonialism outside of the Reich. These colonists continue the imperial projects initiated by the German colonists in Africa. Within Guatemala, similar violence between the colonizers and Indigenous populations affected these German barons' relationship with their Indigenous workers. In the film, German barons, in a paternalistic fashion, discuss their role in Guatemala's progress as "benevolent," at the expense of Indigenous peoples battling land confiscation and human rights abuses.

7. For more on transculturality in the age of the German Enlightenment, see also Zhang 2017.

8. Susanne Zantop argued this in *Colonial Fantasies* (1997).

9. For succinct introductory works on race see Banton 1998; Samson 2005; Chukwudi Eze 1997; Repp 2004. Repp traces how women in Wilhelmine Germany promoted eugenics and the advancement of the white race. As Repp (2004, 123) notes, Lucia Dora Frost, an enemy of the feminist movement, argued that race was "a purely internal, subjective aesthetic sensation" that inspires a noble feeling about the individual herself. Yet Frost also argued in 1914 that as the family was the foundation of the modern state, the fittest German mothers should be encouraged to reproduce; only then would Germany win against the colored races (125).

10. See also Wintzer 1900. Wintzer points out that although the Welser episode had an "unglückliche[n] Ausgang" (unlucky ending) (47), the German émigrés there were very successful in trade (48). See also Haebler 1903. Haebler was the first scholar who completed a systematic study of the Welser period in Venezuela in German.

11. See Fernández de Oviedo's hand-drawn manuscript map of Lake Maracaibo, which accompanies the Madrid copy of *La Historia General*. According to Rudolph Schuller (1917), it was drawn to correspond to the account sent from Venezuela to Spain about Alfinger's death, which probably did not occur until 1533. The map was, at the earliest, drawn later in 1533, but it could also have been created as late as 1536 (see fig. 4.33, above).

12. Castellanos's work deals with the period from 1522 to 1560. The first part of the *Elegías* covers the period up to 1578 but was published in 1589. The second part was written around 1584; the third part, around 1601. Both the second and third parts were only published in 1847. See the previous chapter for more on Castellanos.

13. For more on Hermann Schumacher the Younger, see Grimmer-Solem 2019, 60–66. Schumacher the Younger traveled through the United States with Ernst von Halle, first to the Chicago World's Fair and then to study the country's agriculture, trade, and economics. Von Halle would travel to Venezuela in 1896 to celebrate the Krupp Puerto Cabello railroad and "to offer publicity for German investment and engagement abroad of a status equal to other European powers" (Grimmer-Solem 2019, 153).

14. Until 1889, the *DKZ* was gathered in bands (*Hefts*) and then bound together as a yearbook with an index. It was in 1889 that the newspaper changed format under the editor Gustav Meinecke and was printed weekly. Hathi Trust Digital Library has digital copies of the *DKZ*: https://catalog.hathitrust.org.

15. See Holger Herwig's *Germany's Vision of Empire 1871–1914*, 270–79. Herwig analyzes Passarge's *Wissenschaftliche Ergebnisse einer Reise im Gebiet des Orinoco, Caura und Cuchivero in den Jahren 1901–02* (Hamburg, 1933).

16. The atlas, *Atlas historique ou nouvelle introduction à l'histoire à la chronologie et à la géographie ancienne et moderne etc.*, was published in seven volumes between 1705 and 1719 in Amsterdam by L'Honore & Chatelain.

17. The German Colonial Association (Deutsche Kolonialgesellschaft) began in 1882 as the Deutscher Kolonialverein, a group meant to convince Otto von Bismarck of the necessity of Germany's colonial expansion. In 1887, the Colonial Association merged with the Society for German Colonization (Gesellschaft für Deutsche Kolonisation), which Karl Peters had created in 1884 to facilitate the conquest of East Africa (Pierard 1987, 19).

18. Despite his many critics, Peters was able to return to Germany in 1914, after Emperor Wilhelm II had bestowed on him the right to use the title Imperial Commissioner. During Hitler's rule, Peters was again revived as a national hero, and a propaganda biopic detailing his struggles directed by Herbert Selpin was released in 1941.

19. A. F. Pollard (1906) attested to Haebler's pedigree in the *English Historical Review*: "No one is better qualified to write such a book than Dr. Haebler: the friend of the present King of Saxony, who married the infanta of Portugal and who took Dr. Haebler with him to that country in 1889, his historical studies have centered in the connexion between Germany and Spain and Portugal, a connexion which was particularly close in the early sixteenth century, and which alone made these oversea enterprises of the Welsers possible" (159).

20. Alfinger is again referred to as Dolfinger.

21. *Auf der Jagd nach dem goldenen Kaziken* was one of Hanstein's few histories; he mostly wrote popular adventure books, historical fiction, travel narratives, and science fiction works for children and young adults. A significant amount of his oeuvre was set in the Americas, about which he frequently took a propagandistic tone. For a list of books written by Hanstein, see Klotz 2014, 134–37. A few of his works appeared on a list of proscribed literature, *Liste der auszusondernden Literatur,* that Allied forces distributed in Soviet-occupied Berlin in February 1946. See the *Verzeichnis der auszusondernden Literatur* prepared by the *Abteilung für Volksbildung im Magistrat der Stadt Berlin,* available on the internet archive: https:// archive.org/stream/Abteilung-fuer-Volksbildung-der-Stadt-Berlin-Verzeichnis-der -auszusondernden-Lit/AbteilungFuerVolksbildungDerStadtBerlin-Verzeichnis DerAuszusondernenLiteratur1946187S.Scan.

22. Hugo von Waldeyer Hartz (1876–1942) was a naval officer and writer. He wrote other texts, such as *Von Tsingtau zu den Falklandinseln* (Berlin: Mittler, 1917), that were decommissioned as Nationalist Socialist propaganda in the *Liste der auszusondernden Literatur* from the Soviet-occupied zone between 1945 and 1952.

23. See Gerhard Drekonja-Kornat's essay "What Were the Nazis up to in Latin America" (2004) and Mary Jo McConahay's *The Tango War: The Struggle for the Hearts, Minds, and Riches of Latin America during World War II* (2018).

24. Originally from *Programmheft* (1938, 16); quoted in Schweizer 2007, 41.

25. Junge Generation was a publisher of books for children and youth active during the Nazi State. Other titles were Theo Bohner's *Ae Ntonga! Hallo Freund!*

Unser Leben in Kamerun (1935; Hi Friend! Our Life in Cameroon); Rolf Rumbeck's *Der silberne Kolibri Kriegspfad im zwanzigsten Jahrehundert - Erzählung aus dem Südamerika der Gegenwart* (1940; The Silver Hummingbird's War Path: Stories from Present-Day South America); Heinz Kindermann, ed., *Rufe über Grenzen: Antlitz und Lebensraum der Grenz- und Auslanddeutschen in ihrer Dichtung* (1938; Cries from over the Border: The Face and Territory of Border and Expatriate Germans).

26. It also included Ulrich Schmidl (1510–79), a German explorer who accompanied Mendoza to Argentina; Jakob Leisler (ca. 1640–91), a German-born American colonist; Arthur Phillip (1738–1814), the son of a German father and English mother who became an English captain and founded Sydney; Johann Cesar Godeffroy (1813–85), who established a German presence in the South Pacific; and Kurt Faber (1883–1929), a world traveler.

27. Labeled a "National Socialist propagandist," Faber made it to the list of "Autoren, deren sämtliche Werke aus dem Bestande zu entfernen wird" (authors whose entire corpus of work were to be removed from circulation) in the *Verzeichnis der auszusondernden Literatur* (February 1946), prepared in Soviet-occupied Berlin by the *Abteilung für Volksbildung im Magistrat der Stadt Berlin*. Available at https://archive.org/stream/Abteilung-fuer-Volksbildung-der-Stadt-Berlin-Verzeichnis-der-auszusondernden-Lit/AbteilungFuerVolksbildungDerStadtBerlin -VerzeichnisDerAuszusonderndenLiteratur1946187S.Scan.

28. Johann Filchart (ca. 1545–89), "Ernstliche Vermahnung an die lieben Teutschen" (Serious Admonition to the Dear Germans):

Gott stärke dem edlen deutschen Geblüt
sein anerbtes Adlersgemüt
Seht, das hab als Deutscher ich
aus deutschem Blut treuherziglich
euch, die ihr Stammet her von Helden,
bei diesen Helden müssen melden,
wenn ich dies deutsche Bild blick an.
Gott gebe, dass ihr's könnt verstahn,
und beides, treu seid euern Freunden
und ein Schrecken allen euern Feinden.

———

God, make the German blood strong
its inherited eagle nature
See, as a German I have, out of German blood, naively [trusted]
that you descend from heroes
[we] must ask these heroes
when I look back at this German picture [of German heroes]

God grant that you all can understand
and both, you all be faithful to your friends
and a terror to all of your enemies.

29. Karl Panhorst wrote an article in 1930 in the *Ibero-amerikanisches Archiv* about the links between Simón Bolívar and Alexander von Humboldt in which he called for a biography on Bolívar in German in light of interest in finding out more about the connections between the men; after all, he argued, the baron's conversations with the young would-be liberator in Paris and Rome would be remembered later as having inspired Bolívar to recognize that he was ready to throw off the yoke of Spanish colonialism in Venezuela (Panhorst 1930). In the absence of German inquiry into the matter, Panhortst provides a review of the literature written in Spanish and French about the encounters for a German public. Panhorst also discusses recent findings from his archival research, including a letter from Vicente Rocafuerte, Humboldt's friend who would become the first president of Ecuador, written on 17 December 1824 from London reporting Bolívar's victories and how Bolívar always treasured the advice Humboldt had given him in Paris. This letter was discovered in the Humboldt-Nachlaß der Dokumenten-Sammlung der Preußischen Staatsbibliothek. A second find of significance to Panhorst was seven pages of handwritten notes about Simón Bolívar (without a date or signature) that Humboldt most likely used as a template for a lecture. These were located in the Humboldt-Nachlaß der Autographen Sammlung Darmstaedter der Preußischen Staatsbibliothek. Panhorst's article signals an increasing interest in Bolívar that may have begun in 1929 when the *Hamburger Überseejahrbuch* published an article on Bolívar by Dr. Warhold Drascher. The decade of the 1930s also saw interest in Bolívar and his relationship with Humboldt. More recently, Oliver Lubrich (2003) has discussed the epithet inscribed on the statue of Humboldt outside of the Humboldt University in Berlin at the bequest of the University of Havana. It reads, "Al Segundo descubridor de Cuba. La Universidad de la Habana 1939" (To the second discoverer of Cuba. The University of La Habana, 1939). The origin of this quote is generally ascribed to the Cuban José de la Luz y Caballero (1800–1862) (Lubrich 2003, 74). See also Wulf 2016, 7; Rippy and Brann 1947, 701.

30. See Becker 2004.

31. *Lebensraum* was a National Socialist ideology whose literal meaning is "living room"; it refers to the habitat necessary for the successful development of a nation. In practice, the theory was that racially superior peoples had the right to expand territorially over racially inferior peoples.

32. Ernst Wilhelm Bohle, chief of the NSDAP, state secretary of the Foreign Office, foreword to Pfeiffer 1941.

33. Schmölz-Häberlein (2002) gives the following citation: J. G. Lettenmair: "Mineros Alemanos." In *Nazionalsozialistische Monatshefte* 112 (1939): 292–95.

34. Mamdani's *When Victims Become Killers: Colonialism, Nativism, and the Genocide in Rwanda* (2001) builds on the ideas of his first book to argue that the legacy of colonial violence informed genocidal violence between the Tutsis and Hutus (Lee 2007, 79). Lee (2007) and Mamdani (2001) investigate how British forms of colonial governance present within Africa—a type of dual mandate that relied on locals to exert the will of the colonizer—gave rise to a "descentralized despotism" (Lee 2007, 78). In comparison to Arendt, Mamdani views apartheid as a continuation of a colonial governance that primarily relied on distinctions between "race" and "ethnicity." The latter method became popular throughout the continent, dividing Black political majorities. In turn, this colonial violence informed later genocidal violence between the Tutsis and Hutus. In particular, according to Lee (2001, 79), Mamdani traces how Belgian colonial authorities fomented a division between "settlers" and "natives" by designating Tutsis racially superior and non-Indigenous. As Lee writes, "Tutsis, who had occupied positions of power under colonial rule, found themselves resented and perceived as an 'alien' presence in the postcolonial period" (79).

35. See https://fuggerandwelserstreetdecolonized.wordpress.com. According to the website, the Fuggerstraße encompassed part of the old Augsburgerstraße and the Welserstraße had been renamed from Bayreuther Straße. Both of these name changes took place in the Schöneberg district of West Berlin between 1957 and 1958.

36. See Decolonize HU, https://decolonizehu.wordpress.com/2016/02/16. Accessed 11 May 2017.

CHAPTER 7. The Venezuelan View of German Conquest

1. Britto García is a prominent Venezuelan writer of novels, essays, and plays. Among the latter is his *El tirano Aguirre o la conquista de El Dorado* (1976), which is representative of his use of historical events to critique contemporary society. He has won the Casa de las Américas Prize for his works *Rajatabla* (1970) and *Abrapalabra* (1979). In 2002 he won a lifetime achievement award from Venezuela's National Prize for Literature.

2. Of the von Hutten and Welser deaths at the hands of Carvajal, the Colombian German historian Friede (1961, 400) cites chronicle writers such as Oviedo y Baños and Castellanos in their gruesome depiction and condemnation of these deaths. These colonial writers therefore depicted Carvajal as a traitor for founding the city of Tocuyo, beheading the Germans, and denying them confession before their death.

3. Born in a German town in present-day Poland, Friede came to Colombia by way of Vienna. After studying Colombian Indigenous subjects and the Andakí

people, he decided to approach the history of the Americas not through the chronicles but through the archive. Friede states in his "Note to the Reader" in *Los Welser en la Conquista de Venezuela* that his goal in that work is to investigate the Welsers' role in the colonization and conquest of Venezuela and Colombia and not to come to their defense (7). Nevertheless, Friede holds that the behavior of the Germans was on par with the atrocious nature of conquistadors throughout the New World.

4. Concerning the preference of local authorities to name Juan de Ampies and not Alfinger as founder of Coro, Denzer (2003, 294) states, "The discussion was conducted intensively and even with support from Spain, because modern Venezuelan history began with the foundation of Coro. A national history that begins with the Whites and Indians who live together in harmony corresponds perfectly to the interpretation of history by Venezuelan Positivism, which sees Venezuelan man as a product of the positive characteristics of the different population groups of the country."

5. Guaicaipuro (ca. 1530–68) was a chief of both the Teques and Caracas tribes that led Indigenous coalitions against Spanish rule.

6. *Mestizaje* is described as a process of the mixing of Latin American racial identities (Indigenous natives, Spaniards, and Black Africans) that resulted from the conquest and colonization of the Americas. Latin Americans such as the Mexican José Vasconcelos described this idealized melting pot in his *La raza cósmica* (1925; The Cosmic Race); and in Venezuela, intellectuals such as Arturo Uslar Pietri followed suit. As I have written previously, through his television program and in his publications such as *La creación del nuevo mundo* (1990; The Creation of the New World), Uslar Pietri subscribed to the idea that the originality and inventiveness of Latin America and, in particular, Venezuela was due to its mestizo identity (Montenegro 2012, 11). Such discourses in effect erase marginalized groups such as Afro-Venezuelans and Indigenous Venezuelans from the imagined community of Venezuelan citizens. For more on mestizaje in contemporary Venezuela, see Bonet 2019.

7. "II Seminario Literatura Latinoamericana: Miradas, memoria y fcción en la narrativa histórica y latinoamericana," which took place during the Tenth Venezuelan International Book Fair.

8. This is something that the Venezuelan literary scholar Alexis Márquez Rodriguez also recognized in his *Historia y ficción en la novela venezolana* (1990).

9. In an essay in the same volume, Britto García writes on Uslar Pietri's preference for historical themes for his narrative fiction such as in the novel *El camino de El Dorado* (1947), about Lope de Aguirre's catastrophic expedition. Even in novels from the first part of the twentieth century, such as Enrique Bernardo Núñez's *Cubagua* (1931), the history of conquest and exploitation of the territory appears as a theme. A number of the novel's characters colonize the island of Cubagua in the 1500s and then reappear at different times throughout history. They

serve to reinforce Bernado Núñez's comparison of petroleum exploitation and speculation in the 1920s and 1930s to the mass extraction of pearls from Cubagua in the early 1500s (Britto García 2014, 33–68).

10. See Libardo Vargas Celemín (2007), who analyzes in detail the narrative voice of Ursúa's mestizo narrator.

11. For an ecocritical analysis of the novel, see Kressner 2013.

12. According to Dolle (2014, xi), many historical novels as well as plays have forgotten the real story of Columbus's treatment of Indigenous peoples and choose to represent him in a benevolent light as a "visionary in search of utopias."

13. "Es una crítica de los alemanes, de esa fatal compañía de los Balzares [*sic*], a quienes entregó Carlos V esta tierra para su conquista y población, que tan duramente trataron á los indígenas, y que la historia trata también justamente con tanta dureza; así como lo hago yo en el drama, pues sigo rigurosamente la historia" (Briceño Picón 1903, 8).

14. I have translated Joyogüire's speech as missing verbs just as in the Spanish.

15. Herrera Luque considered himself a psychiatrist first and a writer second. His doctoral thesis in psychiatry served as the basis for his book, *Los viajeros de Indias* (1961), in which he studied the legacy of psychopathic actions and trauma caused by the conquistadors still present in the Venezuelan nation. He wrote *Boves, El Urogallo* (1972), and *Los Amos del Valle* (1979) before writing *La luna de Fausto* (1983). Venezuelan expatriates in Miami started a foundation in his name in 2017.

16. See a reading of La Sayona and María Lionza in Herrera Luque's novel in Jose A. Rodriguez's dissertation, "New Visions of the Past: Reinterpretations of History in the Novel and Cinema of Contemporary Venezuela" (2017, 111).

17. In a letter to his brother Moritz written from Coro, Philipp acknowledged that Faustus had warned him that they would have an unlucky year. See "Philipp von Hutten an seinen Bruder Moritz von Hutten: Brief aus Coro vom 16. Januar. 1540," in Hutten and Schmitt (1999, 128–36).

18. The entry written by Chesney-Lawrence and translated by Anamaría Crowe Serrano (2005) continues, "He made his debut as an actor with the Teatro de la Universidad Central, and while there wrote *Juan Francisco de León* (1959) and *La sopa de piedra* (Stone Soup, 1960). In 1961 he studied at the Piccolo Teatro in Milan. On his return he staged his plays *El extraño viaje de Simón el malo* (The Strange Journey of Simon the Evil, 1961), *Los insurgentes* (The Insurgents, 1962), and wrote or co-wrote a number of works such as *Triángulo* (1962), *En nombre del rey* (In the King's Name, 1963), *Días de poder* (Days of Power), *Testimonio* (1967), *Profundo* (Deep, 1971), and *Acto cultural* (Cultural Act, 1976). In 1967 he formed El Nuevo Grupo together with Román Chalbaud and Isaac Chocrón. After 1976 he turned his attention to writing soaps for television. Other plays include *El día que me quieras* (The Day You Love Me, 1979), *Una noche oriental* (An Eastern Night,

1983), and *Autorretrato de artista con barba y pumpá* (Self-Portrait of the Artist with a Beard and Top Hat, 1990). His last play was *Sonny* (1995), a version of *Othello* about the life of a boxer."

Conclusion

1. All the articles discussed in this section were retrieved from the Stadtarchiv (City Archive) Ulm (G2 Folder: Federmann, Nikolaus).

Epilogue

1. See, e.g., Keenan 2018.

2. See "Fugger-Express," n.d., AugsburgWiki.

3. See the webpage of the Fugger und Welser Erlebnismuseum: www.fugger-und-welser-museum.de/en/. Accessed 17 January 2019.

4. See Vincent Moloi's documentary, *Skulls of My People* (2016).

5. French president Emmanuel Macron has stated that he favors restitution of looted art to its former colonies. On 23 November 2018, he declared that France would return twenty-six works of art to Benin. The British Museum and other institutions are also pondering what to do about looted art. In Berlin, the Ethnological Museum of Berlin holds around 580 objects that are part of the Benin bronzes strewn throughout European institutions.

6. Freedom-Roads! 2015. http://www.freedom-roads.de/. Accessed 11 May 2017.

7. Afrika-Hamburg.de 2005. www.afrika-hamburg.de. Accessed 11 May 2017.

WORKS CITED

Acosta Saignes, Miguel. 1949. *Historiografía de Venezuela: Aguado y Simón*. Caracas: Venezuela, Ministerio de Educación Nacional.

Adorno, Rolena. 2011. *Colonial Latin American Literature: A Very Short Introduction*. Oxford: Oxford University Press.

Aguado, Pedro. 1913. *Historia de Venezuela escrita en 1581 por fray Pedro de Aguado y publicada, bajo la inspección de la mencionada Academia, por disposición del Gobierno del General Juan Vicente Gómez*. Tomo 1. Caracas: [Academia Nacional de Historia] Imp. Nacional. www.cervantesvirtual.com/nd/ark:/59851/bmc5h7r4.

———. 1916. *Historia de Santa Marta y nuevo reino de Granada por fray Pedro de Aguado*. Edited by Jérónimo Bécker. Madrid: J. Ratés.

———. 1987. *Fray Pedro de Aguado: Recopilación Historial de Venezuela*. 2 vols. Edited by Guillermo Morón. Vol. 1. Caracas: Academia Nacional de Historia.

Alcalá, Luis de. 1543. *Tratado de los préstamos*. Toledo: Juan de Ayala.

Alvar, Manuel. 1997. "Carlos V y la lengua española." In *Nebrija y estudios sobre la Edad de Oro*, 169–88. Madrid: CSIC. www.cervantesvirtual.com.

Amin, Samir. 1990. "Colonialism and the Rise of Capitalism: A Comment." *Science & Society* 54, no. 1: 67–72. www.jstor.org/stable/40403048.

Arcaya, Pedro Manuel. 1916. *Narración del primer viaje de Federmann a Venezuela*. Caracas: Lit. y Tip. del Comercio.

Arellano, Fernando. 1987. *Una introducción a la Venezuela prehispánica: Culturas de las naciones indígenas venezolanas*. Caracas: Universidad Católica Andrés Bello.

Arendt, Hannah. 1966. *The Origins of Totalitarianism*. New York: Harcourt.

Arias Lopez, Marie E. 1969. "Un livre américaniste publié en Alsace au XVie siècle." *Bulletin de la Faculté des Lettres de Strasbourg*, 605–10.

Armani, Alberto. 1985. *La genesi dell' Eurocolonialismo: Carlo V e i Welser*. Genova: ECIG.

Assmann, Aleida. 2016. *Shadows of Trauma: Memory and the Politics of Postwar Identity*. Translated by Sara Clift. New York: Fordham University Press.

Auer, Alfred. 1998. *Philippine Welser & Anna Caterina Gonzaga: Die Gemahlinnen Erzherzog Ferdinands II; Schloß Ambras Innsbruck, 24.6.–31.10.1998*. Vienna: Kunsthistorisches Museum.

Augsburg Postkolonial Group. 2019. "Jahresrückblick 2019." https://augsburgpost kolonial.wordpress.com/ueber-die-fugger/.

Aznar, Luis. 1945. "Los Alemanes en las Indias Occidentales." In *Viaje a las Indias del Mar Oceano*. Translated by Nélida Orfida. Buenos Aires: Editorial Nova.

Azpilcueta, Martin de. [1557] 1965. *Comentario resultorio de cambios*. Edited by Alberto Ullastres, José M. Perez Prendes, and Luciano Pereña. Madrid: CSIC.

———. 2014. *On Exchange: An Adjudicative Commentary*. Translated by Jeannine Emery. Sources in Early Modern Economics, Ethics, and Law. Grand Rapids, MI: CLP Academic.

Baer, Wolfram. 1978. "Philippine Welser 1527–1580." Fotoausstellung des Stadtarchivs Augsburg [23 Juni bis 17 September 1978]; [Führer durch die Ausstellung]. Augsburg: [Himmer], 1978.

Banton, Michael. 1998. *Racial Theories*. 2nd ed. Cambridge: Cambridge University Press.

Baralt, Rafael María. 1887. *Resumen de la historia de Venezuela desde el descubrimiento de su territorio por los castellanos en el siglo XV, hasta el año de 1797*. Vol. 1. Curazao: A Bethencourt.

Baranowski, Shelley. 2011a. "Against Human Diversity as Such: Lebensraum and Genocide in the Third Reich." In *German Colonialism: Race, the Holocaust, and Postwar Germany*, edited by Volker M. Langbehn and Mohammad Salama, 51–71. New York: Columbia University Press.

———. 2011b. *Nazi Empire: German Colonialism and Imperialism from Bismarck to Hitler*. Cambridge: Cambridge University Press.

Baron, Hans. 1937. "Religion and Politics in the German Imperial Cities during the Reformation (Continued)." *English Historical Review* 52, no. 208: 614–33. www.jstor.org/stable/553704.

Bauer, Volker. 2013. *Wurzel, Stamm, Krone: Fürstliche Genealogie in frühneuzeitlichen Druckwerken*. Wolfenbüttel: Herzog August Bibliothek.

Beauchesne, Kim. 2011. "'Soy ahora un bandido': La apropiación de la figura del rebelde en el *Tirano Aguirre*, de Adolfo Briceño Picón." *Revista Iberoamericana* 77, no. 236–37: 665–83.

Beaujean, Dieter, and Simon Turner, eds. 2010. [Hollstein's] *German Engravings, Etchings and Woodcuts: 1400–1700. Johann Ulrich Stapf to Hans Stercker*. Vol. 77. Ouderkerk aan den Ijssel, Netherlands: Sound & Vision Publishers.

———. 2016. [Hollstein's] *German Engravings, Etchings and Woodcuts: 1400–1700. Georg Strauch (continued) to Nicolaus Strauss*. Vol. 85. Ouderkerk aan den Ijssel, Netherlands: Sound & Vision Publishers.

Becker, Frank. 2004. *Rassenmischehen, Mischlinge, Rassentrennung: Zur Politik der Rasse im Deutschen Kolonialreich*. Stuttgart: F. Steiner.

Beinart, William, and Lotte Hughes. 2007. *Environment and Empire*. Oxford: Oxford University Press.

Ben-Amos, Ilana Krausman. 2008. *The Culture of Giving: Informal Support and Gift-Exchange in Early Modern England*. Cambridge: Cambridge University Press.

Bergermann, Marion. 2019. "Straßenumbenennung zieht sich." *Neues-Deutschland*, 2 October. www.neues-deutschland.de/artikel/1111946.afrikanisches-viertel -strassenumbenennung-zieht-sich.html.

Berman, Russell A. 1998. *Enlightenment or Empire: Colonial Discourse in German Culture*. Modern German Culture and Literature. Lincoln: University of Nebraska Press.

Bigelow, Allison Margaret. 2019. "Transatlantic Quechuañol: Reading Race through Colonial Translations." *PMLA* 134, no. 2 (March): 242–59.

Blaut, J. M. 1989. "Colonialism and the Rise of Capitalism." *Science & Society* 53, no. 3: 260–96. www.jstor.org/stable/40404472.

Blendinger, Friedrich. 1984. "Die Zunfterhebung Von 1368." In *Geschichte der Stadt Augsburg: 2000 Jahre von der Römerzeit bis zur Gegenwart*, edited by Gunther Gottlieb et al., 150–53. Stuttgart: Konrad Theiss.

Bock, Hartmut. 2008. "Die Familiengeschichtschreibung der Welser." *Mitteilungen des Vereins für Geschichte der Stadt Nürnberg* 95: 93–162.

Bonet, Natalia García. 2019. "The Indian Within: Negotiating Indigenous Identity among Dominant Images of Indigeneity in Venezuela." *Bulletin of Latin American Research* 38.S1: 57–75.

Borja Gómez, Jaime Humberto. 2002. *Los indios medievales de fray Pedro Aguado: Construcción del idólatra y escritura de la historia en una crónica del siglo XVI*. Bogotá: Centro Editorial Javeriano.

Bosl, Karl, ed. 1983. "Wolfgang Moritz Endter." In *Bosls Bayerische Biographie*, 176. Regensburg: Pustet. https://bavarikon.de/object/bav:UBR-BOS-0000P192 XTB00039.

Bouquet, Mary. 1996. "Family Trees and Their Affinities: The Visual Imperative of the Genealogical Diagram." *Journal of the Royal Anthropological Institute* 2, no. 1: 43–66. www.jstor.org/stable/3034632.

Briceño Picón, Adolfo. 1903. *Ambrosio de Alfinger: Los alemanes en la conquista de Venezuela*. In *Teatro andino*, edited by Adolfo Briceño Picón, 191–306. Paris and Mexico City: Ch. Bouret.

Brickhouse, Anna. 2015. *The Unsettlement of America: Translation, Interpretation, and the Story of Don Luis de Velasco, 1560–1945*. Oxford: Oxford University Press.

Britto García, Luis. 2014. "Fundamentos histórico-politicos de la narrativa venezolana: Narrativa y positivismo." In *II Seminario Literatura Latinoamericana: Miradas, memoria y ficción en la narrativa histórica venezolana y latinoamericana. Actas 2014*, edited by Johan López and Francisco Ardiles, 33–68. Caracas: Centro Nacional del Libro.

Brown, Stephen. 2012. "Venezuelan Tribe Angry at 'Sacred' Stone in Berlin." Reuters, 26 June. www.reuters.com/article/us-germany-venezuela-stone/venezu elan-tribe-angry-at-sacred-stone-in-berlin-idINBRE85P1202012 0626.

Buisseret, David. 1992. Introduction to *Monarchs, Ministers, and Maps*, edited by David Buisseret, 1–4. Chicago: University of Chicago Press.

Cabrujas, José Ignacio. 2011. *En nombre del rey*. In *Obra dramática*, edited by José Ignacio Cabrujas, Leonardo Azparren Giménez, and Gloria Soares de Ponte, vol. 3: 65–132. Caracas: Editorial Equinoccio.

Campos, Carlos Alberto. 1985. "Technology, Scientific Speculation and the Great Discoveries." *Revista da Universidade de Coimbra* 33: 485–542.

"Capitulación de los Belzares con la Corona de Castilla." 1528. Madrid. 27 March. www.cervantesvirtual.com/obra-visor/capitulacion-de-los-belzares-con-la -corona-de-castilla-madrid-27-de-marzo-de-1528--0/html/ff6bf908-82b1 -11df-acc7-002185ce6064_2.html#I_0.

Carande Thobar, Ramón. 1943. *Carlos V y sus banqueros*. Tomo 1: *La vida económica de España en una fase de su hegemonía, 1516–1556*. Madrid: Revista de Occidente.

———. 1965. *Carlos V y sus banqueros*. 2nd ed. 3 vols. Madrid: Sociedad de Estudios y Publicaciones.

———. 1967. *Carlos V y sus banqueros*. Madrid: Sociedad de Estudios y Publicaciones.

Cardot, Carlos Felice, ed. 1962. *Venezuela en los cronistas generales de Indias*. Vol. 1. Caracas: Academia Nacional de Historia.

Carman, Glen. 2006. *Rhetorical Conquests: Cortés, Gómara, and Renaissance Imperialism*. Purdue University Press.

Carretero Zamora, Juan Manuel. 1995. "Fiscalidad extraordinaria y deuda: El destino del servicio de las Cortes de Castilla (1535–1537)." *Espacio Tiempo y Forma, Serie IV, Historia Moderna* [en línea], 0.8: n.p. http://revistas.uned.es /index.php/ETFIV/article/view/3325.

———. 2000. "Fiscalidad parlamentaria y deuda imperial." In *El imperio de Carlos V: Procesos de agregación y conflictos*, edited by Bernardo J. García, 157–84. [Madrid]: Fundación Carlos de Amberes.

Castellanos, Juan de. 1962. *Elegía de varones ilustres de las Indias*. Edited by Isaac J. Pardo. Caracas: Academia Nacional de la Historia.

———. 2004. *Antología crítica de Juan de Castellanos: Elegías de varones ilustres de indias*. Edited by Luis Fernández Restrepo. Bogotá: Editorial Pontificia Universidad Javeriana.

Celemín, Libardo Vargas. 2007. "Memoria, identidad y prosa poética en la voz mestiza del narrador de *Ursúa.*" *Revista de Literaturas Modernas*, no. 37–38 (January): 229–46.

Certeau, Michel de. 1988. *The Writing of History.* New York: Columbia University Press.

Chesney-Lawrence, Luis, and Anamaría Crowe Serrano. 2005. "Cabrujas, José Ignacio." In *The Oxford Encyclopedia of Theatre and Performance.* Oxford: Oxford University Press. www-oxfordreferencecom.proxy.binghamton.edu/view /10.1093/acref/9780198601746.001.0001/acref-9780198601746-e-632.

Chukwudi Eze, Emmanuel, ed. 1997. *Race and the Enlightenment: A Reader.* Cambridge, MA: Blackwell.

Clüver, Philipp. 1729. *Introductionis in Universam Geographiam.* Amsterdam: Apud Petrum de Coup.

Columbus, Christopher. 1990. *Journal of the First Voyage (Diario del primer viaje) 1492.* Translated by B. W. Warmister Ife. Liverpool: Aris & Phillips.

Conley, Tom. 1992. "De Bry's Las Casas." In *Amerindian Images and the Legacy of Columbus*, edited by Rene Jara and Nicholas Spadaccini, 103–31. Minneapolis: University of Minnesota Press.

Coronil, Fernando. 2019. "Perspectives on Darkness in El Dorado." In *The Fernando Coronil Reader: The Struggle for Life Is the Matter*, edited by Julie Skurski et al., 123–27. Durham, NC: Duke University Press.

Coronil, Fernando, and Julie Skurski. 2019. "Dismembering and Remembering the Nation: The Semantics of Political Violence in Venezuela." In *The Fernando Coronil Reader: The Struggle for Life Is the Matter*, edited by Julie Skurski et al., 171–230. Durham, NC: Duke University Press.

Cortés, López J. L. 2004. *Esclavo y colono: Introducción y sociología de los negro-africanos en la América española del siglo XVI.* Salamanca: Ediciones Universidad de Salamanca.

Cramer-Fortig, Michael, Peter Fleischmann, and Simone Herde. 2006. *Aus 650 Jahren: Ausgewaelte Dokumente des Stadtarchivs Augsburg zur Geschichte der Reichstadt Augsburg 1156–1806. Beiträge zur Geschichte der Stadt Augsburg.* Augsburg: Wißner.

Cromwell, Jesse. 2018. *The Smuggler's World: Illicit Trade and Atlantic Communities in Eighteenth-Century Venezuela.* Chapel Hill: University of North Carolina Press and Omohundro Institute.

Cuesta Domingo, Mariano. 2010. "Tradición y progreso en la cartografía de la contratación." In *Cartografía hspánica: Imagen de un mundo en crecimiento, 1503–1810*, edited by Mariano Cuesta Domingo and Alfredo Surroca Carrascosa, 21–47. Madrid: Ministerio de Defensa, 2010.

Davies, Surekha. 2003. "The Navigational Iconography of Diogo Ribeiro's 1529 Vatican Planisphere." *Imago Mundi* 55, no. 1: 103–12.

Davis, Elizabeth B. 2000. *Myth and Identity in the Epic of Imperial Spain*. Columbia: University of Missouri Press.

Decolonize HU. 2016. https://decolonizehu.wordpress.com/2016/02/16.

Dehn, Paul. 1886. "Deutsch nationale Kapitalanlagen im Auslande." *Deutsche Kolonial Zeitung* 8. Heft, 231. Berlin: Eigentum und Verlag des Deutschen Kolonialvereins.

Dehner, Diana. 1993. "'El Dorado' brachte kein Glück." *Sudwest Presse*, 15 January.

Denzel, Markus A. 1994. *"La Practica della Cambiatura": Europäischer Zahlungsverkehr vom 14. bis zum 17. Jahrhundert*. Stuttgart: Steiner.

Denzer, Jörg. 2002. "Die Welsern in Venezuela—Das Scheitern ihre Wirtschaftlichen Ziele." In *Die Welser: Neue Forschungen zur Geschichte und Kultur des oberdeutschen Handelshauses*. Edited by Mark Häberlein and Johannes Burkhardt, 285–319. Berlin: Akademie Verlag.

———. 2003. *Die Konquista der Augsburger Welser-Gesellschaft in Südamerika (1528–1556) Historische Rekonstruktion, Historiografie und lokale Erinnerungskultur in Kolumbien und Venezuela*. Munich: Beck.

Derrida, Jacques. 1992. *Given Time: I. Counterfeit Money*. Translated by Peggy Kamuf. Chicago: University of Chicago Press.

———. 1995. *The Gift of Death*. Translated by Peggy Kamuf. Chicago: University of Chicago Press.

Deutsche Kolonialzeitung (DKZ). 1888. "Der portugiesische Vizekönig Don Franzisko d'Almeida, sowie die Augsburger Kaufleute Balthasar Sprenger und Hans Mayr im Jahr 1505 in Kiloa." Berlin, 18 February.

———. 1891. "Die Versammlung der deutschen Kolonialgesellschaft in Nürnberg am 29 und 30. Juni 1891." Berlin, 25 April.

———. 1905a. "Kalender 12 bis 18 Januar." Berlin, 12 January 1905.

———. 1905b. "Aus den Abteilungen." Berlin, 12 January 1905.

Deutsche Welle. 2018. "Germany Returns Human Remains from Namibia Genocide." *DW News*, 29 August. www.dw.com/en/germany-returns-human-remains-from-namibia-genocide/a-45268717.

Diemer, Dorothea. 2010. "Zur Verwahrgeschichte des Codex Argenteus Upsaliensis im 16. jahrhundert: Johann Wilhelm von Laubenberg zu Wagegg." *Zeitschrift für Deutsches Altertum und Deutsche Literatur* 139, no. 1: 1–25. www.jstor.org/stable/25738104.

Dilke, O. A. W. 1985. *Greek and Roman Maps*. London: Thames and Hudson.

Dolle, Verena, ed. 2014. *La representación de la conquista en el teatro latinoamericano de los siglos XX y XXI*. Hildesheim: Georg Olms.

Drekonja-Kornat, Gerhard. 2004. "What Were the Nazis up to in Latin America." In *Revisiting the Nationalist Socialist Legacy*, edited by Oliver Rathkolb, 310–17. New Brunswick, NJ: Transaction Publishers.

Drelichman, Mauricio, and Hans-Joachim Voth. 2011. "Lending to the Borrower from Hell: Debt and Default in the Age of Philip II." *Economic Journal* 121, no. 557: 1205–27. www.jstor.org/stable/41301355.

Eddy, Melissa. 2012. "A Rock Fated to Anger Nations." *New York Times*, 11 July. www.nytimes.com/2012/07/12/arts/12iht-stone12.html.

Eisler, Colin. 2009. "Who Is Dürer's 'Syphilitic Man'?" *Perspectives in Biology and Medicine* 52, no. 1: 48–60. Project MUSE, doi:10.1353/pbm.0.0065.

Eligon, John. 2018. "The Big Hole in Germany's Reckoning? Its Colonial History." *New York Times*, 11 September. www.nytimes.com/2018/09/11/world/europe/germany-colonial-history-africa-nazi.html.

Endriss, Julius. 1936. *Kaspar Schwenckfelds Ulmer Kämpfe.* Ulm: Grüner Hof.

Engels, Johannes. 2007. "Geography and History." In *A Companion to Greek and Roman Historiography*, edited by John Marincola, vol. 2: 541–52. Oxford: Blackwell, 2007.

Escudero, José Antonio. 2000. "El gobierno de Carlos V hasta la muerte de Gattinara." In *El imperio de Carlos V: Procesos de agregación y conflictos*, edited by Bernardo J. García, 83–96. Real Monasterio de Yuste: Fundación Carlos de Amberes.

Eser, Thomas, and Stephanie Armer. 2017. *Luther, Kolumbus und die Folgen: Welt im Wandel 1500–1600.* Ausstellung im Germanischen Nationalmuseum, Nürnberg vom 13. Juli bis 12. November. Nürnberg: Verlag des Germanischen Nationalmuseums.

Eze, Emmanuel, ed. 1997. *Race and the Enlightenment: A Reader.* Cambridge, MA: Blackwell.

Faber, Gustav. 1944. *Deutsches Blut in Fremder Erde.* Berlin: Junge Generation.

Farías, Eduardo Arcila. 1997. "Welser." In *Diccionario de la historia de Venezuela.* 2nd. ed., edited by Manuel Campos Ródriguez, vol. 4: 299–301. Caracas: Fundación Polar.

Federmann, Arnold, and Nikolaus Federmann. 1938. *Deutsche Konquistadoren in Südamerika mit Einem Nachdruck der "Indianischen Historia" des Nicolaus Federmann des Jüngeren Von Ulm.* Berlin: Hobbing.

Federmann, Nikolaus. 1557. *Indianische Historia. Ein schöne kurtzweilige Historia Niclaus Federmanns des Jüngern von Ulm erster raise so er von Hispania un[d] Andolosia ausz in Indias des Occeanischen Mörs gethan hat und was ihm allda begegnet bis auff sein widerkunfft inn Hispaniam auffs kurtzest beschriben, gantz lustig zu lesen.* Haguenau: Sigmund Bund.

———. 1837. *Belle et agréable narration du premier voyage de Nicolas Federmann le jeune, d'Ulm aux Indes de la mer océane, et de tout ce qui lui est arrivé dans ce pays jusqu'à son retour en Espagne.* Edited by Henri Ternaux-Compans. Paris: A. Bertrand.

———. 1945. *Viaje a las Indias del mar océano.* Edited by Nélida Orfila. Buenos Aires: Editorial Nova.

Fernández de Oviedo y Valdés, Gonzalo. 1959. *Historia general y natural de las Indias.* 5 vols. Edited by Juan Pérez de Tudela Bueso. Biblioteca de autores españoles. Madrid: Ediciones Atlas.

Flakin, Wladek. 2012. "Colonial Berlin in 10 stops." *Exberliner*, 25 September. www.exberliner.com/features/zeitgeist/colonial-berlin-in-10-stops/.

Fortique, Jose Rafael. 1976. *Los Welser en la historia de Coro: Trabajo leído en el concejo municipal de Coro el día 29 de octubre de 1976.* n.p.: n.p.

Fortoul, José Gil. 1907. *Historia constitucional de Venezuela.* Vol. 1. Berlín: Carl Heymann.

Frevel, Christian. 1991. "Conquistadoren aus Augsburg." *Schwäbische Zeitung,* 7 September.

Friede, Juan. 1960. *Vida y viajes de Nicolás Fédermann.* Bogotá: Libreria Buchholz.

————. 1961. *Los Welser en la conquista de Venezuela.* Caracas: EDIME.

————. 1964. "Fray Pedro Aguado y fray Antonio Medrano, historiadores de Colombia y Venezuela." *Revista de Historia de América,* no. 57–58: 177–232. www.jstor.org/stable/20138632.

————. 1965. "Einführung." In *Indianische Historia.* Munich: Klaus Renner.

Fröhlich, Michael. 1990. *Von Konfrontation zur Koexistenz: Die deutsch-englischen Kolonialbeziehungen in Afrika zwischen 1884 und 1914.* Bochum: Universitätsverlag Dr. N. Brockmeyer.

Fröschle, Hartmut. 1979. *Die Deutschen in Lateinamerika: Schicksal und Leistung.* Tübingen: Hörst Erdmann.

Fuchs, Barbara. 2007. "The Spanish Race." In *Rereading the Black Legend,* edited by Margaret R. Greer, Walter D. Mignolo, and Maureen Quilligan, 88–116. Chicago: University of Chicago Press.

Fuenmayor, María Gabriela. 2018. "Con un ritual de sanación preparan la repatriación de la piedra 'Abuela Kueka.'" *Panorama*, 11 May. www.panorama.com.ve /ciudad/Con-un-ritual-de-sanacion-preparan-la-repatriacion-de-la-piedra -Abuela-Kueka-20180511-0026.html.

"Fugger-Express." n.d. AugsburgWiki. www.augsburgwiki.de/index.php/Augs burgWiki/Fugger-Express.

Fulcher, James. 2004. *Capitalism: A Very Short Introduction.* Oxford: Oxford University Press.

Galster, Ingrid. 2011. *Aguirre o la posteridad arbitraria: La rebelión del conquistador Vasco Lope de Aguirre en historiografía y ficción histórica (1561–1992).* Bogotá: Editorial Universidad del Rosario and Editorial Pontificia Universidad Javeriana.

García, Jesús "Chucho." 2001. "Demystifying Africa's Absence in Venezuelan History and Culture." In *African Roots / American Cultures: Africa in the Creation of the Americas,* edited by Sheila S. Walker, 284–90. Lanham, MD: Rowman & Littlefield.

Geffcken, Peter. 2021. "Ravensburger." In *Stadtlexicon Augsburg*, edited by Günther Grünsteudel, Günter Hägele, and Rudolf Frankenberger. Augsburg: Wißner Verlag. www.wissner.com/stadtlexikon-augsburg/artikel/stadtlexi kon/ravens burger/5117.

Geffcken, Peter, and Mark Häberlein. 2014. *Rechnungsfragmente der Augsburger Welser-Gesellschaft (1496–1551): Oberdeutscher Fernhandel am Beginn der Neuzeitlichen Weltwirtschaft*. Stuttgart: Steiner.

Grimmer-Solem, Erik. 2019. *Learning Empire: Globalization and the German Quest for World Status, 1875–1919*. Cambridge: Cambridge University Press.

Groebner, Valentin. 2002. *Liquid Assets, Dangerous Gifts: Presents and Politics at the End of the Middle Ages*. Philadelphia: University of Pennsylvania Press.

Grosse, Pascal. 2005. "What Does German Colonialism Have to Do with National Socialism?" In *Germany's Colonial Pasts*, edited by Eric Ames, Marcia Klotz, and Lora Wildenthal, 115–34. Lincoln: University of Nebraska Press.

Gullace, Nicoletta F. 1997. "Sexual Violence and Family Honor: British Propaganda and International Law during the First World War." *American Historical Review* 102, no. 3: 714–47. www.jstor.org/stable/2171507.

Haase, Yorck Alexander, and Harold Stein Jantz. 1976. *Die Neue Welt in den Schätzen einer alten europäischen Bibliothek: Ausstellung der Herzog August Bibliothek Wolfenbüttel = The New World in the Treasures of an Old European Library: Exhibition of the Duke August Library Wolfenbüttel: [30. 6.–22. 8. 1976, Herzog August Bibliothek Wolfenbüttel, 23. 9.–6. 10. 1976, Princeton University Library, January 1977], Newberry Library Chicago*. Wolfenbüttel: Herzog August Bibliothek.

Häberlein, Mark. 2012. *The Fuggers of Augsburg: Pursuing Wealth and Honor in Renaissance Germany*. Charlottesville: University of Virginia Press.

Häberlein, Mark, and Johannes Burkhardt, eds. 2002. *Die Welser: Neue Forschungen zur Geschichte und Kultur des Oberdeutschen Handelshauses*. Berlin: Akademie.

Häberlein, Mark, and Michaela Schmölz-Häberlein. 1995. *Die Erben der Welser: Der Karibikhandel der Augsburger Firma Obwexer im Zeitalter der Revolutionen*. Augsburg: Bernd Wißner.

Haebler, Konrad. 1903. *Die Überseeischen Unternehmungen der Welser und ihrer Gesellschafter*. Leipzig: C. L. Hirschfeld.

Hagemann, Annick. 2015. "Exploring Germany's Colonial Past." 21 April. www .slowtravelberlin.com/colonial-berlin/.

Haliczer, Stephen. 1981. *The Comuneros of Castile: The Forging of a Revolution, 1475–1521*. Madison: University of Wisconsin Press.

Hanauer, Auguste. 1908. *Bibliothèques et Archives de Haguenau*. Strasbourg: Librairie Noiriel.

Hanstein, Otfried von. 1929. *Auf der Jagd nach dem goldenen Kaziken: Die erste deutsche Kolonie der Welser in Venezuela 1527 bis 1555*. Leipzig: Leipziger Graphische Werke.

Hantzsch, Viktor. 1895. *Die überseeischen Unternehmungen der Augsburger Welser.* Leipzig.

Hayes, James, and Benjamin Timms. 2012. "Physical Geography: The Human-Environment Connection." In *Placing Latin America: Contemporary Themes in Geography,* 2nd ed., edited by E. Jackiewicz and F. Bosco, 11–30. Lanham, MD: Rowman & Littlefield.

Herrera Luque, Francisco. 1983. *La luna de Fausto.* Caracas: Editorial Pomaire. Reprint New York: Sudaquia, 2013.

Herwig, Holger. 1986. *Germany's Vision of Empire in Venezuela 1871–1914.* Princeton, NJ: Princeton University Press.

Hess, Peter. 2021. *Violent First Contact in Venezuela: Nikolaus Federmann's Indian History.* University Park, PA: Pennsylvania State University Press.

Hutten, Friedrich K., and Eberhard Schmitt. 1999. *Das Gold der Neuen Welt: Die Papiere des Welser-Konquistadors und Generalkapitäns von Venezuela Philipp von Hutten 1534–1541.* Berlin: Berlin-Verl. Spitz.

Jahn, Joachin. 1984. "Die Augsburger Sozialstruktur im 15 Jahrhundert." In *Geschichte der Stadt Augsburg: 2000 Jahre von der Römerzeit bis zur Gegenwart,* edited by Gunther Gottlieb et al., 248–301. Stuttgart: Konrad Theiss.

Janssen, Johannes, A. M. Christie, and M A. Mitchell. 1896. *History of the German People at the Close of the Middle Ages.* Vol. 11. London: K. Paul, Trench, Trübner, & Co.

Jecmen, Gregory, and Freyda Spira, eds. 2012. *Imperial Augsburg: Renaissance Prints and Drawings, 1475–1540.* Washington, DC: National Gallery of Art in association with Lund Humphries.

Jimenez G[raziani], Morella A. 1986. *La esclavitud indigena en Venezuela.* Caracas: Academia Nacional de Historia.

Johnson, Carina L. 2011a. "Aztec Regalia and the Reformation of Display." In *Collecting Across Cultures,* edited by Daniela Bleichmar and Peter C. Mancall, 83–98. Philadelphia: University of Pennsylvania Press.

———. 2011b. *Cultural Hierarchy in Sixteenth-Century Europe: The Ottomans and Mexicans.* Cambridge: Cambridge University Press.

Johnson, Christine. 2008. *The German Discovery of the World: Renaissance Encounters with the Strange and Marvelous.* Charlottesville: University of Virginia Press.

Karrow, Robert W., Jr. 1993. *Mapmakers of the Sixteenth Century and Their Maps: Bio-Bibliographies of the Cartographers of Abraham Ortelius, 1570.* Chicago: Speculum Orbis Press.

Keenan, Sean. 2018. "Atlanta's Confederate Avenue Could Soon Be Renamed United Avenue." *Curbed Atlanta,* 26 September. https://atlanta.curbed.com /2018/9/26/17904944/confederate-avenue-atlanta-united-grant-park.

Kellenbenz, Hermann. 1984. "Wirtschaftsleben der Blütezeit." In *Geschichte der Stadt Augsburg: 2000 Jahre von der Römerzeit bis zur Gegenwart,* edited by Gunther Gottlieb et al., 248–301. Stuttgart: Konrad Theiss.

Kellenbenz, Hermann, and Rolf Walter. 2001. *Oberdeutsche Kaufleute in Sevilla und Cadiz (1525–1560): Eine Edition von Notariatsakten aus den dortigen Archiven.* Stuttgart: Steiner.

Kießling, Rolf. 1984a. "Augsburgs Wirtschaft im 14. und 15. Jahrhundert." In *Geschichte der Stadt Augsburg: 2000 Jahre von der Römerzeit bis zur Gegenwart*, edited by Gunther Gottlieb et al., 171–81. Stuttgart: Konrad Theiss.

———. 1984b. "Augsburg zwischen Mittelalter und Neuzeit." In *Geschichte der Stadt Augsburg: 2000 Jahre von der Römerzeit bis zur Gegenwart*, edited by Gunther Gottlieb et al., 241–51. Stuttgart: Konrad Theiss.

———. 2002. "Wirtschaftlicher Strukturwandel in der Region—Die Welser-Vöhlin Gesellschaft im Kontext der Memminger Wirtschafts- und Sozial-Geschichte des 15. und frühen 16. Jarhunderts." In *Die Welser: Neue Forschungen zur Geschichte und Kultur der Oberdeutschen Handelshauses*, edited by Johannes Burkhardt and Mark Häberlein, 184–214. Berlin: Akademie.

Kirchner, Gottfried, dir. 1991. *Der Todeszug der Lanzenreiter.* Deutsche Eroberer in Südamerika, Terra X, Episode 26. Aired on ZDF (Zweites Deutsches Fernsehen). www.dailymotion.com/video/x770gqi.

Klekar, Cynthia. 2009. "Obligation, Coercion, and Economy: The Deed of Trust in Congreve's *The Way of the World*." In *The Culture of the Gift in Eighteenth-Century England*, edited by Linda Zionkowski and Cynthia Klekar, 125–42. New York: Palgrave Macmillan.

Klotz, Aiga. 2014. *Kinder-und Jugendliteratur in Deutschland 1840–1950*. Band II. Stuttgart: J. B. Metzler.

Knoll, Arthur J., and Lewis H. Gann. 1987. *Germans in the Tropics: Essays in German Colonial History.* New York: Greenwood Press.

Knoll, Arthur J., and Hermann Hiery. 2010. *The German Colonial Experience: Select Documents on German Rule in Africa, China, and the Pacific 1884–1914*. Lanham, MD: University Press of America.

Kocka, Jürgen. 2016. *Capitalism.* Translated by Jeremiah Riemer. Princeton, NJ: Princeton University Press.

Kreikle, Christian. 1992. "Trügerische Hoffnung auf Eldorado." *Neu-Ulmer Zeitung*, 1 December.

Kressner, Ilka. 2013. "Counter (Current) Discourses: Rivers in William Ospina's *Ursúa* and *El país de la canela*." In *Troubled Waters: Rivers in Latin American Imagination*, edited by Elizabeth M. Pettinaroli and Ana María Mutis. *Hispanic Issues On Line 12* (Spring): 180–94.

Kretschmer, Konrad. 1970. "Die Atlanten des Battista Agnese." *Acta Cartographica* 8: 355–61.

Kristmannson, Gauti. 2019. "Germanic Tradition." In *A World Atlas of Translation*, edited by Yves Gambier and Ubaldo Stecconi, 355–74. Amsterdam: John Benjamins.

Kupčík, Ivan, and Friedrich Kunstmann. 2000. *Münchner Portolankarten: Kunstmann I-XIII und Zehn Weitere Portolankarten: Überarbeitete und Ergänzte Neuausgabe des Originalwerkes von Friedrich Kunstmann aus dem Jahr 1859 mit 13 Erneuerten Farbtafeln sowie Zehn Weitere Seekarten von Anfang des 16. Jahrhunderts, Einschliesslich der Seit 1945 Verschollenen Seekarten aus Münchner Sammlungen.* München: Deutscher Kunstverlag.

Lacan, Jacques. 1988. "Seminar on *The Purloined Letter.*" In *The Purloined Poe: Lacan, Derrida, and Psychoanalytic Reading,* edited by John P. Muller and William Richardson, 28–54. Baltimore: John Hopkins University Press.

Langbehn, Volker M., and Mohammad Salama, eds. 2011. *German Colonialism: Race, the Holocaust, and Postwar Germany.* New York: Columbia University Press.

Las Casas, Bartolomé de. [1552] 2005. *Brevísima relación de la destrucción de las Indias.* Edited by Trinidad Barrera López. Madrid: Alianza.

———. [1597]. *Newe Welt. Warhafftige Anzeigung der Hispanier.* Translator unknown. Frankfurt: n.p.

———. 2003. *An Account, Much Abbreviated, of the Destruction of the Indies, with Related Texts.* Translated by Andrew Hurley. Indianapolis: Hackett.

Lee, Christopher J. 2007. "Race and Bureaucracy Revisited: Hannah Arendt's Recent Reemergence in African Studies." In *Hannah Arendt and the Uses of History: Imperialism, Nation, Race, and Genocide,* edited by Richard H. King and Dan Stone, 68–86. New York: Berghahn.

Legnani, Nicole. 2020. *The Business of Conquest: Empire, Love, and Law in the Atlantic World.* Notre Dame, IN: University of Notre Dame Press.

Leitch, Stephanie. 2010. *Mapping Ethnography in Early Modern Germany: New Worlds in Print Culture.* Basingstoke: Palgrave Macmillan.

Leite, Naomi. 2017. *Unorthodox Kin: Portuguese Marranos and the Global Search for Belonging.* Oakland: University of California Press.

Leitz, Christian. 2003. "Nazi Germany and the Luso-Hispanic World." *Contemporary European History* 12, no. 2: 183–96. www.jstor.org/stable/20081151.

Liebman, Seymour B. 1976. *The Inquisitors and the Jews in the New World: Summaries of Procesos, 1500–1810, and Bibliographical Guide.* Coral Gables, FL: University of Miami Press.

Lindner, Ulrike. 2009. "Colonialism as a European Project in Africa before 1914? British and German Concepts of Colonial Rule in Sub-Saharan Africa." *Comparativ: Leipziger Beiträge zur Universalgeschichte und Vergleichenden Gesellschaftsforschung* 19, no. 1: 88–106.

Lockhart, James. 2003. "Encomienda and Repartimiento." In *The Oxford Encyclopedia of Economic History,* edited by Joel Mokyr. Oxford: Oxford University Press. www-oxfordreference-com.proxy.binghamton.edu/view/10.1093/acref/9780195105070.001.0001/acref-9780195105070-e-0239.

López, Johan, and Francisco Ardiles, eds. 2016. *II Seminario literatura latinoamericana: Miradas, memoria y ficción en la narrativa histórica venezolana y latinoamericana. Actas 2014*. [Caracas]: Centro Nacional del Libro.

Lovera Reyes, Elina. 2011. "El fidelismo de los indios caquetíos de Coro durante la independencia de Venezuela." *Tiempo y Espacio* 21, no. 56. www.scielo.org.ve.

Lowe, K. J. P. 2005. "The Stereotyping of Black Africans in Renaissance Europe." In *Black Africans in Renaissance Europe*, edited by T. F. Earle and K. J. P. Lowe, 17–47. New York: Cambridge University Press.

Lubrich, Oliver. 2003. "In the Realm of Ambivalence: Alexander Von Humboldt's Discourse on Cuba (*Relation historique du voyage aux régions équinoxiales du nouveau continent*)." *German Studies Review* 26, no. 1: 63–80. www.jstor.org/stable/1432902.

Mair, Paul Hector. 1550. *Bericht vnd antzaigen der loblichen Staat Augspurg aller Herren Geschlecht*. Augsburg: Melchior Kriegstein.

Maler, Anselm, ed. 1992. *Fray Bartolomé de Las Casas an Philipp II: Der Widmungsbrief zu den Tratakten "Von den schätzen in Peru" und "Von den Zwölf Bedenken."* Wiesbaden: Otto Harrasowitz.

Maltby, William S. 1971. *The Black Legend in England: The Development of Anti-Spanish Sentiment, 1558–1660*. Durham, NC: Duke University Press.

Mamdani, Mahmood. 1996. *Citizen and Subject: Contemporary Africa and the Legacy of Late Colonialism*. Kampala: Fountain.

———. 2001. *When Victims Become Killers: Colonialism, Nativism, and the Genocide in Rwanda*. Princeton, NJ: Princeton University Press.

Markey, Lia. 2016. *Imagining the Americas in Medici Florence*. University Park: Pennsylvania State University Press.

Márquez Rodríguez, Alexis. 1990. *Historia y ficción en la novela venezolana*. Caracas: Monte Avila.

Martínez, Tomás Eloy, and Susana Rotker, eds. 1992. "Oviedo y Baños: La fundación literaria de la nacionalidad venezolana." In *Historia de la conquista y población de la provincia de Venezuela*, edited by Tomás Eloy Martínez, ix–xlviii. Caracas: Biblioteca Ayacucho.

Martínez-Dávila, Roger L. 2018. *Creating Conversos: The Carvajal–Santa María Family in Early Modern Spain*. Notre Dame, IN: University of Notre Dame Press.

Martínez-Osorio, Emiro. 2016. *Authority, Piracy, and Captivity in Colonial Spanish American Writing: Juan de Castellanos's Elegies of Illustrious Men of the Indies*. Lewisburg, PA: Bucknell University Press.

Martínez Sánchez, Yuly Paola. 2015. "Museo de lo inútil, Ursa, y la Ceiba de la memoria: Entre la crisis y el orden de la representación." *Estudios de Literatura Colombiana*, no. 36: 37–57.

Marx, Karl. 1976. *Capital.* Vol. 1. London: Penguin/New Left.

Maurer, Franz. [1867] 2010. "Outline for the Foundation of a German Colony and Naval Station of the Nicobar Islands, April 1867." In *The German Colonial Experience: Select Documents on German Rule in Africa, China, and the Pacific 1884–1914,* edited by Arthur J. Knoll and Hermann Hiery, 9–11. Lanham, MD: University Press of America.

Mauss, Marcel. 1990. *The Gift.* Translated by W. D. Halls. London: Routledge.

Mbembe, Achille. 2002. "The Power of the Archive and Its Limits." In *Refiguring the Archive,* edited by Carolyn Hamilton, 19–27. Dordrecht: Springer.

McConahay, Mary Jo. 2018. *The Tango War: The Struggle for the Hearts, Minds, and Riches of Latin America during World War II.* New York: St. Martin's Press.

Melamed, Jodi. 2011. *Represent and Destroy: Rationalizing Violence in the New Racial Capitalism.* Minneapolis: University of Minnesota Press.

Melé, Domènec. 1999. "Early Business Ethics in Spain: The Salamanca School (1526–1614)." *Journal of Business Ethics* 22, no. 3: 175–89. www.jstor.org /stable/25074200.

Meurer, Peter H. 2007. "Cartography in the German Lands, 1450–1650." In *The History of Cartography,* vol. 3, edited by David Woodward, 1172–245. Chicago: University of Chicago Press.

Mignolo, Walter. 1982. "Cartas, cronicas y relaciones del descubrimiento y la conquista." In *Historia de la literatura hispanoamericana: Época colonial,* vol. 1, edited by Manuel Alvar and Luis Iñigo Madrigal, 57–116. Madrid: Cátedra.

Mikkelsen, Jon M., trans. and ed. 2013. *Kant and the Concept of Race: Late Eighteenth-Century Writings.* Albany: SUNY Press.

Miller, Shawn William. 2007. *An Environmental History of Latin America.* Cambridge: Cambridge University Press.

Mitgau, Hermann. 1968. "Geschlossene Heiratskreise sozialer Inzucht." In *Deutsches Patriziat, 1430–1740,* edited by Hellmuth Rössler, 1–25. Limburg/ Lahn: C. A. Starke.

Moloi, Vincent, dir. 2016. *Skulls of My People.* Puo Pha Productions. www.idfa.nl /en/film/048bcdc9-47f5-4279-aa90-ebcc8db1e5b7/skulls-of-my-people.

Montenegro, Giovanna. 2012. "Futurism in Venezuela: Arturo Uslar Pietri and the Reviews *Indice* and *válvula.*" *International Yearbook of Futurism Studies* 2: 286–303.

———. 2013. "Textual and Visual Representations of the New World: German and Spanish Perspectives of the Conquest of Venezuela in the Sixteenth Century." PhD diss., University of California, Davis.

———. 2017. "Conquistadors and Indians 'Fail' at Gift Exchange: An Analysis of Nikolaus Federmann's *Indianische Historia* (Haguenau, 1557)." *Modern Language Notes* 132, no. 2: 272–90. http://muse.jhu.edu/article/656912.

———. 2018. "'The Welser Phantom': Apparitions of the Welser Venezuela Colony in Nineteenth- and Twentieth-Century German Cultural Memory." *Transit: A Journal of Travel, Migration, and Multiculturalism in the German-speaking World* 11, no. 2: 21–53. http://transit.berkeley.edu/2018/montenegro/.

Moore, Jason W. W. 2016a. "Anthropocene or Capitalocene? Nature, History, and the Crisis of Capitalism." In *Anthropocene or Capitolocene*, edited by Jason W. Moore, 1–11. Oakland, CA: PM Press. https://orb.binghamton.edu/sociology_fac/2.

———. 2016b. "The Rise of Cheap Nature." In *Anthropocene or Capitolocene*, edited by Jason W. Moore, 78–115. Oakland, CA: PM Press. https://orb.bing hamton.edu/sociology_fac/2.

Morón, Guillermo. 1967. *Historia de Venezuela*. 4th ed. Madrid: Ediciones Rialp.

———. 1971. "Historia de Venezuela." In *Historia de Venezuela*, 5 vols., edited by Guillermo Morón. Vol. 1. Caracas: Italgráfica.

———, ed. 1977. *Juicios de residencia en la provincia de Venezuela. I. Los Welser*. Caracas: ANH.

———. 1992. "Prólogo." In *Noticias historiales de Venezuela de fray Pedro Simón*, edited by Demetrio Ramos Perez, ix–xli. Caracas: Biblioteca Ayacucho.

Moseley, C. W. R. D. 1981. "Behaim's Globe and 'Mandeville's Travels.'" *Imago Mundi* 33: 89–91.

Moses, Dirk. 2002. "Conceptual Blockages and Definitional Dilemmas in the 'Racial Century': Genocides of Indigenous Peoples and the Holocaust." *Patterns of Prejudice* 36, no. 4: 7–36.

Mulzer, Erich. 2000. "Welserhof." In *Stadtlexicon Nurnberg*, edited by Rudolf Endres and Michael Diefenbacher, 1171. Nürnberg: W. Tümmels.

Münzer, Hieronymus. 1920. "Itinerarum hispanicum Hieronymi Monetarii (1494–1495)." Edited by L. Pfandt. *Revue Hispanique* 48: 1–179.

———. 1991. *Viaje por España y Portugal: 1494–1495*. Edited by Ramón Alba. Madrid: Ediciones Polifemo, 1991.

———. 2013. *Doctor Hieronumus Münzer's Itinerary (1494 and 1495): And Discovery of Guinea*. Translated by James Firth. London: James Firth.

Myers, Kathleen A., and Nina M. Scott. 2008. *Fernández de Oviedo's Chronicle of America: A New History for a New World*. Austin: University of Texas Press.

Necker, Alejandro. 1938. "La conquista y el régimen de los Welser." Bachelor's thesis, Universidad Central de Venezuela.

Nemser, Daniel. 2015. "Eviction and the Archive: Materials for an Archaeology of the Archivo General de Indias." *Journal of Spanish Cultural Studies* 16, no. 2: 123–41.

Neuber, Harald. 2020. "Streit beigelegt: Kueka-Stein kehrt aus Berlin nach Venezuela zurück." *amerika21*, 21 January. https://amerika21.de/2020/01/236649/venezuela-deutschland-kueka-piedra-pemon.

Nieto, Lidio, and Manuel Alvar Ezquerra. 2007. *Nuevo tesoro lexicográfico del español (s. XIV–1726)*. Madrid: Arco Libros.

Nirenberg, David. 2015. *Communities of Violence: Persecution of Minorities in the Middle Ages*. Princeton, NJ: Princeton University Press.

Nora, Pierre. 1997. *Les Lieux de Mémoire*. 3 vols. Paris: Gallimard.

Offen, Karl, and Jordana Dym. 2011. Introduction to *Mapping Latin America: A Cartographic Reader*, edited by Jordana Dym and Karl Offen, 1–18. Chicago: University of Chicago Press.

Olegario, Rowena. 2016. *The Engine of Enterprise: Credit in America*. Cambridge, MA: Harvard University Press.

Ospina, William. 2005. *Ursúa*. Bogotá: Alfaguara.

Otte, Enrique, ed. 1959. *Cedularios de la monarquía española relativos a la provincia de Venezuela (1529–1535)*. Vol. 1. Caracas: Fundación John Boulton y la Fundación Eugenio Mendoza.

———. 1963. *Cédulas reales relativas a Venezuela, 1500–1550*. Caracas: Fundación John Boulton y la Fundación Eugenio Mendoza.

———. 1982. *Cedulario de las provincias de Venezuela, 1529–1535*. Caracas: Academia de Ciencias Políticas y Sociales.

———. 1984. *Cedulario de las provincias de Venezuela, 1500–1550*. Caracas: Academia de Ciencias Políticas y Sociales.

Oviedo y Baños, José de. 1987. *The Conquest and Settlement of Venezuela*. Translated by Jeannette Johnson Varner. Berkeley: University of California Press.

———. 2004. *Historia de la conquista y población de Venezuela*. 2nd ed. Caracas: Biblioteca Ayacucho.

Padrón, Ricardo. 2020. *The Indies of the Setting Sun: How Early Modern Spain Mapped the Far East and the Transpacific West*. Chicago: University of Chicago Press.

Palmer, Patricia. 2015. "Response by Palmer to 'Betraying Empire: Translation and the Ideology of Conquest.'" *Translation Studies* 8, no. 3: 357–61.

Panhorst, K. H. 1930. "Simon Bolívar und Alexander von Humboldt." *Ibero-Amerikanisches Archiv* 4, no. 1: 35–47. www.jstor.org/stable/43135712.

Pardo, Isaac J., ed. 1962. *Juan de Castellanos: Elegía de varones ilustres de las Indias*. Caracas: Academia Nacional de la Historia.

Parker, Geoffrey. 1992. "Maps and Ministers: The Spanish Habsburgs." In *Monarchs, Ministers, and Maps*, edited by David Buisseret, 124–52. Chicago: University of Chicago Press.

Peguero Mills, Maria de Lourdes. 2008. "Juan de Castellanos' 'Elegies' and Alonso de Ercilla's 'Araucana': A Comparative Analysis." PhD diss., University of Minnesota.

Pelz, Daniel. 2018. "Berlin's African Quarter to Change Colonial-Era Street Names." DeutscheWelle.com, April 20. www.dw.com/en/berlins-african-quarter-to-change-colonial-era-street-names/a-43474130.

Perera, Ambrosio. 1943. *El Tocuyo conquistado y conquistador*. Caracas: Coromoto.

Pérez de Tudela, Almudena, and Annemarie Jordan Gschwend. 2003. "Exotica Habsburgica: La Casa de Austria y las colecciones exóticas en el Renacimiento Temprano." In *Oriente en Palacio: Tesoros asiáticos en las colecciones reales españolas*, edited by Marina Alfonso Mola and Carlos Martinez Shaw, 27–44. Madrid: Patrimonio Nacional.

———. 2007. "Renaissance Menageries: Exotic Animals and Pets at the Habsburg Courts in Iberia and Central Europe." *Early Modern Zoology* 2: 419–47.

Pérez Salazar, Bernardo. 2006. "Del cuerpo y otras ambigüedades." Review of *Ursúa*, by William Ospina. *Revista de Economía Institucional* 8, no. 14: 305–10.

Perkowska, Magdalena. 2008. *Historias híbridas: La nueva novela histórica latinoamericana (1985–2000) ante las teorías posmodernas de la historia*. Madrid: Iberoamericana.

Petershagen, Henning. 1992. "Federmannomanie." *Südwest Presse*, 14 March.

Pfeiffer, Hans Ernst. 1941. *Unsere schönen alten Kolonien*. Berlin: C. A. Weller.

Pierard, Richard V. 1987. "The German Colonial Society." In *Germans in the Tropics: Essays in German Colonial History*, edited by Arthur J Knoll and Lewis H. Gann, 19–37. New York: Greenwood Press.

Pohle, Jürgen. 2007. *Martin Behaim (Martinho da Boémia): Factos, lendas e controversias*. Coimbra: Cadernos do CIEG.

Pollard, A. F. 1906. "Die überseeischen Unternehmungen der Welser und ihrer Gesellschafter by Konrad Haebler." *English Historical Review* 21, no. 81: 158–59. www.jstor.org/stable/549440.

Ponce de Behrens, Marianela. 1990. "Los capitanes pobladores y la política poblacional de los Welser en la provincia de Venezuela." In *III Congreso venezolano de Historia*. Caracas: Departamento de Investigaciones Históricas de la Academia Nacional de Historia.

Ponce de Behrens, Marianela, Diana Reginfo, and Letizia Vaccari. 1977. *Juicios de Residencia en la Provincia de Venezuela: Los Welser*. Caracas: Academia Nacional de la Historia, Fuentes para la Historia Colonial de Venezuela.

Pons, María Cristina. 1992. *Memorias del olvido: La novela histórica de fines del siglo XX*. Mexico City: Siglo Veintiuno.

Pott, Sandra. 2005. "La *Cosmographei* (1544) de Sebastian Münster, une approche protestante de la cosmographie au tournant du Moyen Age et des Temps Modernes?" *Anglophonia* 17: 75–85.

Pulido, José. [1983] 2018. "Francisco Herrera Luque: 'Al doctor Fausto le salió psiquiatra.'" *El Nacional*, 18 May. www.el-nacional.com/noticias/papel-literario/francisco-herrera-luque-doctor-fausto-salio-psiquiatra_234978.

Pulido, Laura. 2017. "Geographies of Race and Ethnicity II. Environmental Racism, Racial Capitalism and State-Sanctioned Violence." *Progress in Human Geography* 41, no. 4: 524–33. doi:10.1177/0309132516646495.

Puttevils, Jeroen. 2016. *Merchants and Trading in the Sixteenth Century: The Golden Age of Antwerp*. London: Routledge.

Rafael, Vicente L. 2015. "Betraying Empire: Translation and the Ideology of Conquest." *Translation Studies* 8, no. 1: 82–93.

Ramos Pérez, Demetrio. 1965. *La revolución de 1533 contra los Welser y su importancia para el regimen municipal*. Caracas: El Cojo.

Ratekin, Mervyn. 1954. "The Early Sugar Industry in Española." *Hispanic American Historical Review* 34, no. 1: 1–19.

Ravenstein, E. G. 1908. *Martin Behaim: His Life and His Globe*. London: George Philip & Sohn.

Rechel, Ulrike. 2014. "Streit um Straßenumbenennungen." *Tip Berlin*, 24 October. www.tip-berlin.de/streit-um-strassenumbenennungen/.

Reeder, John, and Luis Perdices de Blas. 2003. *Diccionario de pensamiento económico en España 1500–2000*. Madrid: Sintesis.

Reimers, Erich. 1938. *Die Welser Landen in Venezuela*. Leipzig: W. Goldmann.

Reinhard, Wolfgang, and Mark Häberlein. 1996. *Augsburger Eliten des 16. Jahrhunderts: Prosopographie wirtschaftflicher und politischer Führungsgruppen 1500–1620*. Berlin: Akademie Verlag.

Rem, Lucas. 1861. *Tagebuch des Lucas Rem aus den Jahren 1494–1541: Ein Beitrag zur Handelsgeschichte der Stadt Augsburg*. Edited by B. Greiff. Augsburg: J. N. Hartmann. Digitized at www.mdz-nbn-resolving.de/urn/resolver.pl?urn=urn:nbn:de:bvb:12-bsb10377716-6.

Repp, Kevin. 2004. "'*Sexualkrise und Rasse*': Feminist Eugenics at the Fin de Siècle." In *Germany at the Fin de Siècle: Culture, Politics, and Ideas*, edited by Suzanne L. Marchand and David F. Lindenfeld, 81–101. Baton Rouge: Louisiana State University Press.

Restrepo, Luis Fernández. 1999. *Un nuevo reino imaginado: Las elegías de varones ilustres de Indias de Juan de Castellanos*. Bogotá: Instituto Colombiano de Cultura Hispánica.

———. 2002. "Sacred and Imperial Topographies in Juan de Castellanos' *Elegías de varones ilustres de Indias*." In *Mapping Colonial Spanish America: Places and Commonplaces of Identity, Culture, and Experience*, edited by Santa Arias and Mariselle Meléndez, 84–101. Lewisburg, PA: Bucknell University Press.

Richards, John F. 2003. *The Unending Frontier: An Environmental History of the Early Modern World*. Berkeley: University of California Press.

Rippy, J. Fred, and E. R. Brann. 1947. "Alexander Von Humboldt and Simón Bolívar." *American Historical Review* 52, no. 4: 697–703. www.jstor.org/stable/1842308.

Ritter, François. 1955. *Histoire de l'imprimerie alsacienne aux XVe et XVIe siècles*. Strasbourg: F. X. Le Roux.

Rivas, Luz Marina. 2014. "La Conquista en el teatro venezolano contemporaneo." In *La representación de la Conquista en el teatro latinoamericano de los siglos XX y XXI*, edited by Verena Dolle, 149–68. Hildesheim: Georg Olms.

Rodriguez, Jose A. 2017. "New Visions of the Past: Reinterpretations of History in the Novel and Cinema of Contemporary Venezuela." PhD diss., State University of New York at Stony Brook. ProQuest.

Rohmann, Gregor. 2004. *Das Ehrenbuch der Fugger*. Augsburg: Wißner.

Rücker, Elisabeth. 1973. *Die Schedelsche Weltchronik: Das Gröste Buchunternehmen der Dürer Zeit*. Munich: Prestel.

Rudolph, Donna Keyse, and G. A. Rudolph. 1996. "Federmann." In *Historical Dictionary of Venezuela*, 2nd ed., by Donna Keyse Rudolph and G. A. Rudolph, 280–81. Lanham, MD: Scarecrow Press.

Rupprecht, Tobias. 2011. "Gier Nach Gold." *Neu-Ulmer Zeitung*, 27 August.

Safley, Thomas M. 1997. *Charity and Economy in the Orphanages of Early Modern Augsburg*. Boston: Humanities Press.

Samson, Jane. 2005. *Race and Empire*. Harlow, UK: Pearson/Longman.

Sánchez Martínez, Antonio. 2013. *La espada, la cruz y el padrón: Soberanía, fe y representación cartográfica en el mundo ibérico bajo la monarquía hispánica, 1503–1598*. Madrid: Consejo Superior de Investigaciones Científicas.

Sandbach, Francis E. 1899. "Otto Von Diemeringen's German Translation of Mandeville's Travels." *Modern Quarterly of Language and Literature* 2, no. 5: 29–35.

Sarabia de la Calle, Luis. 1544. *La instrucción de mercaderes*. Medina del Campo: Pedro de Castro.

Schlenker, Ines. 2007. *Hitler's Salon: The Große Deutsche Kunstausstellung at the Haus de Deutschen Kunst*. Bern: Peter Lang.

Schmidt, Benjamin. 2006. *Innocence Abroad: The Dutch Imagination and the New World, 1570–1670*. Cambridge: Cambridge University Press.

Schmidt, Sven. 2015. *Das Gewerbebuch der Augsburger Christoph-Welser-Gesellschaft (1554–1560): Edition und Kommentar*. Augsburg: Wißner.

Schmölz-Häberlein, Michaela. 2002. "Kaufleute, Kolonisten, Forscher: Die Rezeption des Venezuela-Unternehmens der Welser in wissenschaftlichen und populären Darstellungen." In *Die Welser: Neue Forschungen zur Geschichte und Kultur der Oberdeutschen Handelshauses*, edited by Mark Häberlein and Johannes Burkhardt, 320–44. Berlin: Akademie.

Schnith, Karl. 1984. "Die Reichsstadt Augsburg Im Spätmittelalter (1368–1493)." In *Geschichte der Stadt Augsburg: 2000 Jahre von der Römerzeit bis zur Gegenwart*, edited by Gunther Gottlieb et al., 153–65. Stuttgart: Konrad Theiss.

Schuller, Rudolph. 1917. "The Date of Oviedo's Map of the Maracaibo Region." *Geographical Review* 3, no. 4: 294–302. www.jstor.org/stable/207430.

Schumacher, Hermann. 1892. "Juan de Castellanos ein Lebensbild aus der Conquista-Zeit." In *Hamburgische Festschrift zur Erinnerung an die Entdeckung Amerikas*, vol. 2, edited by Wissenschaftlichen Ausschuss des Komités für die Amerika-feier, 146–96. Hamburg: L. Friederichsen & Co.

Schwartz, Stuart B., ed. 2004. *Tropical Babylons Sugar and the Making of the Atlantic World, 1450–1680*. Chapel Hill: University of North Carolina Press.

Schweizer, Stefan. 2007. *"Unserer Weltanschauung sichtbaren Ausdruck geben": Nationalsozialistische Geschichtsbilder in historischen Festzügen zum "Tag der Deutschen Kunst 1933 bis 1939."* Göttingen: Wallstein.

Schwenckfeld, Caspar. 1922. *Letters and Treaties of Caspar Schwenkfeld von Ossig: 1538–1539*. Leipzig: Breitkopf and Härtel; Pennsburg, PA: Board of Publication of the Schwenckfelder Church.

Seubert, Adolf. 1856. *Die Sterne Schwabens: Eine Festgabe für Jung u. Alt in Schwaben*. Stuttgart: Schweizerbart. www.mdz-nbn-resolving.de/urn/resolver.pl?urn =urn:nbn:de:bvb:12-bsb10120778-9.

Sheppard, Eric. 2005. "Jim Blaut's Model of the World." *Antipode* 37, no. 5: 956–62.

Sieh-Burens, Katarina. 1986. *Oligarchie, Konfession und Politik im 16 Jahrhundert: Zur Sozialen Verflechtung der Augsburger Bürgermeister und Stadtpfleger 1518–1618*. Munich: Ernst Vögel.

Silverblatt, Irene. 2007. "The Black Legend and Global Conspiracies: Spain, the Inquisition, and the Emerging Modern World." In *Rereading the Black Legend*, edited by Margaret R. Greer, Walter D. Mignolo, and Maureen Quilligan, 99–116. Chicago: University of Chicago Press.

Simmer, Götz. 2000. *Gold und Sklaven: Die Provinz Venezuela während der Welser-Verwaltung (1528–1556)*. Berlin: Wissenschaft und Technik Verlag.

Smith, Adam. [1776] 2003. *The Wealth of Nations*. New York: Bantam Dell.

Sooman, Imbi, Jesma McFarlane, Valdis Teraudkalns, and Stefan Donecker. 2018. "From the Port of Ventspils to Great Courland Bay: The Couronian Colony on Tobago in Past and Present." *Journal of Baltic Studies* 44 no. 4: 503–26.

Specker, Hans Eugen, and Gebhard Weig, eds. 1981. *Die Einführung der Reformation in Ulm: Geschichte Eines Bürgerentscheids*. Ulm: Stadtarchiv Ulm.

Spiegel International. 2012. "Parting with 'Love': Artist Agrees to Return Venezuelan Stone." *Der Spiegel*, 5 July. www.spiegel.de/international/germany /german-artist-agrees-to-give-sacred-kueka-stone-back-to-venezuela-a-842717 .html.

Springer, Balthasar. 1509. *Die Merfart vn[d] erfarung nüwer Schiffung vnd Wege zu viln onerkanten Jnseln vnd Künigreichen von dem großmechtigen Portugalische[n] Kunig Emanuel Erforscht funden bestritten vnnd Jngenomen*. [Oppenheim: Köbel.]

Stelzner, Uli, and Thomas Walther. 1998. *The Civilizers: Germans in Guatemala.* Germany/Guatemala. DVD. ISKA.

Stenglin, Emmanuel. 1682. *Venezuela Provincia in America Occidentali Quam olim Dni. Velseri Patricij Augustani possidebant, a Carolo V. Imperatore ipsis Consignata Venezuela.* [Nürnberg]: Wolfgang Mauritius Endter.

Stoecklin, Jules. 1888. *Les colonies et l'émigration allemandes.* Paris: Louis Westhauser.

Stoler, Ann. 2002. "Colonial Archives and the Arts of Governance." *Archival Science* 2, no. 1: 87–109.

Stolley, Karen. 2013. *Domesticating Empire: Enlightenment in Spanish America.* Nashville, TN: Vanderbilt University Press.

Struck, Wolfgang. 2010. *Die Eroberung der Phantasie: Kolonialismus, Literatur und Film zwischen Deutschen Kaiserreich und Weimarer Republik.* Göttingen: V&R Unipress.

Stuart, Kathy. 1999. *Defiled Trades and Social Outcasts: Honor and Ritual Pollution in Early Modern Germany.* Cambridge: Cambridge University Press.

Sundberg, Juanita. 2008. "Tracing Race: Mapping Environmental Justice Research in Latin America." In *Environmental Justice in Latin America*, edited by David Carruthers, 25–47. Cambridge, MA: MIT Press.

Telesur. 2020. "Venezuela consigue retorno de piedra Kueka desde Alemania." *Telesur*, 20 January. www.telesurtv.net/news/venezuela-consigue-retorno -piedra-kueka-desde-alemania-20200120-0028.html.

Terjanian, Pierre, Adam B. Brandow, Matthias Pfaffenbichler, and Stefan Krause. 2019. *The Last Knight: The Art, Armor, and Ambition of Maximilian I.* New York: Metropolitan Museum of Art.

Tlusty, B. Ann. 2001. *Bacchus and Civic Order: The Culture of Drink in Early Modern Germany.* Charlottesville: University Press of Virginia.

Tortorici, Zeb. 2018. *Sins Against Nature: Sex and Archives in Colonial New Spain.* Durham, NC: Duke University Press.

Tracy, James D. 2002. *Emperor Charles V, Impressario of War.* Cambridge: Cambridge University Press.

Tzanaki, Rosemary. 2017. *Mandeville's Medieval Audiences: A Study on the Reception of the Book of Sir John Mandeville (1371–1550).* Abingdon: Routledge.

Van Groesen, Michiel. 2008. "The De Bry Collection of Voyages (1590–1634): Early America Reconsidered." *Journal of Early Modern History* 12, no. 1: 1–24.

Veracoechea, Emilia Troconis de. 1984. *Historia de El Tocuyo colonial: Período histórico 1514–1810.* Caracas: Universidad Central de Venezuela.

Vieira, Alberto. 2004. "'Sugar Islands': The Sugar Economy of Madeira and the Canaries, 1450–1650." In *Tropical Babylons: Sugar and the Making of the Atlantic World, 1450–1680*, edited by Stuart B. Schwartz, 56–88. Chapel Hill: University of North Carolina Press.

Vila, Marco Aurelio. 1998. *La Venezuela que conoció Juan de Castellanos siglo XVI (Notas geográficas)*. Caracas: Academia Nacional de Historia.

Vilches, Elvira. 2004. "Columbus's Gift: Representations of Grace and Wealth and the Enterprise of the Indies." *Modern Language Notes* 119, no. 2: 201–25.

———. 2010. *New World Gold: Cultural Anxiety and Monetary Disorder in Early Modern Spain*. Chicago: University of Chicago Press.

Villalón, Cristóbal de. 1541. *Provechoso tratado de ca[m]bios y co[n]trataciones d' mercaderes y reprovacion de vsura*. Valladolid: Francisco Fernandez d' Cordoua.

Viña Brito, Ana. 2004. "La Hacienda de Tazacorte (La Palma)." *Anuario de Estudios Atlánticos* 50, no. 1: 545–86. http://mdc.ulpgc.es/.

———. 2012. "Los flamencos en Canarias en el siglo XVI: Una comunidad extranjera. Especifidades en la isla de La Palma." *Revista de Historia Canaria* 194: 161–91. http://mdc.ulpgc.es/.

Viña Brito, Ana, and Nicolás de Kun. 2010. "Lucas Rem y la 'tierra maldita': Vicisitudes de un factor alemán a principios del XVI." *Anuario de Estudios Atlánticos* 56: 115–38.

Wagner, Henry R. 1931. "The Manuscript Atlases of Battista Agnese." *Papers of the Bibliographical Society of America* 25: 1–110.

Waldeyer-Hartz, Hugo von. 1927. *Die Welser in Venezuela: Bilder aus der Frühzeit Deutscher Kolonialgeschichte*. Berlin: Verlag R. Eisenschmidt.

Wallerick, Grégory. 2010. "La guerre par l'image dans l'Europe du XVI e." *Archives de Sciences Sociales des Religions* 55, no. 149: 33–53. www.jstor.org/stable /40930249.

Warsh, Molly A. 2018. *American Baroque: Pearls and the Nature of Empire, 1492–1700*. Williamsburg, VA: Omohundro Institute of Early American History and Culture; Chapel Hill: University of North Carolina Press.

Welser, Marcus. 1682. *Opera historica et philologica, sacra et profana*. Nürnberg: W. Mauritii & J. Andreæ.

Welser, Marx. 1595. *Chronika der weltberühmten reichsstadt Augspurg: Aus dem lateinisch verteutscht durch Engelbert Werlichium*. Frankfurt am Main.

Wey Gómez, Nicolás. 2008. *The Tropics of Empire: Why Columbus Sailed South to the Indies*. Cambridge, MA: MIT Press.

White, Hayden V. 2014. *The Practical Past*. Evanston, IL: Northwestern University Press.

Wintzer, Wilhelm. 1900. *Der Kampf um das Deutschtum: Die Deutschen im Tropischen Amerika: Mexiko, Mittelamerika, Venezuela, Kolumbien, Ekuador, Peru und Bolivien: mit Übersicht über die wirtschaftlichen, politischen und gesellschaftlichen Verhältnisse dieser Länder*. Munich: T. F. Lehmann.

Wissenschaftlichen Ausschuss des Komités für die Amerika-feier. 1892. *Hamburgische Festschrift zur Erinnerung an die Entdeckung Amerikas*, vol. 1. Hamburg: L. Friederichsen & Co.

Wolff, Hans, ed. 1992a. *America: Early Maps of the New World.* Munich: Prestel.

———. 1992b. "The Munich Portolan Charts: Past and Present." In *America: Early Maps of the New World,* edited by Hans Wolff, 127–44. Munich: Prestel.

Woodward, David. 2007a. "Cartography and the Renaissance: Continuity and Change." In *The History of Cartography,* vol. 3, pt. 1: *Cartography in the European Renaissance,* edited by David Woodward, 3–24. Chicago: University of Chicago Press.

———. 2007b. "The Italian Map Trade, 1480–1650." In *The History of Cartography,* vol. 3, pt. 1: *Cartography in the European Renaissance,* edited by David Woodward, 779–91. Chicago: University of Chicago Press.

Wulf, Andrea. 2016. *The Invention of Nature: Alexander Von Humboldt's New World.* New York: Alfred A. Knopf.

Wüst, Wolfgang. 2011. "Die Lateinamerika-Mission des Augsburger Handelshauses Welser." In *Bayern in Lateinamerika: Transatlantische Verbindungen und Interkultureller Austausch,* vol. 40, edited by Peter Clauss Hartmann and Alois Schmid, 51–75. Munich: C. H. Beck.

Zäh, Helmut. 2002. "Konrad Peutinger und Margarete Welser: Ehe und Familie im Zeichen des Humanismus." In *Die Welser: Neue Forschungen zur Geschichte und Kultur des Oberdeutschen Handelshauses,* edited by Mark Häberlein and Johannes Burkhardt, 449–509. Berlin: Akademie.

———. 2012. "Einfürung: Das Geschlechterbuch von Hans Burgkmair d. J. und Heinrich Vogtherr d. J.im Kontext der Augsburger Familien-und Ehrenbücher." In *Das Augsburger Geschlechterbuch: Wappenpracht und Figurenkunst. Ein Kriegsverlust Kehrt Zurück,* edited by Hans-Martin Kaulbach et al., 11–18. Stuttgart: Staatsgalerie Stuttgart.

Zantop, Susanne. 1997. *Colonial Fantasies: Conquest, Family, and Nation in Precolonial Germany, 1770–1870.* Durham, NC: Duke University Press.

Zemon Davis, Natalie. 2000. *The Gift in Sixteenth-Century France.* Madison: University of Wisconsin Press.

Zhang, Chunjie. 2017. *Transculturality and German Discourse in the Age of European Colonialism.* Evanston, IL: Northwestern University Press.

Zimmerer, Jürgen. 2017. "Kolonialismus ist kein Spiel." *Frankfurter Allgemeinen Zeitung,* 9 August. http://plus.faz.net/feuilleton/2017-08-09/der-kolonialismus-ist-kein-spiel/40725.html.

———. 2019. "Die größte Indentitätsdebatte unserer Zeit." *Süddeutsche Zeitung,* 18 February. www.sueddeutsche.de/kultur/2.220/kolonialismus-postkolonialismus-humboldt-forum-raubkunst-1.4334846.

Zimmerer, Jürgen, and Horst Bredekamp. 2019. "War Humboldt Kolonialist?" Interview by Andreas Kilb and Stefan Trinks, *Frankfurter Allgemeinen Zeitung,*

Feuilleton, 3 January. https://zeitung.faz.net/faz/feuilleton/2019-01-03/war -humboldt-kolonialist/250565.html?GEPC=s5.

Zimmerer, Jürgen, and Michael Perraudin, eds. 2011. *German Colonialism and National Identity*. New York: Routledge.

Zuleta, Rodrigo. 2006. "Ursúa: Una novela atiborrada." Review of *Ursúa*, by William Ospina. *Boletín Cultural y Bibliográfico* 43, no. 73: 121–22.

INDEX

Page numbers followed by *f* indicate figures.

GIOVANNA MONTENEGRO
is an associate professor of comparative literature
and director of the Latin American
and Caribbean Area Studies program
at Binghamton University.

www.ingramcontent.com/pod-product-compliance
Lightning Source LLC
Chambersburg PA
CBHW050625280326
41932CB00015B/2533